Regional Integration
and Democracy

Governance in Europe
Gary Marks, Series Editor

Regional Integration and Democracy

Expanding on the European Experience

edited by
Jeffrey J. Anderson

ROWMAN & LITTLEFIELD PUBLISHERS, INC.
Lanham • Boulder • New York • Oxford

ROWMAN & LITTLEFIELD PUBLISHERS, INC.

Published in the United States of America
by Rowman & Littlefield Publishers, Inc.
4720 Boston Way, Lanham, Maryland 20706

12 Hid's Copse Road
Cumnor Hill, Oxford OX2 9JJ, England

Copyright © 1999 by Rowman & Littlefield Publishers, Inc.

British Library Cataloguing in Publication Information Available

Library of Congress Cataloging-in-Publication Data

Regional integration and democracy : expanding on the European
    experience / edited by Jeffrey J. Anderson.
        p.   cm.
    Includes bibliographical references and index.
    ISBN 0-8476-9024-5 (alk. paper).—ISBN 0-8476-9025-3 (pbk. :
alk. paper)
    1. Democracy—European Union countries.   2. European Union.
3. European federation.   4. Europe—Economic integration.
5. International economic integration.   6. Democracy.   I. Anderson,
Jeffrey J.
JN40.R44   1999
320.94'09'049—dc21   98-36858
                                                                    CIP

Printed in the United States of America

∞ ™ The paper used in this publication meets the minimum requirements of
American National Standard for Information Sciences—Permanence of Paper for
Printed Library Materials, ANSI Z39.48–1992.

Contents

Preface and Acknowledgments

As a widening and deepening European Union (EU) heads into the twenty-first century, it confronts a range of challenges—some perennial and others novel—that impinge on the sovereign character of the member governments as well as on their democratic constitutions. These challenges are clearly of the utmost importance not only for Europe but for other parts of the world where democracy is unfolding amid nascent regional integration initiatives. As such, the contributors to this volume believe the evolving relationship between European integration and national democracy provides important models and lessons that can travel beyond the confines of the continent.

This volume addresses an interrelated sequence of theoretical and empirically oriented questions. It focuses on broad theoretical issues relating to integration, democracy, and sovereignty in the EU—specifically, the implications of integration for the exercise of national sovereignty, as well as the EU's "democratic deficit." The volume asks whether the democratic deficit at the European level has a domestic counterpart: Has democracy been altered in any of the member states as a result of regional integration in the postwar period? Finally, it shifts the perspective to the international level and draws parallels and contrasts between the European experience and regional integration initiatives in North America (NAFTA) and the Southern Cone (Mercosur).

The volume has its origins in a series of conversations in spring 1995 among Thomas Biersteker, João Carlos Espada, and myself. With the generous financial and logistical support of the Thomas J. Watson Jr. Institute for International Studies at Brown University and the Luso-American Foundation based in Lisbon, Portugal, Professor Espada and I organized an introductory conference for over twenty European and American participants in Lisbon in November 1995 and a smaller scholars' workshop at Brown in May 1996. This volume grew out of the many stimulating discussions that took place at these events.

In conclusion, I express my profound gratitude to the people whose hard work and invaluable advice made this volume possible: Diogo Freitas do Amaral, Tom Biersteker, Simon Bulmer, Francisco Sarsfield Cabral, Victor Constância, Claudia Elliot, João Carlos Espada, Jaime Gama, Carlos Gaspar, Claus Hofhansel, Jorge Braga de Macedo, Rui Machete, Guilherme D'Oliveira Martins, Adriano Moreira, Paul Pierson, João de Deus Pinheiro, Francisco Lucas Pires, Charles Powell, Fauso Quadros, and Philippe Schmitter. I would also like to thank Jean Lawlor, conference organizer at the Watson Institute, for her flawless work (as usual!) and Susan McEachern, executive editor at Rowman & Littlefield, for her infinite patience and unwavering support.

1

Introduction

Jeffrey J. Anderson

From its inception in the postwar period, European integration has been bound up intimately with democracy. The goal of securing a league of democracies against both threats from within—specifically, widespread economic deprivation and a resurgence of German nationalism—and the external menace of Soviet communism lies at the very core of the formation of the European Economic Community (EEC) in the late 1950s. Since that time, champions of the European project have hailed it first as a beacon and then as a bulwark for postauthoritarian regimes embarking on difficult paths to democracy. The accessions of Greece, Spain, and Portugal were viewed in this light, and similar arguments are heard today about eventual membership for the new democracies in Central and Eastern Europe.

Viewed from this perspective, the democratic credentials of European integration must be judged an unqualified success: They include postwar prosperity, a tamed and constructive Germany, and a failed communist alternative. Yet the relationship between democracy and integration has been and continues to be uneasy. Although integration's original rationale and subsequent effects are often cast in terms of democratic aspirations, after forty years the European project still lacks elemental attributes of democracy. Much has been written about the Community's "democratic deficit."[1] Suffice it to say here that the European Union's (EU) institutional arrangements fail to attain levels of popular control, public accountability, and responsiveness we have come to associate with, and indeed to expect of, democracy at the level of the nation-state.

The EU's democratic deficit represents the starting point for this volume.[2] What are its characteristics and consequences, what are its sources, and why has it persisted and proved so resistant to change? We then go beyond the supranational democratic deficit to consider two interrelated clusters of questions that represent our original contribution to the literature. First, we examine the impact of integration on national democratic institutions and practices. In short, is integration creating or exacerbating domestic democratic deficits among the member governments? To the extent that national democracy has been diminished or otherwise influenced by integration, how can we explain the resulting cross-national patterns of change and continuity? With these questions, we seek to shift the terms of the discussion of integration and democracy, which has concentrated almost exclusively on the supranational level.

Second, we employ the evolving European model of regional integration and democracy as a reference point for evaluating comparable phenomena in other parts of the world. Whether in Latin America, Africa, or Asia, concerted efforts to democratize national political systems and simultaneously to intensify regional cooperation among nations have been under way for over a decade. Despite the apparent singularity of the European experience, its relevance for the purposes of comparison is much broader than is typically acknowledged in the community studies literature, a fact we demonstrate in this volume.

THEORETICAL CONTEXT

This volume brings together three themes: democracy, regional integration, and globalization. It is useful to think of them as nested phenomena ranging from the nation-state (democracy) to the international system (globalization) that share considerable space at the margins. In the next three subsections, these issues are discussed and their potential interrelationships plumbed.

Democracy

Democracy and the processes by which it is achieved are the subjects of a long and venerable literature in the social sciences. After years of debate, a firm consensus has emerged that democracy is best viewed as a set of procedures and institutions rather than a set of normative goals or purposes.[3] Of course, within this consensus approaches differ; some remain content with a streamlined Schumpeterian focus on routinized competitive struggles for the people's vote, whereas others opt for more elaborate conceptualizations.[4] What these approaches share is an emphasis on tangible, empirical attributes of a political system, the presence or absence of which determines whether the system is democratic. This is the approach adopted by the authors in this volume, either explicitly or implicitly; we are interested in the impact of integration not on what democracies ought to be doing or achieving but on how they actually function and what outcomes they produce.

Much less consensus exists about how democracy emerges and why it occurs in some countries and not others. An earlier tradition emphasized the influence of structural factors such as the level of economic development, sociocultural cleavages, and the distribution of economic resources.[5] More recent contributions, although acknowledging the importance of structure and context, depict a more open-ended process in which bargaining outcomes during the transition period play an important role in creating essential preconditions for democracy.[6] In this volume the latter approach carries more relevance; several authors deal with countries that are in the midst of or have recently completed negotiated transitions to democratic rule, and the bargains on which the new regimes are based remain fragile and are therefore subject to both endogenous and exogenous influences.

The sweep of the democracy literature notwithstanding, areas of central importance to this volume exist that are not especially well covered. Democracy as a set of institutions and procedures, whether newly minted or long established, is by no means static. To be sure, we know a lot about the sources of democratic breakdown.[7] Short of catastrophic failure, however, there is still plenty of room for variation in performance. Over time and in comparison to other democracies, the political system may function better or worse. Institutions and procedures can gain or lose in effectiveness, and the outcomes they produce—whether political, social, or economic—can have powerful negative or positive feedback effects on the democratic system itself. The literature on democratic "overload" and the recent contributions by Robert Putnam have attempted to tap the sources of democratic performance.[8] In this volume we seek, among other things, to isolate the impact of an external source of influence—regional integration.

Regional Integration

Regional integration can be defined as "the process whereby an international organization acquires responsibility for taking an increasing number of decisions in areas which were previously reserved to the state."[9] This prosaic but accurate description of postwar developments in Europe also captures the trajectories of nascent regional integration initiatives under way in Asia (Association of Southeast Asian Nations [ASEAN]), South America (Mercosur), and to a lesser extent North America (North American Free Trade Agreement [NAFTA]).

There can be little dispute that regional integration has progressed furthest and fastest in Europe. After forty years few, if any, areas of national policy in the fifteen member states are not in some way—either directly or indirectly—subject to supranational strictures of varying intensity. From a core set of jointly managed policies revolving around the internal market, agriculture, and external trade, European Community (EC) member governments expanded the scope of supranational coordination and authoritative decisionmaking to include regional policy, the environment, foreign policy, and monetary policy.[10] A mark of the advanced stage of integration in Europe is the frequency with which member states submit to decisions and rulings of purely supranational authorities such as the European Commission and the European Court of Justice, which act on the basis of competencies and laws generated by the treaty framework. This feature of the European Union sets it apart from other international organizations and from regional integration projects elsewhere in the world; it also sets up potential nodes of friction and even contradiction with national democratic institutions and processes.

As integration has progressed, the democratic credentials of the supranational edifice have been called into question with increasing frequency. Democracies are in charge of the European project, but their creation, critics argue, is far from democratic. National governments have ceded or pooled sovereignty in key areas, yet the variegated decisionmaking structures and procedures erected at the supranational level have not been endowed with the same democratic safeguards as exist and operate, however imperfectly, back home. A weak European Parliament, opaque decisionmaking procedures in the European Commission and Council of Ministers, and the marginalized state of the national parliaments place severe constraints on the ability of the European *demos*—parceled as it is among fifteen separate nation-states—to exert anywhere near the level of control and to exact anywhere near the degree of accountability it can from its own national governments. Even if, as Joseph Weiler maintains, integration will always result in a diminution of democracy from the vantage point of the nation-state, European arrangements clearly have not been constructed with an eye toward minimizing that loss.[11]

The origins of the EC/EU's democratic deficit are complex, but they can be traced to the desire of the member governments—more precisely, of the national executives—to remain as firmly in control of the integration process as possible. As such, those who seek to eliminate or reduce the democratic deficit face an uphill battle; their agenda, which typically includes a much strengthened European Parliament, is virtually indistinguishable from the agenda of those who seek to push the integration process in the direction of a federal outcome: a United States of Europe. Since the end point of integration has always been bitterly contested among the member states, a situation that has intensified in the post-Maastricht period, it should come as no surprise that progress on eliminating the democratic deficit has often fallen victim to deadlock on these more fundamental debates about integration and national sovereignty. One of the objectives of this volume is to explore the nexus among integration, national sovereignty, and democracy.

Globalization

Globalization (or internationalization) is a ubiquitous yet enigmatic concept.[12] In its economic guise, globalization refers to the growth in economic transactions among countries since the late 1970s—specifically, international trade in goods and services, currency trading, and foreign direct investment.[13] The increased volume of trade and the expansion of international capital markets have many sources, including technological improvements (for example, computerized trading) and the embracing of economic policy variations on a neoliberal theme by governments around the world. As a sociopolitical phenomenon, globalization refers to myriad recent, independent developments: the increased volume and speed of information flows among nations, whether through traditional channels such as the print and broadcast media or through new technologies such as the Internet; the emergence of transnational advocacy communities such as Greenpeace (environment) and Amnesty International (human rights); and the growing influence of international agencies such as the World Bank, the International Monetary Fund, and the United Nations.

Economic globalization is an inherently uncoordinated process driven by countless market actors. Political globalization carries more evidence of human design, yet even here the processes have unfolded in a manner largely beyond the control of any single authority. As globalization progresses, so the argument goes, the implications for nation-states grow more significant. National borders, whether by design or accident, become more permeable both economically and politically, which carries potentially weighty implications for domestic politics and even for elemental regime characteristics.

Most obviously, as globalization progresses, countries grow more interdependent and thereby become more vulnerable to impulses transmitted by the international system. Even a modest decline or rise in prices on international markets can mean the difference between prosperity or penury for individuals, firms, sectors, regions, and even nations. Granted, this is nothing new, but in today's world the speed and scope of exogenous economic shocks are vastly greater than they have been previously. And as nations' vulnerability to exogenous economic shocks has grown, so too has the likelihood of externally induced political crises.[14] Nation-states are also unable to shield the domestic arena from political scrutiny, counsel, and even demands originating in the international community; episodes such as France's contested decision in 1995 to resume nuclear testing in the South Pacific and the Serbian regime's attempt to annul local elections in 1996 demonstrate that "world opinion"—often backed by the implicit or explicit threat of coordinated sanctions—is increasingly a force with which to be reckoned.

Globalization also creates a situation in which the preferences and capabilities of domestic actors—ranging from individuals up to government agencies—become bound up, sometimes intimately and inextricably, with extranational factors. Current research has devoted much attention to two areas in this regard. First, the autonomy of national governments has diminished in the face of globalization, insofar as their standard policy repertoires have lost efficacy because of the undermining influences of international forces.[15] At the extreme, a loss of autonomy translates into a loss of sovereignty. Second, global economic forces have the capacity to rearrange issue cleavages in society and thereby to shape the nature of domestic political conflict. For example, the interplay of international price changes and the relative scarcity or abundance of production factors at the national level have produced shifts in domestic political coalitions with important consequences for government policy choices and outcomes.[16] As economic globalization has progressed, issue cleavage lines at the national level have fallen increasingly along sectoral lines, dividing mobile international capital and its labor forces from capital and labor relatively more rooted to particular production locations.[17] Sectoral politics is expected to become more salient than the traditional politics of class.

With such a complex, manifold phenomenon, tracing its implications for national democracy is a challenging task. One must stress at the outset that these international effects are not necessarily all malign or unhelpful. Thomas Biersteker, for example, argues that several facets of globalization actually prompted or amplified the waves of democratization that have engulfed Latin America, Central and Eastern Europe, Asia, and to a lesser extent Africa in recent decades.[18] The debt crisis of the 1980s plunged authoritarian regimes into political crisis in many parts of the world, marking the beginning of the painful and in many cases successful negotiated transitions to democracy.[19] These transitions were often guided by the conditional support of international agencies. Similarly, the end of the Cold War and the subsequent demise of the Soviet Union created an international opening for politico-economic liberalization programs in the former Soviet sphere of influence. The spread of democratic values, ideas, and models—facilitated by a global media—also contributed to these dramatic developments.

Alongside these beneficial impacts, globalization raises many troubling questions about the future of national democracy, whether long established, newly minted, or coming into being. International economic crises cut both ways—whereas they may have ushered in democratic transitions in many parts of the world, they can also undermine the stability and legitimacy of democratic arrangements, particularly those still in the so-called consolidation phase; recall the example of the Weimar Republic. To the extent that globalization reshapes large swaths of national politics along sectoral lines, it is likely to create unresolved tensions in democracies that are universally based on the principle of territorial representation and that in the vast majority of cases have been organized to address the clash of class-based interests. Finally, to the extent that nation-states attempt to manage the effects of globalization through increased cooperation, including formal political and economic integration,[20] we come full circle in our discussion—that is, we are faced with the need to examine the broader implications of regional integration for contemporary democracy.

RESEARCH QUESTIONS

The intersection of democracy, regional integration, and globalization is of paramount importance as more nation-states turn to democracy and supranational cooperation to address the needs and demands of their citizenries and as globalization proceeds apace. Our focus in this volume is on the immediate nexus between integration and democracy, but it is self-evident that to understand that relationship, both in the abstract and in its geographical-historical manifestations, one must take into account the larger international context. In this section I outline some of the issues one should consider and in the following section relate them to the chapters that constitute this book.

Regional integration impinges on national sovereignty. As the European case demonstrates, integration can take the form of direct transfers of sovereignty from national governments to supranational authorities or the pooling of national sovereignties, in which the member governments retain control but do so jointly or collectively. These cumulative outcomes carry important implications for a democratic polity in at least three main areas.

1. Although this is often overlooked, formal constitutional arrangements that regulate relationships between citizens and their government, as well as those that establish the legal relations among the various levels and branches lodged within the sphere of public authority, rest on national sovereignty. In each democracy citizenship rights and the prevailing system of intergovernmental relations were established on the basis of an intact national sovereignty; thus, for citizenship rights as specified in the constitution to be claimed against the state or for the division of responsibilities between national and subnational governments to operate as speci-

fied in the constitution, the sovereignty of the central public authority must remain unaltered.

To the extent, however, that national sovereignty is transferred or shared through supranational integration, these complex relationships are subject to change and, in extreme cases, transformation. This may happen formally, as when integration necessitates legal reforms and amendments to the existing constitutional structures at the national level. It may also occur on a more informal level, as when integration alters prevailing power relationships between the institutions of government (without affecting constitutionally prescribed relationships or powers) or establishes rights superordinate to those (unchanged) rights existing at the national level. In considering the European experience, perhaps the most problematic developments from the standpoint of national democracy have involved the impact of integration on the powers and responsibilities of the national parliaments and court systems.

2. The national policy process is also subject to change through integration. For example, supranational policies may utilize institutional structures and normative frameworks that privilege certain actors and interests over others by granting them exclusive access to various kinds of resources (for example, information, material benefits, authority). Should these integration-conferred advantages cumulate, they could produce a shift in the terms of intergovernmental, electoral, or group competition at the domestic level. Depending on the circumstances, these domestic shifts could weaken or undermine formal policymaking structures and systems of social concertation and interest intermediation.

European integration has sparked numerous arguments in this vein, some of which have obvious although as yet unexplored implications for national democracy. Since the inception of the EEC in 1957, supporters of the left have argued strenuously that the Community's treaty framework, with its presumption in favor of markets and a hands-off approach by public authorities, privileges business over labor both procedurally and in terms of outcomes.[21] More recently, scholars have argued that the treaty-based nature of European integration, which places national governments at the heart of the complex and variegated bargaining processes in Brussels, gives state actors real advantages over societal groups in the domestic policy process.[22]

3. Integration processes could influence the elemental inputs of the national democratic process by shaping the interests and possibly the identities of individual citizens. This was the expectation (and even the hope) of early functionalists such as Mitrany and Deutsch, who saw in European integration a technocratic force for shifting citizen loyalties inexorably away from the nation-state toward a new supranational political entity. Although the EC/EU has yet to win over citizens' allegiance with a demon-

strable capacity to address difficult problems with higher levels of efficacy and efficiency than the nation-state model, integration processes in Europe and elsewhere clearly retain the ability to influence the way citizens define their interests and where they look for solutions.

Indeed, in what must be considered a splendid irony, in the 1990s the EU has become bound up intimately with mushrooming political backlashes on both the left and the right in many member countries. On the left, critics charge that the goal of economic and monetary union enshrined in the Maastricht Treaty carries a price tag—enumerated in the various convergence criteria for membership—that will ultimately bring down the postwar welfare state. Rejecting government calls for budget austerity and fiscal conservatism, parties of the left and their supporters in the labor movement are seeking to mobilize voter fears and discontent on the basis of traditional class loyalties, this time with an added trace of anti-Europeanism. On the far right, political entrepreneurs have held up the specter of a borderless United States of Europe to stoke economic fears and xenophobia among the general population. It thus appears that within a very short period, European integration has contributed to the weakening of a hallmark of the postwar period: the "permissive consensus"[23] over integration.

Taken together, these various direct and indirect effects of integration could alter the larger context within which democratic institutions and processes operate at the nation-state level. Put another way, by acting on the polity, the economy, or both, integration may serve as a catalyst for significant changes in the political economy of a member state. Yet the cumulative effects of integration are unlikely to be uniform across national boundaries, if only because the recipients of these changes—the member states—are anything but uniform.

Democratic polities are constructed differently; as a case in point, Arend Lijphart identifies two basic variants of democracy in the twentieth century: majoritarian and consensus.[24] Variations in the spatial ordering of the constitution are also fairly common; the most elemental distinction separates federal from unitary states. Institutional differences among democracies are compounded by variations in the age of the regimes. Two countries may sport more or less identical democratic institutional arrangements and yet function very differently—and respond to supranational integration effects in a dissimilar manner—because one has been in business for a century whereas the other has existed for a mere five years.

In addition to distinctions within the regime category *democracy*, democratic institutions are linked to the economy in distinctive ways across space. For example, students of comparative political economy in the postwar period have traditionally distinguished between liberal and corporatist models among the advanced industrial democracies.[25] In the former, the state maintains a more or less arm's-length relationship to the economy and the actors situated therein, whereas the latter is characterized by much more regular, routinized, and institutionalized interactions between state actors and producer groups.

The point is simply this: Even if one can assume that integration generates similar mixes of benefits, costs, opportunities, and constraints for each member state,[26] its impulses fall on variegated landscapes; thus, its effects are likely to differ on the ground, if not from case to case then almost certainly from broad category to broad category. For this reason, we have selected a wide variety of countries for detailed examination in this volume. Yet we also begin with the expectation that, at least in the case of Europe, since the member countries are basically democratic and essentially capitalist, the impact of integration will reveal broadly comparable and systematic patterns. The main questions revolve around what gives rise to these patterns and whether they are reproduced in integration initiatives involving existing or would-be democracies in other parts of the world.

OUTLINE OF THE VOLUME

In Section I of this volume, three chapters explore various aspects of the relationship between regional integration and democracy in Europe, with special emphasis on the supranational level of analysis. The authors focus analytical attention on the implications of integration for sovereignty, legitimacy, and identity within the nation-states of Europe.

In the first chapter of this section, Thomas Biersteker characterizes postwar European integration as an exemplar of the contemporary redefinition of national sovereignty. Beginning with the premise that sovereignty is a social construct, he examines the changing operational meaning of the concept and its core components—authority, identity, and territory—with the goal of devising a new language and theoretical orientation with which to analyze the emerging European polity. Biersteker argues that the number and range of authority claims made by states have changed in recent decades, marking a transformation of the meaning of sovereignty and its exercise by states. Nowhere is this better exemplified than in contemporary Europe; EU members remain sovereign in important respects, but the meaning and content of this sovereignty have changed dramatically since 1957. Given the intimate link between national sovereignty and the democratic model, Biersteker establishes a useful starting point for thinking about the relationship between regional integration and democracy at both the supranational and national levels.

In chapter 3, Wolfgang Merkel begins with an intriguing paradox. For most of the postwar period, European integration proceeded rapidly because of the incompleteness of democratic controls.[27] The uniting of Europe was very much an elite economic game played by political executives who were relatively unconstrained by mass publics or national representative institutions. This changed with Maastricht; integration encroached into core sovereign domains of the member governments, thereby vaulting Europe's democratic deficit squarely onto the agenda. In fact, Merkel argues, democratization has since become a political prerequisite for integration. As such, what was once a paradox is becoming a dilemma: Integrate further, and democracy suffers; democratize, and integration malfunctions.

This "efficiency-democracy" dilemma informs Merkel's ensuing analysis. After exploring the relationship between normative democratic theory and the empirical attributes of the EU's democratic deficit, he concludes that the dilemma is intractable—Europe's elites cannot realize both options simultaneously. Further integration without democratization will cause a profound loss of public support for the European project. Further democratization without system effectiveness will also weaken public attachments. Either way, legitimacy suffers. Thus, Merkel counsels no advance beyond the status quo ante Maastricht until support from political elites and mass publics has become "intense and structured."[28]

Merkel's analysis suggests that one means of escaping the efficiency-democracy dilemma could lie in the development of a common political identity among Europe's citizenries. Specifically, individual Europeans who identified with the larger EU collectivity might be more willing to tolerate any decline in system effectiveness that attended a thoroughgoing democratization of Europe's overarching political structures.

The content and sources of political identity in contemporary Europe and their relationship to the integration process are taken up by Gary Marks in chapter 4. His analysis focuses on the numerous territorial identities that exist in today's Europe—local, regional, national, and supranational—and on how they might foster, either singly or in combination, a democratic EU that enjoys widespread legitimacy among citizens. Based on an evaluation of Eurobarometer survey data and lower-level regional surveys, Marks concludes that the "multiple identities" that incorporate the European territory are not only common but appear to have become more prevalent since regional integration commenced in the late 1950s. Marks argues that this could be the result of more frequent and intense interactions across borders and of shared assessments of the economic benefits of integration. Thus a common identity of sorts already exists in Europe, although it is of a different nature than the national identities that emerged on the continent out of the crucible of state-building, war, and ethnolinguistic commonalities. By pointing out that territorial attachments are strongest where the institutional opportunities for citizen participation are greatest—typically at the national or subnational level, depending on the constitutional form of the polity—Marks hints at a way out of Merkel's democracy dilemma: Democratize the EU further, and (multiple) identities conducive to further integration may grow.

In Section II, five authors look at the impact of European integration on democracy in nine European countries, eight of which are currently EU members and one of which soon will be. Together, these chapters seek to establish whether the political and economic elements of regional integration have opened up or exacerbated democratic deficits within the member governments and, if so, to identify and evaluate the probable consequences.

António Barreto takes up the intriguing case of Portugal, a member whose recent political journey from authoritarianism to consolidated democracy has become virtually synonymous with the therapeutic powers of European integration. He presents a comprehensive and fine-grained analysis that does more than simply document the conventional wisdom about Portugal and Europe; in fact, Barreto points beyond the substantial silver lining to a small but worrisome cloud: Community membership has reinforced the closed practices of Portuguese administration and executive government perfected under authoritarianism. Barreto concludes that Europe's democratic deficit is perpetuating lingering defects in the construction of Portugal's young democracy.

Péter Gedeon then examines Europe's role in the Hungarian transition from state socialism to liberal democracy. He finds that European influences on Hungary, measured in terms of direct leadership effects, have in fact been minimal, with the single exception of Hungary's policies toward its ethnic minorities. Rather, a subtle but pervasive Europeanization of values and institutions, mediated by Hungarian elites, is occurring in the political and economic spheres of Hungarian life. Here, Europe functions as a general orientation point—a coherent, successful model of political economy that can be readily imported. But according to Gedeon, a second and potentially much more direct process of Europeanization is getting under way as Hungary queues up for eventual EU membership. Again spearheaded by domestic economic and political elites, this facet of Europeanization will eventually result in direct, unmediated EU influence on Hungary's ongoing postsocialist transition. It also promises to transform "Europe" into a salient political issue for average Hungarians, who until now have maintained generally positive but relatively unreflective attitudes toward the EU. Gedeon concludes by outlining the clear parallels and subtle contrasts that exist between Hungary's present situation and that of Portugal prior to accession in 1986.

The next three chapters explore the variegated impacts of regional integration on several established members of the European project. Jack Hayward looks at France and the United Kingdom (UK), two countries that despite their many internal dissimilarities and their almost polar roles in postwar Europe are both multinational creations of centralized, unitary states, each steeped in recent imperial pasts. As a consequence, both have experienced profound difficulties with the integration process, particularly when it involves shifts in the locus of democratic decisionmaking from the national to the supranational level. Indeed, Hayward attributes the emergence of the EC/EU's democratic deficit to British and French reluctance to complement functional economic integration, which both countries have ardently supported, with institutional political integration of a corresponding depth. The adversarial style of politics in both countries, which contrasts with the consensualism practiced in smaller member countries as well as in Germany, has also created a more conflictual relationship with Europe. Moving beyond this larger shared European experience of defensiveness, Hayward skillfully reveals the differing contours of domestic reaction and adjustment to the integration process, the causes of which reside in distinctive features of national democracy in each country.

In my chapter on the Federal Republic of Germany, I outline the remarkable level of congruence between the postwar German political system and the evolving European architecture. This bedrock compatibility stemmed largely from the seismic changes in German interests, institutions, and identity brought about by total defeat in World War II. In comparison to other EC members, especially the larger ones, Germany's relationship with Europe was largely harmonious. Elites and masses held that, rather than undermining democracy at home, European integration complemented and extended it. With unification and Maastricht, however, this situation has begun to change. New points of friction between Germany and the European Union have opened up along many fronts, both economic and political. Some of these could potentially transform the traditional German postwar model, particularly the welfare state and the organization of the political economy. As with France and the UK, a democratic backlash occurred in the wake of Maastricht, reinforcing decentralist institutional tendencies in the German system and potentially complicating the future path of integration.

Paulette Kurzer's analysis ranges widely but deeply across four member governments and three policy areas. She begins by unpacking regional integration into distinct components—market integration, European state building, and intergovernmental treaty formation—and then traces their separate impacts on national democratic institutions and conventions. Specifically, she examines the evolution of social concertation in Belgium, the Netherlands, and Sweden; the emergence of regionalist movements in Belgium and Italy; and efforts to develop a European strategy for joint law enforcement. All three varieties of integration have generated tangible, complex effects within the member countries, frequently attended by economic turmoil and political conflict. Market (or "informal") integration has had the greatest impact, leading to extensive curtailments of national policy autonomy and to the demise of institutional mechanisms designed to forge consent between and among state and societal interests. European state-building initiatives have contributed both to an erosion of the state's fiscal autonomy and to shifts in intergovernmental relations within the member states. Nevertheless, Kurzer's case studies reveal that the institutions and conventions of national democracy have exhibited remarkable resilience and adaptability in the face of such consistent external pressures.

The volume concludes with two chapters that explore broader relationships between regional integration and democracy elsewhere in the world. Gustavo Vega-Cánovas examines Mexico in the context of a recent and limited integration initiative embodied in the North American Free Trade Agreement; his chapter is followed by José Augusto Guilhon Albuquerque's study of the much more ambitious Mercosur initiative. Each author seeks to establish the kind of regional integration project his case represents, using the European experience as a reference point, and then to trace the implications of regional integration for ongoing processes of democratization (Mexico) and democratic consolidation (Brazil, Paraguay). In both instances elites viewed regional integration as a means of adjusting to international economic pressures and of creating a zone of economic and political stability in which domestic reforms could proceed.

Nevertheless, the authors identify distinctive features of these initiatives that lead them to different conclusions about the future trajectories of integration in the regions, as well as about the implications of those trajectories for national democracy. In Mexico, NAFTA has accelerated challenges to one-party hegemony that had been building since the early 1980s; at the same time, however, in the minds of many Mexicans it has become inextricably linked, at least since 1994, to austerity politics and the resulting economic hardship and social injustice, with worrisome consequences for the process of democratization. In Brazil and Paraguay, the growth in economic and political stability—often uneven and fitful—paralleled the formation and consolidation of the Mercosur initiative. In Paraguay, Mercosur played a decisive role in strengthening the hand of democrats faced with a military coup. In Brazil, Mercosur appears to have served more as an instrument for the creation of domestic reform coalitions led by strong presidents, but its contribution to domestic stability has been vital nonetheless.

*   *   *

With this book, we seek to shift the terms of discussion of integration and democracy by bringing together a wider range of country cases and regional contexts—including some from outside Western Europe—and a broader range of themes, with special emphasis on the fate of domestic institutions and processes in an integrating context. As such, this volume departs from standard approaches, which are based exclusively on the European experience and direct attention exclusively on the supranational level. With this novel focus, we hope both to reframe the study of the EU's democratic deficit, casting new light on time-honored but heretofore narrowly conceived questions, and to generate promising clues to the dynamic interactions between democracy and integration elsewhere.

NOTES

1. For an early discussion of the democratic deficit with specific reference to the European Parliament, see Shirley Williams, "Sovereignty and Accountability in the European Community," in Robert Keohane and Stanley Hoffmann, eds., *The New European Community* (Boulder: Westview, 1991), 155–76.

2. See Michael Newman, *Democracy, Sovereignty, and the European Union* (New York: St. Martin's Press, 1996); and Antje Wiener and Vincent Della Sala, "Constitution-making and Citizenship Practice—Bridging the Democracy Gap in the EU," *Journal of Common Market Studies* 35 (December 1997), 593–614.

3. Samuel Huntington, *The Third Wave: Democratization in the Twentieth Century* (Norman: University of Oklahoma Press, 1991), 5–6.

4. One example is Dahl, who lists eight institutional characteristics that must be present to guarantee the responsiveness of government to its citizens—a fundamental characteristic of democracy. Robert Dahl, *Polyarchy* (New Haven: Yale University Press, 1971), chapter 1.

5. Good examples of authors writing in this vein include ibid., and Samuel Huntington, "Will More Countries Become Democratic?" *Political Science Quarterly* 99 (summer 1984): 193–218.

6. See for example Giuseppe Di Palma, *To Craft Democracies* (Berkeley: University of California Press, 1990).

7. See, for example, Juan Linz and Alfred Stepan, eds., *The Breakdown of Democratic Regimes* (Baltimore: Johns Hopkins University Press, 1978).

8. See Anthony King, "Overload: Problems of Governing in the 1970s," *Political Studies* 23 (1975): 162–74; Samuel Brittan, "The Economic Contradictions of Democracy," *British Journal of Political Science* 5 (1975): 129–59; Mancur Olson, *The Rise and Decline of Nations* (New Haven: Yale University Press, 1982); and Robert Putnam, *Making Democracy Work* (Princeton: Princeton University Press, 1993).

9. Paul Taylor, *The Limits of European Integration* (New York: Columbia University Press, 1983), 26.

10. This is not to suggest that the EU has unfolded according to some internal logic as described by neofunctionalist theory, to take one example. European integration has proceeded, to use the ubiquitous phrase, in fits and starts and has been subject as much to exogenous shocks and forces as to internal dynamics. For up-

to-date overviews of the European Union in all its complexity, see David Wood and Birol Yesilada, *The Emerging European Union* (White Plains, N.Y.: Longman, 1996); and John McCormick, *The European Union: Politics and Policies* (Boulder: Westview, 1996).

11. Joseph Weiler, "After Maastricht: Community Legitimacy in Post-1992 Europe," in William James Adams, ed., *Singular Europe* (Ann Arbor: University of Michigan Press, 1992), 11–42 at 21. Weiler argues that the way to compensate for this loss of democratic control is to adopt measures at the supranational level, including, that is, the formation of democratic structures that increase the social legitimacy of integration among the affected populations. As many of the country chapters in this volume show, the actual response of EU member governments to the democratic deficit has been to strengthen the control of national institutions over the integration process—that is, to achieve accountability from below.

12. For skeptical perspectives on the globalization phenomenon, see Suzanne Berger and Ronald Dore, eds., *National Diversity and Global Capitalism* (Ithaca: Cornell University Press, 1996); and J. Rogers Hollingsworth and Robert Boyer, eds., *Contemporary Capitalism: The Embeddedness of Institutions* (New York: Cambridge University Press, 1997).

13. For an introduction to the phenomenon that is expressly empirical, see Helen Milner and Robert Keohane, "Internationalization and Domestic Politics: An Introduction," in Helen Milner and Robert Keohane, eds., *Internationalization and Domestic Politics* (New York: Cambridge University Press, 1996), 3–24.

14. Again, this is a matter of degree. Two studies that chart the impact of the international economy on national politics over the centuries are Peter Gourevitch, *Politics in Hard Times* (Ithaca: Cornell University Press, 1986); and Ronald Rogowski, *Commerce and Coalitions* (Princeton: Princeton University Press, 1989).

15. For a review of this general argument, see Milner and Keohane, "Internationalization and Domestic Politics," 16–18.

16. Rogowski, *Commerce and Coalitions*.

17. Jeffry Frieden, "Invested Interests: The Politics of National Economic Policies in a World of Global Finance," *International Organization* 45 (Autumn 1991): 425–51.

18. Thomas Biersteker (with Christine Kearney), "The Global Setting of Contemporary Democratization and Political Reform," unpublished manuscript, Brown University, April 1994.

19. This is the starting point for Di Palma, *To Craft Democracies*.

20. See Stefan Schirm, "Transnational Globalization and Regional Governance: On the Reasons for Regional Cooperation in Europe and the Americas," Center for European Studies, Program for the Study of Germany and Europe, Working Paper no. 6.2, July 1996.

21. Philippe Schmitter and Wolfgang Streeck, "Organized Interests and the Europe of 1992," in Norman Ornstein and Mark Perlman, eds., *Political Power and Social Change* (Washington, D.C.: American Enterprise Institute, 1991), 46–67.

22. Andrew Moravcsik, "Why the European Community Strengthens the State: Domestic Politics and International Cooperation," paper presented at the Annual Meeting of the American Political Science Association, New York, 1994.

23. Leon Lindberg and Stuart Scheingold, *Europe's Would-Be Polity: Patterns of Change in the European Community* (Englewood Cliffs, N.J.: Prentice-Hall, 1970), 74.

24. Arend Lijphart, *Democracies* (New Haven: Yale University Press, 1984). Both variants are well represented in the EU; the UK is Lijphart's template for the majoritarian variant, whereas most small member governments—Belgium, the Netherlands—conform to the consensus model.

25. Peter Katzenstein, ed., *Between Power and Plenty* (Madison: University of Wisconsin Press, 1978); Peter Katzenstein, *Corporatism and Change* (Ithaca: Cornell University Press, 1984); Peter Katzenstein, *Small States in World Markets* (Ithaca: Cornell University Press, 1985); Peter Hall, *Governing the Economy* (Oxford: Oxford University Press, 1986); and David Soskice, "Wage Determination: The Changing Role of Institutions in Advanced Industrialized Countries," *Oxford Review of Economic Policy* 6 (1990): 36–62.

26. As the EU post-Maastricht moved into an era of variable speeds on issues such as social policy and economic and monetary union, this assumption looks more than a little tenuous.

27. Merkel's analysis suggests an interesting contrast worthy of further research; unlike the typical national experience in Europe, where democracy emerged in part as the by-product of the bourgeoisie's pursuit of its economic agenda, in modern Europe the by-product of a supranational economic agenda has been rather unhelpful to democracy.

28. Merkel in this volume, p. 62.

Section I

European Integration and Democracy

2

Locating the Emerging European Polity: Beyond States or State?

Thomas J. Biersteker

The polity emerging within the European Union (EU) resides somewhere between a simple aggregation of separate states and the ideal of a single confederated Westphalian state. It is not an integrated entity or a system of states but occupies the ambiguous space located between or possibly beyond them. The "surrender" of competencies to Brussels, the emergence of transnational lobbying and social movements within contemporary Europe, and the ongoing precedents established by the European Court of Justice raise a host of questions about how to think about the nature of sovereignty in Europe, as well as about the nature of political accountability and its implications for democracy both within states and within the European Union as a whole.

For many scholars of international relations, trapped within the paradigm of the state system and its unitary ideal of the Westphalian state, contemporary Europe presents a paradox. It is either a supranational state in the process of formation or a collection of ambivalent states attempting to hold on to their sovereignty. Every transfer of decisionmaking authority to Brussels is viewed as yet another zero-sum transfer of sovereignty from the individual state. As Alexander Murphy has recently argued, however, that kind of thinking is indicative of "the extent to which the modern territorial state has captured our spatial imaginations. . . . The co-opting has been so far-reaching that we accept it unproblematically."[1] The emerging European polity should be viewed not as paradoxical but as indicative of a more general change in the operational meaning of sovereignty itself. Europe does not indicate the end of sovereignty but provides one of the most important illustrations of its contemporary redefinition. We need to move beyond traditional conceptualizations of state sovereignty to understand the polity emerging within contemporary Europe.

In our recent book on the social construction of state sovereignty, Cynthia Weber and I attempted to historicize state sovereignty, arguing that its meaning is socially constructed through the practices of states and other principal agents in the international system and concluding that although "state sovereignty is important, it is only one among several competing organizing principles for state relations in the international system."[2] A great variety of alternatives have coexisted with state sovereignty in both the past and the present; the Hanseatic League, the Concert of Europe, the early American states-union, European colonial empires, the informal empire of the former Soviet Union, and pan-Arab nationalism are all examples of significant alternatives. These alternative ways of organizing authority sometimes coexist in harmony with state sovereignty and sometimes coexist uneasily. In this context, the emerging European polity should be viewed not as exceptional but as an illustration of an alternative way of organizing authority from the exclusive territorial state and its aggregations.

Many scholarly observers of contemporary Europe invoke an imagery of ambiguity when they attempt to describe the emerging European polity. For some, the European Union is "very far from being a traditional regional organization,"[3] and existing states "are being melded gently into a multi-level polity"[4] or a "multi-tiered, not strictly hierarchical, political-territorial system."[5] For others, the European polity "is well on the way to becoming something new,"[6] is already "a polity of a new kind"[7] or, as former European Commission President Jacques Delors described it, "un objet politique non-identifié."[8] One thing is clear: Many observers believe more is going on here than a simple aggregation of separate states. John Ruggie goes so far as to speculate that Europe "may constitute nothing less than the emergence of the first truly postmodern international political form."[9] Because of the great difficulty in conceptualizing the European polity, many have called for the development of a new language to describe the phenomenon.[10]

In their efforts to conceptualize and describe the emerging polity in contemporary Europe, scholars routinely invoke the concept of *sovereignty*. Alberta Sbragia has described the gradual transformation of "sovereign" states into "member states,"[11] William Wallace and Julie Smith have discussed the "effective loss of state sovereignty,"[12] and Philippe Schmitter has considered the reluctance of individual countries "to insist on their 'sovereign rights.' "[13] Gary Marks, Liesbet Hooghe, and Kermit Blank repeatedly invoke sovereignty in their assessment of European integration since the 1980s, considering it to be a condition, something weakened, something to be maintained, a control, an institution, and something equated with state-centered analysis more generally.[14] With a few important exceptions, however, most notably in the recent works of James Caporaso,[15] Paul Taylor,[16] and Thomas Risse-Kappen,[17] little of this discussion of sovereignty has been linked to contemporary international relations scholarship. Moreover, virtually none has directly engaged the recent theoretical literature on the changing nature and meanings of sovereignty.

This chapter examines the recent international relations literature on sovereignty, first to determine the extent to which the emerging European polity is indicative of a broader change in the nature of sovereignty itself and second to suggest a vocabulary for describing the phenomenon. It will attempt to move the debate beyond two simple and overstated views of the contemporary nature of sovereignty (with significant parallels in contemporary literature on Europe): one that contends that sovereignty is passé (an exaggerated statement of the multilayered governance perspective) and another that maintains that sovereignty remains the preeminent principle for organizing and understanding international relations (a version of the intergovernmentalist perspective).[18] Framing the discussion as a choice between sovereignty's demise and its preeminence is largely the product of a preoccupation with postwar "realism" and its tenets, an obsession common within much of U.S. international relations thinking. It is important to move the discussion beyond this point in the literature on both European integration and international relations. As Wolfgang Streeck has suggested, "Once it is recognized that the political and economic regime that is developing in Western Europe, whatever it may be, is a new kind of animal that is altogether different from the national state, especially in its relation to the economy, the problem . . . changes from how empty or how full the glass is, to what kind of glass we are dealing with and what purposes it may serve."[19]

Sovereignty is a social construct; it is a vessel into which different meanings can be, and historically have been, poured. What is under way in the world today is an important change in the meaning of sovereignty, and not its demise or disappearance as an institution. This has direct implications for the analysis of the European polity. Whereas sovereignty is still claimed and invoked, its operational meaning may have undergone profound change. If we can understand the nature of that change, we may have a better language and conceptual orientation for describing the contemporary European polity.

CHALLENGES TO THE WESTPHALIAN IDEAL OF STATE SOVEREIGNTY

A major revitalization of interest in sovereignty has occurred since the mid-1980s, an interest that accelerated after the end of the Cold War.[20] Much of this revived interest is a reaction to the series of events and ac-

tions that led up to, and were subsequently enabled by, the end of the ideological struggle between socialist East and capitalist West. Moreover, evidence increasingly indicates that the Westphalian *ideal* of state
sovereignty—as a clearly recognized central location of constitutional
(final) authority, recognized as legitimate by a people with an unproblematic identity and living within a clearly defined territorial space—is already
quite far behind us (if it has ever really existed).

Evidence of apparent challenges to state sovereignty abounds, much of
it largely anecdotal. For example, more United Nations peacekeeping operations have been undertaken during the 1990s than in the forty-five-year
history of the organization preceding 1990. Many of these operations involve a direct challenge to Article 2 of the UN Charter, the principle of
sovereign equality and nonintervention in the domestic affairs of all members—rendering as at least problematic recent UN activities in Bosnia,
Cambodia, El Salvador, Somalia, and Haiti. At the same time, the global
human rights regime has been invigorated, altering major state behavior
even in difficult cases such as China and Argentina.[21] Increasingly, adherence to the global human rights regime has become an important criterion
for diplomatic recognition, as it was for several states of East and Central
Europe and the newly independent states of the former Soviet Union.

In the realm of international finance, we are increasingly cognizant of
an extraordinary increase in the flow of capital across national boundaries—exceeding an average of $1.3 trillion per day—which can appear
to challenge state authority in economic affairs. Double the annual gross
domestic product of the United States crosses national boundaries every
day as increasingly every state, regardless of its size, experiences the constraints of decisions taken by international financial managers given the
dramatic increase in short-term, cross-border portfolio investment in the
early 1990s.

Many states have begun to recognize limits on national economic development. Equating development with modernity and the progressive mas-
tery of nature is increasingly a relic of past thinking in discussions of the
global environment. The harms principle in international law—that is, the
view that no state can intentionally engage in behavior that harms its
neighbors and justify its actions under the mantle of sovereignty—is increasingly accepted. There have been other practical political challenges
to state authority claims, as group rights or the rights of peoples have been
recognized in a wide variety of international settings. The European Commission has recognized the rights of the people of Lombardy in certain
domains, and calls for the recognition of group rights have also emerged
in the former Soviet Union and in International Labor Organization declarations about the rights of indigenous peoples in South America. Much of
this has been reinforced by the major expansion of the activities of non-

governmental organizations—not only in their numbers, resources, and membership but also in their political impact and their ability to place issues on the global agenda.

Finally, a number of new forms of regional political organization have embarked on new courses or emerged in recent years. The EU Maastricht Treaty is the preeminent example of this phenomenon, but we have also witnessed the emergence of other regional arrangements, from the North American Free Trade Agreement (NAFTA) to Mercosur, the Association of Southeast Asian Nations (ASEAN), and the evolving confederation of states in the former Soviet Union. At the same time, other states are renegotiating the authority structures within the territorial space they occupy, from Palestinian home rule to proposed revisions of federal arrangements within Canada.

Taken together, these developments add up to what appears to be a significant challenge to traditional conceptions of state sovereignty—what Daniel Deudney describes as the "real-state" that exists in the abstract world of realist theory where states claim absolute and final authority over a wide range of issues, national identities are unproblematic, and the boundaries around territory (the physical jurisdiction) are clear and unambiguous.[22] The end of the Cold War has raised questions about many old assumptions, including those about state sovereignty.

James Rosenau shares the view that the days of absolute and exclusive sovereignty have passed, and contends that as authority crises of the state have deepened, "thus do efforts to reassert the privileges and benefits of sovereignty seem destined to founder, caught up in the entangling networks of competence and agitation woven by newly empowered masses."[23] In his recent work on territoriality, John Ruggie contends that the world of the modern system of states may be fluid and in the process of being remade: "Its remaking involves a shift not in the play of power politics but of the stage on which that play is performed."[24]

THE REALIST COUNTERREACTION

Whereas some scholars have argued that state sovereignty's time has passed, that it is destined to founder, or that it is being remade (as indicated by the dramatic growth in the global movement of capital, ideas, and technology), others quickly counter that the magnitude of transborder transactions is no greater today than it was at the end of the nineteenth century.[25] Moreover, the recent spate of multilateral interventions is not such a unique departure; sovereignty has long been under challenge in one way or another. As Stephen Krasner observes, "Interventions have always been a feature of the international system."[26] Finally, for some observers the apparent challenges to state sovereignty exist only because states allow them to exist.[27] Since states enabled these developments and structures, states can also dismantle them or take them away.

Although compelling at the outset, each of these responses is deficient in certain respects. The first argument, that transborder flows are no more significant today than they were at the end of the nineteenth century (and that we are only now approaching previous levels of integration), fails to consider changes in the structure of flows across state boundaries, as well as the speed with which transactions take place.[28] Changes in thinking and modes of operation can be found in a variety of types of institutions today. They are most visible in the changing structure of individual firms but can also be seen in a variety of nongovernmental organizations (NGOs), in major international institutions (particularly the international financial institutions), and even within the foreign economic policy of individual states.

Individual firms have begun to change their basic modes of operation from a principal concern with national markets to a concern with planning, production, and servicing on a regional and global scale.[29] As Robert Reich has illustrated with his now classic example of a Japanese-owned multinational with a U.S. subsidiary seeking American government support against the unfair trading practices of an American-owned multinational exporting from East Asia, the idea of "national capital" is increasingly problematic.[30] In geographical terms, whereas the locations of research, production, or services might once have been contained within a single state, they are increasingly likely to be dispersed across different enterprises located in different states. An ever growing number of firms has developed a network of global production locations and an investment strategy that spreads corporate risk (and tax liability) on a global scale. This change in the organization of production has been accompanied by a corresponding change in the organization of international finance.[31] Increased financial liberalization has facilitated the emergence of new financial actors that operate on an instantaneous basis across the globe.

This change in the mode of operation of institutional actors is not restricted to firms; evidence also exists of a shift in orientation within nonprofit nongovernmental organizations, which are no longer just thinking globally and acting locally but are increasingly beginning to act globally as well. Many NGOs operating in the area of humanitarian intervention have been called on to deliver services as part of international relief operations. Over 10 percent of total public development aid (approximately $8 billion) in 1994 was disbursed by NGOs, "surpassing the volume of the combined UN system ($6 billion)" excluding the international financial institutions.[32] Human rights NGOs have created issue networks that operate on a global scale and have effectively pressured states accused of violating individual and group rights, as well as states that might sanction their behavior.[33] These networks have the power to draw attention to issues, to mobilize their transnational networks of support, and even to place issues on the national, regional, and global agenda.

The second realist response, that sovereignty has always been under challenge, is more on the mark; however, it is unable to address questions about where ideas about sovereignty came from in the first place or how they have changed over time.[34] This response reflects the ahistorical tendency of much of positivistic social science and is insufficiently self-reflective. Much more is to be gained from a careful historical reconstruction of the changing meaning of core concepts, such as sovereignty, across time and place. Cynthia Weber's empirical work on changing justifications for cross-border intervention chronicles ways in which the meaning of sovereignty has changed over time—both the changing location of sovereignty (in God, the King, and the People) and the changing justifications for intervention (for God, for King, for Country) or for ideology (whether on behalf of the free world or the liberation of oppressed peoples or for the cause of humanitarianism). Whereas intervention may be a constant feature of the international system, the social practices and justifications for intervention are not.

Finally, in response to the third realist response—that challenges to state sovereignty exist only because states allow them to exist—states *are* responsible for the construction of many institutions and practices now attributed as bringing about the demise of the sovereign state as a political form (the United Nations, global financial market liberalization, the European Union). Just because states created these institutions, however, it is not clear that they can simply dismantle them at some future point. Although states may be inclined to dismantle restrictive institutions, in many instances states have become imprisoned by the very institutions they created, rendering largely irrelevant the fact that those institutions were constructions of the state in the first place. The 1948 Universal Declaration of Human Rights and the Internet are both creations of powerful states. The declaration has become a global regime, however, and the Internet (created to be an indestructible, centerless network for command and control as part of a national defense network) may have been extended beyond the capacity of *any* state to contain, despite recent efforts by China, Saudi Arabia, and the United States.

THINKING ABOUT SOVEREIGNTY

How should we proceed to think about sovereignty? How can we come to terms with the widespread perception of significant change in the nature

of sovereignty without overstating its presence and potential consequences? How should we conceptualize the changing meaning of sovereignty? And how can we get beyond sterile debates about whether sovereignty is eroding or being replaced to consider how its scope and meaning
might have changed?

It is helpful to begin with a conception of sovereignty as a social construct. Social construction links identity with practice.[35] Sovereignty is an
inherently social concept. States' claims to sovereignty construct a social
environment in which they can interact (the international society of
states),[36] whereas at the same time the mutual recognition of each other's
claims to sovereignty is an important element in the construction of states
themselves.[37] States create sovereignty as an institution, and the institution
of sovereignty creates states. In this sense, states and sovereignty are mutually constitutive and relationally defined. Moreover, each of the core components of sovereignty—authority, identity, and territory—is also constructed socially.

We can begin our analysis with a provisional definition of sovereignty
as the external recognition (by states) of claims of final authority by states.
This is simple enough, perhaps transparently so; however, these claims are
not absolute.[38] States' authority claims vary from one issue area to another
and are not fixed over time, which is the key to understanding the changing
meaning of sovereignty. The question is not whether sovereignty exists as
a unitary condition or state of being but how claims of authority are issue
specific and change over time.

Therefore, one way to come to terms with the changing meaning of sovereignty is not to search (probably in vain) for an alternative to the system
of sovereign state authority that already exists or is about to appear. The
modern state system we perceive as having emerged out of the Treaty of
Westphalia did not come about as a result of a clear break with the past,[39]
and there is no reason to expect any potential transformation away from
the ideal of the Westphalian state sovereignty system to be any different.
Elements of the past continue in the present; changes can be perceived
only after we develop a vocabulary to describe them.[40] Forms or under-
standings of sovereignty will emerge, like an image out of a fog; they will
come into view only gradually and dimly. We do not have to identify a
clearly defined new global authority or imagine a return to the heteronomy
of the Middle Ages to discuss emerging forms of sovereignty. A more
fruitful way to proceed is to focus on variations in claims of authority.[41]

The concept of authority itself is not free of complexity and ambiguity,
and a long tradition of analysis of the concept exists within political theory. For the purposes of the argument about authority claims in this chapter, however, the close relationship between power and authority is recognized, and authority is taken to refer to institutionalized, or formal, power.

What differentiates authority from power is the legitimacy of the claim (implying rights of some superior or some location of authority and obligations of subordinates or subjects of that authority). Legitimacy implies some form of consent or recognition of authority by the regulated or governed. This consent may be socially constructed through the political and rhetorical practices of political leaders. It is the product of persuasion and trust rather than coercion.

Sovereignty's meaning is variable, therefore, because the authority claims states make (or are recognized by other states to have made) are not fixed in space and time. They vary, and this variance determines the change in the meaning of sovereignty. Many scholars have been stymied by the observation (or declaration in the works of F. H. Hinsley and of Alan James on constitutional independence) that sovereignty is indivisible.[42] Therefore, it is impossible to imagine degrees of sovereignty. It is not meaningful to talk about an "erosion" of sovereignty in a linear or continuous sense. Similarly, the 1970s literature on interdependence was appropriately criticized for confusing sovereignty with influence and control. The degree of control may vary but not the status of sovereignty, or so the traditional argument goes. Rather than claim that sovereignty is indivisible (you either have it or you do not), however, it is more fruitful to argue that the range of issues over which authority is claimed or recognized by others is not fixed. It varies, and its variance determines the changing meaning of sovereignty.

For example, during the age of decolonization that followed the end of World War II, states held very closely to the view stated in Article 2 of the UN Charter that "nothing contained in the present Charter shall authorize the United Nations to intervene in matters which are essentially within the domestic jurisdiction of any state." Operationally this meant states claimed rights to take measures that might include everything from the right to extend rights to individuals to the severe repression of minority groups challenging the goals of the nation-building project. All of this was undertaken in the name of national security, national development, or state building. These claims were tacitly recognized by the inaction (in both word and deed) of other states, and they were defended in the name of national sovereignty and *rights* of sovereign nonintervention. During the 1970s these claims were extended into the economic realm, with declarations of the permanent sovereignty of states over natural resources located in their territories.

Today, these claims sound archaic. Moreover, even the most repressive of the major powers—China—frames the defense of its human rights behavior in terms of a discourse of rights.[43] China criticizes its critics for their failure to address their people's economic and social rights. The fact that China engages in a discourse about human rights and defends itself in these terms, rather than in a repetition of rights of nonintervention in matters that are under "domestic jurisdiction," indicates a change in the nature of authority claims made by states.

Claims of permanent sovereignty over natural resources associated with the new international economic order negotiations in the 1970s have followed a similar course in the 1990s. They are simply no longer being made, particularly as the pace of liberalization and privatization has accelerated across the globe.

Many scholars interested in the study of sovereignty have differentiated between its *internal* and *external* dimensions. The internal dimension generally refers to the consolidation of the territory under a single authority and the recognition of that authority as legitimate by the people, whereas the external dimension generally refers to recognition by other states. This distinction between the internal and external dimensions of sovereignty can be adapted to the argument in this chapter about the issue-specific nature of sovereignty as follows: Both the number and range of authority claims have changed (the traditional "internal" dimension of sovereignty), as have the number and range of claims recognized externally as legitimate (the "external" dimension).[44]

To elaborate on the external dimension, norms of recognition change over time. The criteria for recognition vary according to the global power political structure and the ideational context (the norms in play) of international relations.[45] As Nina Tannenwald has recently argued, there are norms that regulate behavior, norms that constitute identity, and norms that permit certain actions.[46] One of the best recent illustrations is the changing norm of recognition for the countries of East and Central Europe, which now extends to include the establishment of democratic institutions and respect for the rights of minorities. These norms of recognition are not absolute, and they are not uniformly applied (as the cases of Croatia and Bosnia testify); rather, they are constantly negotiated and placed on the diplomatic agenda. The important point for the present argument is that some of these norms of recognition—particularly the establishment of democratic institutions and the protection of group rights—were not norms as recently as the late 1980s.

NEW LOCATIONS OF AUTHORITY

If the range of authority claims is variable, where does the authority over specific issues previously claimed or recognized by states go? Does it disappear? If not, who or what inherits the authority states no longer claim or are recognized by others to possess? The location of authority in the global system has significantly dispersed in recent years; Susan Strange has termed it a "diffusion of power in the world economy."[47] The state is no longer the predominant location of authority on a growing number of issues and faces challenges from other locations. In some cases the state no longer claims to have authority, in other instances it is no longer recognized externally by others as possessing authority in certain domains, and in still other cases it faces competing claims and challenges from other actors. This situation can be illustrated by discussing examples of each of these three types of challenges to traditional (or idealized) state authority claims: the ceding of claims of final authority to other locations, the changing norms of external recognition of claims, and the emergence of competing locations of authority.

First, states may cut back on their range of claims of final authority. The ceding of competencies in certain issue domains from individual states to the European Union is a prime example of reducing claims of authority. It is ironic to note the speed with which the new states of East and Central Europe, in seeking national independence (taken by some to illustrate a trend counter to that described in this chapter) are willing to surrender many of the claims of final authority associated with the Westphalian ideal of potential benefits of membership in the European Union. Similar transference of authority can be seen in the emergent dispute resolution mechanisms within NAFTA. Efforts to harmonize policy in anticipation of the benefits of deepened regional integration further illustrate voluntary disengagement from prior claims of authority, which is taking place at a time when there appears to be a significant expansion of regional institutions throughout the world, as discussed elsewhere in this volume.

Other international institutions are increasingly being ceded a legitimate authority that constrains not only the weakest states but increasingly some of the larger powers as well. States created and therefore willingly abide by the strictures of these institutions. For example, the United Nations has sanctioned humanitarian interventions in a growing number of instances. The operative issue is no longer whether these interventions are justified but whether the United Nations can accommodate the large demand for action in so many different locations. The frequency, extent, and apparent acceptability of conditionality by international financial institutions have also significantly increased. This has ranged from the International Monetary Fund's enhanced surveillance, demands for institutional reform during the Asian financial crisis, and criticism of military spending in member countries to the political conditionality of the World Bank and the European Bank for Reconstruction and Development and the World Bank's interest in environmental conditionality. The growing recognition and use of the dispute resolution mechanisms of the World Trade Organization provide yet another illustration.

Similarly, the International Court of Justice has begun to hear cases that apply the principle of harms in transborder pollution cases, and international lawyers prosecuting international war crimes tribunals have pushed litigation beyond the intentions and wishes of the major powers that initiated the proceedings. Issues that were once unambiguously inside the realm of state responsibility have been delegated to outside institutions. The boundary separating inside from outside has moved—dramatically far—in some instances.

Second, some important changes have been made in recognition, both by other states and by international institutions, of some of the claims previously made by states. For example, states are no longer recognized as legitimate final authorities on the violation of the human rights of individuals or groups within their domains. When it was first promulgated in 1948, the Universal Declaration of Human Rights was just another legal proclamation with no effective international enforcement mechanism. The declaration's influence was often contingent on the backing of major powers, primarily the United States, which applied it when convenient during the Cold War but ignored it when a critical alliance partner was involved.

Today, however, ideas about the universalization of human rights have been institutionalized to the extent that they have begun to challenge some of the prerogatives of traditional state sovereignty. Although important regional variations exist in conceptions of human rights (and a good deal of legitimate debate takes place about their scope, ranging from narrow applications to individuals to broader applications to groups[48]), there is global acceptance of the discourse of human rights. That is, virtually everyone constructs their arguments in terms of different sets of legitimate human rights. This reality is as significant for the development of democracy as was the extension of suffrage throughout the world earlier in the twentieth century.

At the same time, as discussed earlier, some important changes have occurred in the norms of recognition of new states. Until recently, the principal criteria for external recognition were associated with meeting the requirements of internal sovereignty (physical control over the territorial space, acceptance by the subject population, clearly established lines of governmental authority, and the like), along with the Cold War alliance concerns of the superpowers. Increasingly important today, however, are requirements such as the establishment and consolidation of democratic institutions, the treatment of the rights of minority populations, and even the management of the economy.

International institutions have withheld recognition of some of the claims of states not only with regard to the actions of coercive agents of the state against subject populations, such as torture or fundamental violations of individual rights, but also with regard to the protection of other aspects of the lives of private individuals within states. The emergence of third-party human rights law has extended the range of international law to issues such as racial discrimination in housing, gender employment, and relationships within the family (previously considered part of the "private" domain). Other international institutions such as the World Trade Organization have begun to intrude into the previously sacrosanct domestic domain by criticizing some labor policies, consumer product safety standards, and environmental accords as non-tariff barriers to free trade.

Third, competing claims of authority have begun to emerge from non-state locations in the world system—from individuals, groups, and markets. In potentially precedent-setting arrangements, individuals now have the right to challenge the actions of states and international institutions, as manifested in the World Bank's new Inspection Panel schema.[49] If two individuals can claim significant material harm as the result of a World Bank project, they can initiate a quasi-independent review of investment decisions taken by the Bank. Although the Inspection Panel is located within the Bank, it is technically independent. Individuals not only have the power to initiate a review of Bank decisions, but their intervention can lead to the termination of a project. One significant precedent here is that the individuals who initiate the review do not need the sanction or backing of their own government. Hence, individuals are recognized as legitimate agents by both states and the intergovernmental institutions they have created.

Even more significant are the actions of transnational issue networks that operate most effectively in the domains of human rights and the global environment. Transnational issue networks, the global spread of ideas, and the emergence of elements of global civil society have increasingly begun to constrain the actions of middle powers. As already discussed, the global acceptance of the discourse of human rights has been facilitated by systemic technological changes. The global reach of the media has increased the visibility of state actions and increasingly exposed them to potential opinion sanctions from NGO networks operating across the globe. States such as China continue to assert traditional claims of sovereign authority yet increasingly find themselves competing with other sources of legitimate authority in the international system—especially the emerging authority of transnational issue networks, which some have described as evidence of the emergence of a global civil society.[50]

Global civil society sets standards of international behavior that increasingly constrain the actions of individual states. The weight of global public opinion is such that states must increasingly be concerned about the reactions of other states, of the publics of those states, and of nongovernmental organizations to avoid being labeled a pariah state, to gain entry into the society of states, to obtain access to conditional resources, and to enter regional common markets such as the European Union or NAFTA.

Nongovernmental organizations, from human rights and humanitarian assistance organizations to environmental NGOs, have played a critical role in facilitating the emergence of a global civil society and are increasingly recognized as legitimate players in the contemporary global system. Advances in communications technology have gradually increased the transparency of individual states and made it possible for repressed groups and individuals to appeal to potential allies abroad for support. In addition, the changed international context in the aftermath of the Cold War has created a situation in which small states receive (and expect) more intervention, since it is no longer possible to play one superpower against another.

The development of human rights institutions and the emergence of intergovernmental procedures for investigating rights abuses (rights tribunals) have further institutionalized and reinforced the basic ideas. These transnational issue networks operate by drawing attention to issues, mobilizing their networks, and placing issues on the global agenda. The practice of convening of parallel meetings of NGOs alongside major UN-sponsored state congresses has become routine in recent years, ranging from the human rights conference in Vienna to the conferences on the environment in Rio, on women in Beijing, and on social development in Copenhagen. This has further legitimated the role of NGOs as they put issues on the global agenda and in some instances even define the terms of the debate.

Finally, the globalization of finance and the emergence of integrated global financial markets have increasingly begun to discipline *all* states, even the most powerful. A major shift has occurred away from sharply demarcated national financial boundaries—with effective currency controls in place—toward increased financial liberalization, the elimination of currency controls, and increased ease of cross-border financial transactions. This tendency toward financial liberalization has facilitated the emergence of new financial actors (bond traders, currency traders, portfolio investors) who have developed global hedging strategies and operate on an around-the-clock and around-the-globe basis. As a result, the emerging world financial market "is not comprised of linked national markets; in fact, it is not comprised of geographic locations at all. It is a network integrated through electronic information systems that entails . . . more than two hundred thousand electronic monitors in trading rooms all over the world that are linked together."[51]

This network has become a location of authority in the economic world, with an ability to reward (and to discipline) countries that pursue policies it deems prudent (or unsustainable). The network operates, in effect, like a global "hard budget constraint" on the behavior of economic and financial decisionmakers who have participated in the ceding of informal authority to the markets through both their statements and their behavior. When finance ministers or heads of state begin to believe and publicly declare that markets have the power to discipline their actions, they signal their consent and participate in empowering markets as legitimate authorities in certain domains.

The changes in the organization of global finance have rendered ambiguous the traditional territorial imagery of international political economy.[52] We need to unbundle our concept of territoriality.[53] Control over flows and networks is becoming more important than hierarchical control over physical territorial space, as Timothy Luke has demonstrated with reference to Kuwait (where royal family control over the flows of oil and wealth continued even after the loss of control of all of the physical territory once occupied by the regime).[54] The emergence of the "region-state"—economic zones with integrated industrial investment and information systems that straddle national boundaries in an increasingly borderless world—is another manifestation of this blurring of traditional conceptions of territoriality.[55] Nowhere is this blurring of territoriality more apparent than in the intense and growing regional interdependence between the United States and Mexico. The recession in Mexico following the peso crisis in the mid-1990s had severe effects on the regional economy of the American Southwest, so much so that it is not an exaggeration to say that for Los Angeles what happens in Mexico City is more important than what happens in Boston.

The visibility and salience of each of these challenges to the Westphalian ideal of state sovereignty—the ceding of final authority to other institutions, the changes in external recognition of final authority, and the emergence of competing locations of final authority—have increased in recent years. Their ability to challenge the authority of states on an ever growing set of issues has also increased, as we can see throughout contemporary Europe.

THE REDEFINITION OF SOVEREIGNTY IN CONTEMPORARY EUROPE

The way of thinking about sovereignty outlined previously can be readily applied to the analysis of the polity emerging within contemporary Europe. Indeed, many of the best illustrations of ceding authority, changing recognition of authority claims, and emerging competing authorities can be found in Europe today. An issue-specific understanding of sovereignty can be useful in thinking about "sovereignty" in modern Europe.

Philippe Schmitter has recently reanalyzed Leon Lindberg and Stuart Scheingold's classic assessment of the expansion of European Community authority[56] and extended it (with some help from the members of the Consortium for 1992) to consider the potential outcome of the Single European Act and the Maastricht Treaty. Schmitter's analysis is based on projections made from existing treaty obligations and from obligations undertaken as a result of subsequent implementation decisions.[57] He estimates that in the arena of economic policy issues—all of which were decided entirely at the state level in 1950—decision authority will reside primarily at the European Union level by the year 2001 in the areas of agriculture, capital flows, goods and services, employment, money and credit, foreign exchange, and macroeconomic policy. In sectors such as transportation, communications, regional development, competition, industry, revenue and taxation, and the environment, policy decisions will be made at both the state and the EU levels. Only in the energy sector will the bulk of the decisionmaking authority continue to reside at the state level, but even there decisions will be shared to some extent.

A similar pattern emerges in the arena of sociocultural issues where working conditions, education, and labor-management relations will be decided at both the state and European levels. Within the domain of politics and constitutional matters, Schmitter and his associates estimate that justice and property rights issues will be decided mostly at the European level, whereas citizenship matters will be shared. Even in international affairs, all policy decisions will be taken at the EU level in commercial negotiations, and economic and military assistance, diplomacy, and intergovernmental organization membership issues will be decided largely within Europe. Only defense and war matters will remain shared between states and the EU. In sum, Schmitter concludes that "there is no issue area that was the exclusive domain of national policy in 1950 that has not somehow and to some degree been incorporated within the authoritative purview of the EC/EU."[58]

Schmitter's analysis is significant because it provides a way of tracking empirically the range and number of claims of authority that have been ceded to Brussels since the late 1950s. Authority over a wide range of issues has been transferred to the European Union, which offers a concrete illustration of a significant reduction in the range and number of claims of authority previously made by the states of Europe. States may have ceded authority for a number of reasons, including efforts to maintain their authority in other arenas. This does not, however, negate the fact that the operational meaning of the states' sovereignty has been broadly redefined by their practices. Moreover, as will be discussed in further detail later, a certain "stickiness" accompanies the ceding of authority over certain domains. EU member states may discover that it is far easier to give things up than to retrieve them at some unspecified future date.

Beyond the ceding of authority to Brussels, there are also some important examples of change in the recognition of claims of authority made previously by the states of Europe. Throughout much of their history, and certainly since the mid-twentieth century, states in Europe were recognized by other states as legitimate in claiming that their treatment of minorities was their own matter. In many instances the norm was one of integration, rather than consociational tolerance, of different peoples. Ever since the European Commission began to recognize the rights of peoples, however, this claim has been undercut. The Commission's invocation of serving the *nations* of Europe is indicative of the rhetorical turn in its reconceptualization of its role. A state's claims are no longer recognized as legitimate in this vital area.

A more substantial challenge to some of the claims previously made by states has emanated from the European Court of Justice. Ever since the Court determined that treaty decisions had a *direct effect*, "that is, that Treaty provisions had the effect of domestic law within the member states even without explicit implementation at the national or Community level,"[59] states have suffered an important loss of external recognition of their claims of authority. This blow was deepened further when the Court of Justice established the supremacy of Community law over national law in 1974, thereby empowering individuals to make charges regarding the violation of their legal rights by their own states.[60]

In addition to ceding claims of authority and losing recognition of prior claims, states in Europe face an array of other groups and institutions challenging their authority in certain domains. Transnational networks and social movements are no longer contained within the confines of the state and can challenge its authority over issues ranging from human rights to the environment. Business lobbying is no longer restricted to or focused on national jurisdictions and increasingly makes claims on behalf of the private sector throughout Europe. As Marks, Hooghe, and Blank have suggested, it is more appropriate to argue that

> Political arenas are interconnected rather than nested. While national arenas remain important for the formation of state executive preferences, the multilevel governance model rejects the view that subnational actors are nested exclusively within them. Instead, they act directly both in national and supranational arenas, creating transnational associations in the process.[61]

Finally, as with the rest of the world, the states of Europe are increasingly subject to the assessments and decisions of financial markets—not just those located in Europe but those throughout the world.

Thus, although the states of Europe are still "sovereign" in some important respects, the meaning of their sovereignty has changed profoundly. They have ceded authority, lost authority, and confronted new locations of authority. By conceptualizing sovereignty as constituting issue-specific claims (and recognition of claims) of authority, we are able to get beyond the dilemma of deciding whether the indivisible (sovereign authority) is divisible or whether the glass is half empty or half full. Sovereignty is simply not what it used to be.

CONCLUSION

Can these general trends be expected to continue? Will the tendencies toward reduced state claims of authority and a redefinition of sovereignty be reversed? Is the European experience only one variant of the immediate post–Cold War rhetoric about a new world order, millennial thinking, a passing phase, or an order whose end is already in sight?

Individual states can and will resist or ignore some of these pressures, at least for a time. Global technological changes are more or less permanent, however, and have had an important effect on the ongoing struggle over the extension of rights, the perceived need for UN intervention, and the globalization of financial markets. Global technological advances have led to greater transparency about state finances, facilitated the transmission of norms and values, and helped to reinforce the shifting of authority to a growing number of locations outside the traditional territorial state.

Transnational networks have displaced the territorial state in the organization of global production, the distribution of global finance, the provision of emergency relief and assistance, the protection of individual and group rights, and the defense of the global environment. This development, facilitated by the technological change described earlier, will ensure that the redefinition of state sovereignty (as the reduction of the number and range of authority claims made by states) is likely to continue in general terms well into the twenty-first century.

Within Europe the development of institutions has proven to be more important than technology and transnational networks in redefining the sovereignty of its states. Some of this is a product of the unintended consequences of state actions. The creation of structural policy was transformed by the European Commission from a side payment to poor countries to an interventionist instrument of regional policy.[62] The increase in the size of the Community from the original six to fifteen members by 1995 expanded the diversity of state executives, increased the room for contention, and enhanced the specialization and technical sophistication of decisionmaking.[63] In addition to the unintended consequences, however, some European institutions—particularly the European Commission—have proven capable of taking their own initiatives with regard to setting the policy agenda, thus further contributing to the redefinition of the sovereignty of the European state.

Much of the debate over contemporary European integration (probably too much) continues to revolve around the alternative conceptualizations of intergovernmentalism and multilayered governance. They are often presented as virtually incommensurable frameworks, yet a number of scholars have attempted to accommodate the sovereign state as a meaningful entity within a regional institution that is expanding its authority domain. Paul Taylor has suggested that the survival of the European state and the extension of the European Union can be made compatible with the theoretical emergence of a Europeanwide consociationalism.[64] His conclusion that the EU states will remain sovereign "until a fundamentally different order is introduced,"[65] however, does not consider the substantial change in the operational meaning of sovereignty that has already taken place. In a similar vein, Wolfgang Streeck's interesting account of the emerging coalition between nationalism and neoliberalism suggests that states might exchange responsibility for the economy for the preservation of their national sovereignty.[66] His conception of sovereignty, however, also fails to consider its contemporary change in meaning.

Viewing sovereignty as variable in meaning (and not just in location) is intended to contribute to the vocabulary needed to conceptualize the polity emerging within contemporary Europe. Such a view does not solve all of the conceptual problems, but it should help to move the discussion beyond the idea of the indivisibility of sovereignty. Ironically, the absence of a clearly defined constitutional order within Europe facilitates the ambiguity and fluidity of the boundaries between states and state.

NOTES

1. Alexander B. Murphy, "The Sovereign State System as Political-Territorial Ideal: Historical and Contemporary Considerations," in *State Sovereignty as Social Construct*, Thomas J. Biersteker and Cynthia Weber, eds. (Cambridge: Cambridge University Press, 1996), 107.

2. Cynthia Weber and Thomas J. Biersteker, "Reconstructing the Analysis of Sovereignty: Concluding Reflections and Directions for Future Research," in *State Sovereignty as Social Construct*, Biersteker and Weber, eds., 279–280.

3. Alberta Sbragia, "From 'Nation-State' to 'Member-State': The Evolution of the European Community," in *Europe After Maastricht: American and European Perspectives*, Paul M. Lutzeler, ed. (Providence: Berghahn, 1994), 70.

4. Gary Marks, Liesbet Hooghe, and Kermit Blank, "European Integration Since the 1980s: State-Centric Versus Multi-Level Governance," *Journal of Common Market Studies* 34, no. 3 (September 1996), 371.

5. Murphy, "The Sovereign State System," 111.

6. Philippe C. Schmitter, "Examining the Present Euro-Polity with the Help of Past Theories," in *Governance in the European Union*, Gary Marks, Fritz W. Scharpf, Philippe C. Schmitter, and Wolfgang Streeck, eds. (London: Sage, 1996), 14.

7. Wolfgang Streeck, "Neo-Volunteerism: A New European Social Policy Regime?" in *Governance in the European Union*, Marks, Scharpf, Schmitter, and Streeck, eds., 64.

8. Schmitter, "Examining the Present Euro-Polity," 1.

9. John Gerard Ruggie, "Territoriality and Beyond: Problematizing Modernity in International Relations," *International Organization* 47, no. 1 (winter 1993), 139–140.

10. Philippe C. Schmitter, "Imagining the Future of the Euro-Polity with the Help of New Concepts," in *Governance in the European Union*, Marks, Scharpf, Schmitter, and Streeck, eds., 133.

11. Sbragia, "From 'Nation-State' to 'Member-State,' " 87.

12. William Wallace and Julie Smith, "Democracy or Technocracy? European Integration and the Problem of Popular Consent," *West European Politics* 18, no. 3 (July 1995), 148.

13. Schmitter, "Imagining the Future," 129.

14. Marks, Hooghe, and Blank, "European Integration Since the 1980s."

15. James A. Caporaso, "The European Union and Forms of State: Westphalian, Regulatory or Post-Modern?" *Journal of Common Market Studies* 34, no. 1 (March 1996).

16. Paul Taylor, "The European Community and the State: Assumptions, Theories and Propositions," *Review of International Studies* 17, no. 2 (April 1991).

17. Thomas Risse-Kappen, "Exploring the Nature of the Beast: International Relations Theory and Comparative Policy Analysis Meet the European Union," *Journal of Common Market Studies* 34, no. 1 (March 1996).

18. Andrew Moravcsik, "Negotiating the Single European Act: National Interests and Conventional Statecraft in the European Community," *International Organization* 45, no. 1 (winter 1991).

19. Streeck, "Neo-Volunteerism," 65.

20. F. H. Hinsley, *Sovereignty*, 2d ed. (Cambridge: Cambridge University Press, 1986); Alan James, *Sovereign Statehood: The Basis of International Society* (London: Allen and Unwin, 1986); Richard K. Ashley, "Untying the Sovereign State: A Double Reading of the Anarchy Problematique," *Millennium: Journal of International Studies* 17, no. 2 (fall 1988); Stephen D. Krasner, "Sovereignty: An Institutional Perspective," *Comparative Political Studies* 21, no. 5 (1988); Philip Allot, *Eunomia: New Order for a New World* (New York: Oxford University Press, 1990); Robert Jackson, *Quasi-States: Sovereignty, International Relations and the Third World* (Cambridge: Cambridge University Press, 1990); Nicholas Greenwood Onuf, "Sovereignty: Outline of a Conceptual History," *Alternatives* 16, no. 4 (1991); Stanley Hoffmann, "Delusions of World Order," *New York Review of Books*, April 9, 1992; Ruggie, "Territoriality and Beyond"; R. B. J. Walker, *Inside/Outside: International Relations as Political Theory* (Cambridge: Cambridge University Press, 1993); Stephen D. Krasner, "Westphalia," unpublished manuscript,

Stanford University, 1991; Gene M. Lyons and Michael Mastanduno, eds., *Beyond Westphalia? State Sovereignty and International Intervention* (Baltimore: Johns Hopkins University Press, 1995); Jens Bartelson, *A Genealogy of Sovereignty* (Cambridge: Cambridge University Press, 1995).

21. Kathryn Sikkink, "Human Rights, Principled Issue Networks, and Sovereignty in Latin America," *International Organization* 47, no. 3 (summer 1993).

22. Daniel Deudney, "The Philadelphian System: Sovereignty, Arms Control, and Balance of Power in the American States-Union, Circa 1787–1861," *International Organization* 49, no. 2 (spring 1995), 192.

23. James N. Rosenau, "Sovereignty in a Turbulent World," in *Beyond Westphalia?*, Lyons and Mastanduno, eds., 224.

24. Ruggie, "Territoriality and Beyond," 139–140.

25. Robert Wade, "Globalization and Its Limits: Reports of the Death of the National Economy Are Greatly Exaggerated," in *Convergence or Diversity? National Models of Production and Distribution in a Global Economy,* Suzanne Berger and Ronald Dore, eds. (Ithaca, N.Y.: Cornell University Press, 1995).

26. Stephen D. Krasner, "Sovereignty and Intervention," in *Beyond Westphalia?*, Lyons and Mastanduno, eds., 246.

27. Ethan B. Kapstein, "We Are US: The Myth of the Multinational," *National Interest* 26 (winter 1991–1992).

28. Thomas J. Biersteker, "Globalization and the Modes of Operation of Major Institutional Actors," *Oxford Development Studies* 26, no. 1 (February 1998).

29. Not all firms need to respond identically for a significant change to be under way.

30. Robert Reich, *The Work of Nations* (New York: Knopf, 1991).

31. Benjamin J. Cohen, "Phoenix Risen: The Resurrection of Global Finance," *World Politics* 48, no. 2 (January 1996).

32. Leon Gordenker and Thomas Weiss, "Pluralizing Global Governance: Analytical Approaches and Dimensions," in *NGOs, the UN, and Global Governance,* Leon Gordenker and Thomas Weiss, eds. (Boulder: Lynne Rienner, 1996), 25. They argue that 25 percent of U.S. assistance is channeled through NGOs and that while he was attending the Social Summit in Copenhagen, U.S. Vice President Al Gore pledged to increase that amount to 50 percent by the end of the decade.

33. Sikkink, "Human Rights."

34. Cynthia Weber, *Simulating Sovereignty: Intervention, the State, and Symbolic Exchange* (Cambridge: Cambridge University Press, 1995).

35. Biersteker and Weber, eds., *State Sovereignty as Social Construct*, 278.

36. Hedley Bull, *The Anarchical Society* (New York: Columbia University Press, 1977).

37. Biersteker and Weber, eds., *State Sovereignty as Social Construct*, 1–2.

38. This conception of sovereignty is analogous to the idea of property; individuals do not possess absolute authority over the use of the property they own. See especially Friedrich Kratochwil, "The Concept of Sovereignty: Sovereignty as Property," unpublished manuscript, University of Pennsylvania, 1992.

39. Krasner, "Westphalia."

40. Ruggie, "Territoriality and Beyond."

41. We need not restrict ourselves to authority, however. Identity is also crucial because it defines a people over whom authority is exercised, as is territory because it defines a physical domain within which authority is claimed to apply.

42. Hinsley, *Sovereignty*, and James, *Sovereign Statehood.*

43. Sikkink, "Human Rights."

44. It is important, however, not to reify this distinction between the internal and the external because the boundary that separates them is a changing one.

45. This is a variant of John Ruggie's observation about regimes and the lack of direct correspondence between hegemony and support for liberal institutionalism. See John Ruggie, "International Regimes, Transactions, and Change: Embedded Liberalism in the Postwar Economic Order," *International Organization* 36, no. 2 (spring 1982).

46. Nina Tannenwald, "The Nuclear Taboo: The Normative Basis of Nuclear Non-Use," unpublished manuscript, Watson Institute, Brown University, 1996.

47. Susan Strange, *The Retreat of the State: The Diffusion of Power in the World Economy* (Cambridge: Cambridge University Press, 1996).

48. Andrew Hurrell, "International Relations and the Promotion of Democracy and Human Rights." Paper presented at the Queen Elizabeth House conference, "The Third World After the Cold War: Ideology, Economic Development and Politics," Oxford University, July 5–8, 1995.

49. Michael J. Hsu, "Institutional Learning: A Study of the World Bank Inspection Panel," B.A. Honors Thesis, Department of Political Science, Brown University, May 1997.

50. Ronnie D. Lipschultz, "Reconstructing World Politics: The Emergence of Global Civil Society," *Millennium* 21, no. 3 (winter 1992).

51. Stephen J. Kobrin, "Beyond Symmetry: State Sovereignty in a Networked Global Economy," in *Governments, Globalization and International Business*, John H. Dunning, ed. (Oxford: Oxford University Press, 1997), 20.

52. Stephen J. Rosow, "On the Political Theory of Political Economy: Conceptual Ambiguity and the Global Economy," *Review of International Political Economy* 1 (autumn 1994).

53. Ruggie, "Territoriality and Beyond," 171.

54. Timothy Luke, "The Discipline of Security Studies and the Codes of Containment: Learning from Kuwait," *Alternatives* 16 (1991).

55. Kenichi Ohmae, *The End of the Nation State: The Rise of Regional Economies* (New York: Free Press, 1995), 79–82.

56. Leon Lindberg and Stuart Scheingold, *Europe's Would-Be Polity* (Englewood Cliffs, N.J.: Prentice-Hall, 1970).

57. Schmitter, "Imagining the Future."

58. Ibid., 124.

59. Marks, Hooghe, and Blank, "European Integration Since the 1980s," 49.

60. Ibid.

61. Ibid., 5.

62. Liesbet Hooghe, "Building a Europe with the Regions: The Changing Role of the European Commission," in *European Integration, Cohesion Policy, and Subnational Mobilisation*, Liesbet Hooghe ed. (Oxford: Oxford University Press, 1996).

63. Marks, Hooghe, and Blank, "European Integration Since the 1980s," 28–29.

64. Taylor, "The European Community and the State," 109.

65. Ibid., 123.

66. Streeck, "Neo-Volunteerism," 68–69.

3

Legitimacy and Democracy: Endogenous Limits of European Integration

Wolfgang Merkel

European integration has been above all the work of political elites. One of the secrets of the advance of European integration, despite occasional lulls, was that it was guided by national executives and promoted by decisions of the European Commission and the European Court. The control of political decisionmaking at the European Community (EC) level by national and supranational sovereigns has been more diffuse, indirect, and incomplete than any democratic member state could sustain. Neither the European Parliament nor the national parliaments—with the notable exception of the Danish Folketing and to some extent the British Parliament—have been able to control the EC legislative process. Subnational units such as the German Länder, the Belgian regions, and the Spanish Comunidades Autónomas have been excluded from decisionmaking despite their constitutional prerogatives within their countries. Aside from the Danish, the Irish, and sometimes the French, the populations of the member states were not asked for input when the treaty framework was fundamentally revised, as occurred in 1986 and 1992.

The weak and insufficient control these democratically legitimated actors and institutions wielded turned out to be rather favorable for European integration, although that changed with the Treaty of Maastricht and the transition from negative economic integration[1] to positive economic and political integration. Deepening became visible and forced numerous supranational, national, and subnational actors to claim additional rights of participation and control in the European decisionmaking process. The long-standing normative goal of closing the European Community's democratic deficit became a functional prerequisite for further integration as well.

What does all of this mean for the scope, direction, and speed of further European integration? The answers presented by the relevant theories of regional integration seem clear. The federalists—or, better, constitutional-ists—claim constitutionally legitimized decisionmaking on the supranational level is the normative and functional *conditio* sine qua non of European integration. A common supranational constitution must be established to initiate a successful and irreversible process of regional integration. The functionalists and neofunctionalists argue the opposite. They see the initial transfer of technical, nonpolitical functions in one economic sector from the national to the supranational level as the beginning of an expansive logic of integration. When one sector is integrated on a supranational level, it will create strains within other functionally independent economic sectors. To alleviate this friction and save the level of integration already achieved, other sectors must be successively integrated as well. Neorealists reject this functionalist point of view. They perceive national governments as the decisive actors that control the process of European integration. And although the governments of the member states may agree that economic integration should occur to maximize mutual welfare, this process will never spill over into the sphere of high politics.

As mutually exclusive theoretical frameworks, these theories fail to explain the stops and starts of European integration, to say nothing of its future trajectory. Above all, they neglect the role democracy plays in the integration process. My hypothesis holds that until the beginning of the 1990s the lack of democracy was highly functional for the course of economic integration. After the Treaty of Maastricht and the transition from negative economic integration to positive economic and political integration, the democratic deficit became a hindrance to further integration. But however necessary from a functional standpoint, democratization will decrease the efficiency of the decisionmaking process in the European Union. In short, an efficiency-democracy dilemma could emerge.

I will develop my argument in four steps. First, I will describe the kind of legitimacy the European Union (EU) needs to survive. Second, I will explore what sort of democratic deficit exists within the EU, and what it means for further deepening of integration. Then I will discuss whether a dilemma exists between the utilitarian and democratic components of legitimacy. Fourth, I will ask whether it is possible to construct a European polity that could overcome the utilitarian-democratic legitimacy dilemma.

LEGITIMACY AND THE EUROPEAN UNION

The European Union is not a federation or a confederation. It is more than an international regime but less than a supranational state. It has been defined, although vaguely, as a "part-formed political system,"[2] a "would-be polity,"[3] and a system "sui generis."[4] This vagueness reflects, on the one hand, the European Union's incremental, ongoing integration process, which continually defies precise definitions. On the other hand, the vagueness illustrates the difficulty in constitutionally defining the European Union's multilevel decisionmaking. Decisionmaking in the EU occurs through a complex, interwoven pattern of national, intergovernmental, and supranational structures.[5] Therefore, a suitable normative theory of political responsibility and democratic participation does not exist for such an intricate political structure.[6] The incompleteness of the definition, even in the area of jurisprudence (sui generis), shows that the political debate over democracy and constitutional legitimacy refers almost exclusively to sovereign states and their citizens.[7]

The difficulty in defining the European Union according to constitutional and international law is reflected in the following question: What kind of authority sources does this sui generis structure need to legitimately demand subordination to its sovereign power? We must also consider whether any sources of legitimacy would support the development of the EU into a federation. If the European Union were merely an international regime or an international organization of sovereign states, the question of legitimacy would be easy to answer. Decisionmaking would be purely intergovernmental and would be based exclusively on bilateral or multilateral treaties requiring ratification by the national parliaments or popular referenda. These treaties, however, have created supranational institutions (the European Commission, the European Court, the European Parliament) and intergovernmental organs (the European Council, the Council of Ministers) that are authorized to determine secondary European law, which can be interpreted—with the help of a "judicial fiction"[8]—as the means for realizing the purpose embodied in the treaty's original text (*Zweckverbandstheorie*).[9] An increasingly tense relationship has existed between supranational and intergovernmental organs since the beginning of the European Union.

It is obvious, though, that this fiction is no longer plausible. Hans Ipsen's classic argument[10] that the member states are fully in command of the treaties is valid for the original EC law; it cannot, however, conceptually legitimize the secondary EC law or its legal effects on the member states. The treaty framework does not have the same character as a constitution.[11] Therefore, the EC/EU lacks legitimacy. This is compensated for in an ad hoc manner by the indirect democratic legitimacy of the Council of Ministers and by the European Parliament (EP), which shares—albeit marginally—the responsibility for European lawmaking.

The European Union has been granted sovereignty by its member states, and it now practices that sovereignty in their place to the extent of directly affecting each state's internal affairs. According to Dieter Grimm, "Although it is not a state itself, it has all the powers of a traditional state."[12] As such, the classical "nation" concept is clearly of little use in probing the legitimacy of the European Union.[13] Thus, we need a concept of legitimacy that is not based on the nation-state, one that is abstract and open enough to describe the specific legitimacy requirements of this complex, sui generis political system. For this, I turn to political systems theory.

According to David Easton, and Gabriel Almond and Bingham Powell,[14] political systems need a certain amount of specific input, obtained both actively and passively, to survive. Specifically, they need a sufficient level of mass support. The degree of loyalty is expressed through the volume and intensity of mass support essential for each political system to be able to transform demands from the environment into political decisions, which are then implemented. This transformation of inputs into outputs is realized through four fundamental process functions (articulation and aggregation of territorial and functional interests, policymaking, implementation, and adjudication), which in turn are influenced by three system functions (socialization, elite recruitment, and communication). Thus, process functions, the efficiency and democratic legitimacy of which depend to a considerable degree on the system functions, produce the political system's outputs. These outputs appear in the form of political decisions such as laws, decrees, and regulations and reappear through feedback as inputs into the political system.

If the system, because of a malfunction of one of its parts, produces an unpopular output, the system-supporting input of active support and passive mass loyalty decreases. In other words, the way in which process, system, and policy functions work independently has a tremendous effect on the efficiency, transparency, legitimacy, and stability of a political system. This is just as valid for a nation-state as it is for the European Union. Therefore, efficiency and democratic legitimacy characterize the European Union's decisions, its policies, and even its integration prospects. In fact, for the polity of the EU (as well as nation-states) two forms of legitimacy are essential: "formal" (legal) legitimacy and "social" legitimacy.[15]

As an intergovernmental organization, the EU encounters few problems with formal legitimacy. The parliaments of the member states, as well as the citizens (through referenda[16]), have given the treaties their approval and consequently formal legitimacy. Their national constitutions have therefore established the norms and procedures necessary for the member states to transfer sovereignty to the EC. As Grimm has explained, "Once the sovereign powers have been transferred, their execution by the institutions of the Community is no longer dependent on national law."[17] This governmental approval of the treaties, however, no longer covers the resulting supranational character of the EC. Therefore, we must test the degree of new legitimacy that has accrued to the European Union's institutions and sovereignty through democratic procedures other than the one-time treaty ratification.

In his concept of legitimacy, David Easton distinguishes between means and objects of support. The objects of support are arranged in the following hierarchy: political community, regime, and political authorities. The means of support, however, are either specific (depending on the system's outputs) or diffuse (independent of performance). From this we can conclude that the two main elements of a political system's (and in our case the European Union's) "social" legitimacy are the system's efficiency and effectiveness on the one hand and the citizens' trust in the legality of the established order on the other.[18]

In this chapter I discuss whether the institutional structures and process functions of the European Union are capable of producing diffuse support and thus democratic legitimacy. I will also examine the degree to which these supports have established the consensus procedures required in heterogeneous societies.[19] Moreover, I will work out the contours of the self-intensifying tension between democratic and utilitarian legitimacy, or what I earlier characterized as the democracy-efficiency dilemma. Finally, I pose the following question: Which of the forms of European integration discussed here is best suited to circumvent this dilemma?

THE EUROPEAN UNION'S DEMOCRATIC DEFICIT

Within the European Union the democratic deficit can be assessed on three fundamental levels: an imbalance of power and legitimacy, the lack of checks and balances, and the absence of intermediate structures and organizations between social and political interests.

Imbalance of Political Power and Democratic Legitimacy

The basic institutional structure of the European Community has changed little since the Treaty of Rome. At first glance, the intricate web of institutions (the Council of Ministers, European Commission, EP, and European Court) suggests a separation of powers comparable to Western liberal democratic systems.[20] In the European Union, however, an imbalance of powers exists that renders it unique. This imbalance is created by the fact that the Council of Ministers rather than the EP dominates the legislative process.[21] The Council's democratic legitimacy accrues from each member state's democratically elected ministers. From an intergovernmental point of view, the basis of legitimacy is direct and solid. From a supranational point of view, though, the basis of legitimacy can be traced only indirectly and is therefore rather weak. Thus the most important decisions made on the European level are legitimized by democratic procedures lodged within the individual member states.

This structure, however, can continue to function smoothly only if the Council practices unanimous decisionmaking. The revival of (qualified) majority decisionmaking since passage of the Single European Act (SEA) in 1986 has caused the Council's legitimacy to crumble. A group of "victorious" member states could thereby directly intervene in the affairs of the "losing" member states, even though the latter's legitimate national representatives voted against the measure. By comparison, the 1966 Luxembourg compromise, which gave each member of the Council effective veto power, seemed substantially more democratic, at least as viewed from the perspective of normative theory.[22] Joseph Weiler maintains that the member states' veto power was "the single most legitimating element" of discretionary decisionmaking in the European Council and the Council of Ministers.[23] Nevertheless, qualified majority decisionmaking has become more and more crucial to the efficiency of an increasingly heterogeneous European Union. Thus, we can begin to see the contours of a dilemma between democracy and efficiency in the European Union.

Although the European Parliament's powers have increased as a result of the 1986 SEA and the 1991 Maastricht Treaty, the legislature remains shy of obtaining the minimum powers possessed by Western democratic parliaments. The parliament, however, is the only EU institution whose members are directly elected by member states' citizens. The other institutions have considerably more power but have a weaker claim to direct democratic legitimacy.

The European Commission is the European Union's executive branch. It has the right to initiate legislation, as well as the power and responsibility to implement the Council's resolutions, and therefore holds considerable power in the European Union.[24] Commission members are named by the national governments, and only since the Maastricht Treaty came into effect have the appointments needed the approval of the European Parliament. Thus, the Commission's democratic foundation is extraordinarily weak.

The judges of the European Court of Justice are also appointed by member states' chief executives, but thereafter they are essentially independent of national or supranational control. The power of the Court of Justice to interpret Community law has been a critical factor in European integration. The courts of the member states have voluntarily accepted its decisions, although it has no power to enforce them. Lower courts have postponed their decisions in cases that affect European law until the European Court has given its decision. Thus during the stagnation of European integration from 1966 to 1986, the European Court played a decisive role in promoting European union. This strong influence, however, is problematic from the perspective of democratic theory, since the European Court is based on a rather weak principle of democratic legitimacy.[25]

If we examine the European Union's institutional structure from the perspective of democratic theory, two problems emerge. First, the EU is associated with an asymmetric allocation of powers and democratic legitimacy. Second, this asymmetry provokes a permanent constitutional controversy based on the "dual sovereignty"[26] of the EC. This controversy has arisen because the community of independent states has created parts of a supranational regime increasingly able to remove itself from the control of its states. Although direct European elections have constructed a supranational sovereign (the "European voter"), that sovereign remains unaware of its role. Even if it were aware of its role, it would be unable to play the part because of substantial gaps in the EP's legislative powers. Whereas the supranational sovereign is still a fiction, the principles of the national sovereigns have already eroded.

Accountability in Policymaking

As integration has progressed, a loophole has developed in the structure of institutional accountability. Community decisionmaking has increased its independence from national parliamentary control,[27] which has resulted from the progressive transfer of authority from the nation-states to the EC. National parliaments' loss of control over the EC has not been compensated by an adequate increase in the European Parliament's powers of control. The EP's increased role in the legislative process provided for by the Maastricht Treaty (Article 189c, codecision procedure) takes the form of negative veto powers more than positive authority to shape legislation. Even this modest enhancement of the parliament, however, could be achieved only by making the institutional network and decisionmaking so complex that even the best-informed EU citizen could no longer follow institutional proceedings.

Thus the national parliaments, as well as the European Committees,[28] formed mostly in the early 1990s, have been unable to monitor the large number of decisions passed in over one hundred meetings of the twenty various Councils of Ministers convened each year.[29] The so-called package deals, which involve complicated compromises across different policy domains, have proven almost impossible for the parliaments to check. One exception is the Market Committee of the Danish Folketing. This committee meets simultaneously with the Council of Ministers, giving the Danish ministers a kind of imperative mandate in the negotiations. This "Danish model" is the perfect example of parliamentary control. If the other member states followed this example, however, a complete blockade of EC decisions would result.[30] Once again, we see the dilemma between democracy and efficiency in the European Union.

Aggregation and Integration of Social Interests

In Western liberal democratic political systems, the aggregation and integration of social interests are performed by political parties, interest groups, social movements, and the mass media. Aggregation and integration are essential in every democratic order for mediation between society's interests and government decisions to occur. They are irreplaceable institutions and organizations of "integrated interest articulation at various levels"[31] that rest on the pluralistic allocation of society's resources and capabilities. If, however, "a parliament does not secure the constant mediation between the people and the state, then only a hollow shell of democracy exists."[32]

This situation is exactly what we find in the European Union. The level of mediation at the EC level is barely developed.[33] An integrated European party system does not exist. Voter turnout in direct European parliamentary elections since their introduction in 1979 has decreased continually, contrary to federalists' predictions. In 1979, 67.2 percent of eligible voters voted, in 1984 that number decreased to 65.0 percent, and in 1989 only 62.8 percent of eligible voters participated in elections.[34] Voter turnout in various countries varies considerably. Belgian citizens, with 90.7 percent voter turnout in the 1989 European elections, are the most sympathetic to the idea of European union—although they are required by law to participate. At the other end of the spectrum, only 36.2 percent of British voters showed up at the polls that same year, reflecting the deep-seated skepticism toward European unity in that country.[35] The electoral campaigns for the European Parliament carried out by the parties in each member state have concentrated almost exclusively on domestic issues. In return, voters have used those elections to express their approval or disapproval of domestic government policy between national elections without risk.

The Europeanization of interest groups predicted by neofunctionalists also lacks empirical support. This is especially evident in the failure of labor union integration to progress beyond a powerless European Trade Union Confederation. The integration of European labor was stopped "before it ever could get started"[36] by the heterogeneous interests of the individual unions of the member states. Historically, labor interests in Europe have been embedded in the organizational diversity and various patterns of national industrial relations.[37] As long as issues of taxation, welfare, employment, and wages are still negotiated and decided at the national level, parties and interest groups will continue to concentrate their efforts on that level. The Europeanization of these nationally matured, maintained, and sanctioned intermediary structures of interest articulation will probably take decades and will lead to serious conflicts of loyalty between the European Union and the individual member states.[38]

But more than parties and interest groups resisted a rapid Europeanization; the mass media did so as well. Newspapers, journals, television, and radio provide public forums in which modern political discourse can unfold. Just as an integrated party system does not exist in Europe, mass media do not create opportunities "where European politics can be given general character, and, therefore, allow democracy to truly develop."[39] This is the case because discourse and communication, as well as the general public, must be bound by a common language. No lingua franca exists for the European Union that is comparable to the Latin used by the educated class during the Middle Ages. Instead, eleven languages are spoken in Europe—none of which is spoken by more than 20 percent of the people.[40] Without a common language, European information and thereby the fundamental base of European political participation remain restricted to a handful of interested functional elites. It is on this source of informal public opinion, which exists only outside "the structures of a political power,"[41] that the democratic formation of opinion and the freedom of expression in interest groups, parties, and parliaments must rely. Thus a multilevel communication link for the formation of public opinion in Europe does not exist at the supranational level. Consequently, a fundamental component of civil society's infrastructure, one that is essential to every democratic community, does not exist in the European Union.[42]

The three system functions—socialization of the citizens, recruitment of elites, and societal communication—which according to Almond and Powell[43] form the basis of democratic legitimacy and efficiency in a political system, are clearly nonexistent at the European level. As long as this is the case, nation-states will continue to dominate the loyalty and identity of the EU citizens.

DEMOCRACY AND EFFICIENCY: THE DILEMMA OF UTILITARIAN AND DEMOCRATIC LEGITIMACY

The widening and deepening of the European Union during the 1980s and 1990s can be seen as an attempt to meet the challenge of globalization.[44] To counter the U.S. and East Asian economic and technological challenge, European firms and industries had to attain sufficient economies of scale. They could compete only if their home markets became "united rather than fragmented."[45] From this point of view, the single European market and economic and monetary union constituted Europe's answer to globalization. Member governments agreed in 1986 and again in 1991 to deepen and expand their cooperation within the EC/EU to regain influence over economic matters and to deliver the economic goods (growth, prosperity, and employment) that their citizens expected.

Both the governments and citizens had to pay a price, however. European politicians and citizens were confronted with a dilemma: They had to choose between "democracy of the people" and "democracy for the people," or in Robert Dahl's terms, "system effectiveness" versus "citizen participation."[46] The governments opted for system effectiveness—that is, a response to the collective economic preferences of their citizens. Governments had to transfer additional components of national sovereignty to the supranational and intergovernmental institutions of the EU. Once again, citizens and national parliaments lost some of their already reduced capacity to participate and to exercise democratic control over important decisions. Although the problem of international constraints was not new, only since Maastricht have citizens, parliaments, and subnational and national executives begun to realize that a conflict could occur between system effectiveness and citizen participation, or put another way, between the utilitarian and democratic components of a polity's legitimacy.

Prior to the Treaty on European Union, integration had been almost exclusively the domain of political elites. The monitoring and control of their political actions by national and supranational sovereigns, however, have been diffuse, indirect, and incomplete. The virtual exclusion of the European Parliament, insufficient institutional control by the national parliaments, poorly informed regional executives and European citizens, and powerless regional parliaments have all been advantageous for the deepening of European integration. If these actors and arenas were included in European decisionmaking, the result would be a complicated and time-consuming negotiation process at several decisionmaking levels. Instead, the interests and problems of the heterogeneous member states have been represented by the individual national governments in the Council of Ministers. Their ability to compromise and to devise creative package deals linking various policy domains has enabled integration to proceed.[47] If the governments had been required to confer with the European Parliament, the national and regional parliaments, or directly with the citizens, a reciprocal blockade of the EC decisionmaking process would have resulted.

This situation, however, has seemed to characterize European integration after Maastricht. The more sovereign powers the EC acquires, the greater the demand for stronger checks by national and regional forces.[48] The European Parliament, national parliaments, regional executives, and citizens have all demanded a more solid normative-democratic foundation and thereby more inclusion in European Union decisionmaking. Yet as more democratic inclusion, control, and transparency are demanded, member governments will have to make allowances for these demands. The normative claim for more democracy becomes a functional prerequisite for further European integration. Thus a proliferation of actors, negotiation arenas, and decisionmaking organs in the European policymaking process seems an unavoidable part of further integration. Difficulties in reaching common positions within the Council will increase considerably and threaten to create a "policy interlock" even more hopeless than the one Fritz Scharpf described in the mid-1980s concerning the Common Agricultural Policy.[49]

The stronger demand for democratic and parliamentary control following Maastricht confirms the "politicization hypothesis" put forward by Joseph Nye and Philippe Schmitter in 1971.[50] These authors stated that the number of actors wanting to participate in European decisionmaking would increase with the deepening of integration. Whether such politicization will hinder further integration depends on the degree to which relevant actors are equipped with strategic resources and have the will to force their interests on the EC. Thus the problem is, as Nye predicted nearly thirty years ago, "not the politicization itself but the premature politicization before the supportive attitudes [toward European integration] have become intense and structured."[51] This is exactly what happened after Maastricht. The heads of the European governments, apparently overcome by the momentous nature of this special historical situation, neglected the fact that such an extensive step toward integration could no longer be covered by the "permissive consensus"[52] of their citizens.[53]

Thus the European unification process seems to have reached a point at which greater democratic legitimacy is needed before it can proceed. Democratic legitimacy, a factor federalist and neofunctionalist theories of regional integration have almost completely neglected, has become a hard constraint for any further deepening of the European Union. Yet this democratization (which entails greater involvement of the European Parliament, the national parliaments, regional executives, and citizens) will completely overload the EC decisionmaking structure. Nevertheless, democratization is necessary to avoid a situation in which economic crisis and intensified distributional conflicts will lead to a fundamental crisis of EU legitimacy. Until now, efficiency rather than democracy has been the most important source of specific support in the European Community. The previously mentioned deficits and citizens' identification with their own nation-states have rendered the European democracy unable to build diffuse citizen support for the EU. When the democratic deficit is removed at the expense of decisionmaking efficiency, however, a traditional source of legitimacy will dry up. Thus the conflict between European efficiency and European democracy resembles a zero-sum-game, if not a classical dilemma. At this time and under the present institutional configuration of the EU, each gain in democratic legitimacy threatens losses in political decisionmaking efficiency.

TWO POSSIBLE WAYS OUT OF THE DILEMMA

Since the late 1980s, European unification has increasingly progressed from negative to positive integration. The EU has expanded from twelve to fifteen member states and further expansion into east-central Europe seems likely. Thus the European Union faces intertwined challenges: Widening, deepening, and democratization are to be achieved without a loss of decisionmaking efficiency. Two important recent reform scenarios purport to meet these three challenges and simultaneously maintain the EU's relatively efficient decisionmaking.

Scenario 1: Institutional Reforms for a Democratic Union

Political institutions are not institutionalized until they have produced legitimate order and the efficiency appropriate to the situation and society and until they function as a symbolic integrative force in society. These functions can be realized only if institutions take on the political form that matches the needs of the society. As such, what institutional arrangements are appropriate for the "European society"?

If we define—hypothetically—the fifteen member states of the European Union as a single "European society," we would face extreme heterogeneity. Virtually the entire spectrum of functional and territorial cleavages (ethnic, linguistic, religious, historical, and political conflicts) segments the European social structure. These multiple cleavages are overarched by national identities, which leave behind historically embedded and deeply ingrained segments, what one might call the *super cleavages* of European society.

Within these states, societal cleavages are overlapped and reconciled by shared communication (*Kommunikationsgemeinschaft*), shared experiences (*Erfahrungsgemeinschaft*), and a deeply felt sense of national identity (*Erinnerungsgemeinschaft*).[54] This is not the case at the European level, where diversity intensifies segmentation and exclusion. European society, assuming it exists, is much more heterogeneous, segmented, and conflictual than even the national societies of Switzerland, Belgium, and the Netherlands—segmented societies that require special consensual democratic structures and procedures.[55] As the polity of an extremely segmented society, the EU is even more in need of consensual democratic institutions.

Four of the eight institutional principles in Arend Lijphart's definition of consensus democracies[56] are vital to the mitigation of social cleavages in the EU:

- Interelite accommodation—Political elites should engage in consensual decisionmaking that resolves conflicts through inclusive compromises rather than majority decisions that exclude relevant minorities.
- Federalism—A federal order with subsidiary decisionmaking structures should be established; this is the most appropriate institutional answer to territorially distinct subcultures and segmented societies.
- Symmetrical bicameralism—A bicameral legislature should be realized in which national minorities are granted sufficient representation in the second chamber.
- Minority veto—Such a veto allows each structural minority to protect its essential interests.

One can argue, and with good reason, that these consociational principles have already been incorporated in the institutional structures of the EU. Although decisionmaking through qualified majorities has been reintroduced, with the SEA project most Council decisions are still taken by consensus. The federal principle is represented by an asymmetric bicameralism[57] that enables representatives of member states to veto decisions that touch on their vital interests. The principle is strengthened by the fact that national governments appoint commissioners and the judges of the European Court.[58] The European Union therefore already uses many consensual democratic procedures.

These elements of consensus democracy are of a special nature, though. Unlike the relationship found in democratic nation-states in the EU, the federal principle dominates democratic principles. The democratic norm that all votes should carry the same weight is seriously violated by majority decisions within the Council.[59] Moreover, decisionmaking elites are very far removed from the public, and the level of control exercised by parliaments, the mass media, and citizens is extremely low. This dominance of the federal principle is appropriate because of the heterogeneous character of the European society, but it has become an obstacle to further deepening and widening of the European Union. Therefore, the institutional structure must be reformed; a balance between democratic and federal principles needs to be established.

One proposal for such a reform was recently put forward by Werner Weidenfeld.[60] Weidenfeld's proposal is based on the assumption that only a system of double representation and legitimacy can create a level of support sufficient for further integration. The procedures for gaining legitimacy in the member states need to be combined and harmonized with the European sources of direct legitimacy.[61] A bicameral system should be institutionalized at the European level, where all essential EU decisions are made on a basis of equality for both chambers. If the votes in the two houses (European Parliament and Council of Ministers) do not coincide, a joint committee should be invoked to work out a compromise.

In addition, European parliamentary elections should be governed by a uniform electoral code. In the European Council, votes should be weighted in such a way that larger states cannot be outvoted by smaller ones and the interests of smaller states can be appropriately protected.[62] The influence of the member states could be maintained through the European Council if the Council continued to set the course on policymaking.

The European Commission would be transformed into the government of the European Union. Its president would be elected by the European Parliament and confirmed by the Council of Ministers instead of appointed by the heads of the member states. The president of the Commission would be granted the power to guide legislative policy and appoint commissioners with the confirmation of both houses of Parliament.

The European Court of Justice would be expanded to two senates, and the judges would serve no longer than twelve-year terms. The resulting system, adapted from the current French and German constitutions, would resemble a federally organized semipresidential system with a two-headed executive (the European Commission and the European Council).

If such an institutional arrangement ever came about, it would improve the deplorable state of democratic legitimacy in the European Union. The arrangement could raise the level of European citizens' political participation by providing for a more powerful European Parliament and enhancing the transparency of, accountability for, and control over EU decisionmaking. With a reformed Commission, the European Union would also acquire a government with a dual democratic legitimacy ensuing from both supranational and national sources. The consensual features would be weakened, but they would be sustained by the strong position of the European Council and the second house of Parliament, the Council of Ministers. Nevertheless, despite these far-reaching effects, some problems would remain.

1. The relationship between the national parliaments and the European Parliament is unclear. Which decisions will be taken by the member state parliaments and which by the European Parliament? The more the national parliaments control European decisionmaking—indications of such tendencies have emerged since the ratification of the Maastricht treaties—the less chance the European Parliament has to attain full parliamentary powers.[63]

2. The proposal contains a contradiction in terms of constitutional theory. In modern history, parliaments have represented the sovereignty of the people. A true "European people," "European sovereign," or even

"European public," as demonstrated earlier, does not exist. According to constitutional theory, there can be no "European constitution"[64] without a European people. Moreover, according to the theory of parliamentarism, the European Union and "the institution of parliament are principally under [a situation of] unrelenting tension."[65]

3. The separation of power within the executive is too ambiguous. Is the European Commission, which now enjoys its own source of legitimacy, still compelled to follow the European Council's lead? Can it be dismissed by a no-confidence vote by the European Parliament against the will of the European Council, which is normally the case in semipresidential systems?

4. It also remains unclear what would happen if the Joint Committee of the European Parliament and the Council of Ministers cannot reach a compromise. Such an impasse could lead to a de facto veto by the member states. A still heterogeneous European Union with considerable decision-making powers could be plagued by a deadlock. If such a situation were avoided through the introduction of (simple) majority rules, however, resistance within member states that did not agree would threaten the implementation of EU decisions. If such obstructive behavior could not be adequately sanctioned, a prisoners' dilemma could result: Member states could increasingly delay implementation of unfavorable decisions because they would assume that other states would delay as well.

Although Weidenfeld's proposal goes far beyond the reform put forward by the so-called reflection group of the 1996 intergovernmental conference (Maastricht II), it may still be insufficient to maintain the governability of a "one-speed" European Union of fifteen, twenty, or even twenty-five members. This doubt is shared especially by those who have proposed the concept of a "multispeed" or "variable geometry" Europe.

Scenario 2: A Europe of Variable Geometry

The basic reasoning of this scenario is as simple as it is convincing. A union of fifteen or twenty states with a total population of around 360 million people speaking over thirty languages, divided by numerous national and historical cultures, and whose economies are at different levels of development cannot be governed by a single set of political norms, institutions, procedures, and decisions. The reduction of this complexity, however, should not be brought about by the British proposal—widening to prevent deepening—or the French proposal—deepening to prevent widening. The maximal as well as ambiguous proposal of the German government—widening and deepening—appears unrealistic in the medium term. These three proposals were therefore confronted with integration models that dissolve the organizational unity of the European Union.

The concept of a multispeed Europe was developed as early as the 1980s.[66] This concept is based on an explicit consensus among member states regarding the goals of integration and the concrete steps necessary to achieve them. Those states prepared to fulfill the requirements necessary to take the concrete steps are allowed to advance to a new stage of integration. Member states unable to meet the requirements will not be included in the new common policy, at least not until they are able to meet the requirements; they would maintain full membership status in all other EU policy areas, however. In addition, those states will receive special support from the more advanced member states to help them quickly fulfill the requirements.

The "Europe of concentric circles" describes a scenario whereby some countries, defined mostly in historical terms as the founding members of the European Economic Community (EEC), represent the core and the driving forces for further integration, whereas the other member states form concentric circles of varying distances from the center.[67] The six EEC founding states would make up the core because of their developed consensus regarding integration goals and their common level of integration. These states would then promote further integration of the surrounding states.

From a historical point of view, this concept appears likely to succeed. The original EU members, concentrated around the Franco-German axis, have been the driving force in European integration during the past decades. Under the rigid convergence criteria set up by the Maastricht Treaty, however, these original countries no longer represent an optimal core for further integration. For one thing, Belgium and Italy will not meet all of the Maastricht requirements.[68] For another, two member states that entered the European Community only in the 1970s and 1990s (Denmark and Austria) will eventually fulfill the requirements. Another problem this proposal generates involves the discriminatory division of European member states into first-, second-, and third-class members. As a result, the cohesion and willingness of multiclass member states to reach compromises would suffer tremendously.

The most complex and contingent integration model to date is variable geometry, which abandons the concept of a fixed number of member states. The difference between this model and a simple multispeed Europe of concentric circles is that the former is based on variation in both territorial and functional constituencies. This model envisages the emergence of different countries clustered in different policy fields (currency policy, foreign affairs, security, social policy, environmental policy, and the like) that would be both large enough to play an effective role in global and regional affairs and small and homogeneous enough to manage their own complexities within a specific policy area.[69] Within the policy regimes themselves, members would decide whether decisions would be made along intergovernmental or supranational lines. Thus several cores would embrace different but overlapping sets of members, which would make decisions according to different procedural rules. It is expected, though, that a core of states belonging to most policy regimes would evolve.[70] Unlike other utopian forms of nonobligational integration,[71] Josef Janning's proposal of "differentiated integration" insists on the membership of all European Union member states in a single European market. This plan would hold in check the centrifugal tendencies within the EU, by preserving a commonly shared level of integration.

The integration concept of variable geometry takes into account the increased differentiation of integration objectives and interests among the six original EEC members and the states that followed. It replaces the idea of simultaneous deepening and widening, which has become increasingly unrealistic, with a more flexible integration scenario. Deepening would progress in various political fields with different groups of member states. At the same time, EU widening remains feasible.

This postmodern form of integration is a clear deviation from the concepts of a "United States of Europe" and a common *Europe des patries* conceived by the founding fathers. The form could, however, help to avoid some of the efficiency problems within the European Union, although it would not solve the problem of the democratic deficit. In fact, it would be more likely to aggravate this problem. The geometry would presumably be too variable to allow sufficient parliamentary control. Decisionmaking would become even more opaque, and, as before, even the best-informed citizens would be unable to follow the decisionmaking process. A further decline in political participation would be unavoidable. The "Europe of variable geometry" would undoubtedly be even more heavily controlled by technocrats and the executive than is the current inflexible European Union. Moreover, the diversity of supranational and intergovernmental policy regimes, with different member states or subnational units, would increase centrifugal tendencies within the European Union. Competition and conflicts among the various policy regimes could severely diminish decisionmaking efficiency in the EU.[72]

CONCLUSION

Both of the scenarios described in this chapter could only partially solve the problems of complexity that plague the integration process. Increased efficiency would be achieved at the cost of reduced democratic control and vice versa. The deepening of European integration in selected policy domains (currency policy, social policy, environmental policy, and so on) with several groups of the most advanced member states, as protagonists of variable geometry propose, would trigger numerous disintegrating tendencies and would damage—perhaps irreparably—the cohesion of the European Union as a whole. Institutional reforms, as proposed in scenario 1, would only marginally solve the efficiency problem and would seriously aggravate the democratic deficit by making majority rule mandatory.

The problems of political efficiency and democratic participation, which already plague some individual member states, will continue to limit the system effectiveness and the democratic participation and control of European governance as long as national societies are so strongly heterogeneous and a European society with a European identity has yet to emerge. The permissive consensus may hold for the status quo, but there are abundant signals that the consensus no longer presents a mandate to the political elites for further integration. Thus the metaphor used by some unreflective prointegrationists—namely, that European integration requires constant forward momentum just like bicycle riding—is misleading. A fast-paced but premature integration, as demanded by Maastricht, carries a stronger potential for disintegration than that suggested by another misleading metaphor, which compares Economic and Monetary Union to a train on which member states unable to meet the requirements today will jump on board tomorrow. The "uncoupling" and the danger of national isolation and even nationalistic regression within the excluded countries therefore appear much more likely.

Robert Dahl lucidly highlighted a democratic paradox that can also be applied to further European integration:

> In very small political systems a citizen may be able to participate extensively in decisions that do not matter much but cannot participate much in decisions that really matter a great deal; whereas very large systems may be able to cope with problems that matter more to a citizen, the opportunities for the citizen to participate in and greatly influence decisions are vastly reduced.[73]

If one considers, as Dahl justifiably does, system effectiveness and democratic participation and control to be two equal components of democratic legitimacy (democracy *of* and *for* the people), the deepening of European integration, as decided at Maastricht, should not be pushed through at present. The costs to both effectiveness and democracy would be too high. Since Maastricht triggered the politicization of European integration, further deepening should not occur until the supportive attitudes of the political elites and citizens of the member states have become intense and structured, to recall Nye's point.[74] Institutional reforms as outlined in scenario 1 can undoubtedly stimulate those attitudes and generate more intense citizen loyalty to a European polity. They should be complemented, however, by additional reforms, such as the adoption of Europe-wide referenda on fundamental EU decisions and direct election of national representatives to the Council of Ministers.[75] Both of these reforms could help to control the European elite cartels and stimulate a European discourse, the essential base of any European democracy.

Even if these reforms can be successfully implemented, however, they cannot completely dissolve Dahl's democratic paradox. European democracies responded to globalization by deepening and widening their cooperation (democracy *for* the people). In so doing they constrained the opportunity of citizens and parliaments to influence and control political decisions. The existing and proposed democratic institutions of the European Union and its member states could not and cannot overcome the "limitations by scale and time"[76] that inherently limit the realm of democracy. The burdens of information, knowledge, political passion, and interest placed on the "European citizen" outstrip those in the national states, which are already too high for many citizens. Dahl appears to be right when he argues that just as the ancient "city states lost much of their political, economic, social, and cultural autonomy when they were absorbed into larger national states, so in our time the development of transnational systems reduces the political, economic, social, and cultural autonomy of national states."[77]

With the transformation of small city-states into larger nation-states, direct participatory democracy was replaced by a new set of indirect representative democratic institutions—which came into existence in democratic theory and political practice. At the end of the twentieth century, when international regimes, transnational systems, and supranational politics have begun to overtake national governance systems, a new set of transnational or supranational democratic procedures and institutions is not yet in sight, even in the most advanced supranational system—the EU. As long as this is the case, extraordinary efforts must be made to strengthen the institutions of local, subnational, and national democracy to compensate somewhat the loss of democracy that globalization and its transnational political responses have brought forth.

NOTES

1. John Pinder, "Positive Integration and Negative Integration: Some Problems of Economic Union in the EEC," *World Today* 24 (1968): 88–110.

2. Helen Wallace, "The Best Is the Enemy of the 'Could': Bargaining in the European Community," in *Agricultural Trade Liberalization and the European Community*, Secondo Tarditi et al., eds. (Oxford: Clarendon, 1989).

3. Leon N. Lindberg and Stuart A. Scheingold, *Europe's Would-Be Polity:*

Patterns of Change in the European Community (Englewood Cliffs, N.J.: Prentice-Hall, 1970).

4. Hans Peter Ipsen, *Europäisches Gemeinschaftsrecht* (Tübingen: Mohr, 1972).

5. Fritz W. Scharpf, *Optionen des Föderalismus in Deutschland und Europa* (Frankfurt a.m.: Campus, 1994); Markus Jachtenfuchs and Beate Kohler-Koch, "Regieren im dynamischen Mehrebenensystem," in *Europäische Integration*, Markus Jachtenfuchs and Beate Kohler-Koch, eds. (Opladen: Leske and Budrich, 1994).

6. Fritz W. Scharpf, "Die Handlungsfähigkeit des Staates am Ende des zwanzigsten Jahrhunderts," *Politische Vierteljahresschrift* 32, no. 4 (fall 1991): 621–643.

7. Peter Graf Kielmansegg, "Legitimität als analytische Kategorie," *Politische Vierteljahresschrift* 12, no. 3 (summer 1971): 367–401; Ernst-Wolfgang Böckenförde, "Die verfassungsgebende Gewalt des Volkes—Ein Grenzbegriff des Verfassungsrechts," in *Zum Begriff der Verfassung*, Ulrich K. Preuß, ed. (Frankfurt a.M.: Suhrkamp, 1994).

8. Fritz W. Scharpf, "Europäisches Demokratiedefizit und deutscher Föderalismus," in *Jahrbuch zur Staats- und Verwaltungswissenschaft* vol. 6, Thomas Ellwein, Jens Joachim Hesse, Renate Mayntz, and Fritz Scharpf, eds. (Baden-Baden: Nomos, 1993–1994), 169.

9. The term *Zweckverbandstheorie* originates from Ipsen, *Europäisches Gemeinschaftsrecht*.

10. Ipsen, *Europäisches Gemeinschaftsrecht*.

11. This is often asserted in connection with European jurisprudence. Dieter Grimm has, however, convincingly criticized this careless treatment of the term *constitution*. A constitution can be considered valid only when it originates from citizens or can be attributed to them. The treaties of the European Community cannot be traced back to a European people but only to the single EU member states. Dieter Grimm, *Braucht Europa eine Verfassung?* Themen vol. 60 (Munich: Carl Friedrich von Siemens Stiftung, 1994).

12. Ibid., 26.

13. Jachtenfuchs and Kohler-Koch, "Regieren im Mehrebenensystem," 30.

14. David Easton, *A Systems Analysis of Political Life* (Chicago: John Wiley and Sons, 1965); Gabriel Almond and G. Bingham Powell, *Comparative Politics: A Developmental Approach* (Boston: Little, Brown, 1966).

15. Joseph H. H. Weiler, "Problems of Legitimacy in Post 1992 Europe," *Außenwirtschaft,* no. 46 (1991): 411–437.

16. Referenda were obligatory in Denmark, Ireland, and Sweden.

17. Grimm, *Verfassung*, 26.

18. David Easton's "diffuse support" is similar to Max Weber's definition of "rational legitimacy." Max Weber, *Wirtschaft und Gesellschaft* (Tübingen: Mohr, 1956), 159.

19. A European society is pure fiction. If we think of it, though, as the sum of all of the societies of each member state, it is far more heterogeneous than the segmented society in Switzerland or the pluralistic society in the United States.

20. Emanuel Richter, "Die Komplexität der Gesellschaft und die Reduktion von Legitimität. Machtstrukturen in der Europäischen Gemeinschaft," in *Macht der Demokratie*, Michael Th. Greven, ed. (Baden-Baden: Nomos, 1991), 282; Emanuel Richter, *Die Expansion der Herrschaft* (Opladen: Leske and Budrich, 1994).

21. Here "Council" will refer to the Council of Ministers and the European Council established in 1974. The European Council, which brings together heads of state every six months, has increasingly become a legislative superstructure that determines the course of European integration. Richter, *Expansion der Herrschaft*, 283; Wolfgang Wessels, "The EC Council: The Community's Decisionmaking Center," in *The New European Community: Decisionmaking and Institutional Change*, Robert O. Keohane and Stanley Hoffmann, eds. (Boulder: Westview, 1991).

22. Scharpf, "Europäisches Demokratiedefizit"; Peter Graf Kielmansegg, "Integration und Demokratie," in *Europäische Integration*, Jachtenfuchs and Kohler-Koch, eds.

23. Weiler, "Problems of Legitimacy."

24. Peter Ludlow, "The European Commission," in *The New European Community*, Keohane and Hoffmann, eds.

25. Beate Wieland, *Ein Markt—zwölf Regierungen?* (Baden-Baden: Nomos, 1992), 81.

26. Rainer M. Lepsius, "Nationalstaat oder Nationalitätenstaat als Modell für die Weiterentwicklung der Europäischen Gemeinschaft," in *Staatswerdung Europas? Optionen für eine Europäische Union*, Rudolf Wildenmann, ed. (Baden-Baden: Nomos, 1991).

27. Scharpf, "Handlungsfähigkeit des Staates," 170–171.

28. In 1992 all twenty national parliaments contained European Committees. Gerda Falkener and Michael Nenntwich, "Das Demokratiedefizit der EG und die Beschlüsse von Maastricht 1992," *Österreichische Zeitschrift für Politikwissenschaft* no. 3 (1992): 277.

29. Ibid.

30. Scharpf, "Europäisches Demokratiedefizit," 170.

31. Lepsius, "Nationalstaat oder Nationalitätenstaat," 30.

32. Grimm, *Verfassung*, 38.

33. Karl-Heinz Neunreither, "Legitimationsprobleme der Europäischen Gemeinschaft," *Zeitschrift für Parlamentsfragen*, no. 7 (1976): 245–258; Lepsius, "Nationalstaat oder Nationalitätenstaat," 31; Scharpf, "Handlungsfähigkeit des Staates," 132; Kielmansegg, "Integration und Demokratie," 57.

34. Richard S. Flickinger and Donley T. Studlar, "The Disappearing Voters? Exploring Declining Turnout in Western European Elections," *West European Politics* 15, no. 2 (1992): 5.

35. Ibid.

36. Bernhard Ebbinghaus and Jelle Visser, "Barrieren und Wege 'grenzenloser Solidarität': Gewerkschaften und Europäische Integration," in *Staat und Verbände, PVS-Sonderheft 25*, Wolfgang Streeck, ed. (Opladen: Westdeutscher Verlag, 1994), 250.

37. Ibid. Wolfgang Streeck and Philippe C. Schmitter, "From National Corpo-

ratism to Transnational Pluralism: Organized Interests in the Single European Market," *Politics and Society* 19, no. 1 (1991): 133–164.

38. Lepsius, "Nationalstaat oder Nationalitätenstaat," 29; Beate Kohler-Koch, "Die Gestaltungsmacht organisierter Interessen," in *Europäische Integration*, Jachtenfuchs and Kohler-Koch, eds.

39. Kielmansegg, "Integration und Demokratie," 57.

40. According to a representative language test within the EU, 28 percent of Dutch and 15 percent of Danish citizens adequately spoke English, but only 3 percent of French and Spanish citizens and a mere 1 percent of Italians did so. Grimm, *Verfassung*, 42.

41. Jürgen Habermas, *Faktizität und Geltung* (Frankfurt a.M.: Suhrkamp, 1992), 374.

42. Kielmansegg, "Legitimität," 375.

43. Almond and Powell, *Comparative Politics*.

44. Michael Zürn, "Über den Staat und die Demokratie im Europäischen Mehrebenensystem," *Politische Vierteljahresschrift* 37, no. 1 (spring 1996): 33.

45. Keohane and Hoffmann, eds., *The New European Community*, 22.

46. Robert A. Dahl, "A Democratic Dilemma: System Effectiveness Versus Citizen Participation," *Political Science Quarterly* 109, no. 1 (January 1994): 23.

47. Scharpf, "Europäisches Demokratiedefizit," 170.

48. Gerda Zellentin, "Der Funktionalismus—eine Strategie gesamteuropäischer Integration," in *Die Integration Europas*, Michael Kreile, ed. (Opladen: Leske and Budrich, 1992), 70.

49. Fritz W. Scharpf, "Die Politikverflechtungsfälle: Europäische Integration und deutscher Föderalismus im Vergleich," *Politische Vierteljahresschrift* 26, no. 4 (1985): 323–356.

50. This hypothesis of politicization was outlined in Nye's and Schmitter's respective revisions of the neofunctional integration model. See Philippe Schmitter, "A Revised Theory of Regional Integration," in *Regional Integration: Theory and Research*, Leon Lindberg and Stuart Scheingold, eds. (New York: Cambridge University Press, 1971); and Joseph Nye, "Comparing Common Markets: A Revised Neofunctionalist Model," in *Regional Integration*, Lindberg and Scheingold, eds.

51. Ibid., 220.

52. Lindberg and Scheingold, *Europe's Would-Be Polity*, 249.

53. The special historical situation determined the decisions of French and German political leaders. Helmut Kohl wanted to dispell partners' worries about a new European central power by firmly attaching the reunified Germany to the West. François Mitterrand, on the other hand, opted to continue the policy France had followed regarding Germany since 1951: one of containment through integration.

54. Kielmansegg, "Integration und Demokratie," 99.

55. Arend Lijphart, *Democracies: Patterns of Majoritarian and Consensus Government in Twenty-One Countries* (New Haven: Yale University Press, 1984).

56. Ibid.

57. The current legislative branch is dominated by the European Council.

58. Kielmansegg, "Integration und Demokratie," 67.

59. Even if we do not consider Luxembourg because of its special status, the

weight of the votes in the Council in relation to the number of citizens in each country is not proportional. For example, seven citizens of the Federal Republic of Germany have the same voting weight as a single Irish citizen. Even in the European Parliament the smaller states enjoy a weighted advantage.

60. Werner Weidenfeld, "Zur Rolle der Europäischen Gemeinschaft in der Transformation Europas," in *Die Integration Europas*, Kreile, ed., 325; Werner Weidenfeld, ed., *Europa '96: Reformprogramm für die Europäische Union* (Gütersloh: Bertelsmann, 1994); Werner Weidenfeld, ed., *Reform der Europäischen Union* (Gütersloh: Bertelsmann, 1995).

61. Weidenfeld, *Reform der Europäischen Union*, 39.

62. Ibid., 40.

63. Hermann Lübbe, "Föderalismus und Regionalismus in der Europäischen Union," in ibid.

64. If we reverse the term of Sieyés, the constitutional power (*pouvoir constitué*) would constitute the power to draft a constitution (*pouvoir constituant*). Emanuel J. Sieyés, *Politische Schriften* (Darmstadt, Neuwied: Wissenschaftliche Buchgemeinschaft, 1975). The paradox therefore results from the fact that the Parliament, as the constitutional power of the sovereign (the people), helps itself to this power, although this power to constitutionally legitimize the Parliament can only be brought forth by the people.

65. Ibid., 115.

66. Eberhard Grabitz, ed., *Abgestufte Integration—eine Alternative zum herkömmlichen Integrationskonzept?* (Kehl: Engel, 1984).

67. G. De Michelis, "Die EG als Gravitationszentrum: Für ein Europa der vier Kreise," *Integration* 13, no. 4 (1990): 143; Josef Janning, "Europa braucht verschiedene Geschwindigkeiten," *Europa Archiv* 49, no. 18 (1994): 532.

68. Especially not the convergence criteria for total national debts and yearly budget deficits.

69. Peter Glotz, *Die falsche Normalisierung* (Frankfurt: Suhrkamp, 1994), 203.

70. Janning, "Verschiedene Geschwindigkeiten," 534.

71. Peter Glotz perceives the flexible geography of Europe as follows: "In some large regions (Western Europe, Scandinavia/the Baltic, the Danube Region), multinational federations could develop; single nation-states and multinational states (Great Britain?, the Netherlands?, Switzerland?) would maintain their independence; in other areas—the Balkans for example—confederation would dominate." Glotz, *Die falsche Normalisierung*, 203.

72. Philippe C. Schmitter, "The European Community as an Emergent and Novel Form of Political Domination," Working Paper of the Centro de Estudios Azanzados en Ciencias Sociales 26 (Madrid, 1991), 61.

73. Dahl, "A Democratic Dilemma," 28.

74. Nye, "Comparing Common Markets," 221.

75. Zürn, "Über den Staat und die Demokratie," 49.

76. Dahl, "A Democratic Dilemma," 30.

77. Ibid.

4

Territorial Identities in the European Union

Gary Marks

> "We are uniting people, not forming coalitions of states."
>
> —Jean Monnet

Whereas the process of European integration over the past two decades has been driven mainly by economic goals, the founders of the European Union were driven by larger ambitions. Jean Monnet, Robert Schuman, Konrad Adenauer, Paul Henri Spaak, and Alcide de Gasperi conceived the European Union (EU) as a response to the horrors of war in Europe, as a means to tame or at least moderate destructive nationalism.[1] The founders hoped to weaken national animosities by establishing an international legal order that would constrain realist anarchy. They wanted to domesticate international tensions within stable supranational institutions. Their long-term goal was to foster a European identity that would overarch and thereby temper contending nationalisms. Although the founders did not believe nationalism would be replaced by Europeanism, they were convinced that patriotism and attachment to Europe could coexist.

The founders of the EU conceived of European identity as an outcome of European integration. They were prepared to build European institutions in the absence of "Europeans." The idea was to appeal to elites who would see the virtue of collective decision making in specific policy areas at the European level. Institution builders today do not have that luxury. European integration has become politicized. It limits the sovereignty of national states in obvious ways, and unless citizens feel some genuine attachment to the territorial community of Europe, the possibilities for further European integration will be constrained. Identity has shifted to the

69

left side of the equation: it is no longer a passive outcome of integration but now shapes the possibility of further integration.

How, it is asked, can one legitimately allocate values if the losers do not feel they belong to the same territorial community as the winners? Decisions about who gets what often involve redistribution among groups, and those who lose will find such outcomes illegitimate if they do not identify with the larger society. Fritz Scharpf has made the point that representation and majority rule are legitimate only in the context of preexisting collective identity: "As long as the democratic legitimacy of European governance must rest primarily on the agreement of democratically accountable national governments, the citizens of countries whose governments are outvoted have no reason to consider such decisions as having democratic legitimation."[2]

One possible implication of this argument is that it is not worthwhile to deepen democratic institutions to counter the democratic deficit if a European-wide collective identity does not exist.[3] This position is taken by Anthony Smith in his recent book, *Nations and Nationalism in a Global Era:*

> Nations and nationalisms remain political necessities because (and for so long as) they alone can ground the interstate order in the principles of popular sovereignty and the will of the people, however defined. Only nationalism can secure the assent of the governed to the territorial unity to which they have been assigned, through a sense of collective identification with historic culture-communities in their "homelands." . . . Since there is little sign that the competition of states, even in Europe, is being superseded by some completely new political order, the likelihood of the nation which forms the *raison d'être* of the state and its community of will being transcended remains remote. Even if a number of states were to pool their sovereignties and even if their national communities were to agree to federate within a single political framework, the national and its nationalism would long remain the only valid focus and constituency for ascertaining the popular will.[4]

The collective identity that is so crucial to democratic legitimacy in Europe, however, was rarely intended to eclipse national identity. Monnet was well aware that national identities were so deep-seated among most Europeans that any attempt to overwhelm them was bound to fail. His goal, like most of those who came after him, was to gradually erode the vindictive elements of nationalism by planting overarching institutions that would nurture common interests.

This pragmatic conception of identity building in Europe was shared by Karl Deutsch. Integration for Deutsch meant piecemeal transfers of specific competencies to an overarching polity alongside the gradual evolution of a "sense of community." Deutsch argued that this was more feasible than "amalgamation," which involves a central government with exclusive authoritative control over individuals in a given territory. Although Deutsch did not rule out the possibility that amalgamation might be the ultimate destination, he argued that it would be self-defeating to make it the explicit goal. Ambiguity served a useful function. In a remarkably farsighted passage, Deutsch explained that "to encourage this profitable ambiguity, leaders of such movements have often used broader symbols such as 'union,' which would cover both possibilities and could be made to mean different things to different men."[5]

Ernst Haas came to a similar conclusion about coexistence of multiple European and national identities. He rejected the possibility that European identity would replace national identities. Haas coined the term *asymmetrical overlapping* to describe the nonstate form of governance he saw developing in Western Europe. In a passage that presages the concept of multilevel governance, Haas identified the possibility of multiple overlapping sources of governance at different territorial levels and corresponding "tiered multiple loyalties."[6]

More recently, William Wallace has argued that "the emergence of a diffuse sense of European identity has not led to a transfer of loyalties from the national to the European level. . . . What we have observed across Western Europe over the last two decades is a shift towards multiple loyalties with the single focus on the nation supplemented by European and regional affiliations above and below."[7]

In the remainder of this chapter, I frame some expectations about sources of identity in Europe. The questions I ask are straightforward: How have the creation and deepening of the European Union shaped Europeans' diverse territorial identities? How strong and how widespread is attachment to the European Union? How is European identity linked to national, regional, and local identities? How can one begin to explain the pattern of identities we see?

I believe these questions are worth asking, even though the data I bring to bear on them are sufficient only to suggest the causal factors that may be at play. Previous quantitative analysis has focused on various measures of support for European integration rather than on issues of identity, and little systematic attention has been given to questions of multiple identity.[8]

TERRITORIAL ATTACHMENTS IN THE EUROPEAN UNION

First, I present a conceptual frame for analyzing variations in territorial identity (see Figure 4.1). I conceive of three basic types, each of which can be regarded as varying in any combination with the other two to describe individual territorial identity. At *A* in Figure 4.1, an individual has *multiple identities*—more than two coexisting identities; at *B*, an individual has an

Figure 4.1   Framing Territorial Identity

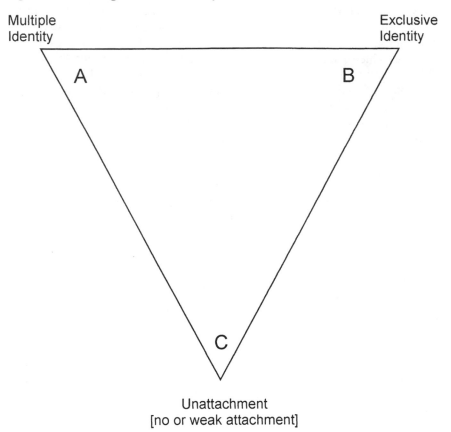

Multiple   Exclusive
Identity   Identity

Unattachment
[no or weak attachment]

exclusive identity, a single identity that overwhelms all others; the third corner of the triangle—*C*—admits the possibility that an individual may be *unattached*—with little or no territorial identity whatsoever. These three possibilities cannot be ranged sensibly along a single continuum, for the strength of territorial identity (and therefore the proximity of an individual to point *C*) is independent of the *character* of an individual's identity—that is, whether the individual has an exclusive identity or multiple identities. Given variations among these three mutually exclusive poles, one may describe an individual's territorial identity as lying at some point in the triangle *ABC*.

    Table 4.1 provides an overview of attachment to different levels of territorial community for fourteen countries (the EU-15 minus Luxembourg). The table is based on Eurobarometer surveys conducted in November

Table 4.1 Territorial Attachment in Western Europe, 1991 and 1995

	Locality 1991	Locality 1995	Region 1991	Region 1995	Country 1991	Country 1995	European Union 1991	European Union 1995
Austria	–	3.5[a]	–	3.7	–	3.5	–	2.3
Belgium	3.3	3.4	3.2	3.5	3.0	3.2	2.4	2.5
Denmark	3.4	3.2	3.6	3.4	3.8	3.7	2.3	2.1
Finland	–	3.1	–	3.2	–	3.6	–	2.0
France	3.1	3.2	3.3	3.4	3.4	3.4	2.6	2.6
Germany	3.5	3.5	3.6	3.6	3.4	3.3	2.4	2.3
Greece	3.7	3.8	3.8	3.9	3.8	3.9	2.5	2.4
Ireland	3.5	3.6	3.6	3.6	3.7	3.7	2.2	2.5
Italy	3.4	3.5	3.4	3.4	3.4	3.5	2.7	2.7
Netherlands	2.9	2.8	3.0	3.1	3.2	3.1	2.1	2.1
Portugal	3.7	3.6	3.7	3.7	3.7	3.7	2.5	2.5
Spain	3.7	3.6	3.7	3.6	3.5	3.5	2.7	2.4
Sweden	–	3.4	–	3.6	–	3.6	–	1.9
United Kingdom	3.2	3.2	3.4	3.3	3.5	3.4	2.2	2.1
EU 12/EU 15[b]	3.4	3.4	3.5	3.5	3.5	3.4	2.5	2.4

Sources: Eurobarometer 36.0 and Eurobarometer 43.1. Data for Eurobarometer 43.1 are presented in *Les Regions pour la Commission Européenne* (Brussels: European Coordination Office, 1995).

Notes: [a] Coding 4 = very attached, 3 = fairly attached, 2 – not very attached, 1 = not at all attached. [b] Average EU 12 and EU 15 attachments in 1995 are identical when rounded to one decimal place.

1991 and May–June 1995. In both surveys attachments at the local, regional, and national levels are comparably high, a noteworthy finding given the emphasis in the popular press and in much scholarly literature on national states as the prime focus of territorial identity. In five countries—Denmark, Finland, Ireland, the Netherlands, and the United Kingdom—attachment to country is significantly greater than attachment at the regional or local level. These are the only countries in which national attachment exceeds subnational attachment by 0.1 or more over both surveys or by 0.2 or more in one of the surveys. In France, Greece, Italy, Portugal, and Sweden, attachment to country is matched by a subnational attachment. In the federal or federalizing societies of Austria, Belgium, Spain, and (western) Germany, country attachment is exceeded significantly by regional attachment.

Attachment to the European Union is much weaker than attachment to smaller territorial units. The difference can be summarized succinctly. Nowhere is mean attachment to the EU greater than 3.0 ("fairly attached"); attachment to all other territorial levels is never less than 3.0. At the individual level, however, a slightly different picture comes into view: 30 percent of the total number of individuals in the national samples are as attached to the EU as they are to their country.

Table 4.2 provides a set of simple correlations for intensity of attachment for individuals across pairs of territorial levels.[9] These data allow one to come to grips with an important issue in the study of territorial identity: To what extent are attachments mutually exclusive or mutually inclusive? Does attachment to the nation come at a cost to EU or regional attachment? The data in Table 4.2 are unambiguous on this score. Attachments are *mutually inclusive*—that is, attachment at one territorial level is associated with *greater* rather than less attachment at other levels. There is no fixed sum of attachment an individual allocates across territorial levels— that is, attachment to the European Union, one's country, region, locality, or town is not a zero-sum competition in which an increase at one level is matched by a loss of attachment at other levels. On the contrary, an individual with a relatively high attachment to any one of these territorial levels is likely to have a relatively high attachment to other levels.

This finding is congruent with responses to questions asked in Eurobarometer 38 (Fall 1992) concerning the relationship of European to one's national identity. Whereas 30 percent of respondents viewed a European Union as a threat to their national identity and culture, 46 percent saw it as a protection. Sixty-two percent saw "a sense of European identity as being compatible with a sense of national identity," compared with 23 percent who envisaged their "country's identity disappearing over time if a European Union came about."[10]

Table 4.2 reveals two additional, second-order features. The first is *contiguity*: Associations between attachments are highest among contiguous territorial units. The strongest associations for any territorial level are those with the next level up or down. The second feature can be termed *parochialism*: Associations across lower territorial levels are stronger than those across higher territorial levels. To take the extremes, the association between attachments at local and regional levels (0.61) is considerably stronger than that at the country and EU levels (0.24). In the aggregate sample, parochialism is stronger than contiguity. The association between

Table 4.2 Correlation Matrix[a]

EC attachment	1.0000	–	–	–
National attachment	0.2367	1.0000	–	–
	(0.0000)			
Regional attachment	0.1786	0.4503	1.0000	–
	(0.0000)	(0.0000)		
Town/Village attachment	0.1345	0.3456	0.6070	1.0000
	(0.0000)	(0.0000)	(0.0000)	

Source: Eurobarometer 36.0.
Notes: [a] Pearson correlation (P value)

local and country attachment (0.45) is greater than that between country and EU attachment (0.24).

Figure 4.2 conceptualizes territorial attachments along two dimensions: the *intensity* of attachment at the local, regional, national, and European levels and the *multiplicity/exclusiveness* of attachment, which I measure as the sum of the differences between an individual's strongest attachment and all other attachments. Intensity varies between 1.0 (no attachment to

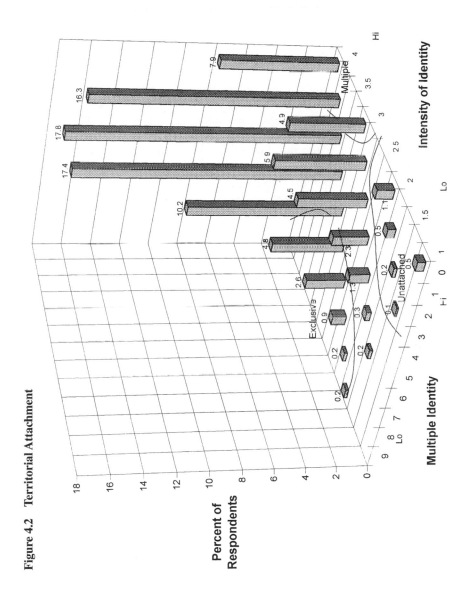

Figure 4.2 Territorial Attachment

any territorial community) to 4.0 (high attachment to one's town or local community, region, country, and to the EU). The multiple/exclusive dimension varies from zero, where attachments across levels are equal in intensity, to 9.0, which describes the combination of a single very strong attachment and the absence of attachment to any other level.

Combining these dimensions, I map the following groupings onto Figure 4.2.

Unattached: Individuals with no strong or fairly strong attachments to any territorial community. At the extreme, in the bottom left-hand corner of Figure 4.2, are individuals who attest to no territorial attachment (1,1,1,1 in ascending size of territorial unit). As one moves up and to the right in Figure 4.2 the level of attachment and its peakedness increase. I include in this category individuals with consistently weak attachment (2,2,2,2). Unattached individuals make up just 2.5 percent of the total sample.

Exclusive: Individuals whose attachments are focused exclusively at one or, at most, two territorial communities. At the extreme is the individual who is very strongly attached to a single level and not at all attached at any other level (all combinations of a single 4 and three 1s). As one moves up and to the left within the exclusive area in Figure 4.2, one finds individuals who have a single very strong attachment and one or two fairly strong attachments (combinations of 4,3,3,1) or, at the border, individuals who have two very strong attachments and two weak or negligible attachments (combinations of 4,4,2,2). Altogether, 8.6 percent of the Eurobarometer sample falls in the exclusive category.

Multiple: Finally are individuals who express strong or very strong attachments to territorial communities at three or all four levels. At the extreme is the individual with a very strong attachment to every territorial level (4,4,4,4). As one moves to the right in Figure 4.2, the degree of multiplicity diminishes. At the border in this category I include individuals with fairly strong attachments if they are consistent across all levels (3,3,3,3) and individuals who have very strong attachments if they are not peaked (i.e., combinations of 4,4,4,3). Individuals with multiple identities constitute 29.1 percent of the sample.

These groupings can be conceived in ideal typical terms. The further one moves to the top left in Figure 4.2, the more multi-attached one is, the further to the top right the more singularly attached, and the further to the bottom left the more unattached. The precise boundaries of these categories are arbitrary. I do not include an individual with a 3,3,4,4 pattern of attachment in the multiple-identity category or one with 3,2,2,1 as unattached or one with 4,3,3,3 as exclusive. At this point, my aim is to chart basic alternatives knowing there will inevitably be gray areas between them.

My larger purpose is to ask the reader to engage identity from a multilevel standpoint. Just as national states in Western Europe form only one part of a multilevel polity that stretches beneath and above them, so national identities form one element in a more complex multilevel pattern encompassing local and regional as well as supranational identities. This much is evident from the data presented here. How identities interact, how they change over time, and how they influence political activity are questions that lead us beyond Eurobarometer data. To make progress with such questions one must dig deeper. In the next section I examine evidence concerning regional and national identities in Catalonia and the Basque Country, and in the final section I engage macrohistorical issues of identity formation.

A NOTE ON CHANGE

The data presented in Table 4.1 suggest that territorial attachment taps deep-seated and therefore relatively stable orientations. Aggregated to the country level, shifts of just 0.3 point on a 4-point scale are rare: There are only three shifts of this magnitude and two shifts of 0.2 point among the forty-eight pairs of data points in Table 4.1. In the remaining forty-three cases, the change, rounded to one decimal place, is 0.1 or less.[11] Of course, the two time periods may straddle a valley or a peak, but the similarity across two time points separated by almost four years indicates that attachments to territorial communities tap diffuse loyalties that are more stable than attitudes concerning the benefits of membership in the European Union.

Given the restricted time period for which commensurate questions were asked in Eurobarometer surveys, we must turn to other sources to probe change in territorial attachments. Some regional surveys for individual countries include questions on regional and national identity that have been repeated over longer time periods, and whereas they cannot give a general picture, they provide one line of sight into the issue of temporal change.[12]

A question analyzed by Juan Linz in his 1986 study of identities in the Basque Country and Catalonia was repeated in surveys carried out by the Centro de Investigaciones sobre la Realidad Social from 1991 through 1994. The first survey was conducted in 1979, the year in which Catalonia and the Basque Country were granted special status in the Spanish constitution. The second set of surveys was conducted roughly a decade after the establishment of regional governments in the Basque Country and Catalonia. Tables 4.3 and 4.4 show the overall frequencies of territorial identities in the Basque Country and Catalonia.

Tables 4.3 and 4.4 reveal that the percentage of people who have balanced multiple identities—that is, who claim to be both Spanish and Basque or both Spanish and Catalan—increased slightly from 1979 to the early 1990s, by 5 percent in the Basque Country and 4 percent in Catalonia. Table 4.5, which combines responses of all those who have multiple identities, whether evenly balanced or lopsided, shows a sharper pattern of change. In the Basque Country multiple identities rose 12 percent from 1979 to the period 1991–1994. In the Catalan case such identities rose 17 percent in the same period.

In both Catalonia and the Basque Country, the proportion of the population that regarded themselves as exclusively Spanish was small, 10 percent in the Basque Country and 16 percent in Catalonia. There was an even larger shift away from exclusive regional identity in the Basque Country, from 38 percent in 1979 to 27 percent in the early 1990s.[13] A significant proportion of Basque citizens no longer view Basque and Spanish identities as incompatible.

The Basque Country and Catalonia are unusual regions in that they have strongly rooted ethnic cultures and distinctive languages, strong regionalist political parties, and entrenched regional governments. But it is worth stressing that the data reveal a shift not toward exclusive regional identity but toward multiple identity. The responsibilities of regional governments in these regions increased considerably during the 1980s at a time of intensive regional mobilization, and the outcome, as these surveys reveal, was

Table 4.3 Distribution of Identities in the Basque Country, 1979, 1991–1994 (in percentages)

Identities	1979	1991–1994
1. Only Basque	38	27
2. More Basque than Spanish	12	20
3. Both Basque and Spanish	26	31
4. More Spanish than Basque	6	5
5. Only Spanish	14	10
Don't know/Didn't answer	4	7
Total	100	100
N	[1,011]	[802]

Sources: The frequencies for 1979 have been excerpted from Juan J. Linz, *Conflicto en Euskadi* (Madrid: Espasa Calpe, 1986), 51.

Notes: The mean frequencies for the period 1991–1994 are derived from five surveys conducted by the Centro de Investigaciones sobre la Realidad Social (CIRES) in June 1991 (525 cases), June 1992 (67 cases), January 1993 (69 cases), January 1994 (69 cases), and June 1994 (70 cases). The question asked by CIRES was: "In general, would you say that you feel more Basque than Spanish, as Basque as Spanish, or more Spanish than Basque? 1. Only Basque. 2. More Basque than Spanish. 3. As Basque as Spanish. 4. More Spanish than Basque. 5. Only Spanish. 6. Do not know. 7. Do not answer."

Table 4.4   Distribution of Identities in Catalonia, 1979, 1991–1994 (in percentages)

Identities	1979	1991–1994
1. Only Catalan	13	16
2. More Catalan than Spanish	11	20
3. Both Catalan and Spanish	33	37
4. More Spanish than Catalan	6	10
5. Only Spanish	28	16
Don't know/Didn't answer	9	1
Total	100	100
N	[1,232]	[1,299]

Sources: The frequencies for 179 have been excerpted from Linz, *Conflicto en Euskadi*, 43.

Notes: The frequencies take into consideration the 9 percent of people who did not answer this question or who gave other responses. Mean frequencies for the period 1991–1994 are from five surveys conducted by the Centro de Investigaciones sobre la Realidad Social (CIRES) in June 1991 (533 cases), June 1992 (191 cases), January 1993 (190 cases), January 1994 (193 cases), and June 1994 (192 cases). The question asked by CIRES was as follows: "In general, would you say that you feel more Catalan than Spanish, as Catalan as Spanish, or more Spanish than Catalan? 1. Only Catalan. 2. More Catalan than Spanish. 3. As Catalan as Spanish. 4. More Spanish than Catalan. 5. Only Spanish. 6. Do not know. 7. Do not answer."

Table 4.5   Percentages of Multiple Identities (Responses 2, 3 and 4), 1979, 1991–1994

	1979	1991–1994
Basque Country (from table 4.3)	44	56
Catalonia (from table 4.4)	50	67

multiple rather than exclusive territorial attachment. Neither survey posed questions about European attachments, but they suggest that the creation of European-level institutions may have deepened multiple identities that include a European component.

EXPLAINING TERRITORIAL IDENTITY

How and why do identities change over time? To make sense of this question one must engage macrosocietal factors including, above all, coercive conflict, culture, socioeconomic interaction, and political institutions. The causal processes linking variations of the initial conditions described by these factors with patterns of identity are undoubtedly complex and conditional, and a theory capable of point-predicting patterns of identity for a given set of individuals is a distant aspiration. But we can still elaborate plausible (and, in principle, empirically falsifiable) statements about particular aspects of identity, and in this section I evaluate prospects for the development of multiple identities that include a stronger European component.

War

Territorial attachments have arguably been shaped more by coercive relations—above all, war and colonial domination—than by any other factors. The solidarity produced within a territorial group engaged in coercive conflict with another group is perhaps the strongest social glue there is. Almost every account of the rise of nationalism and national states in Western Europe, and, more broadly, of ethnic consciousness in a variety of industrial and preindustrial settings, emphasizes the causal role of coercive conflict as a source of identity. As Anthony Smith summarizes his wide-ranging survey of the sources of nationalism and ethnicity, "protracted wars have been the crucible in which ethnic consciousness has been crystallized."[14]

Coercive conflict not only deepens ethnic or national identity but usually makes those identities more exclusive. First, war eliminates attachments that overarch the contending communities.[15] War creates an extreme "us versus them" mentality in which those who have an overarching identity with both communities are forced to make a choice.[16] Second, a war among states weakens substate attachments as it strengthens attachment to the warring community as a whole. Historically, national war has helped to integrate diverse groups into multiethnic societies such as the United States and the Soviet Union. Similarly, war has had the effect of nationalizing territorially diverse societies such as the United Kingdom, France, and Spain. International war not only ratchets up the state's capacity to extract and mobilize resources in a society, but it deepens commitment to the national community in a way that squeezes out other identities. In other words, war strengthens exclusive identity; it presses individuals toward the *A* corner of Figure 4.1.

A distinctive feature of Western Europe over the past half century is that it has not been the site of a major international war. The study of identity in Western Europe is therefore the study of identity in the absence of its most powerful source. This historically anomalous situation provides, I believe, a key to understanding the developments of the past half century. The absence of war has meant the absence of an immensely powerful influence toward exclusive identity, leaving causal space for a variety of other influences that have had the net effect of sustaining significant levels of multiple identity. The deepening of subnational and supranational identities has proceeded without the check of war and the hardening of exclusive national state identities. The past half century has been one of diffusion—diffusion of authoritative competencies among multiple levels of government, diffusion of individual identities among multiple territorial communities.

War shapes identity, but it is possible, indeed plausible, that identity affects a community's willingness to go to war. One of the reasons it is worth exploring the sources of multiple identity is that individuals having some shared territorial identity are perhaps less likely to engage in coercive conflict against each other. To the extent that individuals in European countries share an attachment to a common European Union, we may hypothesize that they will be less bellicose in expressing the identities that divide them.[17] This is one of the more ambitious goals of European integration that takes us back to the origins of the project. Support for the European Union as a means to avoid war among European states appears strong and enduring; when individuals are asked why they favor European integration, consistent majorities cite "peace" as the strongest reason.[18]

For the two centuries or more leading up to World War II, war making in Western Europe had undergirded national states and helped to crystallize national territorial communities. The absence of interstate warfare in the second half of the twentieth century has opened the field to other influences that might otherwise have been overwhelmed, including intensified social interaction and economic and political integration, and I discuss these in turn next.

Culture

Important streams of theorizing about identity emphasize culture—including particularly language, ethnicity, religion, and social transactions—as key to territorial attachment.[19] With respect to language and ethnicity the European Union is extraordinarily diverse and is likely to remain so. To the extent that ethnic and linguistic commonalities are requisites for shared territorial identity, one would not expect to see multiple identities that encompass Europe as a whole.

The most influential line of theorizing, associated with Karl Deutsch, hypothesizes that territorial identities are created as populations integrate socially and economically.[20] This premise rests on the supposition that common identities result from shared experiences and culture that, in turn, are related to the intensity of social and economic interaction among individuals. From a Deutschian standpoint, then, there are grounds for expecting a shift in the direction of a European identity with the increase in intra-European trade and commerce, the decline of border controls, the vast increase in travel within Europe, the creation of Europeanwide political institutions, educational exchanges, and so forth. All of these factors, according to a Deutschian model, contribute to gradual cultural homogenization and increased personal trust among Europeans, thereby leading to shared identity.[21]

One must pay detailed attention to intervening factors, however, to evaluate whether an increase in the density of individual interactions will deepen shared identity. Examples of increasing interaction leading to hostility rather than integration (e.g., in Europe during the first two decades of the twentieth century) suggest that no objective function links social/economic/political transactions to identity. It seems sensible to argue not that the effect of a given level of transaction on individual identity is an objective datum but that it is instead interpreted—and contested—in a political setting.[22]

The process leading from transaction to culture to territorial identity is neither simple nor reflexive. First, the process is shaped by *institutions* (i.e., socially accepted formal and informal rules) that (1) constrain interactions within preestablished networks so that the type and incidence of interaction vary systematically across groups and (2) shape the way a given transaction affects participants—for example, through a setting of schools, labor unions, and firms that can vary across the relevant territory. Second, the process depends on *actors* (i.e., individuals and groups of individuals operating within a given field of institutions) who (1) have prior territorial identities that shape their interpretation of ongoing experience and (2) are influenced by political discourse in their local and national settings.

To evaluate the effects of institutions and actors on the link between transactions and identity demands a disaggregated research agenda. To what extent have student exchanges within the EU had a measurable effect on the patterns of identity of participants? How have orientations (and identities) of particular sets of individuals been influenced by European cable television, structural funding in the poorer regions of the EU, travel abroad, or living in a border region? These are just a few of the basic questions that are essential building blocks for a theory linking cultural convergence to multiple identity, yet we have little systematic information that bears on them.

Transactions across national borders may exacerbate exclusive identities. As Suzanne Berger has observed, "The conjunction of rising global flows of capital with new immigrant flows across borders once politically closed has heightened sensitivities everywhere to territorial facts, the control of frontiers, and national sovereignty."[23] Globalization may lead to irredentist reaction rather than liberal internationalism. Such reaction has been intensified by the efforts of radical right politicians to link economic disaffection to European integration and the decline of national sovereignty.

Clearly, one cannot argue straight from the density of transactions to the creation of identity; too much intervenes. It may be, however, that cultural convergence resulting from increased transactions serves as a necessary but not sufficient condition of multiple identity creation. This would be a weak and perhaps more plausible form of Deutschian theory.

The European Union cannot draw either on solidarity resulting from coercive conflict, or on ethnic or linguistic commonalities, and these are by far the most powerful bases of territorial identity. This alone may explain the relative weakness of European identity compared with identity at the national or subnational level. But it would be premature to stop here, for we still need to explain the positive level of attachment to the EU among significant minorities in the 1990s and the increase in multiple identity that has occurred in particular regions such as Catalonia and the Basque Country.

Economic Interest

Instead of arguing that the sheer density of transnational transactions shapes identities, a number of writers have linked individual economic prospects under international market integration to support for the European Union. More generally, we can hypothesize that attachment to territorial communities is influenced by individuals' perceptions of their economic fortunes under alternative scenarios. This would apply to national as well as international economic integration. The building of national states went along with the creation of national markets and the demolition of numerous local barriers to trade. In the process, village craftsmen and artisans employed in city guilds sought refuge behind traditional local and city privileges against rule making from the center. Conflicts between traditional guilds, based on monopoly rule setting in particular towns and cities, and new entrepreneurs seeking to escape those rules were an endemic feature of early capitalism across Western Europe.

In recent years, the link between economic life chances and the territorial organization of markets has again become transparent. Individual opinions concerning the personal economic implications of European market integration vary widely, from strongly positive to strongly negative, and we might expect that such impressions influence the level of individual attachment to the European Union. Their effect is magnified because the European Union is a relatively recent institutional innovation. In Gabriel Almond and Sidney Verba's terms, individual evaluations of EU policy output are likely to be particularly important because the polity cannot call on reserves of diffuse loyalty.[24]

Literature on the political economy of market integration allows us to relate individual location in the economy to EU attachment. A basic conclusion of this literature is that less skilled workers in protected sectors of domestically oriented industry stand to lose the most under market integration and that owners of export-oriented capital stand to gain the most.

The primary reason is that labor is far less mobile than internationally oriented capital, both across economic sectors and geographically. Owners of capital are able to shift the use of their productive resource in response to market pressures far more effectively than can workers. Although, in principle, freedom of movement exists for labor across national borders, it is limited by cultural and linguistic barriers. The effects of contrasting mobility are amplified by national economic regulation. National governments have a strong inducement to give special consideration to the political demands of international capital because it is so mobile. In seeking to retain existing capital and attract new capital, governments compete to provide a favorable regime for owners of capital, presumably at the expense of other factors of production. Finally, market integration has consequences for the relative organizational power of workers vis-à-vis employers. Employers, particularly those in export-oriented industries, can counter the demands of organized labor by moving—or threatening to move—investment to more accommodating labor markets elsewhere. Workers have been unable to redress their relative immobility by establishing transnational union organizations that encompass workers in relevant product markets.

These expectations are supported by Gary Marks and Richard Haesly in a multivariate logistic analysis of 1991 Eurobarometer data.[25] The authors find that individual attachment to the EU is significantly associated with class position, sense of economic well-being, and respondents' orientation toward the single market. Such relationships hold when controlled for education, political knowledge, and a variety of other individual background variables. This finding is consistent with the work of Agusti Bosch and Kenneth Newton and others cited in this chapter, although in none of these studies are the relationships particularly strong. Marks and Haesly find that on the basis of class, sense of economic well-being, and orientation toward the single market, individual attachment to the EU (on a four-point scale) can be "predicted" with a probability of slightly less than 60 percent.

A substantial body of research suggests a link between economic evaluations and support for European integration. One way to interpret the evidence is to say that specific support for economic integration spills over into generalized support for European political institutions. This has a precedent: Pride in German economic performance after World War II fed into diffuse loyalty toward the democratic institutions of the Federal Republic. If this process took hold in the European Union, it would be possible to speak of an economic route to European political attachment.

Political Institutions

A tradition in political philosophy has argued that identity may arise not only from the ingroup reinforcement of war or cultural commonality but also from a shared experience of political citizenship. Formal political institutions—in particular, parliaments, executives, courts, and civil services—may provide a locus for identity as symbols of a particular territorial community, by providing channels for meaningful political participation, and by making common policy for individuals in a given territory.[26]

If this hypothesis is valid, one would expect to find that patterns of attachment reflect the distribution of political competencies across subnational, national, and supranational political institutions—that is, that there are relatively high levels of regional attachment in federal polities and relatively high levels of national attachment in unitary polities. Table 4.1 confirms this hypothesis. The only countries for which regional attachment is higher than national attachment are Austria, Belgium, Germany, and Spain—federal or federalizing countries. From this standpoint, relatively low levels of attachment to the EU reflect lack of opportunities for participation at that level or a lag between the shift of competencies to the EU and changes in individual attachments.

Individual-level data are broadly consistent with this hypothesis. An extension of the citizenship hypothesis holds that individuals who participate more, have greater political knowledge of the EU, and have high levels of subjective political competence should be more attached to the EU. This is what we find, although the relationships are not very strong.[27]

By the same logic, we would expect to see an increase in European identities as the scope of competencies in the EU has increased. An assortment of data presented in *Public Opinion and Internationalized Governance*, edited by Oskar Niedermayer and Richard Sinnot, supports this notion for the period up to the early 1990s. Bosch and Newton write that "one variable, however, stands out as important—the passage of time. Support for EC membership and for European unification simply grows slowly in the long term. Each year seems to add, on average, about a fifth to a quarter of 1 per cent for approval of European unification and EC membership."[28] Recent surveys reveal that we cannot extrapolate this finding into the post-Maastricht era. EU support follows a jagged path through time. The overall level of EU attachment fell slightly between 1991 and 1995, whereas levels of specific support for European integration declined more sharply.

The citizenship hypothesis suffers from the same disability as transaction theory—it connects two factors that are mediated by actors and institutions. In the post-Maastricht era, European citizenship and identity have become salient issues in party-political competition in several member states. These issues spring from parties to electorates and back again; they are manipulated to gain votes or support for factions within parties, and they are interpreted and reinterpreted in partisan terms by the press. Consequently, it is problematic to model identity as if it resulted from an objective process of increasing transactions or opportunities for political participation.

CONCLUSION

The analysis of territorial identity is in its infancy. We know little about the pattern of individual territorial identities and even less about how and why those identities change over time. Instead of drowning in a sea of data, researchers strive to gain whatever tidbits of systematic information are available. The thrust of this chapter has been to set out a conceptual framework to map individual identity and discuss some factors that may explain what is found in Eurobarometer surveys.

In terms of identity creation, European integration over the past half century has been very different from state building during the previous two centuries. It is not simply that the degree of ethnic and cultural heterogeneity in the European Union is far greater than that in any member state but also that the forces of identity creation in European integration appear to be far weaker than those in the process of state building. European integration has been driven by an economic rather than a war-making logic; as a result, its capacity to transform individuals appears to be weaker.

But I do not draw the implication that common territorial identity is a chimera in the EU. This chapter argues that identity should not be conceived in all-or-nothing terms or as the result of a tradeoff among loyalties at different territorial levels. I have mapped territorial identity along two dimensions: intensity of attachment to a particular territorial community and exclusive versus multiple attachment across one or more territorial levels. It is not unusual to find individuals in the European Union who have relatively intense multiple identities. But the big questions remain unanswered: How can one explain variation among individual identities across time and place? How are different territorial identities mobilized in different contexts? How do individuals act on the basis of different patterns of territorial identity?

The offshoot of this inquiry is that we should regard with skepticism claims that democratic institutions cannot be deepened in the EU because there is too little European identity. Even if we accept the view that identity must precede democratic institutionalization, it is not self-evident that EU identity is lacking. This chapter has explored patterns of territorial identity based on the presumption that individuals may have mutually inclusive territorial identities. We might frame similar questions in studying liberal democracy, for it is not self-evident that by democratizing the European Union one is undermining democracy in national states. If Europe is a multilevel polity in which citizens may have multiple identities, we can envision democratic channels at a multiplicity of levels.[29]

As states and nations lose their grip on authority and identity in the process of multilevel governance, we might expect received wisdom about the virtues of the national state to be questioned. Historically, the national state was the crucible for liberal democracy, but is the national state the only context in which liberal democracy might flourish?

NOTES

I am indebted to Richard Haesly for ideas and Eurobarometer data. I also wish to thank Liesbet Hooghe, Leonard Ray, Jeffrey Anderson, Paul Pierson, Mark Pollack, and João Espada for comments and Tim Burch for editorial assistance.

1. I use the term *European Union* to encompass its earlier incarnations, the European Economic Community and the European Community.

2. Fritz W. Scharpf, "Negative and Positive Integration in the Political Economy of European Welfare States," in *Governance in the European Union*, Gary Marks, Fritz Scharpf, Philippe Schmitter, and Wolfgang Streeck, eds. (London: Sage, 1996), 26. My point of departure in this chapter is to explore the extent and sources of multiple identities, which include identity at the European level. A second response is the one taken by Philippe Schmitter who explores the scope for democracy in the absence of an overarching shared identity: "Why should individuals (and, for that matter, organizations) in the Euro-Polity have to be 'nationals' in some sense in order to act like citizens? Why could they not be loyal to a common set of institutions and political/legal principles rather than to some mystical charismatic founder or set of mythologized ancestors? . . . That, it seems to me, is the major issue. Not whether the eventual Euro-Polity will be able to reproduce on an enlarged scale the same intensity of collective sentiment that was once characteristic of its member nation-states, but whether it can produce an encompassing system of stable and peaceful political relations without such a passionately shared identity or community of fate." Philippe C. Schmitter, "How to Democratize the Emerging Euro-Polity: Citizenship, Representation, Decision-Making," unpublished ms.

3. For an alternative view, see Kees van Kersbergen, "Double Allegiance in European Integration: Publics, Nation-States, and Social Policy," EU Working Papers (European University Institute, Florence, Italy, 1997), 1–31.

4. Anthony D. Smith, *Nations and Nationalism in a Global Era* (Cambridge: Polity, 1995), 154–155; Michael Th. Greven, "Der Politische Raum als Mass des

Politischen: Europa als Beispiel," in *Europäische Institutionenpolitik,* Thomas König, Elmar Rieger, and Hermann Schmitt, eds. (Mannheim: Campus, 1997), 45–65. For a succinct overview of nationalism in Europe, see Roger Eatwell, "Europe of the 'Nation States'? Concepts, Theories and Reflections," in *European Political Culture,* Roger Eatwell, ed. (London: Routledge, 1997).

5. Karl W. Deutsch, Sidney Burrell, Robert Kann, Maurice Lee, Jr., Martin Lichterman, Raymond Lindgren, Francis Loewenheim, and Richard Van Wagenen, *Political Community and the North Atlantic Area* (Princeton: Princeton University Press), 4.

6. Ernst B. Haas, "The Study of Regional Integration: Reflections on the Joy and Anguish of Pretheorizing," in *Regional Integration: Theory and Research,* Leon N. Lindberg and Stuart A. Scheingold, eds. (Cambridge: Harvard University Press, 1971). Haas did not intend this as a mere possibility: "Perhaps the now existing Western European pattern approaches this image" (31).

7. William Wallace, *The Transformation of Western Europe* (London: Royal Institute of International Affairs, 1990), 33. Similarly, Soledad García and Helen Wallace perceive "the potential development of multiple identities in concentric circles which would encourage compatible loyalties from the local to the European level." Soledad García and Helen Wallace, "Conclusion," in *European Identity and the Search for Legitimacy,* Soledad García, ed. (London: Pinter, 1993), 172. See also Daniela Obradovic, "Political Legitimacy and the European Union," *Journal of Common Market Studies* 34, no. 2 (June 1966): 191–221. Brigid Laffan emphasizes that the "extension of political space beyond the nation-state provides a shelter for multiple identities be they local, regional or national." Brigid Laffan, "The Politics of Identity and Political Order in Europe," *Journal of Common Market Studies* 34, no. 1 (March 1996): 81–102. For a trenchant criticism of an exclusive focus on national identity and the notion that democratic legitimacy depends on a homogeneous *Volk,* see J.H.H. Weiler, Ulrich R. Haltern, and Ranz C. Mayer, "European Democracy and Its Critique," in *The Crisis of Representation in Europe,* Jack Hayward, ed. (London: Frank Cass, 1995).

Multiple identities in a system of multilevel governance bear some resemblance to Ernest Gellner's description of *pre*national identity: "A great diversity and plurality and complexity characterizes all distinct parts of the whole: the minute social groups, which are the atoms of which the picture is composed, have complex and ambiguous and multiple relations to many cultures; some through speech, others through their dominant faith, another still through a variant faith or set of practices, a fourth through administrative loyalty, and so forth. When it comes to painting the political system, the complexity is not less great than in the sphere of culture. Obedience for one purpose and in one context is not necessarily the same as obedience for some other end or in some other season." Ernest Gellner, *Nations and Nationalism* (Ithaca: Cornell University Press, 1983), 139.

8. Several of the best quantitative analyses of European identity are contained in a single recent volume: Oskar Niedermayer and Richard Sinnot, eds., *Public Opinion and Internationalized Governance* (Oxford: Oxford University Press, 1995), which was published following an earlier draft of this chapter. See particularly the chapters by Oskar Niedermayer, Richard Sinnot, Bernhard Wessels,

Guido Martinotti and Sonia Stefanizze, and Sophie Duchesne and André-Paul Frognier. For historically informed perspectives see García, ed., *European Identity and the Search for Legitimacy*. Other recent works that bear on the topic are Mark N. Franklin, Cees Van Der Eijk, and Michael Marsh, "Referendum Outcomes and Trust in Government: Public Support for Europe in the Wake of Maastricht," in *The Crisis of Representation in Europe*, Hayward, ed.; Andreas Sobisch and David Patterson, "Public Support for European Integration: A Longitudinal Analysis," presented at the American Political Science Association meeting, Chicago, Illinois, September 1995; Vincent Mahler, Bruce Taylor, and Jennifer Wozniak, "Economics and Public Support for the European Union, 1976–1992: An Analysis at the National, Regional and Individual Levels," presented at the European Community Studies Association meeting, Charleston, South Carolina, May 1995; Richard Eichenberg and Russel Dalton, "Europeans and the European Community: The Dynamics of Public Support for European Integration," *International Organization* 47, no. 4 (1993), 507–534; Christopher J. Anderson and Karl C. Kaltenhaler, "The Dynamics of Public Opinion Toward European Integration," *European Journal of International Relations* 2 (1996): 175–199; Matthew Gabel and Harvey D. Palmer, "Understanding Variation in Public Support for European Integration," *European Journal of Political Research* 27 (1995): 3–19; Ulf Hedetoft in *Signs of Nations: Studies in the Political Semiotics of Self and Other in Contemporary European Nationalism* (Aldershot: Dartmouth, 1995) has written a rich and unusual study focusing on Danish, German, and British identities and analyzing them in relation to European identity. We still lack plausible analyses of how local, regional, national, and supranational identities fit together. This is the topic of a dissertation being written by Richard Haesly at the University of North Carolina at Chapel Hill using focus group data from Wales and Scotland.

9. This table and the data for Figure 4.2 were prepared by Richard Haesly. Table 4.2 is based on data from Eurobarometer 36.0. At the time of writing, data from Eurobarometer 43.1 were not yet released for scholars. The durability of average levels of attachment at the country level from 1991 to 1995 suggests that the patterns I derive from the earlier year are reasonably robust.

10. Karlheinz Reif, "Cultural Convergence and Cultural Diversity as Factors in European Diversity," in *European Identity and the Search for Legitimacy*, García, ed., 139–140; Thomas Risse-Kappen, "Ideas, Communicative Processes, and Domestic Political Change in Europe—A Conceptual Framework and Some Preliminary Results," presented at the International Conference of Europeanists, Chicago, Illinois, March 1996.

11. Because the data for 1995 are rounded to a single decimal place in the source currently available, I have done the same to data for 1991. This section is drawn from Gary Marks and Iván Llamazares, "La Transformación de la Movilización Regional en la Unión Europea," *Revista de Estudios Políticos* 22, no. 1 (1995): 149–170.

12. I thank Iván Llamazares for these data. The ideas in this section are explored in ibid.

13. Some surveys also indicate that the proportion of the Basque population that considers itself exclusively Basque has decreased since the late 1970s. According

to such surveys, from 1979 to 1989 the percentage of those who considered themselves "only Basque" decreased from 39.7 to 35.9, whereas the percentage who considered themselves "more Basque than Spanish" increased from 12.6 to 17.8. See F. J. Llera, "Conflicto en Euskadi Revisited," in *Politics, Society, and Democracy: The Case of Spain*, Richard Gunther, ed. (Boulder, Colorado: Westview Press, 1993), 183.

14. Anthony D. Smith, *The Ethnic Revival* (Cambridge: Cambridge University Press, 1981), 75. Peter Sahlins comes to a parallel conclusion in his comparison of the contrasting identities of Cerdans in the Pyrenees who happened to be on different sides of the French/Spanish border: "National identity is a socially constructed and continuous process of defining 'friend' and 'enemy,' a logical extension of the process of maintaining boundaries between 'us' and 'them' within more local communities." Peter Sahlins, *Boundaries: The Making of France and Spain in the Pyrenees* (Berkeley: University of California Press, 1989), 271.

15. By the same logic, cross-national alliances may deepen an overarching alliance identity as individuals develop attachments both to their respective nations and to the alliance in general. Arguably, this happened among the Allies during World War II. The strongest assertion of such transnational attachment was the sentiment that Britain and France and later Britain and the United States should merge into transnational states.

16. Eric Hobsbawm emphasizes the "us versus them" character of identity in "Nation, State, Ethnicity, Religion: Transformations of Identity," in *Nationalism in Europe Past and Present*, vol. 1, Justo G. Beramendi, Romón Máiz, and Xosé M. Núñez, eds. (Santiago de Compostela: University of Santiago de Compostela, 1994), 33–46.

17. This hypothesis is plausible but, to my knowledge, untested.

18. Reif, "Cultural Convergence and Cultural Diversity," 136.

19. For example, the writings of Anthony Smith. Hans-Jürgen Puhle notes that "to have a regional language and culture of one's own seems to be a minimum requirement for the formation of cultural and hence political nationalism." Hans-Jürgen Puhle, "Nation States, Nations, and Nationalisms in Western and Southern Europe," in *Nationalism in Europe Past and Present*, vol. 2, Beramendi, Máiz, and Núñez, eds., 13–38.

20. Karl W. Deutsch et al., *Nationalism and Social Communication* (New York: Wiley, 1953); *Political Community and the North Atlantic Area*.

21. For a recent argument along these lines, see Alec Stone-Sweet and Wayne Sandholtz, "European Integration and Supranational Governance," *Journal of European Public Policy* 4 (September 1997): 297–317. Chris Shore argues that underlying several of these initiatives is an attempt by the European Commission to create a European identity. Chris Shore, "Inventing the 'People's Europe': Critical Approaches to European Community 'Cultural Policy'," *Man* 28, no. 4 (December 1993): 779–799.

22. This is the approach taken by Benedict Anderson, *Imagined Communities: Reflections on the Origin and Spread of Nationalism* (London: Verso, 1983).

23. Suzanne Berger, "Comments," in *Regional Integration: The West European Experience*, William Wallace, ed. (Washington, D.C.: Brookings Institution, 1994), 117–118.

24. Gabriel A. Almond and Sidney Verba, *The Civic Culture* (Princeton: Princeton University Press, 1963).

25. Gary Marks and Richard Haesly, "Thinking Through Territorial Identity in Europe with Reference to Some Evidence," presented at the International Conference of Europeanists, Chicago, Illinois, March 1966.

26. The political sources of identity are an element of civic, as distinct from ethnic, nationalism. Whereas civic attachment is open to multiple identity, as conceptualized here, ethnic attachment is usually exclusive. On this distinction see Michael Keating, *Nations Against the State: The New Politics of Nationalism in Quebec, Catalonia and Scotland* (London: Macmillan, 1996), and Laffan, "The Politics of Identity and Political Order in Europe." Klaus von Beyme argues along these lines that to the extent that it exists, "citizenship in Europe is set on the road of *constitutional patriotism* (emphasis in the original)." Klaus von Beyme, "Citizenship and the European Union," unpublished ms.

27. Marks and Haesly, "Thinking Through Territorial Identity in Europe."

28. Agusti Bosch and Kenneth Newton, "Economic Calculus or Familiarity Breeds Content?" in *Public Opinion and Internationalized Governance*, Niedermayer and Sinnot, ed., 91. Bosch and Newton carefully note the limits of this generalization and point out that Greece, Spain, and Portugal appear to be exceptions.

29. For a flexible approach to applying liberal democracy in the EU, see Antje Weiner and Vincent Della Sala, "Constitution-making and Citizenship Practice—Bridging the Democracy Gap in the EU?" *Journal of Common Market Studies* 35 (December 1997): 595–614; Philippe C. Schmitter and José I. Torreblanca, "Old 'Foundations' and New 'Rules' for an Enlarged European Union," Working Paper (Instituto Juan March, June 1997), 1–26. A conceptual analysis commensurate with these views is James A. Caporaso, "The European Union and Forms of State: Westphalian, Regulatory or Post-Modern?" *Journal of Common Market Studies* 34, no. 1 (March 1996): 29–51.

Section II

European Integration and the Nation-State

5

Portugal: Democracy through Europe

António Barreto
translated by Elizabeth Plaister

During the brief period between 1960 and the early 1990s, Portugal underwent a process of far-reaching social, economic, and political change that,
in different ways, occurred under European influence. In the course of only
two or three decades, a closed and very homogeneous society, an authoritarian political regime, the last overseas colonial system, a protected and
relatively autarkic economy and a degree of international isolation were
replaced by a democratic regime incorporated in the European Union, an
open economy, an increasingly open society, and a principally tertiary
productive structure.[1]

In the broadest sense, long before Portugal officially became a member
of the European Community (EC) in 1985, European integration was one
of the main driving forces behind these changes. Indeed, social and eco
nomic integration had already begun during the 1960s, particularly
through emigration, tourism, trade, business and television,[2] Until the
1974–1975 revolution, however, and the establishment of the democratic
state in 1976, European political integration did not exist. Portuguese political authorities were not interested in closer contact with Europe that
might imply a reduction of their own power or a change in the political
system. Meanwhile, no pressure was apparent from European countries to
liberalize or democratize the authoritarian corporatist regime. For opposition groups, however, the terms *Europe* and *democracy* were synonymous.

During the revolutionary crisis in 1975, when a real threat existed that
a new authoritarian regime might be established—this time of the left—
democratic forces claimed a European vocation and received pledges of
solidarity, economic aid, and political support from a number of EC member states. Once democracy had been established, its consolidation was
inextricably linked to the project of European integration. Portugal's for-

mal accession, which became effective in 1986, contributed to political stability and relative economic and social success during the following decade. The first economic difficulties experienced by a backward country now open to international competition emerged during the early 1990s. Nonetheless, public opinion appeared to continue to support the European ideal.[3]

Regarding social cohesion, of which the official social security system is an element, European integration appears to have played a positive—although indirect—role by improving economic well-being, opening up trade opportunities, and providing access to structural funds, thereby helping unemployment levels to be kept low.[4] Nonetheless, direct influences on the social security system were limited. Indeed, growth of the Portuguese welfare state had begun at a moderate pace in the 1960s, speeding up considerably after the 1974 revolution; by the mid-1980s, prior to EC membership, the state already provided universal coverage.[5]

In political terms and with respect to the functioning of institutions, European integration may have contributed to the relative modernization of the public administration, although not to the extent that it furthered social and economic modernization. Lacking democratic and parliamentary traditions and with a fragile civil society and a weak private entrepreneurial structure, the Portuguese political regime, although democratic, is not transparent and remains essentially dependent on the executive. The European Union, with its known democratic deficit, has not only failed to contribute to political modernization but has perhaps contributed to the perpetuation of the secretive and closed practices of the administration and the government. Europe played a decisive role in changing Portuguese society and consolidating democracy by creating an atmosphere of general sympathy with European institutions and Western European political regimes, by accepting Portugal as an eventual member, and by supporting the emerging democratic system. But its impact in developing a modern, transparent, and participatory parliamentary democracy has been limited. In a country such as Portugal, which lacks deep-rooted democratic traditions, the European Union will not likely have a direct influence on *enhancing* democracy.

PORTUGAL'S SINGULARITIES

When Portugal officially applied to the European Community in 1977, the country had a number of specific features, some of which were unique. Portugal was the most economically backward country in Europe, with the lowest income per capita, the lowest amount of industrial product, the lowest level of productivity per employee, and the highest percentage of the population making a living from agriculture. Of the European countries with significant emigration, Portugal had the highest percentage of nationals living and working in other EC countries,[6] the highest level of illiteracy and lowest percentage of the population attending higher education, and the smallest amount of social security coverage and public health services. Portugal's population indicators—specifically infant mortality, life expectancy, and birth rate—were more in line with underdeveloped countries than with European states.

Portugal's political features were even more unique. The country had just emerged from two years of extensive upheaval during which a coup d'état was followed, although without extensive violence, by a process of social revolution and a successful counterrevolution. These events had ended Europe's longest dictatorship of the twentieth century: forty-eight years of authoritarian corporatism and single-party rule. The fall of the regime also brought an end to the world's oldest and most enduring empire as Portugal's colonies in Africa were the last to gain independence.

The government that applied for EC membership was the first democratic government, based on free elections and universal suffrage, to exist in Portugal in the twentieth century. From the corporate state and the revolution the Portuguese democratic state—the youngest and least experienced in the Western world—inherited a large bureaucracy and a huge public sector that monopolized every major sector of the economy, together with a complex bureaucratic system of protectionist regulations governing economic activities.[7] In most cases structures and traditions were contrary to those of an open administration and were incompatible with the market laws, free trade and private enterprise current in the EC.

Even more important, Portugal was one of the most unitary countries of Western Europe. Within borders laid down over eight centuries ago Portugal displayed a rare permanence and homogeneity: one nationality, one people, one ethnic origin, one language, one state, and one hegemonic religion existing within a territory that had remained practically unchanged. This unitary nature was so strong that when reinforced by almost five decades of an authoritarian regime not only the political regime but Portuguese society itself "was not plural."[8] Unlike most, if not all, other European countries, within its own borders Portugal had no national centrifugal forces or even regional entities with a strong identity. Finally, given its geographic location and long Atlantic and colonial history, Portugal rarely participated in the great European social, military, and political movements or processes.[9]

BACKGROUND TO INTEGRATION

Portuguese society began to look toward Europe prior to the 1974 revolution and prior to EC membership in 1985. Indeed, the process began in the early 1960s but was restricted primarily to the social and economic fronts. Portugal's participation in the founding of the European Free Trade Association (EFTA) was one of the clearest indications of this new trend. Subsequently, foreign trade, foreign investment, business, and technological development acquired an undeniable importance in society with a growing European presence, prompting a European focus in economic projects and social aspirations.[10] In parallel with these economic developments, during that decade European mass tourism began to include Portugal as a destination, which had the expected impact on the economic, trade, cultural, and human fronts.

Emigration to Europe also increased rapidly during the 1960s, with a major impact on people's behavior and habits, as well as on foreign trade and the balance of payments.[11] At that time traditional Portuguese emigration underwent two major changes. The first concerned the number of immigrants departing annually for other countries, which rose from 32,000 in 1960 to 173,000 in 1970, and then dropped to 120,000 in 1973. The second change lay in their destination. Initially Brazil, followed by the United States, Venezuela, and Canada were the prime destinations; subsequently, emigrants looked to Europe, especially France. Within a little over a decade, over 51 percent of the residents born during that period left the country and settled elsewhere in Europe.

This human and social integration had far-reaching repercussions and was perhaps one of the main factors in social change. Social structures, activities, and occupation of the territory changed, as did patterns of behavior, aspirations, and attitudes. Cultural horizons in a previously closed country underwent extensive change. Bilingualism increased, as did the number of families with dual nationalities. "Emigrant remittances" became the primary means for achieving equilibrium in balance of payments, and for many families, particularly in rural areas, these funds were essential supplements to their income and well-being.[12]

Over the centuries emigration had become structural and traditional, but beginning in the 1960s, a new form of emigration came into being. Previously, emigration had been seen as a permanent break, but it subsequently became a partial or temporary separation. The proximity of the new destination, permanent human and social relationships, and an established unbreakable economic relationship corresponded to a form of integration between nationalities and regions rather than of traditional emigration. Although they lacked formal political frameworks and institutional integration, these developments in combination heralded European integration.

EUROPE AS A DEMOCRATIC ASPIRATION

Political integration, even of an informal nature, did not follow the same course. The authoritarian regime had survived the democratic Allies' victory and the defeat of the fascist and Nazi Axis powers. Although Portugal was only belatedly admitted to the United Nations (in 1955), it had been accepted as a founding member of the North Atlantic Treaty Organization (NATO) in 1949, which in the context of the Cold War was considered a gesture of support by Western powers for the corporatist regime. In 1960 the Portuguese government prepared to resist pressures to decolonize and was the only empire to maintain that position to the bitter end. Portugal was subject to relative international isolation, although that did not worry the regime since António de Oliveira Salazar favored protectionism, the African colonies, and relative autarky in the interest of retaining his power. Portugal's participation in the founding of EFTA had no apparent political or institutional implications, and the country remained relatively aloof from the European integrationist dynamics and debates.

That was the case with government policy. But even before the 1974 revolution the "European option," as it came to be called, had brought democratic pressure to bear on the authoritarian state. In a sometimes veiled manner, although more explicitly at times, members of different branches of the opposition—with the exception of the Communists—frequently stated their preference that the political models of democratic Europe be adopted by Portugal.[13]

From the early 1960s the clandestine or exiled Acção Socialista Portuguesa (ASP) maintained close relations with the democratic parties of Europe, particularly those in the socialist and social democratic camps. When the Partido Socialista (PS) became a party in 1973, the political patterns of a democratic Europe were again claimed as models.

The "European option," however, unlike the African focus and pursuit of the colonial wars, continued to cause internal division and friction among leading groups within the government, public administration, and the economy. The traditionalists were considered "African" and "Atlanticist," the democrats were "liberals" and "European." The Africa versus Europe formula was an explicit synthesis of what, if freedom of expression had existed, might have represented the most serious topic of political discussion, within both society and the regime.[14]

In 1970 the founding of the Associação para o Desenvolvimento Económico e Social (SEDES), a tolerated ersatz of an unauthorized party, was loaded with political significance. One of SEDES's priorities was to give particular attention to Portugal's relationship with other European countries.

Such trends were opposed by the majority of the regime's civilian and military authorities, as well as by the more traditionalist entrepreneurs with interests in Africa. The European option, in their view, constituted a denial of Portugal's permanent interests, particularly its colonial vocation. Franco Nogueira, Salazar's most prominent foreign minister, defended the African or Atlantic option, as it was intentionally labeled in contrast to the

European option, and strove vainly to extend NATO's sphere to the south Atlantic, whereby the Portuguese colonies would have been included.

Hence, *Europe* and *Africa* were euphemisms for *democracy* and *corporatism.* The democratic aspiration and the European option, however, were primarily the fruits of an internal impulse rather than responses to outside stimuli. European pressures for democratization were tenuous or nonexistent. The European partners of the authoritarian regime were largely passive regarding democracy in Europe. Only after over ten years of war in Africa did certain European countries, particularly the Scandinavian ones, condemn the war and the authoritarian regime. In Europe, awareness of the absence of democracy and respect for fundamental human rights in Portugal, where they existed at all, were centered in public opinion rather than in politics and diplomacy. For many years Portugal was the only member of NATO and EFTA in which basic political rights were not respected, democratic elections were not held, a single-party parliament existed, and total censorship was practiced.

EUROPE'S ROLE IN THE PORTUGUESE REVOLUTION

During the 1974–1975 revolution, a return to the former regime became impossible. Two viable political options existed: The first was an essentially authoritarian revolutionary regime with central planning, military participation in the government, and relations with the communist bloc; the other was an essentially liberal, democratic, and parliamentary regime that had a market economy, close to the European democracies, and was aligned with NATO.

After two years of arduous struggle and periodic elections, the second alternative emerged victorious. Europe became almost a slogan—the symbol of parliamentary democracy—indiscriminately representing the Western countries, NATO, the European Community, the market, and private enterprise.[15] In addition, Europe included the countries in which over 1.5 million Portuguese worked.

During the two years 1974 to 1976, most European leaders of all political persuasions visited Lisbon to demonstrate unequivocal solidarity. Europe also represented potential political, economic, and commercial support for a country undergoing a serious reconversion crisis and an economy experiencing acute difficulties. Decolonization destroyed a proportion of foreign trade and brought over 600,000 former colonials—most without funds, residences, or work—back to Portugal. The European recession caused by the first oil shock hit a country with no energy resources that was grappling with a serious social and political crisis. The revolution created its own upheavals, including a drop in investment, foreign trade difficulties, and low international credit. Many entrepreneurs went abroad as a result of political persecution and nationalizations. Hundreds of firms were occupied, and private enterprise was seriously restricted; meanwhile, the public sector failed to evince adequate resources and competencies.

Portugal rapidly found itself on the brink of a payments crisis. During this period joining Europe was not only an aspiration for many Portuguese, but it also played an active role in, and positively responded to, requests for assistance. This aid was forthcoming less from the EC than from some of its individual members, particularly Germany, which were generous in providing credit and emergency loans. A number of countries, perhaps fearing the consequences of increasing unrest in a country that was after all European, actively sought to help solve the Portuguese problem. Political and moral support came from the United Nations, the World Bank, the International Monetary Fund, EFTA, the EC, and the European Investment Bank. Even multinational companies and banking conglomerates showed confidence in the future of Portuguese democracy, although this attitude was not unanimous.

Support from abroad was not limited to Europe. The United States played an important role, both bilaterally and within international organizations. Such support was controversial, however. Some within the U.S. administration and business community considered Portugal to be a lost cause.[16] They were overruled by others who defended a strategy of intervention and assistance.[17] Nonetheless, U.S. support never equaled the type or programmatic nature of the support offered by a number of European countries.

Portugal's young and inexperienced political parties rapidly received interest and receptivity from their European counterparts. Technical assistance, money, expertise in conducting elections, and knowledge of international relations were essential first steps in democratic party life. The Social Democratic Party of Germany (SPD), the Scandinavian Social Democrat parties, and the other parties of the Socialist International collaborated closely with the Partido Socialista. The Centro Democrático e Social (CDS) was immediately welcomed by the European Christian Democrats. The Partido Popular Democrático (PPD), although with fewer ties to European parties, also received outside assistance, particularly from liberal parties. Even the Partido Comunista Português (PCP) established closer relations with European communist parties, particularly in France.

The action of the European Community was modest and discreet, perhaps reflecting the range of members' opinions and the absence of a Community tradition in the area of foreign policy. Even EFTA, to which Portugal belonged but which had no political pretensions, reacted with moderate but unprecedented generosity, perhaps showing more open-minded understanding than the EC.[18]

In addition to these actions by states, international organizations, and political parties, Europeans' interest in events in Portugal and in Portuguese aspirations for European approximation was apparent on many other fronts. In cultural, scientific, academic, artistic, and press domains, a new life appeared to be beginning for a country that for decades had been generally ignored or had sought to be ignored.

In short, at the time of the revolution and in contrast to the preceding period, Portugal's European approximation was the result not merely of internal impetus and a democratic aspiration to achieve European models, but also of real assistance and European interest in the country's political destiny. We can reasonably state that European political leaders considered events in Portugal to be in the European domain. Moreover, European action was important in founding the democratic State. We cannot say that Portugal could not have established a multiparty democracy without European assistance, but when it did so it was with European support.

PORTUGAL'S APPLICATION FOR EC MEMBERSHIP AND THE TRANSITION

Once democracy, however fragile, had been achieved, EC membership again emerged as Portugal's prime political goal and the symbol of collective aspirations. The first constitutional government, which had publicly introduced its program, prepared to apply for membership.[19] Portugal's application was formally submitted in 1977, and subsequently all governments considered European integration a political priority.

Public opinion toward EC membership was extremely positive. Polls demonstrated 70 percent to 90 percent support for integration. All parliamentary parties, except for the communists, supported the goal of EC membership with varying degrees of enthusiasm. Employers and economic and business associations favored membership, as did one of the two trade union federations. Members of intellectual, artistic, professional, academic, and press circles supported the European project. The only opposition was voiced by the communists and extreme left.

From 1977 to 1985, during the application and transition process, virtually no unfavorable opinion of EC membership was expressed by the right. Those associated with the political right used the economic models of European integration as arguments to counter the left and the predominantly socialist 1976 constitution, particularly the excessive size of the public sector, restrictions on private activity, and the presence of the military in bodies that had constitutional power.

Throughout this period no evidence of nationalism emerged, and the more traditionalist sectors received no support from public opinion. The defenders of the African legacy were also to make their voices heard. Interestingly, this political heritage had been revived by individuals and groups of the revolutionary left who supported a national strategy of affinity or approximation with the nonaligned countries of the Third World.

The Portuguese and Spanish applications for EC membership were favorably received in Europe. Within the short time of two years, the authoritarian regimes in power in these countries were brought down, and they sought to join forces with their European neighbors. Simultaneously, relations between Western Europe and the communist East had reached a tense deadlock despite the illusory progress of the Conference for Security and Cooperation in Europe. The United States was experiencing difficulties as a result of the defeat in Vietnam and Richard Nixon's impeachment. Europe, particularly the EC, which was still suffering from the consequences of the oil shocks and was concerned about stagnation, turned its attention inward. Enlargement to include the new democracies of the South was viewed favorably as a path to possible recovery.

The EC did not accept Portuguese membership unconditionally. The nine members offered an affirmative response but imposed a ten-year transition period and relatively short deadlines for dismantling customs barriers. They also demanded rapid withdrawal of administrative obstacles to competition and of excessive state intervention in the market. Similar rules were in force in existing EC countries, and it was to be expected that they would be applied to new members. The impact of enforcing in-depth reforms in a short period of time was inevitably severe.[20] Nonetheless, the EC decided to support Portugal's transition through certain practical means, most notably so-called premembership aid, which allowed Portugal to carry out a number of development projects and to become familiar with Community cooperation mechanisms.

THE FIRST DECADE OF INTEGRATION, 1986–1995

Broadly speaking, the practical conditions of Portugal's transition process were negotiated in two parts: the first prior to 1985, before formal membership, and the second after that date as successive transition phases elapsed. The conditions negotiated prior to membership were more severe: The deadlines for dismantling customs barriers were shorter, anticipated economic liberalization was more rapid, and little specific aid was obtained from the EC. Portugal's desire to obtain a rapid affirmative response to its membership request appeared to prevail over anticipated subsequent difficulties. The political benefit of full EC membership was a priority in the hope that it would help to consolidate democracy and strengthen the system. The severity of membership conditions, however, had no notable impact on consolidating democracy.

The conditions renegotiated after 1985 were more generous and more sensitive to the specific problems of the Portuguese economy and society. Some transition deadlines were extended, but, more important, a series of special programs were drawn up to support the reconversion of production structures and the development of infrastructure.[21] The general improvement in conditions can be explained by the fact that Portugal was now a full member and was therefore in a better bargaining position.

Foreign investment in Portugal, trade, and business—particularly within the European sphere—rose dramatically. New economic and institutional conditions, together with European development funds, were essential in Portugal's recovery and growth during the late 1980s into 1991. During the first four years of membership (1986–1989), financial transactions with the EC were to Portugal's advantage, amounting to 321.6 billion escudos (US$1.93 billion). During the following four years (1990–1993), the figure totalled 1.16 trillion escudos (US$7.0 billion). In recent years EC financial aid has been equivalent to approximately 3 percent of Portugal's gross domestic product (GDP).[22]

Such economic performance was assisted by internal political successes, particularly the achievement of political stability. Although no direct cause and effect existed, in 1987, one year after accession, Portugal entered a cycle of parliamentary majorities and full-term governments. Another factor contributing to internal stability was the successful conclusion of constitutional reviews, without tension, through consensus among the main parties.[23] The role the EC played can be considered decisive in areas other than the specifically economic. The economic model arrived at owed much to integration and to shared European models. The interventionist, protectionist, and regulatory tradition of the Portuguese state was drastically reduced in less than a decade. Through privatizations, the public sector was reduced to dimensions comparable to those in other EC countries.

Today, no economic sector is closed to private enterprise or foreign investment. The powers of the economic administration have also been severely curtailed.[24] State intervention in the economy still exists and to no small extent because the weight of the Portuguese state is supplemented by that of the EC, which is not the best example of a liberal body. Indeed, European trends toward harmonization (industrial, monetary, environmental, fiscal, and so on) have created an extensive network of standards and regulations that must be respected by economic agents. If these agents want to receive Community support, they must adhere to the rules, harmonize their productive processes, submit their projects for approval, and submit detailed accounts to both national administrations and Community bodies. Agriculture is the best-known example of an activity that is so strictly regulated, subsidized, protected, and licensed that little of the market and of classical private enterprise remains.

In comparing the situation today with that of the 1960s and particularly the 1970s, however, it is apparent that far-reaching liberalization has indeed occurred in the economy and is attributed largely to integration.[25] National protectionism has been virtually eradicated.[26] Freedom of establishment and free enterprise are widespread today. The financial system is open, and the capital market has been liberalized. Although the weight of the capitalist state and of local authorities continues to be excessive in many sectors, neither Salazar's corporativism nor the revolution would identify with today's institutions and economic models.

In this new context of a market economy, growth also came to be inextricably associated with integration. Overall, in what can be considered a typical example of strengthening or building up the system, growth and integration were decisive factors in consolidating the democratic regime.[27] Without them it is unlikely, in the context of the formidable internal and external crises Portugal was undergoing, that the democratic regime could have been established in such a relatively rapid and peaceful manner. Portuguese leaders and Community authorities may have considered that support for one part of the democratic system—in this case the market economy—would affect both other parts and the whole.[28]

In economic and institutional praxis, as in that of culture and attitudes, Europe was synonymous with democracy. Europe cushioned losses and attenuated mourning processes that under other conditions might have created calamitous situations: defeat in the African wars; the end of the myth of Portugal's civilizational mission, which had made such an important contribution to the ideology of the former regime; the dissolution of the empire, which until recently had been elevated to being the intrinsic reason for Portugal's presence in the world; and the undermining of the "race" and the nation.[29] In short, the country had shrunk, its historical raison d'être had changed, and its national identity had been lost.[30]

Over many years prior to the 1974 revolution and decolonization, the terms *stronghold of the West, balcony of Europe, most faithful and missionary nation, multiracial, multicontinental, and universalist nation*, and *country of the five departures* had been losing their substance, revealing their ideological vacuum and atavistic nature. Nonetheless, assisted by the war, these myths had endured and exerted some effect. Now, in the course of a few weeks, they had been shattered. The consequences were incalculable.

Without antidote or compensation, it was not easy to live with the effects of such amputations. EC membership meant Portugal and the Portuguese were not left empty-handed, anxious, facing the unknown with no tomorrow. The EC helped the Portuguese to come to grips with the inevitable and to understand that they could survive without the empire. Disaster was averted in exchanging glory and grandeur—an ideology that had flourished for decades—for the routine of work and day-to-day living in a confined space only because the exchange was accompanied by other factors, the first of which was European integration. Even though Portugal was the poorest among richer nations, one of the smallest among larger nations, and one of the most backward among more developed nations, the Portuguese found satisfaction in living side by side with other Europeans and suffered no crisis of self-esteem.

The Portuguese were faced with two possible courses. The first, the revolutionary ideal, involved affinity with socialist and communist countries and sympathy for Third World nations. This was a course of material sacrifice and controlled freedoms but was also one of moral glory and grandeur among the oppressed who had won their freedom. For its supporters, the revolution and decolonization could be held up as examples. The Portuguese revolution would be the first in a new world, ushering in a new historical cycle. Some thought Portugal could overstep advanced capitalism and even bureaucratic socialism. The Portuguese, however, did not respond favorably to the revolutionary ideal, which involved further sacrifices and represented a form of puritanical and moralistic stripping down without, or with uncertain, freedoms. In fact, this revolution proved to be the last of the old world. Since 1974 no revolution has claimed socialism as its philosophy.

The second course, that of the democratic ideal, was symbolized largely by Europe. Europe gave concrete, physical, rooted, tangible meaning to aspirations for freedom that otherwise involve risk. Europe gave the uncertain horizons of democracy territorial and geographical reality. It was a genuine substitute for past glories, a home in which there is always room for one more. In addition to neighborly relations and affinities, Europe represented security.

THE FIRST ECONOMIC IMPACT OF EUROPEAN INTEGRATION

The extensive modernization of communications—particularly highways—carried out largely with EC funds, was an undeniable effect of European integration. The financial, insurance, real estate, and distribution sectors also underwent extensive modernization that was prompted substantially by participation in the common market. But difficulties also arose.

From the early 1990s on, the negative consequences of integration became apparent, to the detriment of certain social groups including those least prepared for the market and competition: small- and medium-scale farmers and rural employees, fishermen, and entrepreneurs and workers in the traditional sectors—particularly textiles, construction, iron and steel, footwear, and the food industries. Unemployment levels, which had been kept exceptionally low, became a cause of concern. A vastly increased number of companies went bankrupt, and for two or three years family income was virtually stagnant.[31]

Another visible consequence of European integration—one that worried certain sectors of the public—was the increasing penetration of multinational and foreign, particularly Spanish, capital into the Portuguese entrepreneurial fabric. Many, however, considered such developments an inevitable consequence of the internationalization of economies. Negative economic effects were attributable directly to the market and only indirectly to the political and institutional processes of integration. In fact, Portugal's European integration coincided with (and may even have been instrumental in) the growing internationalization of the Portuguese economy.

Only with the emergence of the first difficulties did any nationalistic feeling begin to surface. The severity of certain problems (the agriculture and fisheries situation, for example) led some people to express serious reservations regarding Portugal's full participation in EC policies. Such reservations, however, were not echoed by public opinion and had little effect on electoral results; indeed, they appear to have been motivated more by an attempt to reap electoral benefits than by genuine nationalistic conviction. The voices that had once expressed reservations about EC membership are now the most vocal in their desire to retain it.

The CDS, now the Partido Popular (PP), is the most fully developed nationalistic party; it uses its understanding of the national interest as an argument against deepening the EU. But for now the PP's position remains within the union. Specifically, the PP suggests that Portugal should more frequently exercise its right of veto and invoke the country's vital interests, thus opting out of a number of issues. Although it is very conservative, the PP endeavors to reconcile liberalism and patriotism, which it opposes— not toward Europe but toward European federalism. The PP is one of the main supporters of a national referendum on the EU, a proposal it has supported since the signing of the Maastricht Treaty in 1992. Although it defends the primacy of the nation-state and its sovereignty, the PP does not risk placing itself outside the confines of the EU.

The PCP is also nationalistic, a continuation of its thinking since the 1950s. Since the 1993 European elections, however, the PCP stated that the EU was a fait accompli, thus removing the party from the almost deserted camp of those radically opposed to European integration. In a marked departure from its usual practice, the PCP is also supporting a European referendum.

Meanwhile, the strategic thinking of employer confederations has evolved in a particularly interesting manner. During the 1974–1975 revolution and the years that followed, the European option was the prime inspiration of the Confederação da Indústria Portuguesa, the Confederação dos Agricultores de Portugal, and, to a lesser extent, the Confederação do Comércio de Portugal. These groups considered that the models prevailing in the European Community regarding the market, the public sector, private enterprise, and labor should be structured similarly in Portugal. Thus in 1982 and 1989, during the revisions of the constitution, the confederations played an important role in invoking European models and influencing parties.

Since accession in 1985 and particularly following the first difficulties experienced in the 1990s, the confederations' concerns and strategy have shifted. They have opposed adoption of the more advanced labor-related standards, particularly those contained in the Social Charter. They have expressed serious reservations about the rapid dismantling of customs barriers and have even suggested extending transition periods. In short, the confederations have defended moderate external protectionism and supported opting out in the more fragile sectors. They have criticized the government for excessive concessions and have invoked special Portuguese circumstances such as economic backwardness and companies' lack of preparation for the rigors of the single market.[32] During the debates prior to ratification of the Treaty of Maastricht, the confederations were particularly critical of the treaty provisions and in some cases demanded that a national referendum should be held.

The change in attitude among the trade union confederations was less marked. The União Geral de Trabalhadores (UGT) has always supported European integration.[33] It fought for acceptance of the Social Charter and of all legal standards and labor practices in force in European countries that are more favorable to workers than those in Portugal. Meanwhile, the Confederação Geral dos Trabalhadores de Portugal (CGTP) has always opposed integration.[34] For several years it maintained a strong radical opposition, although by the 1990s it had become more moderate. That is, it now seeks to benefit where it can, participating in EC structures and applying for training programs. Like the UGT, the CGTP supports the most advantageous labor standards contained in the Social Charter.

Despite difficulties, European integration can be viewed positively as an essential ingredient in fostering democracy, which would be unlikely to survive without prosperity or some reasonable expectation thereof. Between 1985 and 1992 Portugal experienced considerable economic growth of 3.5 percent to 4.5 percent per year, above the 2.5 percent achieved in other European countries. GDP per inhabitant increased at a comparable rate. Integration appears to have been an essential component of achieving these successes.

Participation in Community structures has affected the attitudes of the principal professional organizations, serving to tone down the most extreme demands for protectionism, reduce radical opposition, and create national and international cooperation programs. Important problems that could affect Portugal and any other EU member country still exist in connection with labor matters. Although social concertation and tripartism are part of the contemporary notion of democracy, both are under threat today and are subject to tensions.[35] On the one hand, no European trade unions exist. On the other, increasing macroeconomic restrictions dictated by European monetary policies are being placed on the freedom to negotiate and on collective bargaining. These processes are currently undertaken within the national context, but several times in recent years in Portugal, rigid limits imposed by monetary and budgetary policy agreed upon with European bodies have proved detrimental to or interfered with national social agreements.[36]

SCIENCE, CULTURE, AND SOCIETY

Significant cultural and scientific activity has resulted from European integration. The most immediate consequences have been the modernization and renewed momentum of activities as a result of the progressive elimination of traditional parochialism. New customs, different cultures, circulation of information, debates involving opposing views, enlargement of areas of scrutiny, and emulation are incomparable advantages of advancing science and culture, as well as of consolidating democracy. Consolidation indeed is not merely the result of political mechanisms and legal provisions; appropriate levels of social and cultural rooting must also be encountered.

For many years the Portuguese lived under the combined effects of a number of realities, including relative poverty, economic backwardness, despotism, nationalism and an African focus in national policies; controlled expression and closed borders were their corollaries. The official versions of national history and culture directly contradicted the opening of ideas or comparing of opinions. Official promotion of culture, the arts, and science paid scant regard to universal criteria but a great deal to the regime's political requirements. European integration has contributed to combating this heritage by promoting free choice and universalism.

Nonetheless, in artistic, literary, and academic circles, demands continue to be heard for protection, as are nationalistic protests. A reluctance to hire foreigners, engage in exchange, or recognize degrees from foreign universities is still encountered. Some corporations still want to create national closed-shop mechanisms, although such aspirations are increasingly obsolete and are rarely taken seriously.

On the cultural, academic, scientific, and technical fronts, European integration has had important results, although they are not readily quantifiable. In the course of approximately a decade, links between Portugal and the other European countries have achieved an unprecedented level.

One of the latest developments has been in the area of education. Finally and after great resistance, European university degrees are now fully and automatically recognized by the Portuguese government and universities. More lecturers and students are going abroad and more foreigners are coming to Portugal than ever in the country's history. Portuguese participation in scientific projects and technological programs at the European level is increasing apace.[37] Technological innovation resulting from private investments has occurred with greater frequency.[38] Increasingly close and substantial relationships have been established between the national press and communications and their European counterparts. All of this depends on other factors, in particular the internationalization of science, communications, the arts, and culture.

Although of limited volume by European standards, Portuguese culture—books, cinema, theatre, music, and so on—has greater access to European markets than ever before. Portuguese contemporary literature in particular has benefited from this wider market, and increasingly translations are being published in other European languages.

The Portuguese cinema industry has benefited from the opening of the European markets, and coproductions with European counterparts are now the rule. Portugal still faces, as with the rest of Europe, the predominance of North American movies. Thus Portuguese authorities, following the European example, are now considering the establishment of a protectionist quota system.

Meanwhile, the development of television (production, broadcasting, and access to foreign channels) does not appear to have been predominantly subject to a specific European influence. The prime influence on Portuguese television has come from Brazil and the United States. Democracy was responsible for opening television to the world, which has little or nothing to do with European integration.

POLITICS AND INSTITUTIONS

In spite of its numerous advantages, several negative consequences of integration emerge on the political front. These consequences are caused directly by European institutions, or are the result of those organizations' association with Portuguese institutions.

The functioning of the European institutions and the European Union decisionmaking processes do not constitute a model for Portuguese democracy. In some cases, on the contrary, they reinforce the trends that restrict democracy, increase separatism, promote bureaucratic power, foster the absence of public scrutiny, hinder political debate, exacerbate scant citizen participation, and boost technocratic power that is not politically accountable.

Decisions that are rerouted to Brussels become more opaque and distant. Many national political decisions in economic and social matters are taken after Community consultation or Brussels' *nihil obstat* ("no objections"). The need to harmonize, or to adhere to Community directives and regulations, eliminates internal political debate. Dependence on European financing even creates a requirement of prior EC authorization.[39] Annual approval of the state budget by the national parliament is preceded by a government commitment to the European monetary authorities, which colors the behavior of members of parliament. The Regional Development Plan, which includes the principal medium-term strategy measures for the economy and society, is approved by parliament only after EC approval. Commitments made in Brussels cannot be changed in Lisbon, except in the unthinkable case of the government renouncing European funds. In such cases the Portuguese parliament operates essentially a passive ratification chamber.

This has become increasingly true as the government's legislative function has expanded considerably, both internally and in participating in European decisions. Many such decisions apply directly to Portuguese society, whereas others are automatically transposed into national legislation—almost always by a decision of the government without participation of the parliament.[40] New decisionmaking processes are taking root, to the detriment of the parliament's political and legislative functions. By tradition, the parliament has had few prerogatives and limited autonomy and has not sought to defend its role as the prime representative body of national sovereignty even in the general context of the new responsibilities emerging from European integration. The European Parliament, however, does not compensate with democratic advantage for the loss of the national parliament's functions.

Whereas government and public administration projects generally undergo prior consultation with associations, local authorities, trade unions, companies, and other interests, this fragmented and low-profile process does not replace political debate. Hearings are also an inadequate substitute for participation. Whereas European institutions may have encouraged social consultation and concertation, although not to the liking of all social partners, that trend has occurred to the detriment of political democracy. In a country with marked corporative traditions, the process has contributed to a relegation of the national parliament.

The Portuguese parliament's participation in European affairs—in defining strategies and assessing policies—has been limited, superficial, inefficient, and, where it has occurred at all, after the fact.[41] The executive informs the parliament of what has occurred, frequently through the press, and does not discuss past events or possible future developments. The government fears a prior negative parliamentary debate would weaken its negotiating position in the Council of Ministers and with the European Commission. The government wants to avoid a situation in which any position it takes that involves a commitment or a yielding of its position—which is inevitable in the permanent negotiations conducted within the EC—might be perceived at home as a defeat. The government does not make its plans public before ascertaining the reactions of other states or knowing what financial contribution it can expect from the EC. A "double scapegoat effect" is frequently seen whereby in difficult situations or in cases of a lack of transparency and of contested decisions the national government blames the European Commission, and the Commission lays full responsibility on the national administration.

The members of the Portuguese executive use secrecy as a working method. For example, until decisions were taken at the Community level, virtually nothing was known about the Portuguese position on important matters such as the drafting of the Treaty of Maastricht, the substance of its main clauses, the competencies of the EU bodies, EU enlargement, policy regarding the former Yugoslavia and the former USSR, the General Agreement on Tariffs and Trade, the Common Agricultural Policy reform, the Franco-German Brigade, assistance to East European countries, and many others.

Portugal's situation may be extreme. That is, of all EU member country legislatures the Portuguese parliament may have the least strength and autonomy, because of the absence of traditions and as a result of other factors that have shaped national political culture.[42] Given the absence of solid regional powers and strong civil society bodies and with scant esprit de corps, the Portuguese parliament is perhaps more dependent on the executive than any other parliament in the EU, and it bears primary responsibility for this situation. Although the European institutions cannot be held responsible, they appear only to perpetuate the situation.

The European institutions may be able to boast of useful results in international cooperation, peace among European countries, and economic relations among members, but in the political sphere they have contributed nothing directly to the democratic system. On the contrary, they have created opaque areas, secret negotiations, and political irresponsibility toward citizens that in the long term could be harmful to the democratic system. Indeed, European parlance has coined the term *democratic deficit* to describe this situation, although the means to end it have been slow to emerge. The stronger parliaments, with more deep-rooted traditions, and other representative institutions frequently protest against the EC's tendency to dominate, whereas the weaker, more dependent parliaments—which include the Portuguese example—simply resign themselves to the situation.[43] The most prominent feature of European institutional construction appears to be the gradual sidelining of national representative institutions from their core spheres of activity—drafting policy and decision-making.

Obviously, this situation eventually generates problems of legitimacy and accountability, particularly in countries where parliamentary and regional institutions have weight and importance. To date, the most significant attempt to resolve this situation led to the creation of the European Parliament, followed by its reforms (direct elections, joint decisionmaking and an increase of certain powers vis-à-vis the European Commission). The intention underlying the establishment of this legislative assembly, which is elected simultaneously in all member countries, was to legitimize and democratize the EC.

This would-be solution has not produced the desired results. In Portugal as in the rest of the European Union, direct election of members of the European Parliament (MEPs) has increased the distance between European institutions and national parliaments while apparently failing to forge a new link with the electorate. In fact, in the first years of membership before direct elections were held, all of the MEPs assigned to Strasburg were members of their respective national parliaments. Therefore, their link to national politics and to the electorate was more visible. Since the first direct elections, their impact on the national scene has been hindered. Their activities are seldom reported by the media and little is known about their political standing.

The European Parliament has no real influence in the countries where, ultimately, it originates.[44] It has little influence on the functioning and decisions of the Council of Ministers. Its powers in choosing the president of the European Commission are insufficient to give it full precedence over the executive. The impact of the actions of the European Parliament and the consequences of its debates for member states are extremely limited. In Portugal at least, such effects are practically nonexistent.

This can be accounted for to some extent by the fact that European elections, from the point of view of national electorates, do not produce results that are proportional to or that correspond to the political choices made by voters. After the European Parliament has been elected, with the consequent alterations in political and party circumstances, the Council of Ministers may remain totally unchanged. Political modifications resulting from elections in an individual country may be cancelled out by elections in other countries. In the European Parliament, Council, and Commission, political choices that follow a given tendency do not correspond to the party choices made by voters.

The absence of European parties may help to explain this phenomenon. Voters in each country vote for the national parties with which they are familiar, and they frequently do so for national, as opposed to European, reasons. Moreover, in the European Parliament, when supposedly national interests are at stake, the MEPs from a given country—although from different parties—will often stand together in a joint position. The reasons are obvious: Their countries are their constituencies. For these MEPs the democratic frameworks of reference continue to be those defined by the national state.

The work methods and decisionmaking processes employed by the European Commission give preference to technical and bureaucratic consultation and occasionally social concertation to the detriment of political debate and responsibility. The EC administration, or the European state under construction, works strictly with Portugal's public administration to the detriment of public opinion and of the elected representative bodies.

This situation may exist in some, if not all, other countries. But there is a difference: Portugal has a very young and weak democratic culture. It has no deep-rooted democratic traditions. Both within society in general and in political, party, and administrative circles, democratic habits are not well established. Meanwhile, in Portugal the European institutions— which are relatively opaque and insufficiently representative—do not encounter a strong parliament, active regional states, parties with long traditions, or solid civic institutions as they do in Germany, Great Britain, the Netherlands, and other countries.[45] In Portugal those institutions encounter a weak civil society and a secretive state that is relatively inaccessible to citizens. In fact, the European institutions and the Portuguese public administration have proved to be kindred entities.

In a number of European countries, through constitutional obligation or following a decision of their leaders, citizens have been required to vote in referenda on important matters relating to European integration such as membership, enlargement, or the amendment of constitutional treaties. In Portugal since 1976, almost all parties have consistently refused to hold referenda. Some have maintained that it is a "plebiscitary" and antidemocratic process.[46] The main parties—the Partido Social Democrata (PSD) and the PS—which together account for two-thirds of the electorate, have shown little sensitivity to matters of legitimacy and citizen participation or have considered that a referendum would not resolve such issues. During the successive stages of EC application (1977), accession (1985), and ratification of the Treaty of Maastricht (1991), these parties fought—sometimes energetically—against the possibility of putting the issue to a vote.[47]

In most European countries, parliamentary debates on European integration are frequent and occasionally unpredictable. In Portugal they are infrequent, predictable, and informative rather than deliberative. The UK, Danish, Swedish, and Dutch parliaments have not abdicated their democratic prerogatives despite the fact that their position may be contrary to EC trends. The German Länder strenuously protect their respective powers vis-à-vis the EC administration. When negotiating the terms of its membership, Sweden made parliament's functions and openness of information its firmest conditions. In Portugal the parliament, local authorities, regional assemblies (Azores and Madeira), and public opinion were shunted aside by the powers of the executive.

Another issue involves economic and social projects that receive European support. In Portugal perhaps more than any other country, these projects are the exclusive responsibility of the state, even when they involve private firms or local authorities. When such projects are financed by European funds, their management becomes centralized. This means that a large proportion of public and private productive investment, as well as infrastructure construction of any size, is undertaken with European support and state approval or not at all. European subsidies and funding, which are fully administered by the state, lie at the root of total political control over investment. Hence, bearing in mind that investments without European backing ipso facto lose some of their competitiveness, European backing for modernization and development has considerably increased the political and technical powers of the administration with no counterweight or moderating influence exerted by civil society or elected bodies.

Shared sovereignty (between the Portuguese state and the European Union), duality of representation (in the national parliament and the European Parliament), vitiation of accountability (the European Commission is not dependent on the Parliament, but on the Council of Ministers, which is composed of governments and is also not dependent on the European Parliament, but on national parliaments), and competing legitimacy (between national and European bodies) create troubling situations in a country in which civil society is weak, parliament is relatively subordinate, and public administration retains habits of secrecy.

No doubt under pressure from European institutions and for reasons emerging from the single market and programs financed by the EC, Portugal's public administration has undergone a process of relative modernization. Since the 1980s bodies specializing in European affairs have been created in nearly all ministries and administrative departments with a range of functions that include studying European legislation and practices, transposing the *acquis communautaire* into Portuguese legislation, training civil servants for specific functions, drafting investment and development programs financed by the EC, and disseminating European rules within the administration, companies, and society in general. The results of such activities appear to have been positive because they have become the main centers of administrative modernization in the public sector.

Certain departments—such as those relating to inland revenue, taxes, public works, and others—have carried out internal reforms with a view to engaging in dialogue with European institutions. More frequently than in the past, attention is given to preparatory studies, financial forecasts, environmental impact studies, and the training of staff involved in investment programs. Nonetheless, there are still no clear signs that such modernization has had any marked influence on relations between the administration and the public. In many areas, even those that have technically been "modernized," old habits persist—including secrecy, the failure to publish studies and assessments, the failure to publicly present accounts, and delays in responding to citizens' requests and carrying out compulsory procedures. Where it has undeniably taken place, modernization of the administration has been either internal and functional, or external in relations with the EC, but it has not occurred in areas connected with the general public.

CONCLUSION

Since before the revolution, the Portuguese have based their democratic aspirations on European political and social models. European states, however, did not take steps or play an active and direct role in promoting democratic trends or reforming authoritarian power.

During the revolution and thereafter, the Portuguese turned to Europe and the EC in the hope of receiving political and economic support in founding a democratic state. To different degrees, some European countries and the EC positively responded to Portuguese requests. Without Europe and the EC, Portuguese democracy would have been more difficult to achieve and might have assumed a different form. Although the EC was not entirely responsible for establishing democracy, its role was undeniably important.

Europe's influence can be described primarily as global and indirect support for democracy, reinforcement of the political and social system, and support for construction of the state. Such influence was not exclusively political and institutional but also had an undeniable social and cultural dimension. An awareness of neighborliness and a sense of belonging were sources of security for the people of a country undergoing a major crisis of rapid transformation. The possibility of integration boosted positive expectations.

Since Portugal acceded to the EC (now the European Union), contact with European institutions has brought pressure for modernization of surviving nondemocratic administrative and business practices. Such modernization, however, is markedly technical and moderately political; there has been no accompanying access to citizen participation. In short, modernization is not necessarily democratization.

In fact, through the European institutions, long-standing, relatively undemocratic administrative and political habits have been encouraged. In Portugal European institutions encounter scant democratic tradition, weak representative bodies, a subordinate parliament, and a weak civil society.

European integration has made an important economic contribution to Portugal's development, thus indirectly supporting the democratic regime. Its political contribution to strengthening democracy has been insufficient. Problems of legitimacy and democracy within the European Union are known in and affect all countries. They have been discussed in all member states since before ratification of the Treaty of Maastricht and increasingly today in anticipation of probable further enlargement and prior to intergovernmental conferences in which future institutional reform is to be discussed. This is a public issue that has been thoroughly analyzed but for which solutions are difficult to find. Portugal constitutes a case apart in that the shortcomings of Portuguese democracy and the weakness of civil society feed the inadequacies of European democracy. Inversely, the European democratic deficit contributes to perpetuating defects in Portuguese democracy.

In all events, contrary to the situation in the late 1960s, Portugal is now a plural society or is on the road to becoming so. This development is closely linked to the way in which society relates to Europe and the state and to the manner in which society is integrated in the European Union.

Portugal acceded to the EC at a time when the country was undergoing an in-depth process of institutional transformation following the 1974–1975 revolution, subsequent decolonization, and the later founding of the democratic state. For this reason the process of Portuguese accession was somewhat different from that of most members, although it did share one essential characteristic: European construction had a very real influence on the nature of institutions created and on political rules.

An interesting problem to be resolved in the future, in Portugal as in all other EU member states, can be summarized as follows: Should the constructors of the European Union give preference to institutions or to social and economic affairs? The first strategy includes an artificial, possibly premature, and certainly willful element: Joint political institutions that are ahead of their time have the effect of molding society and patterns of behavior. In respect of the nonexistence of European political parties, for example, supporters of this method might respond that "if you establish the parliament, the parties will eventually follow." The second strategy advances human, demographic, social, cultural, and economic integration with a view to saving time and to ensuring that the political institutions that follow will take root more naturally. One of the main arguments of those who defend this approach is that political democracy has the nation-state as an essential framework of reference.

The drawbacks of the first strategy include a number of frequently emphasized implications: Political artificiality produces centrifugal effects and damages political rules. Nationalistic tendencies in particular might find a pretext in such a course. The disadvantages of the second strategy are also well-known. Without joint political institutions there is no joint project. The Portuguese case provides arguments for both strategies. The preexistence of institutions forced the pace of and speeded change. But other powerful influences in bringing about political change and opening up society were the result of demographic, social, and economic factors that predated European integration.

NOTES

1. See António Barreto, *A Situação Social em Portugal, 1960–1995* (Lisbon: Instituto de Ciências Sociais, 1996).
2. Portugal is one of the founding members of the European Free Trade Association, which gave rise to important trade relations and expansion of industrial business with other member countries. From 1960 to 1962, instead of their traditional destinations (North and South America, particularly Brazil), Portuguese immigrants went to European countries, especially France. In the period 1957–1959, Portuguese television began regular broadcasts throughout the country. During the 1960s Portuguese beaches became a destination for mass European tourism. In 1961 the Portuguese colonial system experienced the first signs of its final dissolution: War began in Angola (February), and Goa was invaded by troops of the Indian Union (December).
3. Between 1992 and 1995, despite awareness of economic difficulties in various sectors, 70 percent of the public continued to support Portugal's EU membership. See polls in *Público, Expresso, Independente,* and *Diário de Notícias* (newspapers, all published in Lisbon).
4. Between 1985 and 1995 the unemployment rate ranged between 3 percent and 8 percent, generally below the majority of EC members. See Barreto, *A Situação Social*; João César das Neves, *The Portuguese Economy* (Lisbon: Universidade Católica Portuguesa, 1994); and José da Silva Lopes, *A Economia Portuguesa, 1960–1995* (Lisbon: Edições Gradiva, 1996).
5. This is particularly apparent in the traditional spheres of social protection

by the state: education, health, unemployment, pensions, and subsistence benefits. See Barreto, *A Situação Social*; and Henrique Medina Carreira, *As Políticas Sociais em Portugal 1960–1995* (Lisbon: Edições Gradiva, 1996).

6. Almost one and a half million Portuguese were living and working in other European countries, particularly France, Germany, Switzerland, Belgium, England, Spain, and Luxembourg. In the 1970s, Portugal's total population was close to 9 million.

7. The state controlled banking, gas, oil, electricity, urban public transport, railways, heavy iron and steel, cement, aviation, navigation, water, postal services, telephones, television, and armaments with no legal possibility of opening up to private interests. Other sectors with a majority state holding included insurance, the press, road transport, paper and pulp, fertilizers, and chemicals. See Lopes, *A Economia Portuguesa*.

8. See Hermínio Martins, "Portugal," in Margaret Scotford Archer and Salvador Giner, eds., *Contemporary Europe: Class, Status, and Power* (London: Weidenfeld and Nicolson, 1971).

9. In the twentieth century the only instances of significance were sporadic participation in World War I and participation as a founding member of NATO. Both of the cases involved the defense of the empire. Portugal's participation in EFTA suggests a new and different trend.

10. In the early 1960s European countries accounted for less than 50 percent of Portuguese foreign trade; ten years later, prior to decolonization, that figure had risen to 60 percent; by the 1990s it had reached over 80 percent. Meanwhile, African colonies' share dropped sharply from approximately 20 percent during the 1950s and 1960s to less than 10 percent prior to their independence to scarcely 1 percent in the 1990s. See Neves, *The Portuguese Economy*; Lopes, *A Economia Portuguesa*; and Werner Baer and António Nogueira Leite, "The Peripheral Economy, Its Performance in Isolation and with Integration: The Case of Portugal," *Luso-Brazilian Review*, 29 (1992): 1–43.

11. See António Barreto and Carlos Almeida, *Capitalismo e Emigração em Portugal* (Lisbon: Edições Prelo, 1970); and Lopes, *A Economia Portuguesa*.

12. *Emigrant remittances* was the term applied to regular, private financial transfers from emigrant workers to their families, either for consumption and subsistence or for building homes and purchasing properties.

13. Several generations of politicians—such as Humberto Delgado, Mário Soares, Sousa Tavares, Salgado Zenha, Ribeiro Telles, and other younger politicians—as well as intellectuals including Eduardo Lourenço and Virgílio Ferreira made European democracy an obligatory political and cultural reference.

14. The liberal wing of members of Parliament from the Acção Nacional Popular (the party of Marcelo Caetano, Salazar's successor since 1969) and some members of government considered the European option to be a new strategy for the national economy and politics.

15. The slogan *A Europa Connosco* (Europe with us) became a rallying cry of the Socialist Party, the main winner in the two democratic elections in 1975 and 1976.

16. This group included in particular U.S. Secretary of State Henry Kissinger

who defended the idea that Portugal was a "vaccination" against leftist tendencies in other European countries.

17. Specifically Frank Carlucci, the U.S. Ambassador in Lisbon, who actively advocated intervention.

18. Attention is drawn, for example, to the creation in 1976 of an EFTA Fund for Portugal to support industrial companies; this gesture was unique in the history of that organization.

19. This was the first socialist government, headed by Mário Soares. Medeiros Ferreira was the foreign minister who conducted the early negotiations in the successful submission of the application.

20. The political discourse of those interested in integrating the different political parties was similar and can be summarized by the frequent statement "what we have to do would be necessary anyway. It is better to do it with integration than without it." It is interesting that years later the same argument is voiced regarding Hungary's application to the European Union. See chapter 6 in this volume.

21. Special plans were drawn up for industry, agriculture, and, for the first time in EC history, education. Other programs with specific features contributed to the construction of highways, development of communications, modernization of the textile industry and fisheries, vocational training, and others.

22. A considerable proportion of this aid was channeled into public investment, particularly construction of communications infrastructure—primarily highways. Public works programs, financed largely by the EC, were a principal factor in keeping unemployment down (between 3 percent and 6 percent), one of the lowest levels in the EC. The annual balance of financial flows between Portugal and the EC, however, was lower than emigrant remittances or earnings from tourism.

23. With the decisive votes of the PSD and the PS, constitutional reviews were ratified in 1982, 1989, and 1991. Through these amendments Portuguese institutions and main constitutional rules were brought into line with the European democratic and parliamentary tradition, as well as with the principles of the market economy. Indeed, the 1991 review was motivated primarily by the need to adapt the text of the constitution to European requirements—namely, the Treaty of Maastricht and monetary union.

24. The traditional powers of the administration included indexing or monitoring all of the main consumer products; virtually freezing rents; subsidizing production activities, particularly prices of food products; and imposing severe licensing requirements for initiating or setting up business activities.

25. Adherence to Community patterns was the main justification expressed by politicians and authorities for any major liberalization reforms that had to be carried out. In a sense, it is not always possible to speak of "direct European influences" because a sort of internationalization of market standards was practiced by the Portuguese elites. See in parallel chapter 6 in this volume.

26. Although in many cases it has been replaced by a form of Community protectionism.

27. See chapter 9 in this volume.

28. See in this connection chapter 8 in this volume.

29. For decades the term *Portuguese race* was frequently employed, even in official terminology. For many years, National Day was called Race Day.

30. All of these myths had prevailed during the past century. One writer even said that "the Portuguese have too much identity." See Eduardo Lourenço, *O Labirinto da Saudade* (Lisbon: Publicações Dom Quixote, 1978), and Eduardo Lourenço, *Nós e a Europa* (Lisbon: Imprensa Nacional-Casa da Moeda, 1988).

31. See the annual reports *Relatório do Banco de Portugal*, Lisbon.

32. The government criticized was that of the PSD headed by Cavaco Silva. A few years earlier he had drafted amendments to the terms of membership, thereby obtaining advantages for Portugal. During the 1990s, however, the government was more interested in obtaining the greatest possible amount of European funds and development aid. Negotiations eventually centered on less protection for agriculture, fisheries, and industry and more financial aid.

33. The main political influences in this confederation are those of the PS and the PSD.

34. Here the main influence is communist.

35. See in this connection chapter 9 in this volume.

36. More specifically, indirect pressures are being brought to bear on democracy in this way. Indeed, tensions caused by European macroeconomic policies more directly affect the national independence and freedom of capitalist states, which are not synonymous with democracy. See in this connection chapter 2 in this volume.

37. Although no reliable indicators exist, proportionately and in comparison with its partners Portugal may have less participation in such European programs. Nonetheless, the extent of these activities is still far greater than it was ten or twenty years ago.

38. The largest foreign private projects ever undertaken in Portugal have occurred since the early 1980s, in part because of European integration. Indeed, these projects have been of European origin: Volkswagen, Ford Europa, Siemens, and Renault.

39. The dimension of financial participation eventually comes to play a role of genuine authorization. Some of the Portuguese authorities' major projects were obliged to seek such approval. Without European funds the Portuguese state would have lacked the necessary resources. To obtain such funding the state must accept rules imposed on it, which have frequently involved modification of projects. Cases in point are the reorganization plan for TAP, the Portuguese national airline; construction of the Lisbon bridge over the Tagus; the motorway plan; the high-speed rail network; the Ford Volkswagen plant; and the natural gas grid.

40. According to European Union and European Court data, Portugal is one of the countries with the highest level of transposition of directives into national legislation and the lowest number of complaints against the state for failure to adhere to those directives.

41. The socialist government of António Guterres, which began its first term in November 1995, shows some signs of change, particularly through a commitment to discuss before parliament, both before and after European summits. Still in office at the end of 1998, Guterres has kept his word, more or less; he discusses European issues in parliament less often than he promised, but regularly nevertheless.

42. Other chapters in this volume suggest that despite their declining role, other national parliaments have retained more prerogatives than the Portuguese parliament and have fought harder to maintain their functions. See chapters 7, 8, and 9.

43. Among the strong parliaments that have recently spoken out against the dominating trends are those in Germany, the United Kingdom, Denmark, and Sweden. Meanwhile, the German federal states, or Länder, a strong and essential element in that country's democratic system, have effectively opposed all plans that marginalize any national or regional institutions except for the national executives.

44. As reflected in the extremely high level of abstention in European elections.

45. See chapters 7, 8, and 9 in this volume.

46. This was true in particular of the Socialist Party and the Communist Party.

47. The circumstances surrounding the Treaty of Maastricht were particularly significant: The referenda were held in a number of countries, and surveys showed that the majority of people believed that they should be held. It is interesting that the majority of those questioned also supported ratification of the treaty, which rules out the hypothesis that supporters of a referendum are hostile to the European Union. In Portugal, the demand for a referendum does not appear to constitute a procedural disguise for radical opposition to European integration.

6

Hungary: Europeanization Without EU Leadership?

Péter Gedeon

State socialism was an economic and political system that reinforced the division between Western and Eastern Europe after 1917. State socialism was seen by the new communist elite in Russia and later in Eastern and Central Europe as a universal solution to the problems of modern capitalism, although in practice it proved to be nothing else but a failed attempt to catch up with that capitalism under the circumstances of underdevelopment.

The state socialist economic model responded to the challenge of economic backwardness with forced industrialization. The classical path of capitalist economic development meant the extension of profit-oriented activity based on private ownership through selling and buying labor. In the process of historical emergence of capitalism, private ownership and profit-oriented economic activity were connected to market coordination and the commodification of labor. By setting up state socialist institutions the communist elite chose a way opposite to classical capitalist modernization. In state socialist industrialization the linked elements of capitalist economy became separated. The commodification of labor was mediated by the abolishment of private property and the suspension of price-regulating markets and profit motivation.

State socialism constituted an attempt to create capitalism without capitalists. The paradox proved fatal for this attempt. The commodification of labor developed by socialist industrialization, and the socialist industrial regime institutionalizing the use of money in the economy, sooner or later demand market coordination and private ownership as its institutional basis. When the process of the establishment and reestablishment of private ownership and market coordination begins, the seemingly autonomous history of state socialism comes to an end.

Therefore, the transformation of state socialist societies in Eastern and Central Europe has been a turn and return to those economic and political institutions developed historically in Western Europe. Consequently, a turn toward the European Union (EU) is deeply rooted in the nature of postsocialist transition in Central and Eastern Europe. For the new political elites of the postsocialist countries, the EU and its member states, along with North America, represent the successful pattern of modernization as opposed to the failed socialist pattern.

The communist elite identified itself with the socialist model by contrasting that model to European and U.S. capitalism. It is unavoidable that the postsocialist elite should distance itself from the socialist model by identifying itself with the model of modern capitalism. EU membership allows these elites to acquire and maintain guarantees for successful modernization in Central and Eastern Europe. The main tasks of the transition to modern capitalism, however, whatever its specific forms will be, have been fulfilled not within but without the framework of the EU. The EU did not play a direct role in shaping the past process of the postsocialist transition in the region. In the first phase of the transformation the Europeanization of domestic structures in the European postsocialist countries has taken place without European leadership.

POLITICAL TRANSFORMATION

In Europe the collapse of state socialism was sealed with the institutionalization of multiparty competition—that is, with the emergence of political democracy. The state socialist system was doomed to failure in part because it could not satisfy the needs it generated, whether military needs represented by the expectations of the *nomenklatura* or those of final consumption nurtured by the great number of households. The one-party system that sheltered both the state and itself from any competing political alternatives and actors was necessary to perpetuate the centrally planned economy based on state ownership and bureaucratic coordination. Privatization and marketization, the two pillars of systemic change in the economy, could take place only if the party that was ruling the state and the economy was uncoupled from the economy. Political democracy institutionalizing party competition was the mechanism that could achieve this. For this reason democratization of the political system proved to be the point of departure for the postsocialist transition in the European socialist countries.[1]

Democratization in Hungary was a peaceful process; it was negotiated between the elites in power and the elites in opposition. The negotiations leading to the major reforms of the political system took place between actors that lacked democratic political legitimation on both sides; the goal of the reforms negotiated by these elites was to set up the rules of the democratic political game. In other words, the negotiations were seen by the actors on both sides as a tool to set up a political system that gives them legitimation.

In Hungary the actors of the negotiated transition were already relatively well differentiated at the time of the so-called roundtable talks.[2] The agreements that designed the institutions of the new democratic order came about as compromises among the different political groupings. The institution-building process was driven by domestic interests, although the outcome may in part have been justified by the actors in terms of international comparisons or adoptions. The roundtable talks served as the constitutional phase of political decisionmaking: The participants had to agree on the rules of the democratic game behind a veil of uncertainty, but they sought to protect and represent their interests through strategic behavior.

The agenda of the roundtable talks included, among others, issues about the status of the new president and Constitutional Court, the party law, the electoral law, and guarantees of a peaceful transition. These talks created the constitutional basis of the new Hungarian democracy. The constitutional decisions reached in the roundtable talks were influenced mainly by the considerations and interests of the representatives of the new party formations and not by suggestions of European or other foreign actors.

Elections for the new Parliament took place in 1990. Six parties could be represented in the Parliament. The winner was the Hungarian Democratic Forum (HDF); the loser was the Hungarian Socialist Party (HSP).[3] The results of the election are shown in Table 6.1.

Following the election results a conservative ruling coalition was formed

Table 6.1   Distribution of Parliamentary Seats Among Parties, 1990–1998

Parties	Distribution of Seats (in percentages)		
	1990	1994	1998
Hungarian Democratic Forum (HDF)	42.5	9.8	4.4
Independent Smallholders' Party (ISP)	11.4	6.7	12.4
Christian-Democratic People's Party (CDPP)	5.4	5.7	–
Hungarian Socialist Party (HSP)	8.5	54.1	34.7
Alliance of Free Democrats (AFD)	23.8	17.9	6.2
Alliance of Young Democrats (AYD)	5.4	5.2	38.3
Party of Hungarian Life and Truth (PHLT)	–	–	3.6
Other	3.0	0.6	0.4

Sources: Sándor Kurtán, Péter Sándor, and László Vass, eds., *Magyarország politikai évkönyve 1995* (Political Yearbook of Hungary 1995), (Budapest: Demokrácia Kutatások Magyar Központja Alapítvány, 1995), 444; and "OVB: Végleges választási eredmény" (National Electoral Committee: Final Results of the Election), *Népszabadság*, June 3, 1998, 4.

from the Hungarian Democratic Forum, the Independent Smallholders'
Party (ISP), and the Christian-Democratic People's Party (CDPP) with
strong leadership by the HDF. The opposition consisted of the two liberal
parties (Alliance of Free Democrats [AFD] and Alliance of Young Democrats [AYD]) and the Socialist Party. The new president was elected by the
Parliament as part of a package deal concluded by the HDF and the AFD,
the body's two biggest parties.[4] Thus the skeleton of Hungarian democracy
was built. The result was a system of parliamentary democracy with a
strong prime minister and a weak president. Power was centralized in the
hands of the prime minister. Members of the cabinet were responsible not
to the Parliament but directly to the prime minister, and because of the
institution of a constructive vote of no-confidence the prime minister could
be dismissed by the Parliament only if a successor could be elected by the
same vote. The power of the president was constrained, and the president
was elected by the Parliament. A Constitutional Court was erected to safeguard the new democratic political order.

The new democratic political institutions emerged from the compromises of the domestic political actors—the party elites—who tried to push
their own interests through this process. This early but fundamental phase
of institution building took place with no direct influence by the EU. On
the other hand, in their programs and election campaigns all six parties
represented in the Parliament emphasized strongly that they were committed to having Hungary join Europe (at that time the European Community). The political elite had internalized those values that served as a uni-
fying basis for modern European societies.

The József Antall government considered human rights, pluralist democracy, and a social market economy to be a common basis for European
and North Atlantic states.[5] The government explained its commitment to
joining the EU through the necessities of Hungarian modernization: "The
main goal of Hungarian foreign policy is to join the process of integration
being conducive to the emergence of European unity, and hereby to provide for those conditions in the field of foreign policy, security and the
economy, that are necessary for the comprehensive modernization in our
country."[6]

Europeanization has had a double meaning for the postsocialist political
elites. First, it denoted the structural change that would lead to the institutionalization of modern capitalism in Hungary. In this sense, Europeanization is not a specific concept related to the European region but a generic
notion of a modern society that developed a market economy linked to
political democracy and the welfare state, first in the West European and
North American states.

Second, Europeanization has meant an integration process within which
Hungary is going to join the EU. This meaning is already linked to the

European region as contrasted with North America. This second form of Europeanization is instrumental to, and at the same time limits, the first one: Hungary will be able to institutionalize the structures of modern society only if it becomes a member of the EU.

Joining the EU, however, is a decision to adopt one of the European versions of modern capitalism. The concept of Europe is broad enough to generate a political consensus among the conservative, liberal, and socialist political groups. The consensus is made possible by the extrication from state socialism. In the postsocialist transformation the different political parties and actors contrast the concepts of the old and the new social order. This brings them to a notion of Europeanization that is broad enough to serve as the basis of a general consensus on the main values of the new economic and political order and that leaves open ideological space for variations and alternatives about the specifics of the transition among the competing political groups. Disagreements among the different political forces over the specific road Hungary should take appear under the umbrella of the concept of Europe.

The new political elite in power saw a coincidence of the pursuit of national interests with the process of joining European integration, which brings with it supranational governance structures. Multiple political identities are characteristic of this elite,[7] in part because of the strength of the political preference to overcome economic and social backwardness and to guarantee the new economic and political structures by joining the European institutions created by the integration process. It is relatively easy for the majority of the political elites and many of the citizens of Hungary—which became a small state after World War I and was disciplined to remain a small state after World War II—to accommodate and live with supranational structures, especially if doing so promises economic and social progress.

The political institutions and the rules of the political game set up early in the transition proved remarkably stable even later. Substantive political processes, however, showed tension and a great amount of change and instability. The most conspicuous sign of instability within a stable framework was provided by the 1994 elections (see Table 6.1).

The electoral volatility of the democratic processes was seen in the fact that the loser, the HSP, and the winner, the HDF, of the 1990 elections changed places in 1994. The stability of democratic institutions was confirmed by the smooth process of passing and taking over power and by the fact that the same six parties remained in the Parliament.

The defeat of the HDF can be explained mainly by voter dissatisfaction. In the 1990 election campaign most parties blamed the communist regime for the economic stagnation in Hungary and proclaimed the idea of joining Europe. The implication of this strategy for the voters was that the postsocialist transition would bring an improvement in welfare within the foreseeable future. The transformational recession ruined those expectations, and the voters punished the coalition in power.

After the 1994 elections a new coalition was formed by the Socialists and the Free Democrats. This coalition maintained the country's European orientation and kept Hungary's EU membership on the agenda. The socialist-liberal government did its best to bring Hungary into the EU and the North Atlantic Treaty Organization (NATO). In 1997 the fact that Hungary, together with the Czech Republic and Poland, was chosen in the first round to be accepted into NATO was celebrated by all of the parliamentary parties. NATO membership was seen by the political elite not merely as an end in itself but also as a means to further Hungary's admission into the EU. Since the major political parties in Hungary agree on this matter, the results of the 1998 parliamentary elections did not call into question the country's prointegration policy line.

ECONOMIC TRANSFORMATION

Economic transformation had already begun during the last reform-communist government, but it gained new impetus after 1990. The economic transformation included institution building and macroeconomic stabilization, which were connected. Institution building engendered macrotensions that constituted the phenomenon of transformational recession and invited stabilization policies that, in turn, might have fed the recession.

The institutions that were linked internally to each other and were seen as indispensable for an efficient economy were private ownership and market coordination. Privatization had to create or re-create the incentive structure that mobilizes economic actors to undertake only profitable economic activities. Although in itself privatization is a series of transactions that follow a universalistic economic logic, privatization of the state socialist economy was a unique historical process.[8]

In Hungary the characteristics of privatization emerged as a consequence of the initial conditions of the postsocialist transition. The state socialist economy created a lack of capital on the demand side of the privatization transactions. The weak economy that emerged out of the transformational recession compelled the state to seek revenues by selling state-owned assets and did not endow the government with economic resources that could have been mobilized for a costly but rapid privatization program. The weak state, facing and at the same time trying to avoid legitimation deficits, may have proceeded too slowly with privatization.

At the end of 1994, about 40 percent of state-owned assets were privatized.[9] After a year of hesitation the socialist-liberal government, under serious economic pressure to raise revenues for the state budget, speeded up the privatization process. In 1996 the minister in charge of privatization announced that by the end of that year, 70 percent of formerly state-owned assets would be privatized. In 1997 the privatization process would officially come to an end; only 109 assets, valued at 350 billion HUF (Hungarian forint), would remain in long-term state ownership.[10]

The scarcity of domestic capital invited foreign investment in the privatization process. Although U.S. participation was notable, the majority of foreign investments came from the EU member states (see Table 6.2). Of the total $5.5 billion in foreign direct investment to Hungary, 60 percent came from the EU.[11]

The Antall government took important measures to liberalize the economy and to exert market pressure on economic actors. By 1993 the extent of liberalization (deregulation and price liberalization) had reached 80 percent of product prices in the domestic market and 90 percent of import prices. The proportion of economic subsidies to gross domestic product (GDP) sank from 13 percent in 1989 to 4 percent in 1993. The bankruptcy law introduced in 1992 led to 4,200 bankruptcy cases that same year. Enterprises that had a one-third share in the 1991 Hungarian export went bankrupt.[12] These measures led to inflation associated with a drop in output. Liberalization of prices and the reduction of subsidies under the initial

Table 6.2 Foreign Investment in Hungary, 1990–1997 (in billion HUF)

	No. of Companies	Billion HUF	Share (in percentages)
Germany	106	292.35	27.86
United States	42	168.80	16.08
France	43	103.17	9.83
Austria	115	53.01	5.05
The Netherlands	20	50.37	4.80
Italy	28	34.76	3.30
Belgium	9	33.93	3.23
United Kingdom	34	20.04	1.91
Switzerland	18	18.41	1.75
CIS[a]	16	10.46	1.00
Sweden	12	5.73	0.55
Finland	2	4.62	0.44
Israel	3	2.32	0.22
Greece	3	1.92	0.18
Other	26	5.12	0.49
Public issue of shares	26	244.53	23.30
Total	503	1,049.54	100.05

Source: "Privatization Monitor," Privatization and State Holding Company, Budapest, December 1997, 4.

Notes: The data exclude so-called greenfield investments—that is, investment in brand-new production sites. [a] Commonwealth of Independent States (Russia and other).

conditions of a shortage economy directly fueled inflation. Import liberalization and bankruptcies led to shrinking domestic output; consequently, output not only faced a demand constraint but also shrank because of supply-side factors. This situation could launch a downward spiral in which supply shrank faster than demand, which could only result in recession coupled with inflation. Monetary policy to fight inflation also contributed to the recession that created open out of hidden unemployment.

In Hungary total production in 1992 reached only 80.9 percent of that in 1989; industrial production in 1992 was only 63.8 percent of that in 1989. This recession was deeper than the Great Depression between 1929 and 1933.[13] Inflation remained around 20 percent, with a peak of 35 percent in 1991. Unemployment remained about 10 percent. The fall of production in the early 1990s was associated with a positive or a small negative balance of payments. In 1991 the balance of payments was positive (with a surplus of $267 million), and the budget deficit was 1.4 billion HUF. In 1992 the balance of payments was still positive ($325 million), but the budget deficit had grown to 114.2 billion HUF. In 1993 the Hungarian economy started growing—the rate of growth was around 3 percent—but that growth was coupled with increasing fiscal imbalances. The balance of payments became negative ($3 billion), and the budget deficit reached 214.7 billion HUF—about 7 percent of GDP.[14]

In 1994 the growth rate of the economy reached 3 percent. That growth, however, was linked to further worsening of monetary indicators. The balance-of-payments deficit reached $3.9 billion, and the budget deficit was 8 percent of GDP.[15] Hungary risked losing the confidence of the international business and financial community, which would have been fatal to the country and the government since the government was dependent on the inflow of foreign capital to finance the country's foreign debts.

Any turn in economic policy occurs under both economic and political pressures, since a restrictive monetary and fiscal policy must face the legitimation constraints rooted in democratic politics. Internal political tensions in Hungary were expressed in public debates among members of the coalition. The smaller coalition partner, the Free Democrats, was pressing the government toward a restrictive economic policy. But before March 1995 the necessity for a stabilization policy was debated within the Socialist Party. The lack of determination by the Socialist Party and the prime minister to stand behind this unpopular program led the Socialist minister of finance to resign. The pressure of economic exigencies (internal and external imbalances) and growing criticism from the international financial and business community, organizations, and the press forced the prime minister to opt for the economic policy of austerity.

In March 1995 newly appointed Minister of Finance Lajos Bokros and the new president of the National Bank of Hungary, György Surányi, announced a strict monetary policy, radical fiscal reforms, and successive devaluations of the forint. By the end of 1995 the balance-of-payments deficit had been reduced to $2.5 billion, and the ratio of the budget deficit had also diminished. Real wages dropped by 12 percent, and productivity rose by 16 percent. International business confidence was restored, and a minimum 1–1.5 percent economic growth was secured. The price paid for these results, besides the decrease of real wages, was rising inflation, which reached 28 percent in 1995.[16]

The economic transformation in Hungary has been a major achievement, but voters have paid an unforeseen price. By 1996 the Hungarian economy had become an open economy, bureaucratic coordination had been replaced by a price-regulating market, and the private sector produced more than 60 percent of GDP. The economy seemed to have entered a new path of growth. The rate of growth was 1.3 percent in 1996 and reached 4 percent in 1997, and it may reach around 5 percent in 1998. On the other hand, in 1995 real wages declined, inflation was above 20 percent, unemployment was around 10 percent, and social services were continually cut.[17] Poverty reached one-third of the population, and the gap between the poorest and the wealthiest strata of the population has been growing.

All of this means that between 1990 and 1995 Hungary accomplished half a turn toward Europe: The new institutions of political democracy and market economy were introduced or reintroduced in Hungary, but because of the transformational recession that was an unavoidable consequence of the reform measures, the lag between Hungary and Western Europe in substantive terms—such as the rate of economic growth, GDP per capita, the rate of inflation, the mortality rate, impoverishment, and so on—may have even grown. The Europeanization of economic institutions was taking place, but the economic processes that accompanied the change in institutions showed that in terms of material welfare and a number of economic indicators—among them the Maastricht monetary targets and the rate of economic growth—the distance between Hungary and the EU countries had grown.

In the early phase of postsocialist transformation, the Europeanization of institutions was not directly coupled with that of the material conditions of the population and the monetary and fiscal conditions of the economy. The painful reforms, however, have created the conditions for a new economic boom. Since 1995, for the first time in twenty years, the Hungarian economy has produced a positive rate of growth without increasing internal and external indebtedness. This gives hope that the Hungarian economy has entered an export-led path of steady growth. A constantly growing economy can provide the material basis for raising the standard of living, easing social tensions, and catching up with Europe. In 1997 real incomes increased by 4 percent.

The economic transformation took place without intense EU participation or influence.[18] Economic reforms were initiated by the political elites in power who internalized the values shared by the European Community. Another segment of reform measures, those in the areas of state budget and social policy, was initiated under the pressure of international economic constraints imposed by the International Monetary Fund (IMF) and the World Bank and also by the reactions of the international business community to Hungarian economic policy and performance.

The role of the EU and its member states in the economic transformation of Hungary between 1990 and 1995 could be seen mainly in the area of capital investment (discussed earlier), in foreign trade, and in EU influence, which was, in the marketization process, connected to the issue of trade. The share of the twelve EU member states in Hungarian export grew from 24 percent to 53 percent between 1989 and 1994; in 1995 the EU share (combined with Austria, Sweden, and Finland) reached 65 percent.[19] The EU had become Hungary's most important trade partner.

In 1991 Hungary concluded an Association Agreement with the EU. This agreement foresaw the gradual and asymmetric reduction of tariffs in trade between Hungary and the EU; furthermore, by contributing to the opening up of the Hungarian economy the EU could assist in strengthening market coordination of Hungary's economy. Because of existing differences in market competitiveness and in spite of the asymmetric character of trade liberalization, however, the Hungarian economy is the more vulnerable party in this process. The EU already maintains a positive balance of trade with Hungary. The Association Agreement treats 40 percent of goods exported from Hungary to the EU as exceptions from tariff cancellation. According to the agreement, in 2001 the percentages of tariff-free goods in trade between Hungary and the EU will be 74 percent for the EU and 95 percent for Hungary.[20] Thus the EU has been successful in protecting its interests in negotiations with Hungary.[21]

In spite of possible resentments toward it, the Association Agreement is seen by the political elite in Hungary as a first and necessary step toward full EU membership. Although the first phase of economic institution building was shaped mainly by domestic politics and international economic constraints, the application for full membership[22] may give the EU greater influence on the postsocialist transition in Hungary in the future.

The fine-tuning of Hungarian institutions to meet EU requirements is and will continue to be taking place.[23] This process, however, will happen at different speeds in different policy areas. Harmonization of law is considered a relatively easy process by Hungarian specialists, who state that Hungarian regulations are already 60 to 70 percent EU compatible. In the case of agricultural policy, Hungary's low-cost agricultural export potential makes that export competitive with that of EU members. After 1990 the agricultural markets of the Central European states were flooded by the goods of EU members. By 1994 only Hungary could maintain its position as a net exporter to the EU in the region.[24] Whether to admit Hungary into the framework of the Common Agricultural Policy (reformed or not) is a politically sensitive issue for both the EU and Hungary.

Another difficult policy area involves Hungarian adjustment to EU monetary targets. Hungary is unlikely to be able to join the new European monetary regime very soon. Because of the effects of the transformational recession, Hungarian monetary indicators have been and remain far from the Maastricht criteria. In 1995 in Hungary the state household deficit reached 7 percent of GDP (rather than 3 percent as mandated by the Maastricht convergence criteria), the ratio of the state debt to GDP was 82 percent (instead of 60 percent), and the rate of inflation was 28 percent (far more than 1.5 percentage points above the best performing EU members). Although these figures have improved, inflation was still around 18 percent in 1997, and the government does not expect single-digit inflation before the year 2000.[25]

Although economic policy may be able to reduce the distance between the Hungarian monetary and fiscal indicators and the Maastricht criteria in the coming years, under the given circumstances the government may be unable to follow a stable exchange rate policy. Although the end of the recession has eased the pressure on the country's external and internal indebtedness and has created more favorable economic conditions, it may be years until policymakers will be ready to sacrifice certain tools of autonomous economic policymaking in exchange for the advantages of joining the EU.[26] For now, the economic constraints stemming from the transformational recession and the political constraints stemming from democratic politics prevent the government from exchanging part of its monetary policy autonomy for a reliable and stable national currency.

The process of negotiations over admission into the EU will be tedious. The expectations of the Hungarian postsocialist elites regarding the EU have never been completely met. Balázs has pointed out that the EU has followed a very cautious policy with respect to the postsocialist states. The EU provided economic concessions in response to the political changes in Eastern and Central Europe and tried to minimize the extent and effects of these economic measures. The strategy of the postsocialist governments, in turn, was aimed at receiving economic concessions from the EU in exchange for political reforms in their countries.[27] In this bargain, "the Central-East-European party has no economic trumps in its hands, because they were already thrown away in the élan of the systemic change. The EU export, flowing in through the open gate of liberalized imports, has preserved for itself a dominant market share."[28]

The commitment of the government and even of the majority of politicians of parties opposed to the European integration process, however, does not depend on an economic cost-benefit calculus; it is a political decision formed by historical experience. The political parties in the Parliament are ready to sacrifice a part of national sovereignty to the supranational powers of the EU. In exchange, the postsocialist political elites have expected and would still like to receive much more economic aid from the EU in the transition period in order to be able to consolidate democracy and to avoid mass dissatisfaction with the transition. So far, the EU has not seemed to respond to these demands.

THE MINORITY ISSUE

Although in general the EU did not play a dominant role in the postsocialist transition in Hungary, some policy areas constitute an exception to the general trend. The case of minority policy is an important exception.

As a result of the 1920 Treaty of Trianon and the Treaty of Paris in 1946, Hungary became a small, relatively homogeneous ethnic state, but large numbers of Hungarians now live in neighboring countries, especially Romania and Slovakia.[29] The minority problem has become a significant political issue in these countries, mainly because of domestic politics. The Antall government tried to use international and European fora to protect the interests and rights of Hungarian minorities against their domestic governments. The minority issue has created tensions in Hungary's relationship with Romania and Slovakia that have hindered the European integration of these countries. Representatives of the EU and EU member states, as well as other (most importantly U.S.) foreign politicians, have warned the countries about the possible consequences of unsolved political tensions—making it clear that the EU does not want to import tensions among its member states into the integration process.

The EU and its member states have also insisted that Hungary, Romania, and Slovakia must normalize their relationships. This demand coincided with the goals of the Antall government to find internationally acknowledged norms and even binding guarantees and to conclude interstate treaties to protect the rights of Hungarian minorities. Therefore the government was ready to respond to the EU demand. The Antall government suggested that basic treaties be signed between Hungary and its neighbors.[30] The realization of these treaties seemed to serve Hungary's goal of European integration and the protection of Hungarian minorities abroad. The Antall government, however, lost the 1994 election before coming to terms with either Slovakia or Romania. After the 1994 election, the new socialist-liberal government did its best to conclude treaties with the neighboring countries. The treaty with Slovakia was signed in Paris in 1995, and intensive negotiations with the Romanian government were concluded in 1996, with ratification by the Hungarian Parliament coming in 1997.

The Hungarian-Slovak treaty was based on mutual compromise. Hungary declared that it would not question the borders between the two countries, and in exchange the Slovak Republic agreed that the treaty could contain the Council of Europe's Recommendation 1201, passed in 1993, which codifies European norms on the rights of minorities. It was important for the Slovak Republic to receive a confirmation of borders from Hungary; for Hungary it was important to include internationally valid norms regarding minority rights in the treaty, since Hungary could then ask EU to monitor those rights. The Hungarian-Slovak agreement was also important for the Gyula Horn government as proof of its sincere desire to seek accommodation with its neighbors. Hungary could demonstrate to the EU that it insisted on good relationships with its partners and was willing to follow European norms. Nevertheless, the Hungarian-Slovak treaty was criticized by Hungarian opposition parties.

In August 1996 the Hungarian and Romanian governments suddenly announced that they were ready to sign a basic treaty. The agreement was made possible by a compromise on Recommendation 1201 of the Council of Europe. The Hungarian government insisted that the recommendation be included in the treaty; the Romanian party first disagreed and then gave its consent with the condition that the treaty include a qualification about the recommendation that excluded the exercise of collective rights and territorial autonomy by ethnic minorities. The Hungarian government accepted this compromise, although the opposition parties in the Hungarian Parliament and the representative organization of the Hungarian minority in Romania the Democratic Alliance of Romanian Hungarians found it unacceptable. These groups accused the Hungarian government of sacrificing the interests of the Hungarian minority to European integration and possible NATO membership. In any case, the sudden compromise may have come about because of pressure from European and U.S. political forces, which wanted to see the two states come to terms with each other. In sum, the treaties reveal a policy area in which direct EU influence, as well as that of other international actors, could be demonstrated.

PUBLIC PERCEPTION OF THE EUROPEAN UNION

The political elite that came to power in Hungary after 1989 saw no alternative policy choice to European integration. The elite believed the damage done by the East Europeanization of Hungary[31] could be rectified only by joining the EU. The EU was considered to provide both an institutional guarantee for successful modernization and a pool of resources that could be mobilized to help Hungary catch up.[32] Consequently, the Hungarian elites in power are committed to EU membership and are ready to pay the price, including constraints on economic and political sovereignty.[33]

Hungarian citizens are also favorable toward membership, although that positive feeling has diminished over the past several years. Opinion polls showed that in 1994, 29 percent of Hungarian citizens had a positive impression about EU goals and activities, and only 8 percent expressed negative feelings (28 percent were neutral, the rest had no opinion). When asked who profits more from closer relationships between the EU and Hungary, 20.1 percent answered Hungary, 39.6 percent said both, and 13.6 percent said only the EU.[34] In a 1996 survey, 69 percent of the Hungarian population thought joining the EU would be beneficial for the country, and only 15 percent said it would be disadvantageous (16 percent did not know).[35]

This positive attitude may result from a desire to move closer to the welfare standards of the developed European countries. The differences in standards cause the Hungarian population to see EU membership as a way to diminish these developmental differences. One legacy of the socialist system in Hungary after the 1956 revolution was that it created needs for increasingly higher levels of consumption, and people expect that joining the EU means moving closer to the average standard of consumption of EU members. That motivation cannot be found in developed European countries that have recently aspired to full EU membership.

In contrast to the situation in some developed EU member states, in Hungary a political backlash by citizens against the EU is unlikely. As a result of the hardships and uncertainties brought about by the postsocialist transition, a legitimation deficit has existed and continues to exist in Hungary. The former conservative government lost the 1994 election because it was not able to fulfill citizen expectations of a higher standard of living. The socialist-liberal government was forced to initiate reforms that led to a drop in real wages and cuts in social benefits in 1995.

This situation was rooted in the nature of the postsocialist transition and in the circumstances of the transformational recession in Hungary. The burden of economic adjustment had been taken up in a period that preceded EU membership; consequently, the social and political costs have not yet been tied to membership in the eyes of the public. The government's legitimation deficit, accumulated as a result of the economic policy of austerity, does not directly spill over onto possible EU membership since the EU was not a central player in the transition. This circumstance may ease the process of joining the EU, especially because it seems to be coinciding with the end of the economic recession. An economic upswing at the time of entering the EU and internalizing the economic and political constraints that are the consequences of EU membership may generate the necessary legitimacy for the move.

EARLY OR LATE ADMISSION INTO THE EU: PORTUGAL VERSUS HUNGARY

The transition to democracy and the process of joining the European Union in Hungary show similarities to those in Portugal.[36] The common features of the transition are rooted in the structurally similar historical conditions of Portuguese and Hungarian political and economic development that served as a point of departure for democratization and integration into the EU. As a result of political dictatorship, a strong, centralized state and a weak civil society emerged in both countries. Within the framework of authoritarian rule and politicized economies, a more or less homogeneous society was maintained. Both states were resized from large to small in history, and in both countries the political elites of the present era still had to face some of the consequences of these changes.

These similarities in the initial conditions of democratization largely explain why in both countries the political elites of the transformation internalized the European norms of political democracy, social welfare, and market economy and why they were looking in a similar way at the EU (or, earlier, the EC) as an important vehicle of domestic political and economic modernization. The political elites' endeavor to become members of the EU is based primarily on political considerations; potential economic costs are outweighed by these considerations, if they are taken into account at all.

The process of extrication from dictatorships also reveals certain differences between the two cases. In Portugal the collapse of a right-wing dictatorship resulted in a new political democracy that was closed to the right and open to the left. Right-wing populism was not a viable option. Left-wing political parties had a strong influence on the first phase of political and economic transition in Portugal. In the area of economic policy, this influence resulted in the nationalization of economic assets.

In Hungary the collapse of a left-wing dictatorship led to a political system that was closed to the left and open to the right. Conservative and liberal political forces and values had the strongest influence on the first phase of political and economic transition. In the area of economic policy, this influence resulted in the privatization of economic assets. Because of the openness of the political system to the right, in Hungary there is some chance for right-wing nationalistic populism to reenter the political stage.

Consequently, whereas in Portugal a leftist opposition may emerge against European integration, in Hungary it is the populist right wing that may turn against the European integration process.

Some other differences between the two states are rooted in the different international circumstances, the changing role of international actors in the process of democratization and European integration. Although democratization in both states took place under the primacy of domestic politics, we can observe an important difference in the role of foreign actors in this process.

In Portugal the EC/EU and certain member states, such as Germany, provided political support and economic aid for the democratization process. This influence was reinforced by Portugal's relatively early admission into the EC. International political assistance could be sought against the leftist forces in Portugal and in pressing for liberalization of the economy.

In the Hungarian case, pressure and assistance were less important.[37] Economic liberalization and privatization were initiated by domestic actors. EU economic support to Hungary between 1990 and 1995 was at an order of magnitude less than that to Portugal. Hungary cannot expect early admission to the EU and must adapt to a changing EU from the outside, whereas Portugal can adapt from the inside.

CONCLUSION

In the process of postsocialist transition, the concept of Europe has gained special political importance for domestic political actors in Hungary and in East-Central Europe. Europe represents a successful model of modernization that has institutionalized political democracy, market economy, and social welfare in Western Europe. Postsocialist political elites have considered EU membership an indispensable means of catching up with the developed world. Staying out of the European integration process has signaled the danger of preserving backwardness.

In the process of extrication from state socialism, the postsocialist elites in East-Central Europe have inevitably internalized the values of modern capitalism, which has been represented by the West European countries—which, in turn, have been represented by the European Union. Although the turn of postsocialist elites toward West European models, structures, and institutions is inviting the EU to take an active role in the transition, the first and most important phase of transformation, which has created new path dependencies for the future of these states, has been dominated mainly by domestic actors. The new political and economic institutions have been shaped by domestic actors driven by domestic interests.

The first phase of the Europeanization of East-Central Europe has taken place without European leadership. This does not mean that European or other international influence does not exist but that such influence is mediated by the way domestic actors internalize institutional patterns that have emerged in modern capitalism and how they react to the external constraints of international economic and political exigencies. The primacy of domestic politics is emerging from a complex process of interaction between domestic and international actors, institutions, and policies.

Thomas Biersteker and Christine Kearney distinguish four potential international sources of democratization: leverage and conditionality, transnational linkages to domestic interests, global effects of the international economic and political system, and international norms and ideas.[38] These factors have played different roles in the different stages of the democratization process in Hungary. Leverage and conditionality—that is, the direct foreign policy actions of foreign powers and the explicit use of conditionality by international organizations—contributed to the creeping liberalization process that emerged as an at least partly unintended consequence of the economic reforms after 1968. The new Ostpolitik in Germany and the bilateral relationships of Hungary with Western states contributed to the country's relative openness. As a consequence, the Hungarian ruling elite and the citizens who could travel abroad became more open to Western ideas.

It was important for the peaceful collapse of the system that by the end of the 1980s, as a result of the erosion of socialist values, the socialist vision was lost even for those in power. Hungary's growing foreign debts from the late 1970s increased economic dependence on the West. The global effects of the international economic and political system, such as the two oil shocks that signaled a new era of global technological and institutional changes in the world market, revealed the economic vulnerability of the socialist system. This realization increased the political weight of reformers in Hungary and thus also triggered the collapse of the regime. In Hungary between 1968 and 1989, a democratic opposition made up of a small group of internal dissidents and public opinion expressed through samizdats emerged that was tolerated by the officials in power. This group established connections with the transnational network of civil organizations fighting for civil rights.

The turn from restricted political and economic liberalization toward democratization and marketization was made possible by an important change in the international political system. The withdrawal of the Soviet Union from East-Central Europe was decisive for the collapse of the socialist system in Hungary because it freed domestic political actors to initiate the peaceful transition from a one-party to a multiparty political system. During the ensuing institution-building process, international norms and ideas—among them the idea of a European Community—internalized

by the political actors played an important role in the postsocialist transformation in Europe. This internalization process made leverage and conditionality dispensable. Transnational networks contributed to the democratization process by helping the newly emerging parties and other actors
of civil society, among them unions, to shape and confirm their new identities. Anonymous systemic forces of the international economy and international organizations pressured the Hungarian government to carry out a
stabilization program and to begin the unpopular reform of the welfare
state.

Hungary's membership in the EU may increase European influence in
the future. In the negotiations on Hungary's membership, in contrast to
the earlier enlargement involving the southern European states, the EU
will exercise leverage and conditionality. It will have less effect on the
main characteristics of the new institutional structure of Hungary's polity
and economy and more on the nature of specific policies and policy regimes. This procedure will be somewhat controversial and painful for
Hungary—especially in the areas of agricultural and monetary policy—
not just for economic reasons but also for political reasons, since these
problems have a direct link to voter satisfaction. Accommodation to EU
requirements in agricultural and monetary policy may hurt the interests of
large groups of Hungarian voters. The institutionalization of EU norms
into the Hungarian legal system will also be a part of the membership negotiations, but that process will probably be smooth.

Two distinct but connected processes channel European influence into
the postsocialist transition. The first follows the impersonal logic of the
market by embedding the Hungarian economy into the European common
market; the second follows the deliberations of political actors in the formation of new institutions.

The process of embedding the Central European economies into European structures is well on its way, and it enforces myriad adaptations by
economic actors on the microlevel. This process can also trigger economic
tensions, attached to the countries' modernization deficit, on the macro-
level. The opening up of the markets of small Central European states to
European competitors leads to macrotensions and to deficits in the balance
of payments and the balance of trade and may crowd out potentially competitive domestic producers from these markets.

The second process is connected to the future membership of Central
European countries in the EU and to outcomes in terms of further institution building. The EU has played only a minor role in this phase of the
postsocialist transformation in which the outlines of the new institutional
order were formed and the stabilization policies leading to legitimation
deficits in some of these countries emerged. In other words, the EU may
take this first phase of transition, which occurred outside of the EU, for

granted and may build on it in the next phase when the Central European countries enter the EU as full members. We can expect that in the second phase the postsocialist countries that will be accepted as members will carry out a series of adjustments to the EU.

From the point of view of the elites of the Central European countries, it is important that the hardships of the transformational recession in the first phase of the transition not burden the process of being accepted as EU members. Since the bulk of economic losses suffered by the population was not tied to the countries' European integration process but to the domestic transformation process that took place outside the EU, there is a chance—depending on prospects for economic recovery—that the integration process may not create major political obstacles.

Although the EU's abstention from a more active role in assisting the East-Central European states in the period that precedes their admission may count as a gain forgone for these countries in their efforts to strengthen their democracies, the long-term economic and social benefits[39] of a successful adaptation process may keep integration attractive to those in power. The Hungarian state will preserve its willingness to exchange the new political constraints on national sovereignty for the desired economic and social benefits of integration.

NOTES

1. Offe shows the dilemmas attached to the primacy of democratization and points out that this primacy is a unique feature of East and Central European transformation. See Claus Offe, "Capitalism by Democratic Design?" *Social Research* 58, no. 4 (winter 1991): 865–892.

2. On the history and logic of the roundtable talks in Hungary, see László Bruszt and David Stark, "Remaking the Political Field in Hungary: From the Politics of Confrontation to the Politics of Competition," *Journal of International Affairs* 45, no. 1 (June 1991): 201–245; and András Bozóki, "Hungary's Road to Systemic Change: The Opposition Roundtable," *East European Politics and Societies* 7, no. 2 (spring 1993): 276–308.

3. The HSP was formed by the reform communists following a split in the Hungarian Socialist Workers' Party (the official name of the Hungarian Communist Party) in October 1989.

4. The agreement of the roundtable talks delineated numerous laws that needed a qualified two-thirds majority to be passed in the Parliament. Prime Minister József Antall asked the Free Democrats to agree to limit the number of these so-called two-thirds laws for the sake of governability. In exchange, he asked the Parliament to elect a leading member of the AFD, Árpád Göncz, as the new president.

5. "As a result of changes in Europe and especially in East-Central Europe a unified European-North-Atlantic area is going to emerge that is being built on fundamental human, political and economic values, such as the provision of human

rights (among them individual and collective rights of national minorities), pluralist democracy, [and a] social market economy." *A nemzeti megújhodás programja* (The Program of National Revival) (Budapest, 1990), 17.

6. Ibid.

7. For this concept see chapter 4 in this volume.

8. See David Stark, "Path Dependence and Privatization Strategies in East Central Europe," *East European Politics and Societies* 6, no. 1 (winter 1992): 17–54.

9. Privatization does not necessarily mean the former state assets are now possessed by private owners; there is a great amount of mixed ownership and cross-ownership. See David Stark, "Recombinant Property in East European Capitalism," *American Journal of Sociology* 101, no. 4 (January 1996): 993–1027.

10. See "Medgyesi: Túlteljesül a tervezett reálbércsökkenés" (Medgyesi: The Foreseen Cut in Real Wages Will Be Surpassed), *Népszabadság*, Budapest, May 25, 1996, 1.

11. Béla Kádár, "Cui prodest Európai Unió?" (European Union: Whose Interest?), *Magyar Tudomány* 103, no. 2 (February 1996): 160.

12. Béla Kádár, "A magyar átalakulás optikája: Kívülről és belülről" (The View of the Hungarian Transformation: From Without and from Within), *Külgazdaság* 39, no. 9 (September 1995): 57.

13. János Kornai, "Transformational Recession," Discussion Paper no. 1, Collegium Budapest/Institute for Advanced Studies, June 1993, 2–6.

14. Zita M. Petschnig, *Jelentések az alagútból: Jelentés a gazdasági átalakulás 1990–1993 közötti folyamatairól* (Reports from the Tunnel: Report on the Processes of Economic Transformation Between 1990–1993) (Budapest: Pénzügykutató Részvénytársaság, 1994), 27–69.

15. Központi Statisztikai Hivatal, *Magyar Statisztikai Zsebkönyv 1997* (Hungarian Pocket Book of Statistics 1997) (Budapest: Központi Statisztikai Hivatal, 1998), 126, 164.

16. Ibid., 43, 126, 152, 162.

17. Ibid., 126, 128–129, 152, 242.

18. For example, EU financial aid to Hungary within the framework of PHARE, the EU's assistance program for Eastern Europe, between 1990 and 1993 was less than 0.2 percent of Hungary's GDP for the same period. Kádár, "Cui prodest," 162.

19. Ibid., 158.

20. See Péter Balázs, "Az EK közép-kelet-európai és mediterrán társulásainak összehasonlítása" (Comparing EC Associations: East-Central-Europe Versus the Mediterranean), *Európa Fórum* 2, no. 4 (December 1993): 3–19.

21. Margit Rácz, "EK-csatlakozás: Magyar érdekek és közösségi feltételek" (Accession to the EC: Hungarian Interests and Community Conditions), *Európa Fórum* 4, no. 3 (November 1994): 77–91.

22. Hungary officially applied for full membership in the EU in April 1994 and was admitted into the first round of negotiations for full membership in 1997.

23. See András Inotai, *The System of Criteria for Hungary's Accession to the European Union* (Budapest: Institute for World Economics of the Hungarian Academy of Sciences, 1994), 19.

24. See András Inotai, "A társulási egyezménytöl a teljes jogú tagság felé?" (From the Association Agreement to Full Membership?), *Gazdaság* 29, no. 1 (spring 1996): 36–37. By 1994, however, Hungary's relative position had deteriorated from an earlier 6:1 export-import ratio to a 1.7:1 ratio. Inotai, "A társulási egyezménytöl," 36–37.

25. Központi Statisztikai Hivatal, *Magyar Statisztikai Zsebkönyv 1997*, 253; and Kádár, "Cui prodest," 164.

26. This is the usual tradeoff for small West European states. See Paulette Kurzer, "Placed in Europe: The Low Countries and Germany in the European Union," in *Tamed Power: Germany in Europe*, Peter Katzenstein, ed. (Ithaca: Cornell University Press, 1997), 108–141.

27. See Péter Balázs, "A periferizáció határai" (The Limits of Peripherization), *Európa Fórum* 5, no. 4 (December 1995): 95–98.

28. Ibid., 96.

29. Hungary's population is 10 million. About 2 million Hungarians live in Romania and eight hundred thousand Hungarians live in Slovakia.

30. See Péter Kende, "A Trianon-szindróma és a magyar külpolitika" (The Trianon Syndrome and Hungarian Foreign Policy), *Külpolitika* 1, nos. 3–4 (fall-winter 1995): 13.

31. Soviet-style industrialization led to controversial results. In 1973 the region again reached 45 percent of the GDP in Western Europe, but subsequent stagnation and decline, beginning in 1973, brought the GDP in the Central and East European region down to roughly 25 percent of the GDP in Western Europe by 1992. The gap grew from a ratio of 1:2 to almost 1:4. Iván T. Berend, "Európa! De miért?" (Europe! But Why?), *Népszabadság*, 28 January 1995, 17.

32. In the opinion of former Minister of International Economic Relations Béla Kádár, the modernization of Hungary is costly, but integration into the EU does not create these costs; they are faced even in the absence of integration. What is more, integration may actually reduce the relative costs of modernization by finding new resources in the EU. As a result of integration, Hungary could receive financial assistance that would reach 3 percent of GDP as opposed to the present 0.3 percent of GDP. Kádár, "Cui prodest," 162–163.

33. Former State Secretary to the Ministry of Foreign Affairs János Martonyi noticed that the Central European states were more strongly committed than some other EU member states to fulfill the obligations set by the EU. János Martonyi, "Csatlakozásunk az Európai Közösséghez" (Hungary's Joining the EC), *Európa Fórum* 2, no. 1 (June 1992): 8. Kádár emphasized that under the circumstances of the globalization of the world economy, voluntary regional integration limiting national sovereignty may help in defending national interests and appreciating the bargaining power of a small state. Kádár, "Cui prodest," 154.

34. Zoltán Molnár and Antal Tóth, "Közép-és kelet-európai vélemények gazdaságról, politikáról és az európai együttmüködésröl" (Public Opinion on the Economy, Politics, and European Cooperation in Central and Eastern Europe), in *Magyarország politikai évkönyve* (Political Yearbook of Hungary), Sándor Kurtán, Péter Sándor, and László Vass, eds. (Budapest: Demokrácia Kutatások Magyar Központja Alapítvány, 1995), 593, 596.

35. György Csepeli and Tibor Závecz, "Várakozások, remények, félelmek: Az Európai Unió képe a magyar közvéleményben" (Expectations, Hopes, Fears: The Image of the European Union in Public Opinion in Hungary), in *Magyarország Politikai Évkönyve 1996-ról* (Political Yearbook of Hungary for 1996), Sándor Kurtán, Péter Sándor, and László Vass, eds. (Budapest: Demokrácia Kutatások Magyar Központja Alapítvány, 1997), 663.

36. On Portugal, see chapter 5 in this volume.

37. Before 1990 Western politicians sometimes tried to impede the political liberalization process in Hungary, warning reform communists and opposition politicians to move more cautiously with political reform. Simply put, they feared possible Soviet intervention. That fear did not exist in the case of Portugal, which was not part of the Soviet sphere of interest.

38. See Thomas J. Biersteker and Christine A. Kearney, "International Sources of Contemporary Democratization," in *International Dimensions of Economic Liberalization and Democratic Consolidation*, Laurence Whitehead, ed. (Oxford: Oxford University Press, forthcoming).

39. László Csaba makes it clear that the real economic benefits of integration are not those of direct monetary aid from the different EU funds. This is even more true in the case of East-Central Europe because aid cannot reach the amounts that were poured into the economies of the Southern European states. The real economic gain in joining the EU for a small state such as Hungary is that the domestic economy becomes more competitive and more attractive to foreign investors. László Csaba, "A rendszerváltozás második fordulója és az EU keleti kibövülése" (The Second Round of Systemic Change and the Eastern Enlargement of the EU), *Valóság* 39, no. 8 (August 1996): 17–18.

7

France and the United Kingdom: The Dilemmas of Integration and National Democracy

Jack Hayward

From its ephemeral origins in the Greek city-state, democracy has endeavored to retain the intimacy of a political community that is close to its citizens while at the same time giving accountable leaders sufficient authority to act effectively. When it acquired a new lease on life at the end of the eighteenth century, democracy in large states became representative of the electorate, which no longer directly decided for itself. The legitimacy of this wider community was conferred by the membership of a nation whose essentially spurious identity was shrouded in historical myth and enforced when necessary by state coercion.

In the context of the European integration process, the salient political dilemma has been how to achieve greater decisionmaking accountability while partially shifting the community basis of democratic legitimacy from the national to the European Union level. This dilemma has posed especially intractable problems in Britain and France.

CONFRONTING POLITICAL DILEMMAS: NATIONAL IDENTITY, STATE SOVEREIGNTY, REPRESENTATIVE DEMOCRACY

In Western Europe the new representative democracy was the political manifestation of the state-nation, with the nation frequently an artifact of the state. This was particularly true of Britain and France, whose sense of national identity was forged in the dynastic wars they fought with each other interspersed with civil wars to create an integrated state. In France this state took the form of an absolute monarchy, whereas in England and, by extension, Britain a constitutional monarchy or crown-in-parliament became the repository of sovereign power. After the convulsions of the French Revolution, in the nineteenth and early twentieth centuries both France and Britain strove to establish stable national democracies; this process occurred gradually and only after struggles that were especially prolonged and bitter in the case of France. No sooner had they established democracies than, after World War II, they were confronted with the need to move from national to European integration, a challenge Britain accepted much more reluctantly than France.

Unlike Germany, however, where the state is a recent creation of a preexisting nation, Britain and France have found it especially difficult to extend the democratic boundaries of their political systems and to accept an authority that implies a community much wider than that of their state-nation because it is assumed that doing so presupposes a suprastate and a supranational community. Thus they have engaged in functional integration, especially in economic matters, as reflected in the earlier designation of the European entity created as a Common Market. Particularly in Britain, with its global free-trading traditions, this posed less of a political problem than it did in state interventionist France, which was much more comfortable with the 1960s protectionist agricultural Community preference than with the liberalizing trends from the mid-1980s.

By the 1990s, constitutional issues had been brought to the forefront of political debate in relation to the Maastricht Treaty, which raised issues of defense, foreign policy, and the police that were regarded as the core of the "regalian" functions of the sovereign state, together with the currency and monetary policy functions that have been regarded as its concomitants. In conjunction with the prospect of successive enlargements of the European Union, this meant the functions, composition, and relative weight of the Council of Ministers, the European Commission, and the European Parliament became much more controversial. Further, the interpretive role of the European Court of Justice—which had imparted to the loose institutional arrangements a capacity to adapt to circumstances in an integrationist direction—came under attack, notably by the British Conservative governments of Margaret Thatcher and John Major, who were pressured by the Europhobic elements in their parliamentary party.

Although it was a French president of the republic, Valéry Giscard d'Estaing, who took the lead in creating a directly elected European Parliament to compensate for the strengthening of the intergovernmental features of the Community with the establishment of a European Council of heads of government, France, like Britain, has been uncomfortable with the idea of a shift of democratic legitimacy from the parliaments of the member states to the European Parliament. The member governments have enjoyed the privilege of power without effective accountability because they have operated in a constitutional no-man's land. Although governments have enjoyed the power to legislate, subject to propositions being forthcoming from the European Commission and to the European Court's capacity to adjudicate, national parliaments have found it difficult to hold them to account because they are forced to make concessions and compromises presented subsequently as faits accomplis. In practice, the European Parliament's increase in formal powers is ineffective because its inability to command the loyalty of the citizens it represents—as reflected in declining electoral turnout—means it cannot even exercise the powers it already has, such as rejecting the Commission president selected by the Council of Ministers. There is a more fundamental reason, however, for Anglo-French unease with the workings of European Union institutions now that they are impinging intrusively on the autonomy of national governments: these institutions' consociational nature.

As Joseph Weiler has pointed out, European governance has three aspects—the international, supranational, and infranational—and the consociational model helps us to understand only the international aspect.[1] Because of the need to preserve at least the semblance of national accountability and the discretion of member governments while overcoming the tendency toward inertia that arises from the capacity of each government to block decisions requiring unanimity, leaders must strive for consensus. Faced with an interdependence that makes the pursuit of independent state action impractical, the customary recourse to majorities—in which the winning coalition can impose its will on recalcitrant minorities—is inappropriate.

Unlike the Netherlands and Germany, where elite bargains leading to package deals gave rise to what Ralf Dahrendorf called government by a "cartel of elites," in France and Britain adversary politics decrees that it is usual to see politics in terms of winners and losers. By extension from intrastate politics to European Union politics, it is not the Lijphart-Daalder-Dahrendorf emphasis on cooperation to overcome interstate conflicts of interest but the Finer stress on the competition between opposed interests asserted with intransigence that characterizes the domestic politics of Britain and France and their approach to European negotiations.[2] Charles de Gaulle and Margaret Thatcher were extreme exemplifications of this propensity. Both were compelled by circumstances to adopt this proclivity—de Gaulle through France's special relationship with Germany, Thatcher in Britain's more subordinate relationship with the United States—but in their conception of Community affairs they were inclined to revert to type.

The Maastricht-exacerbated fear that a supposedly minimalist European Community (EC) might be escalating into a potentially maximalist European Union (EU) mobilized the latent hostility of sections of the political class, which complained that they had not noticed how far the incremental process of European integration had already gone. This belated reaction took different forms in Britain and France—more parliamentary in Britain and more populist in France, although popular hysteria was whipped up in Britain in the mid-1990s. These two countries were conspicuous in the low-level and relative loss of support for the European Community, even before the Maastricht Treaty was signed. Whereas France had been at the heart of the enterprise of European integration from the start, Britain early on laid claim to be at its spleen. Until the advent of the Tony Blair Government in 1997, British governments had adopted the role within the EU played by the former USSR in the United Nations during the Cold War years when Foreign Minister Molotov frequently vetoed proposed actions with a curt *niet*.

Ever since Britain's immediate postwar reluctance to play the leading role in the initial moves toward European integration left France to take over this function, there have been both persisting contrasts and enduring affinities in the two countries' approach to adapting national democracy to the needs of intergovernmental and supranational collaboration. Having created state-nations in the late medieval and early modern periods, France and Britain had subsequently achieved a relatively high measure of national integration and a firm commitment to democratic institutions that gave most of their citizens a keen sense of distinct identity and a loyalty to their governments as both the symbolic and practical manifestation of that identity. (One should not forget, however, that they are both multinational unitary states, so *national identity* is an artifact that has not eliminated substate identities.) Two world wars, the globalization of the world economy, and the increasing role of governments in economic management and welfare state provision to promote social cohesion and economic competitiveness have provided the context within which France and Britain confronted the need to accept closer integration within Western Europe.

Unlike Germany, which has accorded conceptual as well as historical priority to the nation over the state, Britain and France have unified multinational communities through state action. Some protagonists of European integration have argued that sufficient cohesion exists to underpin a European Union.

> The problem is that this argument simply does not ring true. For most Europeans any sense of European identity defined in ethno-cultural or ethno-national terms would be extremely weak. . . . To insist on the emergence of a preexisting European Demos defined in ethnocultural terms as a precondition of constitutional unification or, more minimally, a redrawing of political bound-

aries, is to ensure that this will never happen. The No Demos thesis which is presented by its advocates as rooted in empirical and objective observation barely conceals a pre-determined outcome.[3]

Whereas for historical reasons Britain and France are predisposed to conceive the basis of democratic legitimacy in citizenship rather than ethnic terms, they are also wedded to their separate identities and are reluctant to create a European state. The result has been an uneasy disjuncture between instituting a piecemeal, incremental process of functional integration and retaining traditional state structures. The consequence has been the much deplored "democratic deficit" through which powers transferred to the European Union level have not been matched by corresponding institutional integration. Member state ministers and officials have exercised power without accountability. The European and national parliaments and even less their citizens are not in a position to exercise control over those who are making ever more extensive and usually desirable interventions in policy matters.

To delegitimize the integration process, critics have focused on the EU's democratic deficit—a cliché that repays close analysis. The fact that both antagonists and protagonists of increased European integration support the assertion that is encapsulated in the term does not mean it is as well-founded as is usually assumed. The empirical evidence shows that the difference in public satisfaction with the working of democratic institutions in the member states and in the EU is small. In a 1994 Eurobarometer survey the average difference between the satisfied was 3 percent (40 percent to 43 percent) and that for the dissatisfied was 5 percent (48 percent to 53 percent) for Europe and the member states, respectively.[4] The trends in turnout for EU elections have not reflected the increasing powers of the European Parliament, which refutes the claim that the declining voter turnout is a consequence of the public's perception of the insignificance of European elections.[5]

Furthermore, as David Judge has argued, insofar as the relatively low public satisfaction with both national and European parliaments is correlated with a "dual democratic deficit," this is a result of *all* parliaments' limited control over governments rather than the differential between strong national parliaments and a weak European Parliament.[6] This was reflected in the fact that among the original six members of the European Economic Community (EEC), no provision was initially made for parliamentary scrutiny of the French government's activities—not merely because of Parliament's circumscribed role in the Fifth Republic but also because Community affairs were treated as part of foreign policy.[7] By contrast, both houses of Parliament established select committees to deal with EC legislation in 1974, soon after United Kingdom (UK) accession, whereas the French National Assembly waited until 1979—more than twenty years after France's accession—suggesting that differences in executive-legislative relationships in the two countries were merely projected onto their respective ways of dealing with the scrutiny of EC legislation.

This view would be too simple. The scrutiny system established in both chambers of the UK Parliament to consider EC directives went beyond the usual practice. Whereas the national UK Parliament plays no part in the crucial formative, prelegislative phases of decisionmaking, it was given the capacity to do so in EC matters: "Once a document is received by the UK Government, the Government deposits it in both Houses of Parliament and within ten working days must also deposit an explanatory memorandum, signed by a minister, on the document's implications for the United Kingdom and the Government's policy towards it. The documents and memoranda are available not only to Members of Parliament but also to the public."[8] In both houses the EU Select Committee is chaired by a member of the opposition, reflecting an institutionalization of its role that does not exist in France—in part because the absence until recently of a dominant party that has formed the government and can be expected to do so again renders such a practice difficult to establish. There are more profound reasons: A winner-takes-all mentality in a country where all opposition was treated as (and often was) subversive toward the political regime prevents the acceptance of the institution of a loyal opposition as integral to the working of the political system—a process that required more than a century to take root in Britain and even longer in Northern Ireland.

A 1980 resolution of the House of Commons ringingly asserted that body's determination to have its say before UK ministers made decisions in the EC Council of Ministers: "No Minister of the Crown should give agreement to any proposal for European legislation which has been recommended by the Select Committee on European Legislation for consideration by the House, before the House has given it that consideration." This "scrutiny reserve" was accepted by the European Council of Ministers in "recognition of the fact that parliamentary control over European legislation has developed further in the United Kingdom than in most of the Community."[9] We shall see that in practice, even after the House of Commons revised the 1980 resolution in 1990 to deal with the post–Single European Act situation created by Qualified Majority Voting, the UK Parliament's scrutiny arrangements have proved incapable of keeping up with the European decisionmaking process.

THE EUROPEAN UNION CONTEXT

The intimidating difficulties of moving from member country to European parliamentary and party representation, and the absence of a "European people" that can provide the mass democratic underpinning for the institutions that have been established, mean that essentially European elites—political, business, bureaucratic, military, and educational—have operated with little reference to their national constituencies. In the case of the political elites, this situation has created great resentment among members of the national parliaments, who lost their institutionalized link to European decisionmaking following the direct election of the European Parliament in 1979.

The weakness of the representative link to national electorates has been compounded by the fact that there are no genuine European parties. Each "European" election is fought as a series of separate, if almost simultaneous, national elections on national issues. Since 1979, direct elections to the European Parliament have had only a modest effect in creating genuine transnational parties, to the extent that Rudy Andeweg has argued that "it may be better to speak of a seventy-nine (national) party system than of a nine (transnational) party system in the European Parliament."[10]

In the 1994 election the British Labour Party (63 members of the European Parliament [MEPs]) and, to a lesser extent, the French Socialists (14 MEPs) were important components of the largest transnational party group (198)—the Party of European Socialists—although the German (40), Spanish (22), and Italian (18) national party delegations also carried great weight. The second-largest group was the European People's Party (EPP), of predominantly Christian democratic inspiration, joined belatedly by the British Conservative Party with 19 MEPs in 1994—having formed a separate European Conservative Group in 1973. The latter was mortally weakened in 1989 by the transfer of the Spanish Popular Party (PP) to the EPP, where the British Conservatives had a modest place relative to the German Christian Democratic Union (CDU) (47 MEPs) and the Spanish PP (30).

The French right has been plagued with splits at the European level, both electorally and in terms of which party group to join subsequently. The 1989 split between the Rassemblement du Peuple Français/Union pour la Democratie Française (RPR/UDF) list and the Centrist list and the 1994 competition between the RPR/UDF list and the dissident list of Philippe de Villiers and Sir James Goldsmith, *L'Autre Europe*, led to a subsequent three-way dispersion among the EPP (13 MEPs) and the European Democratic Alliance (14), whereas the 13 MEPs elected from *L'Autre Europe* formed the bulk of the Nations of Europe group.[11]

In Britain, party discipline ensured that the voters could not choose between pro- or anti-integrationist Conservative or Labour candidates, although in 1994 the campaign polarized (rather artificially) a relatively Euro-enthusiastic Labour Party and a Euro-skeptical Conservative Party. The poor showing of the latter, however, reflected its domestic unpopularity rather than the dithering over its EU policy and contributed to the weakening of John Major prior to his electoral defeat in 1997.

Despite the divisions within parties over European integration policies and the tendency for MEPs to be more integrationist than their national counterparts, the fault lines within the European Parliament (EP) are national: "When Groups fail to vote cohesively, it is usually because one or more national delegations have decided to opt out of a Group position."[12] The weakness of transnational parties is reflected in the vague nature of their manifestos, as well as in the poorly financed and feeble extraparliamentary linkages with the voters. Candidates are selected within each country, thus reinforcing the insularity of national parties, especially where—as in France—selection is based on a list system.

Although European elections have allowed some parties to make a breakthrough into national politics, as occurred with Jean-Marie Le Pen's National Front in 1984, such an occurrence is exceptional. Le Pen's breakthrough turned out to be not a flash protest vote but the launching pad for a sustained presence within French domestic politics. In the case of de Villiers, his European electoral success in 1994 on an anti-Maastricht platform did not, as he had hoped, carry through to the 1995 French presidential election where he failed badly, winning less than 5 percent of the vote. A different example of the way in which European elections can relate to national politics was the poor showing of the French Socialist list in 1994, which resulted in its leader, Michel Rocard, resigning from his post and withdrawing from the subsequent presidential campaign. Thus despite attempts to dismiss European elections as second order and second-rate, they can have significant national political consequences.

In practice, the European Parliament—fragmented among nine loose transnational parties, requiring a coalition to achieve a majority, and without the cohesive effect of the need to support a government—has relied on achieving consensus between its two largest groups, the Socialists and the EPP. Facing an intergovernmental Council of Ministers rather than a European government and a Commission recruited through nomination by the governments of the member states, whose loyalty to the European Union is somewhat equivocal, the EP majority coalition identifies the extension of its powers with the promotion of the integration process. Particularly since the extension of its legislative powers under the Maastricht Treaty, the EP "is obliged to muster absolute majorities in the cooperation, codecision and certain assent procedures and even larger majorities for certain budgetary amendments. Even where simple majorities would be sufficient, the Parliament makes great efforts to muster large, cross-party majorities, and its political and constitutional resolutions are considered weak and ineffectual unless they command such big, and broad, majorities."[13] This nonadversarial "grand coalition" approach to EP politics is another powerful factor in making it difficult to link democratic party politics within nonconsociational member states, such as France and the UK, to the EU.

The way in which the EU has conducted its affairs has favored piecemeal, functional, secretive, technobureaucratic collaboration between national and Eurocratic officials. Around thirty thousand insiders—three-quarters of whom are national officials—form a network that goes by the unattractive name of *comitology*. The bulk of the preparatory work of negotiating compromises between the separate national interests falls on them. Thus even within the ministerial structures of the two states, which are generally considered the ones best organized to secure coordinated national control over intra-EU activities, the practice of frequent meetings in Brussels has tended to concert viewpoints to lead to a convergence that does not always commend itself to their political masters in Paris and London.

The habit of give and take in the secluded environment of closed committee politics provides a marked contrast to the tendency of ministers to assume intransigent public attitudes for domestic consumption. The fact that the ministers usually have to settle for a compromise means their assertive rhetoric loses its credibility. They are also regarded as having "sold out" the national interest by outsiders who are frequently unrealistic about what is obtainable. This situation offers an underdog mass of potentially resentful citizens to the populist demagogues of both the right and the left, who can deploy their antiestablishment skills to show that the mainstream leaders are betraying their peoples in pursuit of their supranational utopia.

Understanding more about the Community method of decisionmaking helps to explain the underlying cause of what is loosely called the democratic deficit. The French term *engrenage* encapsulates the way in which Eurocratic insiders work. George Ross, in his book *Jacques Delors and European Integration*, has defined the process as "an 'action trap' in which agents, once set on a specific course of action, find themselves obliged to take a set of further and much broader actions that point them in a direction in which they did not necessarily intend initially to go."[14] The Delors presidency (1985–1994) of the European Commission demonstrated the use of this technique—imported from France—in masterly fashion, in which a largely French-staffed cabinet with a clear set of objectives was able to coax and compel a diversity of national and EU decisionmakers in a direction whose further implications and ultimate (federalist) destination they initially had only dimly perceived. However effective, such an approach feeds the paranoid propensities of the Euroskeptics and has become less effective in the 1990s.

EUROPEAN INTEGRATION'S CHALLENGE TO DEMOCRACY:
FRANCO-BRITISH CONTRASTED RESPONSES

In marked contrast to the British government's sustained lukewarm disposition toward the development of the European Coal and Steel Community (ECSC)—EEC—EC—EU, joining belatedly what it could not prevent or delay and reluctantly accepting those policies from which it could not escape or opt out (with conspicuous exceptions such as the Single European Act), France has acted as the driving force of the European integration process. France quickly adopted a partnership relationship with Germany but one in which it was politically and militarily the senior partner. This relationship was accepted by a divided Germany until what had been an economic preponderance has become in the 1990s, following reunification, a demographic and increasingly political preponderance. Particularly with the 1958 return to power of de Gaulle, France advanced a confederalist conception of European integration whose first version was the 1961–1962 Fouchet Plan. This was a resolutely intergovernmental program of comprehensive collaboration in pursuit of a "European Europe" that was not dominated by the United States. The intention was to preserve national independence while securing the benefits of intra-European regional collaboration based on close cooperation with Germany.[15]

Ironically, although Britain was much more sympathetic to de Gaulle's conception of European institutions, it was excluded from EC membership because of its deference to the United States. This, in turn, paralyzed both the intergovernmental and federalist possibilities of an advance toward closer integration because most other member states would accept concessions on supranationalist arrangements only if Britain were admitted. By the time that happened, the loss of impetus had reached the point at which federalism had largely disappeared from the political agenda. Thus the additional British ballast has accounted for only part of the difficulty in resuming progress toward closer political integration—toward a genuine European Union and not simply a market based on free trade and thus open to the world at large.

Because, as we have seen, Britain and France are both multinational creations of unitary states, they find it particularly difficult to accept integration within a federal political system in the way Germany and Italy are inclined to do. Self-consciously former imperial powers with a worldwide reach, these countries regard the de jure loss of formal sovereignty as adding insult to the injury of the de facto loss of the capacity to control their own destinies. As Stanley Hoffmann eloquently put it over thirty years ago:

> The French may not have a sense of national purpose, but, precisely because their patriotism has been tested so often and so long, because the pressures of

the outside world have continued throughout the postwar era to batter their concerns and conceits, and because modernisation, now accepted and even desired, also undermines traditional values still cherished and traditional authority patterns still enforced, French national consciousness opposes considerable resistance to any suggestions of abdication, resignation, *repli*—so much so that the "Europeans" themselves have to present integration as an opportunity for getting French views shared by others instead of stressing the "community" side of the enterprise.[16]

Hoffmann was writing at a time when de Gaulle was still the head of state affairs and was capable of imposing a halt to the Monnet-style process of European integration of which he disapproved. Hoffmann excluded the United Kingdom because of its subservience to the United States after its admission took up the defense of national sovereignty. It has done so, however, without pursuing the elevated Gaullist ambition of a "European Europe." Britain has also disappointed the hope of Monnet who believed that once it joined the EC it would be swept along by integration dynamics, although he did say in an advance warning against opt-outs that the British "will be good partners on one condition: that there are no exceptions for them in the rules."[17]

Although the UK joined the EC fifteen years after France, it preceded France in seeking a measure of accountability for ministers and officials engaged in Brussels negotiations with the UK Parliament. The major difference between the British and French conceptions of democracy is that in Britain in the past the electorate has expressed its political preferences only as mediated indirectly through parliamentary representation, whereas in France a triple channel exists for the expression of popular sovereignty. In France the people's will can make itself explicit through its election of the president, the election of deputies to the National Assembly, or directly by referendum.

Referenda have been used in France on two occasions relating to EC issues—the admission of three new members (including Britain) in 1972 and the ratification of the Maastricht Treaty in 1992—whereas in Britain a referendum was used in 1975 to confirm the terms of British membership. If the Blair Government were to decide to join a single EU currency, it would not do so without putting the choice to a referendum. Whereas in Britain the referendum is regarded as an exceptional divergence from the principle of parliamentary sovereignty and was not used to ratify the Maastricht Treaty, in France the use of the referendum (on the initiative of the president of the republic) was extended in 1995 without the safeguard of prior approval by the Constitutional Council. This change was part of President Jacques Chirac's populist 1995 electoral campaign to strengthen his link to the mass public, but in compensation the annual sessions of

Parliament were extended from six to nine months to increase the parliament's capacity to exercise more effective control over EU activities.

Despite attempts to link national parliaments and the European Parliament for mutual support in strengthening legislative powers vis-à-vis national and EU executives, in practice the two are more competitive than collaborative. The real problem has been that national parliaments have usually exercised little effective control over their national governments—although there have been conspicuous exceptions such as Denmark, which took the form of "binding parliamentary scrutiny" as soon as it joined the EC (along with the UK) on January 1, 1973.[18] How have France and the UK responded to the challenge to national democratic practices raised by European integration? The Fifth Republic has restricted the French parliamentary sovereignty characteristic of the Fourth Republic, whereas the UK continues to assert a parliamentary sovereignty that in practice is largely usurped by the government. How has parliamentary scrutiny of EC matters evolved over the last quarter of a century in the UK and France? As this process began five years earlier in Britain, I begin with the House of Commons.

The Commons Select Committee on European Legislation was set up in 1974 to examine three kinds of EC documents it judged to be of "legal and political importance"; in practice, these documents are contentious ones that affect UK law and have financial implications. Of the approximately one thousand documents it receives each year, one-third are considered to fit these categories and about ninety are referred (since 1991) to one of the two European standing committees. Both the select committee and the standing committees receive evidence and examine witnesses—usually the appropriate minister, although that power is rarely used. "Each week, a paper is circulated by the Select Committee on European Legislation to the departmental select committees informing them of relevant European legislation. However, relatively little time is given over by the committees to European issues." Nevertheless, "the Foreign Secretary and the Home Secretary do now appear before the foreign affairs and home affairs committees respectively before each meeting of the European Council," although no regular scrutiny process exists.[19] The House of Commons holds two annual general debates prior to European Council meetings. The work of the House of Lords European Communities Committee is if anything more authoritative than, although complementary to, its House of Commons counterpart. The latter seeks breadth and reports quickly, whereas the House of Lords deals with fewer documents in greater depth.

In France, only with the end of dual membership in the EP and the national parliament in 1979 and the direct election of the EP did the two chambers set up parliamentary committees (called *délégations*) on EC activities. The committees had no investigative powers and were seldom given information by the French government before the Council of Ministers discussed a matter, despite an official government obligation to do so. The foreign minister or the minister for EC affairs would occasionally provide evidence, but the National Assembly and Senate standing committees largely ignored them, and "many parliamentarians were unaware of their existence."[20] The enfeebled nature of the French Parliament in matters of European policy contrasted sharply with its status in the mid-1950s, when the Parliament rejected the proposal to create a European Defence Community.

The situation changed with the Single European Act (SEA, signed in 1986 and operative from July 1987), which replaced the prevalence of unanimous decisionmaking on a range of EC matters with Qualified Majority Voting (QMV). QMV required about 70 percent of the votes cast in the Council of Ministers. Because national ministers could now be outvoted, member state parliaments could no longer even nominally enforce accountability effectively. Furthermore, as a result of the "cooperation procedure" established by the SEA, if an absolute majority of MEPs supported an amendment accepted by the Commission, it would prevail unless member states in the Council of Ministers were unanimously opposed.

Since 1987 the right of member state veto has fallen into abeyance, "although the British and French governments claim that the Luxembourg Compromise still exists as a safeguard of the last resort."[21] Consensus at all costs has been sacrificed to decisionmaking capacity, which has extended and speeded up legislation. As a result of this

> constitutional turning point . . . the leisurely scrutiny processes national parliaments had established were suddenly inundated with large amounts of legislation. This could be expected to have two consequences. In the first place, the Community's legislative process was very much more evident to national parliaments. In the second, the scale of the legislation involved necessarily meant that national parliamentary scrutiny (in the majority of the Member States scrutiny mechanisms did not change substantially) became more perfunctory.[22]

This was not the case in Britain, however, as we have seen, or in France.

Alarmed by the press of complex legislation and the conspicuous loss of democratic control, the Michel Rocard Government (1988–1991) sought to strengthen French parliamentary scrutiny of EC legislation. The government sided with the more cautious line taken by the Senate rather than with the National Assembly, which had sought to acquire a coordinating function. Nevertheless, the work of the EC committees was linked with the standing committees of the National Assembly and the Senate because of overlapping membership. The membership of the EC committees was doubled from eighteen to thirty-six. They were to receive all EC proposals in time to make their views heard before being faced with faits accomplis. A 1990 act institutionalized the practice of ministers giving evidence to the EC committees, a practice that could be extended to EC officials. Finally, the committees could choose matters on which they wished to report and make recommendations, and the reports had official status.[23]

Meanwhile, President François Mitterrand, in a 1989 speech to the EP, advocated joint meetings with representatives of member state parliaments to try to avoid competition among them prior to the Maastricht Treaty negotiations and to meet objections over inadequate democracy prior to the Intergovernmental Conference (IGC) on Political Union. The joint meetings of members of both the EP and the national parliaments took place in Rome in November 1990. It predictably supported increased cooperation and exchanges of information between the groups and supported giving the EP ratification powers over future treaty amendments equivalent to those enjoyed by national parliaments. This proposal was not accepted in the Maastricht Treaty, with the British government in particular unfavorable to such extensions of the role of the EP.[24]

During the 1991 pre-Maastricht IGC, the French government again took the initiative in establishing what came to be called the Conference of the Parliaments. Because of the addition of two intergovernmental pillars to the EC (one dealing with a common foreign and security policy and the other with justice and home affairs), it was necessary to establish a consultative assembly with a broader remit than the EP to cover EU matters. This proposal met with opposition, particularly from the UK government, and was weakened notably when it was left unclear whether all member state parliaments would have to agree for the conference to meet. Such agreement is unlikely; the Commons Foreign Affairs Select Committee asserted in 1993 that "we see greater merit in the development of a series of bilateral contacts between the European Parliament and each national parliament and the further development of national parliaments' pre-legislative role."[25] Thus matters relating not merely to the two intergovernmental pillars but also to Economic and Monetary Union (EMU) will have no EU parliamentary forum.

Nevertheless, the Conference of European Affairs Committees (CEAC) of the national parliaments and the European Parliament meets twice yearly to discuss ways to improve parliamentary scrutiny and has secured regular progress reports from EP committees to share with member state parliaments. An EP computerized system to track legislative proposals and amendments—the European Interinstitutional Legislative Observatory—provides information to national parliaments.[26] Such modest steps toward cooperation, however, cannot overcome governments' reluctance to increase parliamentary involvement in EU-related legislation.

The ratification debates over the EU Maastricht Treaty were used by national parliaments to increase their role. This was especially true in France, where a constitutional amendment (article 88-4) now requires that the government must submit to Parliament all legislative proposals from the European Commission to the Council of Ministers. Parliament can then— exceptionally—adopt resolutions on its own initiative. In July 1994 Prime Minister Édouard Balladur sent a circular to ministers asking them and their officials to delay discussion of matters for Council decision until the (nonbinding) resolutions of the French Parliament have been received. This procedure, however, does not apply to the common foreign and security and justice and home affairs pillars of the treaty.

The French Parliament has changed its rules and procedures to deal with the consequences of the post-Maastricht constitutional amendment. This has strengthened the role of the two EU committees because the standing committee to which proposed resolutions are sent must respond within a month. To increase the likelihood of acceptance by the standing committee, one of its members is selected to act as rapporteur. This, in turn, increases the likelihood that the resolution will be debated in Parliament.

The National Assembly's EU committee is more active than that of the Senate in deciding which matters require no further action because they are too unimportant or have been overtaken by EU legislation and those that need further attention. (Because it usually takes a month for proposals to reach the French Parliament, intervention by the EU committee often comes after legislation has already been approved by the Council of Ministers; hence the Balladur circular referred to earlier.) The committee decides by appointing a rapporteur, tabling a resolution or expressing its views to the government. It takes into account the need to amend national legislation and the attitudes of French interest groups toward the proposals.

Between August 1992 and June 1994, the National Assembly EU committee dealt with 265 EU legislative proposals, of which 38 proposals expanded into 41 resolutions being tabled—mostly (25) by committee members and the rest by party groups (10) or chairs of the standing committees (6). Of the 41 resolutions proposed, 23 were adopted. National Assembly debates occur on Mondays and Thursdays, however, which are notorious for the number of absentees (on these days deputies devote themselves to their local offices) and poor attendance.[27]

Although it is difficult as yet to assess what influence the French Parliament has begun to exercise and complaints have been made that the government prefers to keep major political matters to itself while referring the bulk of minor technical ones, some procedural improvements have been made. French ministers taking part in Council negotiations now receive their Parliament's resolutions, and the ministers' officials are supposed to take those resolutions into account when preparing negotiation positions.

The resolutions are used selectively and tactically to strengthen ministers' positions when they correspond to the French government's viewpoint. Since the 1993 influx of Euroskeptics into the National Assembly following the landslide right-wing election victory, its EU committee has attracted many of those who want to increase the national Parliament's role in EU affairs, making it much more active than it had previously been.[28]

Thus although it started to take scrutiny seriously somewhat later than the House of Commons, in a forlorn attempt to hold ministers to account the French National Assembly—under the sympathetic aegis from 1995 to 1997 of its anti-Maastricht President Philippe Séguin—at last began to flex its flaccid muscles. This could be seen as part of the attempt to overcome the growing gap between the mass public and the government by easing the curbs the Fifth Republic has imposed on the French Parliament. There has been little evidence, however, that the French executive will release its grip on the decisionmaking process since the Lionel Jospin Government took office and Laurent Fabius replaced Séguin as National Assembly President in 1997.

In Britain the 1993 European Communities (Amendment) Act extended parliamentary scrutiny to the especially controversial matter of EMU. The British government had obtained an opt-out in the Maastricht Treaty, and this act required that it report to Parliament on its proposals for the coordination of economic policies, its role in the European Council of Finance Ministers (ECOFIN) in pursuit of Article 2 treaty objectives, and the work of the European Monetary Institute in preparation for EMU. Given the move to greater independence of central banks on the way to the creation of a European Central Bank, it is significant that the governor of the Bank of England now reports annually to Parliament and the government's medium-term economic and budgetary assessment must obtain parliamentary approval of the convergence criteria stipulated in the Maastricht Treaty.[29]

Such changes in a matter so pivotal to the activity of both national and EU politics make clear that sweeping assertions of a unilateral "democratic deficit" should be qualified. Parliaments do not merely legitimize the actions of their governments; they want to play an active part in decisions such as the move toward a single European currency. This flies in the face of the wish of governments to retain an uninhibited capacity to reach bargained agreements in the EU arena. Compelled to sacrifice an increasing portion of their discretionary power to EU institutions, ministers are extremely reluctant to concede much of what remains to parliaments—especially when doing so exposes dissensions among their parliamentary supporters to damaging public view. Hence, although lip service will be paid to increasing the involvement of the legislature, the executive will jealously protect such freedom of action as external and internal constraints permit.

Within France and Britain significant splits over European integration are found between political and economic elites and among public opinion, parliamentary parties, and leaders; contrasts also exist between the two countries. Businesspeople in both countries have generally favored increased economic integration, although there have been conspicuous exceptions—such as Sir James Goldsmith, founder of the ephemeral UK Referendum Party, and Jacques Calvet of Peugeot. The flood of mergers and joint ventures since the late 1980s accepts the logic of the Single Market, and EMU is regarded as its corollary. As business is aligned with the right, we might assume that right-wing political parties would adopt a similar policy. This has been decreasingly the case in the British Conservative Party in its currently weakened state, although in the 1980s Thatcher had already played the nationalist card with little inhibition. Euroskepticism "from below" has since become increasingly influential, as backward-looking public suspicion has been transmitted through the parliamentary party to the William Hague–led opposition.

Meanwhile under Blair the "New Labour" Party, in which the "Little Englander" elements had previously been active, veered toward a more prointegrationist line as it came to recognize that a continental social market economy did at least preserve some of the features of the postwar social democratic consensus at a time when socialism had receded from the political agenda. Furthermore, the working of adversary politics in Britain has meant that as the Conservative Party shifted toward Euroskepticism, it was natural for the Labour Party to adopt at least a moderately Euro-enthusiast stance. Each party, however, retains a significant minority within its ranks that is uneasy with, if not hostile to, the official line. Britain is the brake in the European vehicle, or to pursue the motor car metaphor, Britain seems condemned to invent a variable geometry vehicle with a gear box that allows the Euro car to move at several speeds simultaneously, with Britain happiest in reverse. Is France still the accelerator?

In France political confusion is, if anything, even greater than that in Britain. In the 1980s European integration policy had been a matter of consensus among the mainstream political parties, leaving the extreme parties of right and left—the National Front and the communists—to oppose integration. With Delors in charge in Brussels (1985–1994) and Mitterrand in control in Paris (having made the momentous decision in 1983 to put European integration before socialism in one country), the policies furthered by Giscard d'Estaing in the 1970s continued.

The Maastricht Treaty referendum exposed a split in the main right-wing party, the RPR, between those who wished to pursue it and those who did not; meanwhile, de Villiers was clearly outdistanced by Le Pen and the National Front in the competition for the anti-European vote. The socialists were deprived of their top presidential candidate, Jacques Delors, who judged inter alia that in the prevailing political atmosphere he would be unable to carry out the policies required by his integrationist objective. The same argument could also be applied to the centre-right Raymond Barre, former EC commissioner and prime minister, who decided not to stand for election.

The European issue was largely ignored in the 1995 presidential election campaign. Federalism was the love that dared not speak its name.[30] Within a context of high unemployment, since Jospin became prime minister in 1997 the Socialist Party has held to the monetary union calendar despite the temptation to exploit the loss in popularity of a deflationary policy associated with the previous government led by Alain Juppé and bound up with its electoral downfall.

PROPOSALS FOR EU INSTITUTIONAL REFORM

The 1996–1997 Intergovernmental Conference led to a flurry of proposals for institutional reform that was accelerated by the prospect of further enlargement, which will make the already cumbersome decision processes unworkable. Regarding the second pillar, only France and Britain have a global foreign and defense policy and nuclear arms to back it up. This has posed problems for the creation of a European policy in these areas—traditionally considered central to the life of the state—particularly because France and Britain have adopted very different approaches to them. Whereas Britain has accepted a loss of national sovereignty within the North Atlantic Treaty Organization (NATO), France from de Gaulle to Mitterrand tried unsuccessfully to promote a common European defense under its leadership outside the NATO framework. Despite recent French policy changes, ambiguity remains over how much the French government would pool its sovereignty as part of this proposal (it will doubtless insist, as has Britain, on unanimity) and whether joint control over nuclear weapons would be either practicable or desirable; such an arrangement, in any event, appears unlikely for the foreseeable future.

Turning specifically to the institutional issues that relate to EC-pillar activities within the EU, the extension of majority voting in the Council of Ministers is a fundamental issue. The capacity to override objections voiced by a minority of states raises a major point of confrontation between those states—such as intergovernmentalist Britain—that want to restrict majority voting and the federalists, led by Germany, which seek to extend it. The latter view, expressed forcibly in the 1994 Christian Democratic Union/Christian Socialist Union (CDU/CSU) Parliamentary Group Report "Reflections on European Policy,"[31] authored by Wolfgang Schäuble and Karl Lamers, was predicated on the claim that the sovereignty of the nation-state has "long since become no more than an empty envelope," that it requires an extension of the powers of the European Parliament as well as the pursuit of a "Europe of the Regions" to implement the principle of subsidiarity—neither of which is favored by the UK and French governments. In pre-IGC hearings conducted by the French National Assembly EU Committee, Lamers stressed that it was not the nation but national sovereignty that was "an empty envelope" because it could not resolve an increasing number of important problems, whereas European federalism could preserve national identities despite limited sovereignties.[32]

Qualified majority voting is linked to the issue of weighted voting, with the larger states seeking to correct what they regard as an increasing imbalance in favor of smaller states, which will predominate among future candidates for entry into the EU. Only about a quarter of the issues to which QMV applies are decided by a vote in the Council of Ministers, and these are often on technical matters. There is no evidence that large and small states usually vote on opposite sides. Because of small states' opposition to increased weighting for large states, there has been a convergence in favor of a "double majority" system of both states and population (characteristic of bicameral federal systems). Whereas France accepts that this is an acceptable quid pro quo for an extension of QMV to matters under the EC or "pillar one,"[33] the UK government has adamantly rejected any extension of QMV while pressing the case for greater weight for the four large states: Germany, France, the UK, and Italy. The idea that these states should have a veto—such as exists in the UN Security Council—is anathema to the smaller states, which regarded with skepticism Britain's episodic attempts to appeal for their support against the Franco-German condominium. Discussions are also taking place over requiring even greater majorities on certain sensitive issues, as well as on the use of "positive abstention" or "consensus bar one" as ways to weaken insistence on unanimity and to provide more flexibility in IGC negotiations.

The key issue at stake behind the bargaining over QMV lies in the term *majority*. Is there willingness to accept any kind of majority decision as legitimate? If so, on which issues and with what measure of disagreement? Thus in 1995 the RPR-dominated EU Committee of the French National Assembly, while referring favorably to British advocacy of a realistic and pragmatic Europe as opposed to a visionary and futurist Europe, rejected a Europe à la carte or "l'Europe self-service" that pushed flexibility too far through opt-outs. To avoid paralyzing Council of Ministers decision-making, it was proposed that unanimity be confined to a few matters such as defense and that larger QMV be accepted for issues such as political cooperation.[34]

The attempt to make QMV the general rule in EC matters and to extend it selectively into EMU policy, foreign and security policy, and justice and home affairs matters has placed the legitimacy of majority voting under increasing strain. Whereas the Conservative UK government—in part for domestic parliamentary reasons—entered the IGC negotiations in 1996 with almost no room for maneuver, the French government—in part to achieve a compromise with Germany—seemed willing to be sufficiently flexible to make a package deal possible prior to persuading most of its "partners" to accept what the de facto senior partners—Helmut Kohl and Jacques Chirac—had agreed.

The Conservative government's March 1996 White Paper, *A Partnership of Nations*, developed immediately preceding the March 1996 IGC in Turin, adopted the variable geometry view of a flexible EU of the self-service kind the French have rejected.[35] Opposing the claim that the EP should acquire new powers and reiterating that national parliaments should be the instrument for ministerial accountability, the report sought to steer the EP toward concentrating on monitoring propensities toward massive fraud and mismanagement—notably in relation to the Common Agricultural Policy. As well as offering ritual reaffirmations of support for subsidiarity (confined to EU member states and not to include the substate level), the UK government concentrated on reasserting the right of member states to defend their national interests and to act on their own when they deemed it necessary, particularly in matters of defense, foreign policy, justice, and home affairs. The government also suggested, however, a number of practical ways to improve the working arrangements for managing the Common Foreign and Security Policy.[36]

It is ironic that although it was in England (and then Britain) that judge-made common law was an essential instrument of political unification, the UK government objected to the constitution-building role of the European Court of Justice.[37] In sum, this negotiating position transparently gave tactical priority to defending national interests to please a shaky parliamentary majority over adopting a strategic posture calculated to maximize influence over the final decisions of the IGC. This very negative approach was accentuated by the 1996 controversy over "mad cow" disease, which was used to make a virtue of UK isolation rather than as an opportunity to promote cooperation to deal with a common problem.

Both the UK and French governments, before and since their 1997 swing from right to left, have been critical of the activist European Commission in the Delors style but are unwilling to make it even more accountable to the "federalist" European Parliament. Instead, they want to make the Commission accountable to the intergovernmental European Council and strengthen the role of national parliaments as ways of curbing the Commission's activist propensities. The French National Assembly EU Committee went as far as to support a two-chamber European Assembly with national parliament representatives forming the first chamber, as advocated by French Euroskeptics such as Séguin; pro-European Conservatives such as Michael Heseltine and Leon Brittan have made similar suggestions.[38]

Although proposals to deprive the European Commission of its monopoly over legislative initiative have in practice been abandoned, its capacity to keep issues on the agenda is threatened by proposals to adopt a "sunset clause" if the Council of Ministers misses a deadline to follow up on Commission initiatives. Even though Commission members are not supposed to be protagonists of national interests, suggestions to reduce their number in line with the necessary portfolios (ten to fifteen) have met with stiff resistance. This resistance might be diminished if the Commission were made accountable to the Council of Ministers as well as to the European Parliament, which would give it a "double legitimacy."[39]

Despite the persistent criticisms of Commission activism, the number of proposals emanating from it has notably decreased, falling from 185 in 1990 to 75 in 1993—even during the Delors presidency. The number has since declined further. Nevertheless, few would be willing to go as far as former French Socialist minister for European affairs and justice minister Elizabeth Guigou, who has advocated giving the Commission president the right not merely (as at present) to be consulted on national nominations to the Commission but also to select from national lists, with the right to dismiss candidates.[40] For his part Chirac, in a pre-presidential election speech entitled "For a Strong Europe," championed increasing the term of office of the president of the European Council to three years rather than strengthening the powers of the president of the Commission. The inconsistency in the French viewpoint was pointed out by a pro-federalist French MEP of the UDF, Jean-Louis Bourlanges, who argued that France is the "prisoner of an extraordinary contradiction: we want a strong Europe, like the Germans, but weak institutions like the British."[41]

Nevertheless, at the end of the debate France will doubtless come down on the German side and accept stronger EU institutions than it would prefer because of the need for an effective capacity to act. Particularly given President Chirac's activist temperament, British governments would be deluded to presume that reticence on the issue of conceding the power to decide for oneself will preclude institutional concessions to secure collective policy achievements. The October 1997 Amsterdam Treaty proved incapable, however, of making a significant advance on institutional reform preparatory to EU enlargement, although majority voting is to be used more in the Council of Ministers and codecision will be extended between the Council and the European Parliament.

Integration by stealth is no longer possible once EU activities have ceased to be foreign affairs conducted by elites and to have no close parliamentary scrutiny or public concern.[42] Parliaments and peoples—especially in former imperial countries such as Britain and France, which are accustomed to think of themselves as great powers—find it extremely difficult to face the humiliating consequences of the fact that they no longer control their own affairs in an ever widening number of matters that affect their daily lives. When European courts—both the European Court of Justice and the non-EU European Court of Human Rights—"interfere" with the activities of their national governments, patriotic pride is mobilized against judicial elites whose prime concern is not electoral popularity. The painful learning process involved in adapting to an integration process that combines intergovernmentalism and supranationalism as complementary approaches rather than alternatives is more a matter of "muddling through" than one of spectacular changes, although such changes sometimes become necessary under the pressure of unpredictable circumstances.

The ephemeral illusion that the end of the Cold War balance of terror would lead to the replacement of power politics with bargaining between peoples devoted to innocent money making and engaged in commercial exchange has been brutally dissipated. We are back to nasty little local wars between would-be sovereign powers. The belief that the EU could be a self-restrained, maxi, common marketeering, peace-loving, herbivorous nonstate has been shattered by the self-assertion of mini, nationalistic, warmongering, carnivorous states. Some states, such as the UK, are tempted to adopt a minimalist response, recoiling from the new context of the 1990s by relying on intergovernmental remedies to threats of mass immigration, environmental pollution, and the need for rapid-reaction military interventions or humanitarian expeditions. The Blair Government has preferred to proceed prudently despite the pretentious rhetoric associated with the launch of the UK presidency in the first half of 1998.[43]

In hopes that NATO will be able to cope with the new situation by keeping the United States committed to Europe and not leaving the EU to fend for itself, countries such as the UK seem content to improvise incremental ways of containing specific problems. The rest of the EU countries, however, seem unwilling to accept the consequences of fleeing forward ensconced metaphorically on a variable-geometry multicycle with an increasing number of people pedaling in a variety of directions at different speeds. Although France may look back nostalgically with regret at its former state-centered sovereignty, despite hesitations and public disenchantment it seems determined to make the most of its diminished circumstances. This means accepting the fact that national democracy must be adapted to the encroaching demands of European integration.

The March 1996–June 1997 IGC discussions offered a context for creative unofficial thinking on this subject and sought to ameliorate the problem of reconciling EU accountability to national parliaments with rapid decisionmaking. If these parliaments were to contribute to public confidence in European decisions, they would have to exercise influence at an early stage in the legislative process, before prearranged agreements had been reached between EU member state governments. This would require that they hear evidence from EU commissioners and seek to influence Commission proposals to the Council of Ministers. Scrutiny of proposed measures would require more time (perhaps a minimum of thirty days), and this procedural requirement could be included in the EU's treaty arrangements. In any event, the 1997 Amsterdam Treaty pleased no one and achieved relatively little. The United Kingdom obtained a further opt-out from the incorporation of the Schengen provisions on visas, asylum, and immigration.[44] It has opted in to the Social Chapter, however, thereby conforming to the traditional British disposition to do too little too late in the process of European integration.

Whereas both France and Britain are on the defensive vis-à-vis the EU, Britain seems more reluctant to swallow its national pride and share in shaping collective decisions to which it will be subjected with or without the benefit of its willed participation. This is particularly true of the adoption of a single European currency by the majority of EU member states.[45] Yet national pride will be better preserved if the limits of national decisions are appreciated and the opportunities offered by integrated decisions are grasped. The Blair Government has decided to postpone this choice to the next millennium.

NOTES

1. Joseph J.H. Weiler with Ulrich R. Haltern and Franz C. Mayer, "European Democracy and its Critique," in *The Crisis of Representation in Europe*, Jack Hayward, ed. (London: Frank Cass, 1995), 24–31.

2. See Arend Lijphart, "Consociational Democracy," *World Politics* 21, no. 2 (1969): 207–225; Hans Daalder, "The Consociational Democracy Theme," *World Politics* 26 (1974): 604–621; and S. E. Finer, ed., *Adversary Politics and Electoral Reform* (London: Wigram, 1975). On the notion of "cartel of elites," see Ralf Dahrendorf, *Society and Democracy in Germany* (London: Weidenfeld and Nicholson, 1968), 276. For the extension of the notion of consociationalism to the European Community, see Paul Taylor, "The European Community and the State: Assumptions, Theories and Propositions," in *The European Community After 1992: A New Role in World Politics?*, Armand Clesse and Raymond Vernon, eds. (Baden-Baden: Nomos Verlagsgesellschaft, 1991), 64–79.

3. Weiler, "European Democracy," 16–17.

4. See European Commission, *Eurobarometer: Public Opinion in the Euro-*

pean Union (July 1994), 1–3, reported in Rudy Andeweg, "The Reshaping of National Party Systems," in *The Crisis of Representation*, Hayward, ed., 59.

5. For turnout figures in elections to the European Parliament from 1979 to 1994, see Julie Smith, "The 1994 European Elections: Twelve into One Won't Go," in *The Crisis of Representation*, Hayward, ed., 210.

6. David Judge, "The Failure of National Parliaments?" in *The Crisis of Representation*, Hayward, ed., 80–82.

7. John Frears, "The French Parliament and the European Community," *Journal of Common Market Studies* 12 (1975): 140–158.

8. Philip Norton, "The United Kingdom: Political Conflict, Parliamentary Scrutiny," *Journal of Legislative Studies* 1, no. 3 (autumn 1995): 96; special issue, National Parliaments and the European Union.

9. Quoted in Judge, "The Failure of National Parliaments," 87.

10. Andeweg, "The Reshaping of National Party Systems," 65.

11. For the 1994 European Parliament election results in seats by party group and country, see table 5 in Smith, "The 1994 European Elections," 212.

12. Francis Jacobs, Richard Corbett, and Michael Shackleton, *The European Parliament*, 2d ed. (Harlow: Longman, 1992), 82.

13. Martin Westlake, *A Modern Guide to the European Parliament* (London: Pinter, 1994), 110–111. On the perplexing complexity of the various majorities required, see table 5, pp. 261–263.

14. George Ross, *Jacques Delors and European Integration* (Oxford: Polity Press, 1995), 254, note 24.

15. See Jack Hayward, "La Cinquième République et l'Intégration Communautaire," in *De la Cinquième République à l'Europe*, François d'Arcy and Luc Rouban, eds. (Paris: Presses de Sciences Po, 1996), 23–43.

16. Stanley Hoffmann, "Obstinate or Obsolete: The Fate of the Nation-State and the Case of Western Europe," *Daedalus* 95, no. 3 (summer 1966): 891.

17. Monnet's comment to German Foreign Minister von Brentano is quoted in François Duchêne, *Jean Monnet: The First Statesman of Interdependence* (London: Norton, 1994), 303; cf. 356.

18. David Arter, "The Folketing and Denmark's 'European Policy': The Case of an 'Authorising Assembly'?" *Journal of Legislative Studies* 1, no. 3 (autumn 1995): 110–123.

19. Norton, "The United Kingdom," 99; cf. 96–98, 100–102, 107.

20. Franco Rizzuto, "The French Parliament and the EU: Loosening the Constitutional Straitjacket," *Journal of Legislative Studies* 1, no. 3 (autumn 1995): 47; cf. 48.

21. Anthony Teasdale, "The Politics of Majority Voting in Europe," in *Institutional Problems of the European Union*, Alain Guyomarch ed. (Aldershot: Dartmouth, forthcoming).

22. Martin Westlake, "The View From 'Brussels'," *Journal of Legislative Studies* 1, No. 3 (Autumn 1995): 167.

23. Rizzuto, "The French Parliament and the EU," 50–52.

24. Westlake, "The View from 'Brussels'," 171; and Judge, "The Failure of National Parliaments," 89–90. When considering the many obstacles to strength-

ening the EP, it is important to recall that membership in national parliaments is still the way for politicians to attain ministerial office in Britain and usually in France.

25. Unpublished document quoted in Westlake, "The View From 'Brussels'," 172.

26. Judge, "The Failure of National Parliaments," 90.

27. Rizzuto, "The French Parliament and the EU," 55; cf. 52–54, 57. Despite successful pressure to secure Strasbourg as the permanent home of the European Parliament, French MEPs are among the most frequent absentees.

28. Ibid., 56–57.

29. Judge, "The Failure of National Parliaments," 93–94.

30. For an outspoken defense of European federalism, see Dusan Sidjanski, *L'Avenir Fédéraliste de l'Europe: La Communauté des origines au traité de Maastricht* (Paris: Presses Universitaires de France, 1992).

31. CDU/CSU Fraktion des Deutschen Bundestages, "Reflections on European Policy," September 1, 1994, mimeo.

32. Cited in Nicole Catala and Nicole Ameline, *Quelles réformes pour l'Europe de demain?* Rapport d'information no. 1939 of the Délégation pour l'Union Européenne of the National Assembly, Paris, February 8, 1995, 111. For a similar viewpoint to that of Lamers on the need to pool weakened national sovereignty, see the comments by the Breton Socialist deputy Charles Josselin, who abstained on the EU committee's report (Catala and Ameline, *Quelles réformes*, 229–230).

33. See the comments of European Affairs Minister Michel Barnier in *Le Figaro*, Paris, July 10, 1995.

34. Catala and Ameline, *Quelles réformes*, 53–54, 82. Even in military security matters France now favors "concerted deterrence" and is much more integrated into NATO.

35. Foreign and Commonwealth Office (FCO), *A Partnership of Nations: The British Approach to the European Union Intergovernmental Conference 1996*, Cmnd. 3181 (London: HMSO, March 1996), 6.

36. Ibid., 17–22. See also annexes B, C, and D for detailed proposals. For a post–Amsterdam Treaty assessment of the Common Foreign and Security Policy, see Marie-France Durand and Álvaro de Vasconcelos, eds., *La PESC. Ouvrir l'Europe sur le Monde* (Paris: Presses de Sciences Po, 1998).

37. FCO, *A Partnership of Nations*, 16–17.

38. Ibid., 95–96; cf. 85–86. Séguin's proposal appeared in an article in *Le Figaro*, December 7, 1994. See also Michael Heseltine, *The Challenge of Europe: Can Britain Win?* (London: Weidenfeld and Nicholson, 1989), 35; and Leon Brittan, *The Europe We Need* (London: Hamish Hamilton, 1994), 226.

39. Renaud Dehousse, "Constitutional Reform in the European Community: Are There Alternatives to the Majoritarian Avenue?" in *The Crisis of Representation*, Hayward, ed., 132. This viewpoint was also advocated by Charles Josselin in his note of abstention to the National Assembly. Catala and Ameline, *Quelles réformes*, 232.

40. Catala and Ameline, *Quelles réformes*, 145.

41. For Chirac's speech, see *Revue des Affaires Européennes* 1 (1995): 30. For

Bourlanges's remark, see *Le Figaro*, June 26, 1995. For other views on France's relationship to the EU, see the issues of *Pouvoirs* on "L'Europe, de la Communauté à l'Union," 69 (April 1994); Laurent Cohen-Tanugi, "Europe: La vacance française," *Le Débat* 83 (January-February 1995): 36–40; and Maurice Duverger, *L'Europe dans tous ses états* (Paris: PUF, 1995).

42. See my conclusion "Has European Unification by Stealth a Future?" in *Elitism, Populism and European Politics*, Jack Hayward, ed. (Oxford: Clarendon, 1996), 252–257.

43. Maurice Fraser, ed., *Britain in Europe* (London: Stratagems, 1998).

44. The suggestions favored by joint roundtables of the European Policy Forum and the Hansard Society for the Study of Parliamentary Government in the UK in conjunction with the UK office of the European Parliament on June 24 and December 2, 1996, in London are summarized in Graham Leicester, *Westminster and Europe, Proposals for Change: The Role of National Parliaments in the European Union*, King-Hall paper 4 (London: European Policy Forum, April 1997).

45. For an authoritative British view, see David Currie, *The Pros and Cons of EMU* (London: Economist Intelligence Unit, 1997).

8

Germany: Between Unification and Union

Jeffrey J. Anderson

This chapter explores the impact of European integration on the German polity broadly conceived—specifically, the formal institutions, rules, and procedures of democracy, as well as key elements of the German model of political economy. As a founding member of the European Economic Community (EEC), Germany has had a long and intimate association with the European project, which increases the probability that the effects of integration on the polity will be both consequential and conspicuous. This hunch is strengthened by the fact that the Federal Republic of Germany (FRG) was and is no ordinary member. As a young, fledgling democracy in the 1950s, Germany embraced European integration with a markedly different approach to national sovereignty than that of other large European countries. Specifically, the FRG exhibited a strong inclination to vest elements of national sovereignty in supranational institutions and, more generally, displayed an ingrained, even exaggerated support for multilateralism.[1] These reflexes—which can be traced back to internalized lessons drawn from the Nazi experience, as well as to firm international expectations about appropriate West German conduct on the world stage—left the country even more open to supranational influences.

The outline of this chapter is basically chronological. First, I establish central features of the West German model as it developed in the postwar period and examine its relationship to the evolving European project. I then discuss the separate yet synergistic impact of unification and European Union on the German model and present a general analysis of the main findings. Like many other authors in this volume, I uncover a mix of system-reinforcing and system-weakening/transforming influences levied by regional integration on national institutions and processes of democracy.

THE WEST GERMAN MODEL

Relative to other advanced industrial nations, West Germany (1949–1990) looked big but acted small. According to Peter Katzenstein, "West Germany comes closer than any other large industrial state to the logic by which political life in the small European states is organized."[2] Institutionally and ideologically, the Federal Republic's political economy approximated the neocorporatism of its smaller Scandinavian neighbors, based on principles of consensualism, international liberalization, and domestic compensation.[3]

The origins of postwar German distinctiveness are to be found in the domestic legacies of its Second and Third Reich incarnations, as well as in the period of Allied occupation. Its small state political economy and brand of decentralized democracy were also products of conscious choices by West German political and economic elites to adapt to a transformed international system. The West German model, renowned for its stability and capacity to perform, rested on the interplay between interlocking sets of institutional arrangements and a firm yet flexible belief system about the functioning of the economy and its relationship to public authority. The model drew on a deeply rooted societal consensus.

The defining features of the German model are often described in purely institutional terms. The organization of the economy, in conjunction with the organization of the polity, generates a complex distribution of (in)capacities and (dis)incentives for public and private actors alike. Scholars of postwar German political economy link these institutional affects to both economic performance and general characteristics of the policy process, including its tendencies toward continuity, incrementalism, and coherence.

Pride of place in institutional analyses of the West German model is usually accorded to the industry-finance nexus. Unlike British or U.S. firms, which garner investment capital through retained earnings, short-term bank financing, or the stock market, large German concerns tend to rely on long-term financing from a major house bank that typically owns stock in the firm and exercises proxy votes for other shareholders.

The industry-finance nexus in Germany is significant for three reasons. First, it generates a long-range planning and investment horizon for management. Second, the interpenetration of finance and industrial capital, in conjunction with a decentralized German state (discussed later), confers on the private sector the capacity to undertake sector-wide adjustment initiatives. And third, viewed from a macroeconomic perspective it is the connective tissue of German "organized capitalism" in the postwar period, buttressing the higher levels of industrial concentration and greater incidence of interfirm cooperation, that has set the German economy apart from its competitors since the end of the nineteenth century.[4]

West Germany's institutional distinctiveness extends to the system of industrial relations. Among the large industrial democracies, the FRG comes closest to the classic Scandinavian model of neocorporatism. In contrast to the now virtually defunct Scandinavian model—premised on peak bargaining between the social partners and the state—negotiated adjustment in the Federal Republic takes place almost entirely within the private sector, below the rarefied heights of the national level and outside formal parliamentary-electoral channels.[5]

Thus German associational life is well developed and highly articulated; interest groups enjoy ready access to and legitimacy within the policy process. That said, the Federal Republic is not especially known for its participatory culture along the lines of the United States despite such notable examples as the greening of German politics in the 1980s, which entailed strong bottom-up, grassroots mobilization. Politically, German citizens tend more toward conventional, passive modes of participation; public opinion polls in the 1980s began to pick up signs of increasing political disaffection and apathy, with the mainstream political parties and "politics as usual" coming in for the brunt of the criticism.

Trademark institutional features of the German model are not confined to the economic sphere. Indeed, the patterns of coordination and decentralized negotiated adjustment are replicated to a remarkable degree inside the state. The symmetry between the public and private spheres is an important aspect of the postwar German model.

A defining characteristic of the German state is its decentralized structure. The starting point here is the FRG's postwar constitution, the Basic Law, which prescribes a territorial and functional separation of powers that sets the postwar German state model apart from most of its western counterparts. Territorially, decentralization takes the form of federalism—more precisely, administrative or horizontal federalism. State governments (Länder) enjoy significant political autonomy vis-à-vis the central government and play a key role in implementing national policies because of the federal government's lack of a field administrative apparatus.[6] In contrast to the American or vertical variant of federalism, the Land governments, each based on a regional parliamentary majority, play a formal role in the national legislative process through direct representation in the upper house, the Bundesrat. Thus the national government is drawn into regular negotiations with the Länder over large portions of its legislative agenda, a process that is often complicated by the injection of partisan politics into federal-state relations.

Functional decentralization at the heart of the federal (i.e., national) apparatus takes essentially three forms. The first is the constitutionally guaranteed independence of the Bundesbank.[7] Thus although fiscal instruments remain under the control of elected officials ultimately subject to parliamentary accountability, monetary policy has remained effectively insulated from political pressures—a situation that, in turn, has generated firm, predictable parameters for governments, business, and labor alike.

The second element of decentralization in the state apparatus springs from the autonomy of individual national ministries. The West German doctrine of ministerial autonomy (*Ressortprinzip*) creates a fairly broad scope for individual minister initiative and necessitates a greater need for coordination mechanisms at the highest echelons of government. The result is that the German policy process is more compartmentalized than is the case in other parliamentary democracies, a characteristic observers describe as "policy sectorization."[8]

Finally, decentralization also results from largely extraconstitutional factors, such as the organizational strength of political parties (*Parteidemokratie*) and the perennial fact of coalition government.[9] In sum, the West German constitutional-political order generates competing centers of authority and power within the state apparatus along both territorial and functional lines. This has contributed to many of the trademark characteristics of the German policy process—specifically, the premium placed on concertation, consultation, and shared power among institutional actors.

The FRG has also been characterized by ideational consensus, captured by the term *social market economy,*[10] which assigns roles and relationships to public and private actors and prescribes economic policy approaches in a way that dovetails harmoniously with the institutional characteristics of the German model described earlier. Where societal production, allocation, and adjustment functions are concerned, social market orthodoxy assigns primacy to the market, defined not in terms of the perfect competition sketched in the economic textbooks or of the American vision of cowboy capitalism but according to the historical legacy of Germany's organized capitalism.

Vis-à-vis the market, state tasks fall essentially into two categories. The first is to uphold the self-regulating economic order by establishing a facilitative framework of rules and regulations (*Ordnungspolitik* or *Rahmenpolitik*). From this principle are derived many traditional economic policy priorities of postwar German governments, whether center-right or center-left. These priorities included price stability; the privileging of investment over consumption, especially as regards the export sector; an open international economy; an arm's-length industrial policy; and an anticartel policy.

The second responsibility of the state is to ensure that the dislocation generated by the operation of market processes is addressed through government social policy broadly conceived. With a rationale many observers trace back to the Bismarckian state, West German policymakers generated a "social" component to the market economy that entails a comprehensive welfare policy, programs designed to address regional economic inequalities, and a limited industrial policy that leaves adjustment strategies to market actors but aims to ease the hardship imposed on individuals and regions by the decline of traditional industrial sectors (e.g., coal, agriculture).

Thus the state is assigned responsibilities and tasks that take it beyond the night watchman state endorsed by neoclassical economists. On the other hand, in the German social market economy the state falls well short of its interventionist and at times omnipresent counterparts in countries such as Japan and France.

The close harmonious fit between ideas and institutions in the West German political economy rested on a deep consensus in society concerning the market and the state and their relationship to one another. Societal agreement over fundamentals manifested itself indirectly in a number of ways, including the high level of policy continuity that characterized the postwar period despite a fair amount of partisan turnover in government, as well as the generally depoliticized manner in which policy was carried out.[11] The consensus was permissive in the same sense that social market economic doctrine was flexible. That is, it afforded policymakers considerable leeway in formulating concrete policy choices and debating their relative worth but at the same time imposed well-understood limits on what was considered acceptable practice in both the public and private sectors.

The outer edges of a societal consensus over institutions and ideology are always contested ground, and the social market economy between 1949 and 1990 is no exception. The political left and the trade union movement tried repeatedly to strengthen the interventionist capabilities of the state; the Social Democratic Party of Germany (SPD) achieved modest success during the 1970s with its concept of *Modell Deutschland*.[12] The lukewarm neoliberalism with which the conservative coalition under Helmut Kohl wrested power from the SPD was an attempt to reorient the consensus toward orthodoxy. Finally, the postmodern challenge issued by the environmental movement in Germany resulted in a greening of the German model as major political parties on both the left and the right have responded to the electoral threat by moving into the ecological issue space, but these changes fell far short of a wholesale reform of the political economy.[13]

Debates over the content of the German model unfolded within clear parameters, however. Although left and right might disagree over the limits of state intervention or labor and capital might differ on the extent of worker participation in management, at no time during the postwar period were the core institutional and ideational features of the West German political economy placed on the table for discussion.[14] The Bonn model served the interests of a cross-class productive coalition centered in the export sectors of the economy and drew on the unswerving support of the state bureaucracy responsible for economic policy.

INTEGRATION AND THE WEST GERMAN MODEL

West Germany was not simply a truncated version of its prewar incarnation but a new polity with tender democratic roots and uncertain economic prospects. And so, based on hard-nosed instrumental calculations, German elites embraced multilateralism, in particular European integration. Economic integration combined with collective security through the North Atlantic Treaty Organization (NATO) offered the Federal Republic concrete opportunities to consolidate democracy, regain elements of its forfeited sovereignty, create the foundations for economic reconstruction and recovery, and hold the door open for eventual reunification with East Germany. In this manner, early German support for European multilateralism can be linked directly to domestic interest politics.

"Polity" interests drove the West Germans toward Europe during the late 1940s and 1950s. With the exception of the left, political elites viewed participation in a community of Western European states as a means to anchor democracy permanently on German soil.[15] These same political groupings, located on the right and in the liberal center, also valued integration as the unavoidable yet ultimately acceptable price for regaining elements of state sovereignty relinquished in the aftermath of total defeat.

Achieving an "equality of rights" with its European neighbors was viewed in Bonn as the sine qua non for both the international rehabilitation of the new German republic and the domestic objective of reunification.[16] It was also seen as central to the country's economic recovery and reconstruction. Regaining economic sovereignty, in other words, required a multilateral approach to Europe.[17]

The coincidence of European integration and polity consolidation in the Federal Republic meant that "integration became a key part of postwar economic and political values in the FRG."[18] Interest groups and citizens alike saw the economic benefits of the *Wirtschaftswunder* as inextricably linked to German membership in a larger European mission.[19] Political and economic elites, for their part, saw the EEC not only as a source of concrete economic and political benefits but also as a means of preserving and strengthening the defining ideational and institutional features of the German model of political economy.

Interest politics alone, however, cannot fully account for much of Bonn's external behavior, including its pacifist military security policy, its approach to national sovereignty, and its reluctance to engage in unilateralism. One must look beyond material and political interests to the politics of identity in postwar Germany.[20]

Initially, the new collective identity took shape as the antithesis of the Third Reich. It also reflected foreign expectations about acceptable German behavior on the international stage.[21] European integration reinforced this process of national identity formation. The multilateral frameworks created by the Paris and Rome treaties provided welcome shackles for a new and untested democracy and allowed Germany to signal its changed and ultimately benign identity and intentions to the rest of the world.

Over time, new dimensions materialized in postwar German identity, ones characterized more by what the country had become than by what it once was.[22] This evolving collective identity manifested itself in Germany's approach to integration; its general goal in European Community (EC) politics was to erect institutional and normative frameworks at the supranational level that would nurture or otherwise support its successful domestic economic formula. Bonn's objectives in various EC policy areas were to preserve these supranational frameworks and adapt them to changing domestic and international circumstances.

Indeed, up until 1989 Germany's domestic and supranational policies stood in harmony with one another; each set parameters for the other, and each reinforced the principles underpinning the other. By the end of the 1980s, a high level of congruence had emerged between the Federal Republic and the European Community.[23]

Institutionally, both entities were characterized by cooperative federal arrangements in which authority and competencies are shared among executive branches at multiple levels within the larger political system.[24] In each system the policy process is highly sectorized, encompassing a diversity of segmented governance regimes.[25]

Parallel ideational principles underpinned the rules of the game in each system. Political and economic actors in the Federal Republic and the EC valued and practiced consensualism, a logical normative component of a constitutional order based on cooperative federalism.[26] Similarly, the norm of subsidiarity was firmly established in each system. This principle, which is again consistent with the institutional features of each system, prescribes that "policy decisions be made on a level as close as possible to the one on which they are implemented while remaining consonant with the basic principles of social justice."[27] One has only to look at Britain or France to observe a fundamentally different set of domestic political assumptions at work, as chapter 7 in this volume amply documents. In the economic sphere, the two systems view the relationship between public authority and the market in similar terms; that is, much of the German doctrine of the social market economy finds a counterpart in the social-liberal orientation of the EC's common market.

Finally, the content of German and EC policies dovetails sufficiently to suggest broad areas of common interest between German policymakers and Community officials. Many of these areas were touched on earlier; they include essentially liberal external trade and internal market policies, price and structural support for agriculture, the social compensation principles underlying regional economic policy, and the price stability orientation of Economic and Monetary Union (EMU).

Congruence, it should be stressed, was the result of reciprocal influence and convergence and not strictly the outcome of Germany's projection of its model onto the rest of Europe. As a member of the EC, Germany consistently sought to intensify and expand the multilateral principles on which the European project rested. Politically, this strategy remained viable throughout the postwar period because it satisfied the expectations of other Community members as to the acceptable face of German participation and influence in Europe. This approach also drew on a firm but permissive domestic consensus about the German model and the country's place in Europe, a consensus nurtured by economic prosperity. Public opinion either approved or took little notice of the political leadership's policy of exchanging long-term intangible benefits for short-term material costs.

When one observes the constellation of ideas, interests, and institutions that comprised the West German model of democratic capitalism and traces out their relationship to the institutions and policies of the European Community, it is difficult to avoid using the term *equilibrium*. Each drew on the other for support, and each influenced the other as adjustment imperatives thrust themselves onto the political agenda from within and beyond the permeable borders of the Community. The principal issue addressed in the following sections is whether unification and union have had an impact on this equilibrium.

THE GERMAN MODEL AND UNIFICATION

Unification resulted in a wholesale transfer of the West German model in Europe to the new eastern territories. The floodgates were opened after the March 18 elections in the German Democratic Republic (GDR), which handed both reform communists and democratic socialists a stunning defeat by the Alliance for Germany and the Alliance of Free Democrats—both closely linked to the coalition parties in Bonn. The East German electorate voted in overwhelming numbers for markets, democracy, and unification and rejected in no uncertain terms a "third way" between democratic capitalism and state socialism.[28]

Nationally, unification was accomplished in two stages. The State Treaty

(*Staatsvertrag*), which went into effect on July 1, 1990, transferred the West German social market economy to the east. Political unification was ushered in on October 3, 1990, by the Unification Treaty (*Einigungsvertrag*). With few exceptions, it replaced the GDR political system with the West German system. GDR demands for concessions ranging from the symbolic (a new flag and national anthem) to the structural (a federal ministry of reconstruction, provisions for direct democracy, a constitutionally guaranteed right to work) went nowhere. Supranationally, in 1990 Bonn and Brussels reached a complex package agreement on transitional arrangements that acknowledged the special needs of the *Beitrittsgebiet* (literally, "acceding area") while safeguarding the interests of the other member governments and Bonn's commitment to a rapid transfer to the former GDR of the EC's demanding *acquis communautaire*.

The metaphor of institutional transfer should not obscure the tangible changes to the German model wrought by unification. For example, although the extension of West German democracy to the GDR was accomplished with little or no change to the basic principles underpinning the system, national institutions required some recasting to accommodate the territorial expansion. The lower house (Bundestag) expanded from 518 to 656 seats to accommodate the east's members of Parliament. The number of seats in the upper house of the federal Parliament, the Bundesrat, was expanded from 11 to 16. Weighted voting arrangements in the Bundesrat were also changed to reflect the addition of new members; as a result the four largest Länder (North Rhine-Westphalia, Bavaria, Baden-Württemberg, and Lower Saxony)—all located in the former West Germany—now have enough votes to block proposed amendments to the constitution, which require a two-thirds majority.[29]

In addition to formal changes in structure, the transfer of West German federalism generated new stresses and strains. The sheer increase in the number of Länder has complicated the process of consensus building, both among the sixteen Länder and between the Länder and the federal government.[30] Adding to the problems of intergovernmental consensus formation are the much larger disparities between rich and poor regions that have opened up since October 3, 1990—a dividing line that finds expression in the Bundesrat, where the poorer states now hold a numerical, if not a party-political, majority.[31]

Alongside these admittedly modest changes to the formal constitution, unification altered—at least in the short term—some standard features of the German political process, or what is sometimes referred to as policy style. In the context of great uncertainty and increasingly desperate economic conditions in the former GDR, West Germany's "Grand Coalition State"[32]—characterized by close concertation among government and opposition parties, the federal bureaucracy, state (Land) governments, and peak associations—gave way to a considerable number of autonomous, centralized initiatives on the part of the political executive, centered around the chancellor's office. In short, the Federal Republic's "enabling state" transformed itself, perhaps only temporarily, to meet the specific challenges raised by the formal unification process.[33]

Beneath the formal process of institutional transfer, an ongoing transfer—or perhaps better put, projection—of West German interests and ideas took place, the success of which is in the end far more problematic. Business, agricultural, and labor organizations began to extend into the eastern territories shortly after the breaching of the Berlin Wall, in many cases imposing a western German interest agenda on their new eastern members and thereby sowing the seeds of future east-west discord. The projection of West German ideas—especially identity—was also a prominent feature of official government statements, parliamentary speeches, press interviews, and election campaign rhetoric. The goal of ideational-identity transfer went largely uncontested in the vacuum that reigned in the postcommunist GDR.[34] And although GDR citizens in the aftermath of November 9 appeared to shed their "double consciousness," seeking refuge in "a larger national identity,"[35] this by no means guaranteed a long-term transformation. In fact, institutional transfer did not automatically entail its ideational counterpart. Public opinion polls conducted in East Germany in 1989 and 1990 revealed substantial opposition to West Germany's security identity (i.e., NATO membership), skepticism toward European integration, and lingering support for social and economic principles that would be difficult to reconcile with social market orthodoxy.

THE GERMAN MODEL AND EUROPE AFTER MAASTRICHT

The Treaty on European Union (TEU) was negotiated at Maastricht in December 1991 and was signed by the leaders of the twelve member governments in early February 1992. With some notable caveats and exceptions, the member governments committed themselves to the twin and inseparable objectives of economic and political union. Germany's support for the TEU sprang from deep-seated convictions about the integration process to be sure, but that cannot be divorced from concern about the impact of unification on relations with its European partners. In effect, Bonn asked for "the golden handcuffs"—that is, continued anchoring in the West— and its European partners obliged.[36]

The impact of European integration on Germany during this period— essentially the 1990s—can be divided into two categories: formal political institutions and state-society relations. The following subsections catalog these various changes; a discussion of their implications appears in the chapter's conclusion.

Formal Institutions of German Democracy

As elsewhere in the Community, ratification of the Maastricht Treaty raised several constitutional issues in Germany. Some were technical in nature, involving the need to bring Germany's Basic Law in line with specific provisions of the treaty; for example, amendments were required to allow European Union (EU) nationals residing in Germany to vote in local and European elections and to enable the government to transfer the functions and competencies of the Bundesbank to a European central bank at some later date. Others went much deeper, however, raising fundamental questions about the direction of integration and whether the TEU represented a sea change in the relationship of the EC/EU to its member governments—thus requiring a comprehensive reformulation of the principle of integration in the national constitution. This issue provoked a wide-ranging constitutional debate in Germany, one that ultimately led to a significant reordering of formal relationships among the main institutions of government.

Since the 1950s, integration had been regulated by Article 24(1) of the Basic Law, which states that "the Federation may by legislation transfer sovereign powers to intergovernmental institutions." There was general consensus among political elites that a new amendment was necessary in light of Maastricht, both to clarify institutional relationships and to reassure an increasingly restive public (discussed later).[37] Major disagreements, however, which in many cases cut across party divisions, opened up among government ministers, Bundestag members, and representatives of the Länder regarding the appropriate constitutional language for achieving these objectives.

The charge against the prevailing constitutional underpinnings of integration in the Basic Law was led by the federal states, which since ratification of the Single European Act (SEA) in 1987 had voiced growing concerns about EC encroachments on their sphere of competence, aided and abetted by Bonn through Article 24(1).[38] In essence, the Länder argued that EC politics increasingly constituted not foreign affairs but "European domestic policy," and as such the Länder were entitled to territorial representation on EC legislation that impinged on their powers and competencies.[39] Since formal ratification of the treaty required Bundesrat approval, Länder demands carried considerable weight in discussions with a skeptical coalition government and deeply concerned civil servants.[40]

Overlapping this debate over Europe and federal-state relations was a heated discussion of the democratic merits (or lack thereof) of the TEU.

Led by representatives of the SPD but drawing on supportive statements by coalition members and Bundesbank officials, critics of the treaty argued that Germany had given away core elements of sovereignty—symbolized by the fate of the deutsche mark under EMU—in exchange for very limited and ultimately inadequate provisions to strengthen the democratic features of the Community. In short, the democratic deficit would widen still further because of Maastricht, with political union lagging well behind the inexorable march of economic and monetary union.

A concrete result of these wide-ranging discussions was a new Article 23.[41] Essentially, the new article moves the German commitment to participate in European integration from the preamble to the body of the constitution and makes this commitment conditional on specific features of the supranational entity that result from the integration process. Specifically, "the European Union must rest upon democratic, social, and federal principles, adhere to the rule of law and the principle of subsidiarity, and guarantee fundamental rights and freedoms on a level essentially equivalent to that guaranteed by the Basic Law."[42] The article authorizes the government to transfer authority to the EU only after conducting elaborate and early consultations with the lower house of Parliament and, more stringently, obtaining the formal consent of the Bundesrat. Indeed, EU initiatives that fall mainly or exclusively within the sphere of authority of the Länder (as defined by other articles of the Basic Law) are subject to a Bundesrat veto, for all intents and purposes. Moreover, on domestic matters of exclusive Länder competence, as set out in other parts of the Basic Law, Article 23 stipulates that the right to represent the FRG's position in the Council of Ministers will be transferred to an official appointed by the Bundesrat.

The sense that Maastricht had prompted a democratic-institutional backlash in Germany was further reinforced by the Federal Constitutional Court's ruling of October 12, 1993, on the constitutionality of the TEU, particularly with respect to basic principles of democracy and the rule of law.[43] Although the court rejected all complaints against the Maastricht Treaty, clearing the way for formal ratification, its decision reaffirmed the role of the national Parliament—specifically the Bundestag—in securing democratic legitimization of the integration process. In affirming the constitutional compatibility of the TEU with the Basic Law, the court also repeatedly delved into the realm of the hypothetical, stating "that Community acts not covered by the constituting treaties are not binding in Germany, that they must be disregarded by German state organs, and that the Court itself will examine Community acts to see if they exceed legal competences."[44]

This statement, combined with the court's consistent references to the European project in language that bespoke a presumption of intergovernmentalism—referring to the EC as a "community of states" (*Staatenge-meinschaft*) and a "federation of states" (*Staatenbund*)—also served, albeit subtly, to place tangible constraints on the integration process. In short, without considerable strengthening of the European Parliament and the creation of a European citizenship, the road to a United States of Europe would eventually become fundamentally incompatible with the principles of the Basic Law. The ruling identified the Bundestag and the Federal Constitutional Court itself as the principal guarantors that such a fundamental incompatibility would not come to pass.

Shifts in State-Society Relations

Regarding the broad structure of state-society relations in Germany, Maastricht and its aftermath have yet to produce fundamental shifts—Katzenstein's characterization of a decentralized state interacting with a centralized society is still accurate—but change is nonetheless apparent, some of it potentially significant. Europe not only represents a parallel focus of group activity, but it is beginning to influence some of the defining features of the postwar German model.

As in the case of formal institutions, the Länder have been at the forefront of change in this area. Dating from the early 1980s, when the Länder began to set up independent offices in Brussels to monitor the policy process and represent their interests, the federal states have pushed hard to establish an institutional presence at the supranational level—not only for themselves but for the regional level of government throughout the Community. The "Europe of Regions" initiative, which began with a conference sponsored by Bavaria in 1989 and culminated with the creation of a Committee of the Regions within the treaty framework at Maastricht, can be interpreted as a German-led mobilization effort designed to create a "third-level" voice in EU affairs.[45]

To date, the impact of this regionalist dynamic at the supranational level has been modest. The Committee of the Regions has evolved little beyond its treaty-defined role as a consultative (and not a decisionmaking) body. This lack of progress is in part a result of the constraining effects of treaty rules, but it can also be ascribed to two other influences. First, the political assertiveness of the German Länder has not been matched by their counterparts in other member countries, except in the Belgian regions. Institutionally weak and therefore dependent on their national governments, regional authorities elsewhere in the EU are simply not in a position to advance the regionalist agenda set out by the Germans. According to Charlie Jeffery, "Indeed, it would not be completely unfair to say that at the moment the Länder to all intents and purposes *are* the 'third level' in Europe."[46] Second, the national governments have proven very adept at wrapping themselves in the mantle of regionalism or at least its practical corollary of subsidiarity. The effect is to dilute the distinctiveness and power of the regionalist agenda in Brussels.

Nevertheless, the regionalist dynamic is having significant effects *within* Germany. Länder efforts in Brussels have opened the door to alternate sources of information, finances, and political support that have enabled them to shore up their position in the domestic policy process. As institutional actors, the voice of the Länder has been strengthened vis-à-vis both the federal government and their own municipal authorities.

Interest associations, especially business and labor, have also responded to the intensification of integration with organizational and strategic adjustments that reveal a combination of opportunistic and defensive motivations. Matters have progressed farthest among business interest associations (BIAs), the members of which have faced directly the consequences of both internal market liberalization and the expansion of regulatory competences in Brussels.[47] At both the sectoral and peak association levels, BIAs have attempted to strengthen European umbrella groups and to improve their own organizational capacities to monitor and influence the EC/EU policy process.

Strategic shifts have also emerged. With the expansion of Qualified Majority Voting in the Council of Ministers since the 1980s, German BIAs have had to rethink their standard methods of operation in Brussels. No longer able to rely on the national veto, BIAs have begun to think in terms of building cross-national alliances to increase the chances that their positions line up with the likely winners in the Council.

Despite these organizational and strategic imperatives wrought by integration, many German industry associations have already lost their monopoly of representation in Brussels, as larger member firms (e.g., BMW, Daimler-Benz, Siemens) set up offices in response to what they see as a decline in the quality of service provided by the European and national umbrella associations. Thus German industry associations face a difficult challenge—coping with the consequences of organizational fragmentation at the European level.

German BIAs will no doubt continue to represent their members' interests in Brussels but at a diminishing level of performance. The only member firms able to compensate would be the large corporations capable of and willing to maintain their own offices in Brussels. Indeed, in recent years the European Commission—ever starved for informational resources and ever vigilant for key political allies—has demonstrated a willingness to bypass the cumbersome Euro-groups and national umbrella associations and instead work directly with individual corporations. Since the success of the German economy has not rested solely on the performance of Daimler-Benz and Siemens but on hundreds, indeed thousands, of innovative small and medium-sized firms, and since continued economic success is increasingly bound up with the flow of Community affairs, the transformation of the Brussels interest group scene into a club for the truly wealthy would be a problematical development for German industry as a whole.

The distinctive role of finance capital in Germany has also grown more open to supranational influences, although the effects resemble opportunities rather than threats from the vantage point of the banks. Already beset by larger forces of globalization, German finance responded to the liberalization of European capital markets—launched with the single market initiative and reinforced by the prospect of a single currency by decade's end—with ambitious buyouts and mergers that have given the sector an increasingly international profile. This process, combined with the possible impact of domestic legislation designed to reduce the equity-based influence of the banks on industrial concerns, could transform the industry-finance nexus in Germany, with as yet unforeseeable consequences.

The challenges confronting German labor are equally fundamental and perhaps more immediate. The gains registered at Maastricht in the realm of European social policy, coupled with subsequent initiatives such as the European Works Councils directive, have seen an enhancement of labor's presence in Brussels, to be sure, with German unions at the forefront.[48] The neoliberal projects embodied in the single market initiative and EMU, however, are taking place largely and literally over its head, as organized labor in general continues to play a modest part in EU affairs.

Perhaps the biggest supranational threat to German labor comes, ironically, from Eastern and Central Europe—that is, the former Soviet zone of influence. Germany's post–Cold War *Ostpolitik*, which entails free trade in the short term coupled with formal enlargement of the EU eastward in the long run, poses a tangible threat to the high-wage German economy. Friction is already apparent in the eastern parts of Germany, where cheap "black" labor from Poland has caused acute labor unrest in the construction industry. Left unaddressed, this issue—in combination with the EU policy effects outlined next—could eventually weaken German labor's long-standing support for both integration and the principle of free trade.

Europe's impact on state-society relations in Germany is also felt through concrete policy initiatives launched in Brussels, occasionally with the enthusiastic support of the Bonn government. In some cases these initiatives have redrawn the balance of power between center and periphery, albeit on a modest scale. A good example can be found in the recent history of the structural funds, the EC/EU policy instrument designed to ameliorate regional economic disparities. An eastern German lobby, led by the Land governments, drew on the support of the European Commission, as well as allies in the federal bureaucracy, to secure the importation of an EU regional development model, fashioned after the needs of the European periphery—over the objections of the Bonn ministry responsible for overseeing the program. What was greeted in eastern Germany and Brussels as a victory for subsidiarity was decried in the Federal Ministry of Economics as an unwarranted intrusion on the federal government's constitutional obligation under Article 72 of the Basic Law to bring about equality of living standards within Germany.

Europe presents a more profound challenge to a key element of the German model—namely, concrete policies that comprise the "social" component of the social market economy. The SEA/TEU liberalization project combined with unification to generate a new edition of an old debate: the question of Germany's status as an attractive location for manufacturing industry. The impetus for this revived discussion was provided by the business community, which began to question whether the country—which for many years has qualified as a high-cost production location—could continue to conduct business as usual under radically changed circumstances. Industry peak associations and individual firm management blamed the unions and government policies for weakening *Standort Deutschland* to the point where Germany now ranks number one in Europe on a variety of cost factors: the highest wages, the shortest work week, the most vacation days, the most burdensome business taxation system, and the most stringent environmental standards.

Europe played a central role in business's case. The BDI, joined by the other peak business associations, maintained that the SEA and the push for EMU would generate intensified competition not just between firms but also between national production locations in the EC.[49] Industry associations called on the government, in effect, to converge unilaterally to the European norm, whether in the area of business taxation, environmental standards, or the "social wage." In short, they argued, the prospect of an integrated European economic space places a new onus on Bonn: the need to take account of the current practices in other members' countries and to reconcile the competitive needs of industry with those practices when legislating. Failure to do so will result in an exodus of investment and, therefore, jobs.

The federal government has also embraced self-imposed constraints emanating from its commitment to EMU. Specifically, the EMU convergence criteria, particularly the criterion governing the size of the annual budget deficit, played a part in the government's decision in 1996 to introduce a comprehensive austerity program to Parliament that included a public-sector wage freeze and cutbacks in social policy expenditure.[50] Welfare retrenchment alone was supposed to save the government DM50 billion, or approximately US$33 billion, in 1997.[51] The proposals elicited swift and total condemnation from union representatives and leaders of the main opposition party, the SPD, who accused the government of undermining the very foundations of the postwar German social contract. Employer associations and conservative economists criticized the proposals for not going far enough.

In the midst of these myriad reverberations, it is perhaps no surprise to find that European integration is playing to a more skeptical German public. The permissive consensus regarding Europe began to fray with the signing of the Maastricht Treaty, which many German citizens believed represented an unnecessary and unwarranted encroachment on their national currency and all it stands for.[52] German public opinion toward Europe has been unsettled further by the Community's loss of momentum post-Maastricht, bitter conflicts with the British and others over EC/EU priorities, and perceptions that Brussels is becoming more an obstacle than a facilitator.[53] A recent European Commission clampdown on industrial subsidies in eastern Germany, which exposed illegal aid practices involving large firms such as Volkswagen in Saxony and Bremer Vulkan shipbuilders in Mecklenburg–West Pomerania, has led to a souring of attitudes toward the EC in the new Länder. Indeed, it is a measure of just how much the permissive consensus on Europe has softened since the Maastricht summit that the SPD could begin seeking electoral advantage after 1995 by presenting a more Euro-skeptical position on EMU and enlargement.

Sometimes leading and sometimes following public opinion, German political elites now express a more sober outlook on the long-run goals of integration—a change in tone unprecedented in the history of the Federal Republic. For example, in November 1993 Bavarian Ministerpresident Edmund Stoiber stated, "We are no longer striving for a federal state. I want a simple confederation." Although government officials immediately distanced themselves from his comments, grandiloquent talk of a United States of Europe is no longer heard in official Bonn circles. Chancellor Kohl, in prepared remarks when he received the Schumpeter Prize in 1993, declared that the EU must not develop into "a European superstate. I find it understandable that people want to be Europeans, but at the same time remain Germans, Frenchmen, Italians or Spaniards. The creation of an European Union does not mean that still essential national and federal structures disappear."[54]

CONCLUSION

Europe is beginning to occupy a pivotal position in divisive struggles over distribution within domestic German politics, as well as over the allocation of sovereignty between the national and supranational levels. This is not only a novelty in postwar German politics but portends major changes in the way in which the German model will function in the future.

If asked to characterize the impact of European integration on Germany in recent years, I would argue that a shift has taken place away from mutually reinforcing dynamics—the national-supranational equilibrium established in the postwar period—to a much more differentiated pattern. Whereas in the past, German governments looked to Europe for multilateral frameworks that supported core features of their domestic model of politics and economics, the situation since unification and union has grown less clear-cut.

System reinforcement still occurs, but it is confined largely to the realm of formal political institutions. The latest round of integration politics, which began with the SEA but hit its stride in the early 1990s, prompted institutional responses from the German Parliament and the federal court that have worked against centralizing dynamics in the sphere of governmental authority. TEU-inspired shifts in the country's federal arrangements provide the clearest example of the reinforcing effects of integration on Germany's decentralized political constitution.

Counterbalancing these outcomes, however, are integration effects—often amplified by pressures and changes associated with unification—that can only be described as system transforming or even system debilitating for the traditional German model of democratic capitalism. The vast majority of these are concentrated in the societal sphere (e.g., public opinion) or at the nexus of state and society (trade unions; the banking system; the welfare state). It remains to be seen whether these "membership effects" carry far-reaching implications for the German political economy and its democratic constitution, to say nothing of the larger European project.

NOTES

1. Multilateralism is an institutional form that "coordinates relations among three or more states on the basis of generalized principles of conduct." Two corollaries follow from multilateralism: (1) The generalized principles of conduct "logically entail an indivisibility among the members of a collectivity with respect to the range of behavior in question," and (2) expectations of diffuse reciprocity among members generally flow from successful multilateralism. John Gerard Ruggie, "Multilateralism: The Anatomy of an Institution," in John Gerard Ruggie, ed., *Multilateralism Matters* (New York: Columbia University Press, 1993), 11.

2. Peter Katzenstein, *Small States in World Markets* (Ithaca: Cornell University Press, 1985), 31. See also Peter Katzenstein, "Stability and Change in the Emerging Third Republic," in Peter Katzenstein, ed., *Industry and Politics in West Germany* (Ithaca: Cornell University Press, 1989), 347; and Kathleen Thelen, *Union of Parts: Labor Politics in Postwar Germany* (Ithaca: Cornell University Press, 1991), 4. Even those who do not expressly note this paradox of size end up placing the postwar German case in the company of the small European democracies. See Peter Gourevitch, *Politics in Hard Times* (Ithaca: Cornell University Press, 1986), 207.

3. Katzenstein, *Small States in World Markets*, 68–69.

4. On the subject of organized capitalism, a term coined by economist Rudolf Hilferding, see Christopher Allen, "The Underdevelopment of Keynesianism in the Federal Republic of Germany," in Peter Hall, ed., *The Political Power of Economic Ideas* (Princeton: Princeton University Press, 1989), 263–289.

5. Andrei Markovits, *The Politics of the West German Trade Unions* (New York: Cambridge University Press, 1986); Fritz Scharpf, *Crisis and Choice in European Social Democracy* (Ithaca: Cornell University Press, 1991).

6. Arthur Gunlicks, *Local Government in the German Federal System* (Durham: Duke University Press, 1986), 117. For a brief but thorough overview of German federalism, see Philip Blair, *Federalism and Judicial Review in West Germany* (Oxford: Clarendon, 1981), 1–6.

7. For a study of the Bundesbank in comparative perspective, see John Goodman, *Monetary Sovereignty: The Politics of Central Banking in Western Europe* (Ithaca: Cornell University Press, 1992).

8. Kenneth Dyson, "West Germany: The Search for a Rationalist Consensus," in Jeremy Richardson, ed., *Policy Styles in Western Europe* (London: Allen and Unwin, 1982), 45; Simon Bulmer and William Paterson, *The Federal Republic of Germany and the European Community* (London: Allen and Unwin, 1987), 25–31.

9. For example, the tendency toward ministerial autonomy is further enhanced by the prevalence of coalition government in the Federal Republic; ministers of different party affiliations face strong incentives to use their autonomy to enhance their party's profile in the coalition.

10. The phrase was coined by Alfred Müller-Armack, *Wirtschaftslenkung und Marktwirtschaft* (Hamburg: Verlag für Wirtschaft- und Sozialpolitik, 1948).

11. Katzenstein, *Policy and Politics in West Germany* (Philadelphia: Temple University Press, 1987), 363; Dyson and Wilks, "Conclusions," in Kenneth Dyson and Stephen Wilks, eds., *Industrial Crisis: A Comparative Study of the State and Industry* (New York: St. Martin's, 1983), 257.

12. Josef Esser and Wolfgang Fach (with Kenneth Dyson), " 'Social Market' and Modernization Policy: West Germany," in Dyson and Wilks, eds., *Industrial Crisis*, 106.

13. See Jost Halfmann, "Social Change and Political Mobilization in West Germany," in Katzenstein, *Industry and Politics in West Germany*, 51–86.

14. Observers have noted the absence in the 1980s of a German neoliberal revival à la Thatcherism or Reaganism; see Katzenstein, "Stability and Change in the Emerging Third Republic," 328, and Paul Pierson and Margaret Smith, "Bourgeois Revolutions?" *Comparative Political Studies* 25 (January 1993), 487–520. This element of German exceptionalism suggests an underlying level of consensus over fundamentals among political and economic elites.

15. The SPD opposed all facets of a western integration strategy in the 1950s on economic grounds and because such a strategy would stand in the way of reunification, which required Soviet consent.

16. Alan Milward, *The European Rescue of the Nation-State* (Berkeley: University of California Press, 1992), 197–198. See also Bulmer and Paterson, *The Federal Republic of Germany and the European Community*, 5–6.

17. Milward, *The European Rescue of the Nation-State*, 67–70.

18. Bulmer and Paterson, *The Federal Republic of Germany and the European Community*, 8.

19. Wolfram Hanrieder, *Germany, America, Europe* (New Haven: Yale University Press, 1989), 340–341.

20. National identity refers to "(a) the nationally varying ideologies of collective distinctiveness and purpose and (b) country variation in state sovereignty, as it is enacted domestically and projected internationally." Ron Jepperson, Alexander Wendt, and Peter Katzenstein, "Norms, Identity, Culture and National Security," in Peter Katzenstein, ed., *The Culture of National Security: Norms and Identity in World Politics* (New York: Columbia University Press, 1996), 59.

21. Scholars working in this tradition emphasize the extent to which identity is shaped by the broader environment, including the expectations of other actors. See ibid.

22. See, for example, Thomas Berger, "Norms, Identity, and National Security in Germany and Japan," in Katzenstein, ed., *The Culture of National Security*, 317–356.

23. The following paragraphs are based on Simon Bulmer, "European Integration and Germany: The Constitutive Politics of the EU and the Institutional Mediation of German Power," in Peter Katzenstein, ed., *Tamed Power* (Ithaca: Cornell University Press, 1997), 47–79.

24. In Germany, cooperative federalism embraces the federal government (Bund) and the states (Länder), whereas at the EC level parallel institutions bring together the member governments and supranational actors such as the European Commission. See Fritz Scharpf, "The Joint-Decision Trap: Lessons from German Federalism and European Integration," *Public Administration* 66 (autumn 1988): 239–278; and Alberta Sbragia, "Thinking About the European Future: The Uses of Comparison," in Alberta Sbragia, ed., *Euro-Politics* (Washington, D.C.: Brookings Institution, 1991), 257–291.

25. Bulmer, "European Integration and Germany," 68–69.

26. Community observers are fond of pointing out that even with the increasing legitimacy of Qualified Majority Voting in the Council of Ministers during the 1980s, most decisions were reached on the basis of consensus, or informal unanimity, so as not to stretch the fabric of consensus among EC member governments. See Wolfgang Wessels, "The EC Council," in Robert Keohane and Stanley Hoffmann, eds., *The New European Community: Decisionmaking and Institutional Change* (Boulder: Westview, 1991), 133–154.

27. Peter Lange, "The Politics of the Social Dimension," in Sbragia, ed., *Euro-Politics*, 231.

28. The final election results (in percentages) were as follows:

Alliance for Germany	48.1
SPD	21.9
PDS	16.4
Alliance of Free Democrats	5.3
Other	8.3

Source: Konrad Jarausch, *The Rush to German Unity* (New York: Oxford University Press, 1994), 126.

29. Hartmut Klatt, "German Unification and the Federal System," in Charlie Jeffery and Roland Sturm, eds., *Federalism, Unification, and German Integration* (London: Frank Cass, 1993), 5. See also Heinrich Mäding, "Die föderativen Finanzbeziehungen im Prozeß der deutschen Einigung," in Wolfgang Seibel, Arthur Benz, and Heinrich Mäding, eds., *Verwaltungsreform und Verwaltungspolitik im Prozeß der deutschen Einigung* (Baden-Baden: Nomos Verlagsgesellschaft, 1993), 319.

30. Manfred Schmidt, "The Domestic Political Economy: Germany in the post-1989 Period," Paper prepared for the International Political Science Association Convention, Kyoto, March 25–27, 1994, 8.

31. Ibid., 9. This imbalance threatened to strengthen the importance of territory over party in the Bundesrat. On the latter cleavage, see Gerhard Lehmbruch, *Parteienwettbewerb im Bundesstaat* (Stuttgart: Verlag W. Kohlhammer, 1976).

32. See Schmidt, "The Domestic Political Economy," 5.

33. Wolfgang Streeck, "German Capitalism: Does It Exist? Can It Survive?" in Colin Crouch and Wolfgang Streeck, eds., *Political Economy of Modern Capitalism: Mapping Convergence and Diversity* (London: Sage Publications, 1997).

34. Witness the anemic and ultimately failed efforts of supporters of the "third way." On the subject of identity politics in the two Germanys at this time, see Hans-Joachim Veen and Carsten Zelle, "National Identity and Political Priorities in Eastern and Western Germany," *German Politics* 4 (April 1995): 1–26.

35. Konrad Jarausch, *The Rush to German Unity*, 127.

36. Timothy Garton Ash, *In Europe's Name* (New York: Random House, 1993), 358.

37. There were dissenting voices to be sure, with some constitutional scholars and political actors arguing that Article 24 was sufficient to accommodate the TEU.

38. Charlie Jeffery, "The Länder Strike Back: Structures and Procedures of European Integration Policy-making in the German Federal System," Discussion Papers in Federal Studies FS94/4, University of Leicester, September 1994, 4.

39. Ibid., 13; Thomas Christiansen, "The Länder Between Bonn and Brussels: The Dilemma of German Federalism in the 1990s," *German Politics* 2 (August 1992), 239–263 at 245–246.

40. Officials in the Foreign Ministry and the Federal Ministry of Economics were fundamentally opposed to any constitutional changes that would diminish or otherwise complicate their positions in the EC policy process, both at home and in Brussels.

41. The old Article 23, after defining the territories to which the Basic Law applied as of the date of inauguration, stated: "In other parts of Germany it shall be put into force on their accession." This article had been used to bring the Saarland into the Federal Republic in 1959, and it provided the vehicle for unification in 1990. With unification, its wording became problematic since it raised the specter of irredentism (e.g., East Prussia or the Sudetenland), and so it had to go, thereby opening up a space in the Basic Law for a new article on European Union.

42. George Ress, "The Constitution and the Maastricht Treaty: Between Cooperation and Conflict," *German Politics* (December 1994): 49.

43. The court considered a number of complaints. Several were lodged by German members of the European Parliament (EP), who contended among other things that the TEU violated basic principles of democracy because it failed to strengthen the EP sufficiently. A separate complaint was filed by a former European Commission official, Manfred Brunners, who argued that the treaty, particularly the provisions relating to EMU, contravened basic principles of democracy guaranteed in the Basic Law.

44. Ress, "The Constitution and the Maastricht Treaty," 65.

45. Jeffery, "The Länder Strike Back," 9–12.

46. Ibid., 20; emphasis in original.

47. See Jeffrey Anderson, "German Industry and the European Union in the 1990s," in Volker Berghahn, ed., *Quest for Economic Empire: European Strategies of German Big Business in the Twentieth Century* (Oxford: Berghahn Books, 1996).

48. See Lange, "The Politics of the Social Dimension," 230–233; and Stephan Leibfried and Paul Pierson, eds., *European Social Policy: Between Fragmentation and Integration* (Washington, D.C.: Brookings Institution, 1995).

49. See, for example, Bundesverband der Deutschen Industrie, "Antworten des BDI auf den Fragenkatalog zur Standortdiskussion der CDU/CSU-Bundestagsfraktion," Cologne, April 1992.

50. The relevant criterion limits annual budget deficits to 3 percent of GDP; in 1995 the Federal Republic missed the target by 0.6 percentage points. Terence Gallagher, "Waigel Tries to Rally Support for German Austerity," *Reuter*, May 13, 1996.

51. Henry Engler, "EU Likely to Show Bonn, Paris Miss EMU Criteria," *Reuter*, May 12, 1996.

52. Hans Rattinger, "Public Attitudes to European Integration in Germany After Maastricht: Inventory and Typology," *Journal of Common Market Studies* 32 (December 1994): 525–540.

53. The government's penchant for using Brussels as a scapegoat to justify unpopular measures—something by no means unique to Germany!—contributes to public disenchantment with Europe. Support for the EU in eastern Germany has become more tenuous of late, in part because of the tough stance taken by the European Commission in recent years on federal and state subsidies to ailing firms in the region.

54. Quentin Peel, "Bavaria's PM Exposes Split on European Union," *Financial Times*, November 3, 1993, 1; "Kohl spricht sich gegen 'europäischen Superstaat' aus," *Frankfurter Allgemeine Zeitung*, May 19, 1993, 2.

9

Belgium, the Netherlands, Sweden, and Italy: Does Market Integration Affect National Democratic Structures?

Paulette Kurzer

Have European state building and integration in any sense changed or transformed national democratic institutions and conventions? A succinct and precise answer is difficult to formulate because regional integration consists of several distinct components, each of which pulls democratic procedures, norms, and institutions into a different direction. The overall effect is therefore far from uniform and unilinear and is difficult to analyze. A sensible first step is to disaggregate the process of European integration into its constituent parts and examine how each dimension interacts with domestic structures and institutions. Even this will not yield any definite answers, although an apparently fruitful way to explore the relationship among regional integration and national democracy is to distinguish between informal integration (market integration), European state building orchestrated by the European Commission and the European Council, and intergovernmental treaties ratified by all or some member states.

Informal integration, in contrast to deliberate intergovernmental treaties and agreements, involves market liberalization and deregulation and is directly correlated with the cross-border movement of people, trade, jobs, and investments. The 1987 Single European Market is the primary force behind increased market integration, whereas the internationalization of production and financial deregulation has further abetted the mobility of capital, goods, and services. Aside from market liberalization and deregulation, measures voted by the heads of governments and executed by the Brussels bureaucracy also possess the potential to reshape the foundation of democratic institutions.

The European Monetary System (EMS)(1979) exemplifies a type of European-level arrangement to provide joint solutions to common problems. Its aim was to create a "zone of monetary stability" in a world of great currency fluctuations, and by definition its creation necessitated the transfer of government decisionmaking authority to a European committee of national ministers of finance and central bank governors. The successor to EMS (European Monetary Union [EMU]) is even more ambitious and involves the introduction of a single currency in Europe, which will further constrain the ability of elected officials to respond to the demands and needs of national electorates.

Another assembly of institutions (Cohesion Funds) arose to enlarge and administer regional or structural funds to ensure an equitable distribution of the anticipated benefits of faster economic growth and innovation. Regional and subnational governments were encouraged to approach the Commission outside formal central government channels to submit proposals or applications for European Union (EU) funding.

A third element of European integration consists of various intergovernmental agreements or accords, concluded by all or part of the EU member states, to lay the foundation of closer political union. The attempt to construct a European judicial and policing framework illustrates this third variant of integration. Schengen, signed by the majority of EU member states, and the creation of Europol, which is at last a legal entity, symbolize the intergovernmental accords to coordinate political action among the member states.

Interestingly, as Thomas Biersteker points out in chapter 2 of this volume, the recent European achievements in setting up multilateral institutions or frameworks do not necessarily imply the end of state sovereignty. Instead, European countries recognize the limits of unilateral action in certain areas and have reconceptualized the meaning of state sovereignty by accepting a supranational framework, for example, for monetary or fiscal policy and exchange rate determination. In contrast to the challenges associated with international production and global deregulation, however, which have undermined the authority of national governments, police cooperation and harmonization of criminal justice procedures lag behind in terms of an established European regulatory regime precisely because they touch on sensitive aspects of state sovereignty and on national definitions of democratic liberties. Statehood therefore still matters, but its importance varies according to policy regime and institutional structure.

The three components of European integration can therefore be arranged according to their actual impact on national democratic structures, institutions, and procedures. Financial and economic integration (informal integration) produced extensive loss of national policy autonomy and of mechanisms through which democratic consent was forged and functional participation of interest groups in policy fields was fostered. European regional aid (which still accounted for one-third of the EU budget in 1997) may lead to a possible modification of the constitutional structures and political discourse of a nation-state with existing territorial divisions. The expansion of European regional aid is associated with the growth of anti-systemic or radical right political parties, which articulate a certain contempt for social solidarity and universality. By comparison, an intergovernmental treaty to pool resources and information to combat transnational crime has made little impact on national democracy because it touches directly on core areas of national sovereignty, and heads of government feel ambivalent about deepening political cooperation in this field.

Each form of regional integration is discussed in the following sections. The case studies are meant to address the extent to which the three variants of regional integration—market integration, regional institution building, and intergovernmental treaties—constrain, redefine, or enhance national democratic institutions, practices, and procedures.

SOCIAL CONCERTATION AND EUROPEAN INTEGRATION: BELGIUM, THE NETHERLANDS, AND SWEDEN

Economic convergence, driven by market integration and capital mobility, affects both constitutional and informal arrangements that define state-society relations. One kind of social arrangement is the participation of labor market agents (business and unions) in the formulation of macroeconomic policy and in the determination of wage and pay levels through centralized collective bargaining. European member states evolved at least two different renditions of social partnerships in the 1960s. The Christian democratic kind (Belgium and the Netherlands) vested government officials with powers to interfere in income and wage policy, and trade union federations were divided into competing religious or linguistic organizations. In the social democratic model, as exemplified by Sweden, specific agreements kept government officials out of collective wage bargaining and out of the employer-union relationship. In contrast to Dutch and Belgian union organizations, the Swedish trade union federation was highly centralized and comprehensive, and it bargained from a position of strength because the Swedish Social Democratic Party—a natural ally of organized labor—governed Sweden for most of the postwar period. Officials from the ruling Social Democratic Party indirectly mediated between unions and employers by providing extensive social benefits and securing full employment through labor market programs.

Informal integration, growing out of European legislation and capital mobility, has sharpened the tradeoffs between solidarity and efficiency and between social security contributions and corporate productivity. Capital mobility has increased economic vulnerability by exposing domestic markets to the whims of foreign exchange markets and uncontrollable currency speculations. Moreover, the single currency project, negotiated during the Maastricht summit in 1991, obliges government officials to shrink central government budgets to 3 percent of gross domestic product (GDP) and to reduce gross national debt to 60 percent of GDP if it stands higher. Because nearly every country in Western Europe—as a result of demographic pressures, stagnant unemployment, and sluggish growth—copes with runaway social security expenditures, governments everywhere care deeply about ways to relieve business from certain kinds of regulatory and tax burdens. The race to join the single currency gives added urgency to the goal of stabilizing labor costs and social security.

Whereas the threat of fiscal bankruptcy, brought about by a rapidly aging population and a growing number of claimants and the pressure to qualify for EMU, should be sufficient motivation for labor and business to reach agreements on the restructuring of payroll taxes and social welfare entitlements, in fact the greater mobility of capital has eroded employers' willingness to seek compromises with representatives of organized labor. In the meantime, governments have fewer discretionary tools with which to induce union cooperation, influence wage demands, and persuade employers to bargain with union representatives. The trend in countries with a tradition of collective bargaining and social partnerships is toward decentralization and plant-level negotiations. From a distance, it seems obvious that progress in regional integration is coupled to the decline of participatory models of policymaking in Europe.

The 1987 Single Market project prompted central governments to emphasize macroeconomic efficiency and performance at the expense of full employment, public service expansion, and social policy expenditures.[1] Frequently, union leaders and left-of-center politicians admit to the need to raise business confidence and productivity. An improvement in profits and productivity, so the reasoning goes, will ultimately translate into more jobs and stronger economic growth. With union leaders accepting neoliberal viewpoints on economic growth, the national policy discourse focuses on how to lessen labor costs and regulatory restrictions.

The new political context has shifted power relations in the political arena to the detriment of unions and the left. Industrial restructuring has generated high unemployment and a decline in union membership density. But the unions and their allies have also lost terrain with the widespread rejection of steering capitalist economies and of using welfare provisions to achieve full employment and income redistribution.[2] As labor unions have lost much of their prestige in light of stagnant unemployment and a more market-oriented environment, employer and business associations have become more assertive in demanding a restoration of management discretionary power and in striving for fewer labor market regulations and lower social security contributions.

From this, it seems obvious that regional integration is damaging to social concertation. Contrary to expectations, however, the industrial relations systems and social partnerships of the three countries under review—Belgium, the Netherlands, and Sweden—muddled through the new constraints arising from informal integration.[3] Purely domestic developments, moreover, are equally destructive to the industrial relations system and policy consultative style of each country. Regional integration has simply added another layer of complications, whereas the range of solutions has narrowed with the surge in capital mobility and cross-border movement of jobs and goods.

Dutch unions organize only 25 percent of the workforce, down from 37 percent before 1979.[4] Yet the decline in union density rates has only moderately reduced the influence and position of Dutch union leaders because wage accords are frequently extended automatically to entire industry sectors. Unions continue to be important partners in the government process of consensus building because wage costs are considered critical tools for overcoming the handicap of a strong guilder. Government forecasters and business still rely on modest pay agreements to stay competitive. In Belgium, union density is about the same as it was a decade ago (60 percent), and government coalitions are eager to obtain the endorsement of labor leaders to institute social welfare reforms in attempts to consolidate budget deficits. In Sweden, organized labor has also survived the transformation of the Swedish economy, although the trade union federations seem to have suffered the greatest setbacks, as seen in the shocking deterioration of the employment situation.[5]

Of the three national social partnerships, the Dutch kind seems to have found a new lease on life, whereas divisions in the Belgian labor movement are a recurrent problem and continue to interfere with a more constructive relationship with government and business. The Swedish social partnership has witnessed the most striking change, in part because the left and organized labor have occupied an exceptionally strong and influential position in the postwar era.

Belgian Labor Relations in the 1990s

In Belgium, economywide concertation was deadlocked for years and was revived in the late 1980s. In April 1996 the federal government, composed of Christian and social democrats, brokered an agreement that involved an exchange of wage restraint for job creation. The unions were asked to accept a mechanism to limit wage increases to the average in neighboring countries in return for a (vague) promise of halving Belgium's 14 percent unemployment by the early twenty-first century. The accord ran into trouble when the socialist trade union federation refused to sign since the accord did not specify how new jobs would be created. Instead, a reduction in social security taxes and more training and flexible working patterns were supposed to combat high unemployment.[6] In the end, despite two months of intensive consultations between government officials and representatives of the different union and employer organizations, the entire endeavor collapsed.

This attempt to reach a consensual agreement on budget expenditures and job creation caps years of direct government involvement in wage formation. After 1983, the Belgian central government gained more influence over private-sector pay development and used its new powers to intervene in the wage bargaining process. Real wages remained frozen until 1986, and in 1989 a competitiveness norm was legislated that restrained wage gains to what was recorded in common currency in seven trading partners. In 1993 the new law on competitiveness was applied for the first time as the first Jean-Luc Dehaene cabinet announced a three-year wage freeze coupled with social welfare reforms and changes in the cost of living index. Announced in October 1993, the plan contained provisions for a three-year wage freeze (until 1996); drastic cuts in social security payments, health care, and child benefits; and new taxes on property and investment income. The Belgian trade union federations reacted by calling for a general strike in November 1993. Intimidated by union militancy, the cabinet withdrew several measures except for the wage freeze and some cutbacks in social spending. Enabling legislation extended government power to intervene in the wage formation system beyond 1996 to ensure that Belgium qualified for entry into EMU.

Institutions for exchange and conflict resolution still exist in Belgium, although the country has an extremely cumbersome and complicated system in which central agreements set out broad guidelines, sectoral negotiations flesh out the details of the central accord, and company-level bargaining between union delegations and management complete the negotiations. Collective bargaining was at an impasse in the 1980s. In the 1990s it broke through the deadlock of the earlier decade although the minister of employment retains the right to impose parameters for national wage accords and to nullify sectoral agreements.[7] These negotiations have never been easy because the Belgian union movement is split along both ideological and regional lines, and relations between labor and business are often conflictual and precarious.

But unions have been successful in preventing a major restructuring of the social security system. For now, Belgian unions have thwarted a reorganization and rationalization of the archaic social security administration, which is organized in separate social insurance funds managed by labor officials. Whereas the Belgian government had to rely increasingly on general revenues to finance the shortfall in payroll taxes, labor organizations still directed the administration of those funds. Union officials are reluctant to yield control because as a result of their administrative responsibilities, a potentially devastating decline in organizational density has been averted. Union management of the social insurance fund is one of the main reasons union density figures for Belgium are so high in spite of stagnant mass unemployment. Belgian coalition governments are cautious about labor objections because social security reform and restructuring carry enormous distributional implications for Belgian society.

Unemployment in Wallonia is twice as high as that in Flanders (18 percent versus 9 percent, respectively, in 1997), and the former also has an older population. The Walloon dependency ratio on social security is higher than that of Flanders, and the French-speaking socialist-affiliated trade union movement is emphatically opposed to administrative reforms and social expenditure cutbacks, which would disproportionately hurt Wallonia. Because social and economic conflicts in Belgium coincide with regional division and polarization, Belgian cabinet officials must be careful not to aggravate the already deep animosity between the two regions and their political representatives. As a result of the dissension among the social partners, Belgian cabinets routinely resort to enabling legislation to overcome obstructions from labor and its allies in Parliament while modifying its goals to prevent major unrest and opposition.

Labor Relations in the Netherlands

In the Netherlands, governments have also recurrently intervened in the wage formation system and with more success. In the 1970s corporatist consultations led to immobility and deadlock, often broken only by statutory pay intervention by the Ministry of Social Affairs. Between 1970 and 1982, despite many efforts, no wage settlements or social accords were concluded, and government officials issued pay increase ceilings. In 1982 a newly installed cabinet under Prime Minister Ruud Lubbers (a Christian democrat) decided to withdraw from the arena of income policies with the unexpected result that the Netherlands witnessed a resurgence of bipartite consultations and wage determination. The main reason for the revival of bipartite voluntary wage negotiations was the rising fear among unions over the continual deterioration of the labor market. Sluggish corporate performance worried both unions and employers, and the latter also feared constant government intervention if private-sector negotiations failed. Even after 1982 the right-of-center cabinet threatened to implement a price-wage control policy.

Dutch employers have kept collective bargaining alive because they prefer the certainty of bureaucratic unions and routinized procedures to the unpredictability of weakened unions, delegitimized industrial relations, and unwieldy conflicts. Moreover, collective bargaining also encompasses numerous legal regulations pertaining to health and safety in the workplace, equal pay for women, youth training, affirmative action for the disabled, and tax subsidies for the long-term unemployed. Dutch unionism has been saved from oblivion by the conviction of employer associations that unions still serve a meaningful role in society.[8]

Although sectoral consultations are back in vogue in the Netherlands, since 1982 the key policy strategy has been wage restraint to restore business profitability and employment growth. Whereas many accords have been signed between trade union and employer representatives to deal with youth unemployment, the minimum wage, part-time work, and disadvantaged workers, the real action has been aimed primarily at controlling wage development. Successive wage pacts have been effective because total labor costs in manufacturing in common currency are 20 percent lower than those in Germany and 7 percent lower than those in Belgium.[9] Thus Dutch corporatism has carved out a new existence by addressing issues arising from the deepening process of European integration and market liberalization.[10]

In the areas of job creation, budget deficits, and price stability, the Netherlands scores some impressive results, leading observers to speak of the "Dutch miracle." In the 1990s, coalition governments began the difficult task of altering the policy core of the social welfare state.[11] The restructuring of the social security system took place along three fronts. Legislative reforms (in 1994 and 1997) reduced administrative agencies' discretionary power to decide eligibility by drafting precise legal rules on the duties and obligations of beneficiaries. Municipalities were always in charge of social provisions, but the new system introduced a basic allowance for all claimants and a variable supplement or deduction to reflect the recipient's particular living conditions. Because municipalities must pay for the supplemental benefits and can save money by reducing the basic allowance, they have become more exacting about who is eligible for what level of benefit.[12]

The second area of restructuring involved semi-privatizing insurance risk to create new incentives for employers to desist from relying on the social safety net to lay off personnel. Employers must still finance sickness and disability benefits, but they can insure that risk through the private insurance market. Premiums for sickness and disability insurance go up if the number of claimants in the firm rises. Such privatization of risk forces employers to think twice before they push older and less productive employees into disability and sickness programs.[13]

The third reform objective aimed to dismantle the prominent role played by parapublic actors—unions and employer associations—in the administration of the system. Until 1994, unions and employer associations were responsible for the administration and supervision of social insurance programs. Together they treated the availability of generous benefits as an easy solution to dismiss redundant employees during economic downturns or recessions. The cost of dismissals was then passed on to the taxpayer while the recipient received relatively high disability and sickness allowances. In 1994 the parapublic corporatist Social Insurance Council was replaced by an independent professional agency and industrial insurance boards were, in 1997, privatized.[14]

Social welfare reforms and wage restraints have produced two remarkable developments. First, official unemployment is just over 6 percent of the labor force and is below the average for the European Union. Labor participation rates, which stood at 55 percent of the working-age population (fifteen to sixty-four years of age) in 1994 rose to 60 percent in 1997. This is an improvement over the last fifteen years, although it conceals some surprising trends because a large proportion of employees work part-time, defined as working at least twelve hours a week or more. If full-time equivalent employment is taken as a starting point, the labor force participation rate is probably no more than 50 percent. But the Netherlands has gone further compared to Belgium to encourage flexible labor market rules toward part-time employment and has introduced stricter rules concerning the ability of entitlement recipients to refuse paid employment.[15]

The second surprising discovery is the lack of friction that could have been expected in light of the social welfare reforms. To be sure, most of the reforms took place incrementally after extensive consultation with the private sector and union organizations.[16] Many observers agreed that something was amiss with the Dutch welfare model, because 15 percent of the Dutch labor force received a disability allowance between 1988 and 1995. Politicians and union leaders generally recognized that the social legislation provided distorted incentives and encouraged abuse or misuse.

It has helped, to say the least, that Dutch social organizations unanimously accept European projects such as the Single Market and the single currency.[17] In the absence of debilitating disagreements on critical issues, social actors and state officials have been ready to correct and revise the role of the caring state. The negotiated consensus produced both winners and losers. From 1977 to 1994 the average inequality in the distribution of aggregate disposable income (meaning income after all taxes and transfers) in the Netherlands increased from 12 to 25 percent, depending on the measure. Thus whereas the average level of inequality remains low by international standards, the distribution has clearly widened, and some people became better off relative to others over the period. One group whose situation has worsened over time is ethnic minorities, whose jobless rate is nearly 25 percent and triple that of the ethnic Dutch population.

Compared to Belgium, however, the Netherlands performed noticeably better in the 1990s, and the level of conflict or friction was much lower. Because distributive conflicts between the two major language communities and divisions within organized labor made negotiated consensus harder to reach in Belgium, governments stepped in directly to settle pay issues. The Belgian case is also different from the Dutch case because most concertation takes place between organized labor and central government officials. Business and employers are not directly engaged in the deliberations on pay-wage policy and social security reforms. But the dominant political bloc in Belgium, the Flemish Christian Democratic Party, has close contact with Flemish business and automatically defends the interests of Flemish employers and firms.[18]

Business and Labor in Sweden in the 1990s

Sweden joined the European Union in 1995 and is an interesting test case as to whether informal nongovernmental integration rather than direct membership in the European Union accounts for the difficulties experienced by labor market institutions and industrial relations systems. In pursuing the "third way,"[19] Sweden combined a vigorous market economy with an activist state and a strong and independent trade union movement. A vast and comprehensive welfare state provided a safety net for the victims of industrial restructuring. In contrast to Belgium and the Netherlands, in the 1980s Sweden did not waver from its postwar course of full employment and public-sector expansion.

By 1994 the Swedish model had gone the direction of Dutch and Belgian postwar commitments. In 1997 the Swedish jobless rate was 12 percent, including those who participated in active labor market schemes. Apparently, Swedish authorities were no longer capable of or willing to pursue a mix of policies and programs to conserve, if not create, jobs.[20] The labor shedding took place prior to Sweden's accession to the European Union, a point which many Swedish voters conveniently ignore in their disenchantment with EU membership.

The rise in unemployment is symptomatic of the irrelevance of the Swedish model in the 1990s, in Sweden and elsewhere. As early as 1982 and more than a decade before EU membership, Swedish engineering employers resisted centralized bargaining and withdrew from peak-level negotiations to strike a separate deal with unions in the metalworking sector.[21] Their decision in the 1980s to abandon centralized wage bargaining terminated the postwar era of class compromises, made famous in the writings of many U.S. academics. In February 1990 the employer organization literally disbanded its central bargaining office and put a definite end to a long and mostly fruitful partnership with labor. Leading the fight against the Swedish model were the most important international firms: Volvo, Ericsson, and SKB.[22]

The breakdown in the Swedish industrial relations system is frequently explained by the competition between blue- and white-collar workers in large firms and its detrimental consequences for the pay structure of Swedish companies. In Sweden the main trade union federation primarily represents blue-collar workers, and a separate labor organization speaks for white-collar workers. In the 1980s the distinction between blue-collar and white-collar work was blurred, yet pay rates differed sharply. Skilled factory workers received less pay than white-collar workers, although they performed similar tasks. In the following years, the trade union federation had to yield to pressures from the rank and file, which demanded increased compensation for its skilled members. In turn, the added category of highly paid workers trickled down and drove up the pay scales for all wage earners. Employers abandoned centralized bargaining to obtain greater wage flexibility because the institutions of centralized wage bargaining could not cope with technological innovations and new job classifications.[23]

In spite of employer success in moving toward enterprise- or industry-level negotiations, nominal wages increased faster in Sweden than in the rest of Europe. Wages in the sheltered sectors, such as public services, continued to gravitate toward manufacturing wages in the first half of the 1990s.[24]

The reason, according to a 1997 report by the Organization for Economic Cooperation and Development (OECD), is that pay solidarity and equity still govern the thinking of union negotiators—even at the industry level—who are loath to yield on the issue of wage compression. Low-skilled workers subsequently find themselves priced out of the job market. In the past, equity considerations, which pushed up overall labor costs, had been checked by periodic devaluation to boost export earnings and limit real wage gains. Until the late 1980s, real wages responded to cyclical fluctuations because a currency devaluation improved the price competitiveness of Swedish exports, and the new gains were only gradually absorbed in subsequent rounds of wage accords.

But global inflation rates have declined in the 1990s and competitive devaluation is no longer a viable option. Each currency devaluation was followed by accelerating inflation, which eventually put new pressure on the currency and prompted another devaluation. In an era of global disinflation and European exchange rate stability, Swedish real wages have become rigid and inflexible. As the pay of low-productivity workers is relatively high, private firms fail to hire sufficient numbers to sustain full employment, and the public sector can no longer absorb job seekers.[25]

Domestic pressures or tensions in the industrial relations system, flowing from technological innovation and new job classifications, contributed to the decline of collective bargaining and social partnership between labor and business. But informal integration also played a role in the decline of the Swedish model. It is not without irony that the Single Market, the pet project of the Delors Commission, stimulated tremendous capital outflows from Sweden, a nonmember of the EC.[26] In turn, as Swedish firms became more established across borders, they sought to integrate employees locally and individually and wanted to see union solidarity weakened at home. They wanted to reward employees through bonuses, profit-sharing schemes, stock options, and share ownership because they treasured certain kinds of employees more than others and wanted to be able to recruit the most skilled and appropriate labor force. As their operations spread over dozens of countries, they demanded the same flexibility they enjoyed abroad at home.[27]

Swedish export firms became increasingly oriented to foreign direct investments abroad during the late 1980s. Thus between 1982 and 1987, foreign direct investment holdings stood at around $2.4 billion. In 1993 the stock of foreign direct investment abroad was over $50 billion, compared with inward foreign direct investment of $14 billion.[28] With such rapid international expansion, the proportion of employees in foreign affiliates of Swedish firms rose to 61 percent of the total workforce of Swedish transnational corporations in 1990, up from 41 percent in 1986.[29] To put this in another perspective, during those four years 200,000 jobs were created in foreign affiliates of Swedish companies and 80,000 jobs were lost in Swedish firms in Sweden.[30] Between 1989 and 1993, one of every four industrial employees lost his or her job because of corporate downsizing and a dramatic decline in capital spending. The unexpected devaluation of the krona in November 1992, following the turmoil in the EMS, improved the cost-price structure and increased exports of finished goods by nearly 9 percent in 1993.[31]

Yet labor force participation rates did not recover to precrisis levels. Swedish firms used their profits to reinforce their presence in, access to, and dominance in foreign markets.[32] Moreover, much capital deepening took place to offset the compression of pay differences, which generally keeps wages high and those of highly technical personnel lower than their marginal productivity.

Capital outflows, rising unemployment, and increased cross-border ventures do not tell the whole story of the decline of Swedish labor-business concertation. Informal integration, which is only partly driven by EU institutions and measures, has altered the calculations of the different participants in the bipartite arrangements. In the past, governments papered over the cracks in the Swedish model by providing special inducements to both labor and business. These incentives generally fueled inflation, which Swedish citizens accepted as the price of full employment. But higher than average inflation rates in a world of highly mobile assets meant that investors, who lost confidence in the exchange rate target, speculated against the currency. Official refusal to yield to speculative pressures in the late 1980s decreased speculative trading in the krona. During the turmoil in European currency markets in late 1992, the Swedish currency fell by 25 percent. Yet this price advantage for Swedish exports did not translate into job creation.

At present, the social democratic minority cabinet, which must rely on the Center Party for parliamentary support, is as eager as any conservative government to placate international markets and build confidence in Swedish macroeconomic management. For this reason Swedish authorities have embraced a less expansive, more German-oriented monetary regime, although the social democratic leadership is abstaining from European Economic and Monetary Union. A mixture of asset sales, tax increases, and spending cuts reduced the country's budget deficit by 12.3 percent of GDP in 1993 to the current projection of a surplus of 1 percent of GDP in 1998.

The committees and advisory councils in the workplace still operate as before, but the central negotiating framework barely exists. Social democratic cabinets are using a language that is alien to the union movement, a language of marketization and dramatic public finance cuts. Years after employers moved away from central wage bargaining, the social democratic establishment embraced EMU criteria and fiscal austerity to prevent devastating exchange rate fluctuations and to attract corporate investments. Considering the current disenchantment with the EU, the social democratic leadership consistently insists that Sweden will not be among the first wave of single currency participants. Whether Sweden joins or not, however, many Swedish international corporations are considering adoption of the euro for handling invoices, transactions, and balance sheet accounting. Rapid conversion to the euro by listed companies could undermine demand for the krona, leading to an outflow of over $16 billion a year. To stem a flood toward the euro, the cabinet must inspire confidence through an economic policy course that sustains a surplus in the central government budget and is geared to price stability. If it does not, many companies will opt for the euro, with severe political consequences for the current government.[33]

Organized interests and elected governments in Belgium and the Netherlands adjusted to the need to stabilize exchange rates and keep inflation in check earlier than their Swedish counterparts. The Dutch encountered the fewest difficulties because social concertation was built on wage restraint and moderation, and that tradition was revived in the 1980s to neutralize an appreciating currency and combat inflationary pressures. The Belgian industrial relations system and labor market organizations never reached the same level of cooperation found in Sweden or the Netherlands. Rather, unions and governments occasionally signed broad social accords to address a particularly acute issue. This erratic ad hoc form of social concertation survived the 1980s and was used to launch a debate on job creation and social security reforms in spring 1996. The Belgian union movement, however, is deeply split along ideological and linguistic-regional lines, and the high unemployment rate in Francophone Belgium (Wallonia) requires that the predominantly socialist union movement block any radical surgery on the social security system. Social concertation is therefore hampered by the divergent and competing interests of labor and the dominance of business conglomerates on the employer side.

To conclude, informal integration exerts extraordinary demands on domestic social partnerships. Problems with social provisions and legislation and imbalances in the labor market are magnified by the cross-border movement of capital, jobs, and goods. But core groups of participants in the previous system of tripartite or bipartite concertation have been able to defend their privileges and access to power. The way this was accomplished and the actual size of the core group vary across countries, but abundant evidence suggests that the accumulation of pressures and constraints has not entirely demolished postwar social partnerships. In the Netherlands a negotiated consensus ushered in new social legislation to reduce benefit claims and expenditures and to keep wage formation under control. In Belgium torturous discussions between the government and different branches of the labor movement have thus far preserved many of labor's privileges. The Swedish social welfare state, in spite of its trimmings, still provides a huge safety net.

EUROPEAN INTEGRATION, DEMOCRACY, AND REGIONALISM: BELGIUM AND ITALY

Regional integration affects the balance of power in the labor market. The same mixture of forces also influences the relationships between different levels of government in the member states. Spurred on by the reduced spending capacity of central government and the widening web of European regulation, subnational politicians in territorially divided countries reevaluate their respective interests and resources and must show greater willingness to commandeer more decisionmaking powers for themselves.

To be sure, territorial claims have increased in countries with regional cleavages or differences. Even then, in countries with noticeable territorial differences such as Italy and Belgium, regionalism as a political movement is the unintended outcome of the loss of policy autonomy, which has diminished the centrality of the nation-state as a political and economic unit as well as the divergent impact of global restructuring and capital mobility on the constituent territories.

In addition, the European Commission intensifies the centrifugal pressure in countries with regional divisions by increasing the size of structural funds (regional aid) and by establishing partnerships with regional and local authorities to enhance the efficacy of its financial assistance to poor regions. Moreover, the Commission has actively solicited regional and local government authorities to submit more fund applications and it has required that national governments consult with local and regional authorities in drafting program applications. Special consultative bodies have been set up to oversee the distribution of structural funds, and the Commission has outlined goals and targets for each eligible region. In 1991, following ratification of the Maastricht Treaty, a Committee of the Regions was formed that had the right to be consulted by the Commission and the European Council of Ministers.[34]

On the one hand, EU assistance, which is targeted to underdeveloped areas, has hastened the formation of regional decisionmaking structures in disadvantaged regions. On the other hand, in Italy as well as Belgium, it is noteworthy that the greatest push for autonomy has come from the rich regions—Flanders in Belgium and northern Italy—which do not qualify for any special EU funding. Regions in Belgium and Italy react to a different set of stimuli, such as the proliferation of European regulation and the desire to manage their own fiscal affairs in light of widely acknowledged economic differences between different parts of the country. European debates on regional decisionmaking autonomy have popularized the concept of greater regional autonomy, even though the most strongly secessionist territorial voices do not directly benefit from EU largesse.

Belgium and Italy share certain peculiarities that help to explain why the drive for regional autonomy is led by the wealthy areas. Both countries have accumulated a public debt stock of over 100 percent of GDP, and both governments have struggled with sizable budget deficits. Consolidation of the central government budget was complicated by the fact that in 1997 net interest payments accounted for between over 8 percent of GDP in Belgium and 10.5 percent in Italy. In spite of these hurdles, Belgian and Italian policy officials and government leaders were eager to join the first wave of EMU members and be part of the core group of single currency countries; therefore, the budget situation required drastic action. Considering the considerable disparities in wealth and income between northern

and southern Italy and between the French-speaking and Flemish prov-
inces, the wealthy regions sought greater fiscal and economic autonomy to
untangle their financial obligations and be released from subsidizing or
transferring funds to the less advantaged regions.[35]

The political momentum for devolution transformed the Belgian state
into a federal structure in 1993. In Italy, federalism is part and parcel of
the ongoing political debates over the modernization of the republic and its
postwar political system. Devolution of state responsibilities is perfectly
compatible with liberal democracy in that territorial decentralization
brings decisionmaking authority closer to the electorate. Subnational authorities can be more responsive to local concerns, which are ignored by
central government officials, and the formation of new representative offices opens the way for younger politicians and new political parties to
capture power from the established elite. In this sense, devolution reinforces fundamental liberal democratic structures and practices.

But in the case of Italy and Belgium, at least some activist groups in the
nationalist-regionalist movement articulate views and goals that challenge
the basic philosophy of democratic universality. Certain elements within
the Flemish political class and the Italian Northern League want to split
the common good and promote the welfare and protection of rights of citizens who belong to the culture of the subnational community. In that
sense, Flemish nationalists and Northern League politicians articulate a
decidedly antidemocratic message of exclusion and repudiate the idea of
social solidarity within a single nation-state.

In Italy, the Northern League, established in 1990, calls for the creation
of a minirepublic in the north. Since most public-sector deficits and debt
can be attributed to the funds spent on the south, a "velvet divorce" would
free the north from subsidizing the south and from paying off the accumulated debt obligations. By its own account, northern Italy has more in common with Baden-Württemburg than with Calabria. In spite of the creation
of regional governments in 1970, the fiscal powers of the new agencies
were restricted and were dependent on general-purpose transfers by the
central government. Supporters of the Northern League, thanks to which
legal changes in 1994 have given regional governments greater revenue
autonomy, are eager to move to fiscal federalism.[36] Then they can position
themselves in the new Europe without having to consider a backward, unproductive, and parasitic south.

In Belgium Flemish nationalists argue for a separation from Wallonia,
which they believe "sponges off" prosperous and industrious Flanders and
is the main reason for the large public debt. Two Flemish nationalist parties—the Flemish Bloc and *Volksunie* (People's Alliance)—are pushing
for a transfer of fiscal policy, health care, and social security to the subnational governing structures so affluent Flanders no longer has to finance

Walloon social security entitlements. Walloon unemployment is twice as high as that of Flanders (18 percent versus 9 percent), and the population is older in that part of Belgium. Some voters allege to be fed up with subsidizing "lazy" Walloons. In turn, the mainstream Christian democrats (the party of Jean-Luc Dehaene) who govern Belgium must pay lip service to the appeals of the extreme separatists with the result that they propose solutions couched in terms suggestive of the discourse associated with the Flemish nationalist parties.

One major contrast with Italy is that the language-regional issue has deep roots in Belgium and in 1993 turned that country into a genuine federal state with three separate regional authorities—Brussels, Flanders, and Wallonia. In Italy regional distinctions existed at the time of the founding of the Italian monarchy in the late 1860s, but for decades the elite or ruling class was able to ignore and thus diffuse regional differences.[37]

The Belgian party most closely associated with separatism is the Flemish Bloc, which received around 13 percent of the Flemish vote in the May 1995 parliamentary election. The Flemish Bloc favors splitting Flanders off from Belgium and returning to a more stable, secure society with no room for the foreigner, the state, and the multinational company. The group was formed in 1978 and won one or two seats in Parliament over the following ten years. The party was propelled into the limelight by its victory in municipal elections in 1988 and its representation in the European Parliament (EP) in 1989. In the EP the Flemish Bloc joined other European right-wing parties and adopted a more recognized right-wing program by calling for the forced repatriation of all non-Western-born residents. The Flemish Bloc experienced a national breakthrough in the 1991 national elections. Along with its anti-Belgium rhetoric, the party espouses common themes of the far right on immigration, the defense of European culture and values, and opposition to liberalism and market capitalism.

Although the Flemish Bloc is shunned by the establishment and its leaders are ostracized, its ability to mobilize unskilled native-born workers and small businesspeople has forced the mainstream to pay careful attention to its platform.[38] The party's success has alarmed politicians and commentators. The party's hard-core supporters' endless vitriol against Belgium and its large migrant population shocks the liberal establishment, especially since a sizable minority of voters identifies with this hateful message.

If the Flemish Bloc is unacceptable to the majority of voters, the *Volksunie* is the old-guard nationalist Flemish party. As early as 1981 the party broached the possibility of splitting Belgium's social security system, which would leave Wallonia in penury and would free Flanders from financing the unemployment and pension benefits of Walloon workers. At that time, the party issued a manifesto that stated "no half measures; Flemish money in Flemish hands and a Flemish state."[39] In the 1990s the attempt to consolidate the budget deficit and reduce the principal public debt set off sharper distributive struggles, and both Flemish and Walloon leaders now offer suggestions to pass the pain of retrenchment onto the other region.

Since 1993 Belgium has been a federal state, and European institution building and treaty negotiations involve the participation and consent of the regions. The federal government must consult the regions (territorial units) and communities (language entities) on EU treaties that impinge upon the competencies delegated to subnational structures. Article 146 of the Treaty for European Union (TEU) permits the direct representation of subnational structures in EU Council meetings that involve areas in which the three communities or regions are exclusively or predominantly competent. Representation rotates and one delegation from a particular subnational entity speaks for Belgium.[40] This has given the territorial and language regions an important role in a policy field usually identified with the powers of the central government and has augmented the visibility and capacities of the regions to project their own separate agenda and also to formulate regional objectives. The imminent arrival of the single currency, however, will diffuse secessionist incentives because a united Belgium is more likely to be able to adjust to external shocks than is a cluster of small semisovereign regions.

In Italy, the Northern League under the leadership of Umberto Bossi resembles the *Volksunie* more than the radical right-wing Flemish Bloc. Founded as the quixotic Lombard League in 1982, the group quickly propelled other regionalist leagues to enter the fray. In 1990 six northern regions banded together to found the Northern League, which secured 17 percent of the national parliamentary vote in 1992 and 11 percent in the 1994 election. The party had a surprisingly strong performance in the 1996 election when it obtained 10 percent of the parliamentary vote and 40 percent of the vote in its heartland, northeastern Italy.

At first some leaders of the leagues claimed to represent the true, pure Italian race and suggested a return to a preunified Italy. Most of this rhetoric has been dropped in favor of a more "cosmopolitan" and less racist campaign, which nonetheless uses questionable ethnoregionalist terms to analyze the differences between "European" and "Mediterranean" Italy, or the north and the south.[41] Although less stridently antiliberal than the Flemish Bloc, the league plays the secessionist card to escape Rome and its clients in the south and has made immigration a major issue that has eventually been incorporated into the platform of other major parties. The Northern League consciously employs blunt, even violent language to mark the boundary between the hardworking folks in the north and the corrupt political class in Rome.[42] Nevertheless, in contrast to the Flemish

Bloc, the Northern League is more of a free market movement, supported by the self-employed and lower middle classes but also by small entrepreneurs who detest the central administrative system.[43]

After its unexpected electoral success in April 1996, the Northern League transformed the vague idea of "Padania," the new republic in the north, into a strategic objective. Relying on a range of powerful symbolic gestures and novelties, the Northern League convened the Parliament of Mantua (where Northern League politicians occasionally meet) and created a force of "Green Shirts" to serve as a militia. The flurry of publicity stunts attracted wide media coverage and legitimated a new turn in the debate on northern grievances against the south. Although few voters really aspire to an independent minirepublic, the Northern League treats the idea of an independent state as a serious option. League activities force Rome to consider it a threat to national unity, and it has placed secession in the middle of the debate. The Northern League has also made the resolution of northern concerns more difficult to achieve since its leaders claim to be content only with the dissolution of the Italian Republic. Most Northern League supporters do not endorse a ministate along the banks of the River Po, but they are deeply dissatisfied with the public institutions, political system, and social organization of the state.[44]

Regionalism in Italy has become a legitimate mobilization point as competitive export-oriented firms view the organization of the Italian state and economy as incompatible with the new Europe of the Single European Market and European Monetary Union. League supporters are pro-Europe and prefer to expand the authority of the European Parliament rather than the structures of regional governments.[45] The supporters of the Northern League want to dilute the ties between the north and the south because European integration has in fact weakened Italy's internal cohesion.

Beginning in the 1950s extra funds and welfare benefits went to the south to enable that part of the country to purchase industrial goods from the north. Rome's proconsumption policies increased demands for goods manufactured mostly in northern industries. But as a result of market liberalization, part of this money is now spent on goods from the EU, whereas the budget crisis and capital flow constraints have reduced the absolute level of spending in the south.[46] Economic ties between the north and the south have been altered, with the result that the north is less tolerant of the waste and inefficiency in Italian state institutions. Basically, European institutional development has offered league supporters a viable alternative to the decaying institutions of the Italian state.

As in Belgium, Europe offers emancipation from the central government in Rome as long as it intervenes less in people's lives than the Italian state. The mayor of Milan, a Northern League politician, worked earlier for the European Commission before entering Italian politics. In an interview he extolled a united Europe of fifty regions but dismissed the idea of a Europe of twelve nations. Northern League politicians exploit the prospects for a closer EU to justify the founding of an Italian federation or, better yet, a new political unit, smaller than its parent but with easy access to Europe. Just like their Flemish counterparts, who want to cast off the declining industrial rust belt of Belgium, league politicians want to get rid of the huge, inefficient Italian state and the unproductive south. In both countries, the TEU placed the idea of "federalism" in the middle of the political agenda. In Italy it is the norm to be a "federalist" even though most advocates have only a vague idea of what that means.

Market liberalization and European state building erode the fiscal autonomy of the central government and spur the quest for self-rule. Although decentralization of decisionmaking structures is usually associated with the strengthening of participatory channels, the regional parties in Italy and Belgium challenge the idea of national solidarity and social citizenship. The regional movements want greater decentralization of state power by asking voters to stop identifying with struggling sections of the country. Their attack on the nation-state is part of the general offensive of revitalized right-wing opinions that blame existing economic misfortune and rising disparities in wealth on individuals in particular regions.

At the same time, membership in the European Union also prevents further territorial fissures. First, the decisionmaking organs of the EU do not accept "regions" as genuine active participants except in debates on regional funding and social cohesion. Second, national sovereignty has been redefined in an age of global financial markets, a borderless Europe, and European institution building. For the regions secession from the nation-state does not guarantee increased autonomy and independence. Although statehood may still confer important advantages in the global economy and in intergovernmental negotiations, it is dubious whether these future ministates will ever possess the limited advantages of statehood. Third, the European Union gives national governments extra resources to diffuse internal tensions among regions. The extra money designated for southern Italy or Wallonia reduces spending claims on the central government's budget.

Finally, the creation of European Monetary Union with a limited number of member states will strengthen the representational importance of central government agencies in Belgium and Italy. Quasi-independent regions will never be allowed direct representation on the European Central Bank Council or even in the European System of Central Banks. National central banks will be the key actors in the new monetary union. Monetary union also places a premium on market size relative to currency area because a larger product market eases adjustments during periods of external turbulence or shocks. In a single monetary regime the regional economies of Italy and Belgium will be better able to address economic shocks if they remain joined.[47]

Therefore supranational organizations also help central governments to resist pressures for devolution and decentralization by providing extra resources and fresh pretexts for mollifying secessionist claims. European integration exerts a paradoxical influence by simultaneously fueling demands for autonomy and restricting those demands to a decentralized decisionmaking authority. The declining importance of statehood and the growing availability of EU funds to level economic disparities moderate demands for genuine independence or secession. European Union and market integration generate at once system-reinforcing and system-threatening effects on member states with existing territorial divisions.

EUROPEAN INTEGRATION, DEMOCRACY, AND LAW ENFORCEMENT: THE NETHERLANDS

One prominent feature of statehood is control over law enforcement and criminal justice. During the Maastricht summit (1991), national governments reluctantly agreed to include police collaboration as one of the nine areas the member states regarded as matters of common interest to achieve the objectives of the European Union, in particular the free movement of persons.[48] Since then, Justice and Home Affairs is housed in the intergovernmental level, the so-called third pillar, and requires unanimity in the Council of Ministers. The Council of Ministers is responsible for establishing uniform attitudes and for promoting all forms of cooperation to actualize the EU objectives. Although resolutions and conventions require unanimity, measures to implement the principles decided upon in the council can be adopted through Qualified Majority Voting.

The preliminary negotiations on the Treaty of Amsterdam (1997) proposed a revision of the Treaty of European Union in the area of internal security, in part to bring Europe closer to the citizen. As a result Justice and Home Affairs received a new title in the Treaty of Amsterdam and are now called "provisions on police and judicial cooperation in criminal matters." The practical importance is that the Council can adopt "framework decisions" to approximate member state laws—which leaves the choice of form and methods of implementation to the member states—and the European Court of Justice receives limited jurisdiction to settle disputes between member states.

In practice, the complicated gyrations of treaty making and amendments have not resulted in better cross-border police cooperation. Each member state firmly believes that its judicial system is superior, and distrust among different national police corps is legendary. Europol, established in 1994

in The Hague, is the first unionwide system for exchanging police information to fight drug trafficking and the criminal organizations involved in
money laundering. Its convention is still unsigned by Belgium, Greece,
Italy, and Luxembourg and its operations have been effectively restricted
to fighting organized crime. Even if Europol becomes fully operationa-
lized in the near future and is working alongside domestic police forces to
investigate cross-border crime, different judicial and legal systems pose
impossible obstacles to better cross-border cooperation. Common rules
and standards must be set so that, for example, a German police official
who captures a criminal driving a stolen Belgian car can return the car to
its rightful owner and indict the thief. For now, no common procedures are
in place to bring cross-border crimes to a satisfactory resolution. In spite
of the overwhelming logic behind the concept of transnational police cooperation to stem transnational crime, progress in this area has been disap-
pointing because policing and criminal justice are indivisible components
of national sovereignty.

An example of the way different definitions of crime and standards employed by EU member states obstruct sound European police and criminal
justice cooperation is the case of Dutch drug policy, widely considered by
other heads of government to be a major impediment to cross-border police cooperation because it is, at the least, unconventional. In 1968, when
heroin began to flood the Dutch market, the Dutch government commis-
sioned a working group to study the increased prevalence of illegal substances.

The report was published years later; it summarized the state-of-the-art
research at that time on drugs and discussed domestic and international
legal conventions. The report's conclusion followed a simple philosophy:
It argued that the risk of a particular drug should determine the extent to
which the authorities became involved in its regulation and prosecution.[49]
Legalization of drugs was not an option because that would contradict the
Single Convention on Narcotic Drugs (1961), which gave nations ample
discretion to pursue their own drug policies but prohibited the legalization
of substances covered in the Convention. But the Dutch government could
amend the 1919 Opium Act to distinguish between drugs with acceptable
and unacceptable risks. Soft drugs carried acceptable risks, and medical
research could not pinpoint the damaging physiological effects of hemp
products. The report also pointed out that the entire foundation of antidrug
legislation would lose legitimacy and effectiveness if such an obvious difference between the two categories of drugs continued to be ignored. It
therefore seemed advisable to decriminalize the private consumption of
soft drugs. An additional benefit of differentiating between soft and hard
drugs was that it kept young middle-class users of cannabis products out

of the clutches of organized crime and shielded recreational drug users from hard-core drug addicts.

Law enforcement and the judiciary concurred with the aims of the new law. The approval of law enforcement is probably counter-intuitive because police corps often appear to be the most antidrug, proprosecution voices in national debates. But the 1886 Dutch Criminal Code vested the judiciary with wide margins of discretion to assess the psychological, social, and economic background of a perpetrator during sentencing.[50] "A crime should not always lead to punishment" was the basic reasoning behind this principle. In the postwar period such thinking dominated, and the public prosecutor's office acquired vast discretionary powers to permit an out-of-court settlement by allowing an offender to pay a large fine. Local police forces and the office of the mayor were also allowed to interpret criminal law legislation to promote the resocialization of an offender.

In this atmosphere of compassionate sentencing and punishment, many municipalities subsequently ignored the commercial trade of soft drugs in certain designated areas where middle-class consumers could legally buy small amounts of soft drugs for personal use. Over time, this indifference gave rise to special kinds of "coffee shops" that served a range of food items made from hashish or marijuana. The "coffee shops"—which number more than a thousand—are forbidden to sell hard drugs, and as a rule they do not trade in hard drugs.

The "coffee shops" and the Dutch legal system's habit of dismissing cases for prosecution helped to spread the message of a country with a tolerant, favorable view toward drug consumption. Admittedly, 50 percent of all cases referred to the prosecutor's office were dropped, but those convicted in drug cases received long prison sentences.[51] In the 1990s the law has become more strict, and prison sentences now vary according to the amount of drugs confiscated.[52] At present, the fact that a crime has been committed is not regarded as sufficient reason for prosecution.[53] But it is important to note that Dutch authorities are no more indulgent and lenient toward the illegal import and export of drugs than officials in other countries.[54] Kilos of illegal drugs have been confiscated year after year, and large contingencies of police officials are occupied with intercepting drug loads and capturing the major figures behind the illicit trade. Dutch prisons are filled with drug offenders, and new cells are quickly taken by new offenders convicted under the Opium Act. Dutch leniency does not extend to the supply of drugs.[55]

Yet "coffee shops" and the lack of repression in the retail trade of soft drugs have treated an image of an open, tolerant, accepting society—an image that has great appeal among young people in neighboring countries. Foreign tourists buy local drug products in Dutch border towns for resale or consumption back home. The lively cross-border drug trade has angered and exasperated neighboring countries and foreign law enforcement agencies. Moreover, although the distribution and production of wholesale drugs—whether innocent hemp substances or dangerous drugs—are prohibited, the "coffee shops" get their wares from somewhere. Neighboring countries have therefore accused the Netherlands of keeping the European drug trade alive by tolerating the operation of "coffee shops," whose owners must deal with organized crime to procure various cannabis products. Because hashish and marijuana are cultivated in areas outside Europe, the supply of soft drugs destined for the "coffee shops" regularly passes through other EU member states.

France, in particular, insists that the Netherlands should comply with wider European norms on drug use and close down the notorious "coffee shops" because they stimulate drug trade and contradict European anti-drug trafficking actions. Most countries subscribe to the War on Drugs model that uses repression and coercion to stamp out drug use and trade. But after so many years Dutch authorities are unwilling to admit that the humane experiment in fighting drug abuse is flawed and the public, although critical of the nuisance "coffee shops" create for local residents, nonetheless condone the concept of decriminalization. Dutch politicians cannot in good faith change the law enforcement culture and policing objectives of the Netherlands to comply with standards that are alien to the Dutch collective experience.

In the age of market integration, a single currency, and fiscal austerity, law enforcement and criminal justice are among the few remaining symbols of national sovereignty. Policing and criminal justice are related to the evolution of liberal democracy, and Dutch officials have always been suspicious of concentrating power in an agency that is not accountable to the electorate. To alter the direction and nature of the Dutch police and legal system to meet alleged "European" standards would affront the sensibilities of all Dutch civil libertarians, democrats, and patriots.

Yet European police cooperation is severely hamstrung unless conflicting standards, operating procedures, and objectives are reconciled to some extent. Without common judicial and policing sensibilities and standards, cross-border cooperation is stymied. Although this is good news for organized crime, it is also in the interest of European citizens for national norms and liberal democratic standards to continue to guide elected officials. As long as European institutions and treaties are free from democratic oversight, European policing should not replace national law enforcement functions and agencies.

CONCLUSION

This chapter has focused on the ways in which the various components of European integration encroach on or redefine democratic institutions and processes. Generally, seen from a distance it appears that European integration has added to the economic turmoil and political resentment that have rocked many European societies in the 1990s. Integration has reinforced and deepened global trends toward market deregulation and liberalization and has contributed to the decline of postwar styles of government intervention and social concertation.

My empirical case studies also demonstrate, however, that social institutions in each country cope with external pressures in their own fashion and have to various degrees adapted to new exigencies. Thus in the Netherlands, the institutions of the industrial relations system found a new lease on life by holding back pay demands and sanctioning an overhaul of the postwar social security system. In Sweden, perhaps because the country joined the EU so much later, the full weight of global financial markets and capital mobility emerged only in the 1990s. By then, internal contradictions had already complicated coordination inside the union movement and had caused a shift in orientation among employers. But sectoral wage accords are still signed, and the social safety net still operates with a high level of funding and compensation.

In Belgium organized labor is still regarded as a discussion partner of the government, although the trade union movement—split along regional-linguistic and ideological lines—has failed to formulate a joint strategy based on a common outlook. The considerable disparities between Flanders and Wallonia in joblessness and in the social welfare dependency ratio obviate joint action, although their combined strength is sufficient to block controversial policy proposals. In all three countries, regional integration and the Single European Market tend to accentuate existing fiscal, financial, and labor market predicaments by magnifying the difficulties and reducing the number of options available to governments to address the multiplication of problems.

Formal European institutions also exert modest influence on democratic institutions. They, too, interact with and thus intensify incipient developments, as is seen in the increase in funding and the scope of EU structural funds to aid distressed regions—which have mobilized regional movements and parties in countries with historical territorial divisions. European integration has legitimized the territorial ambitions of linguistic, ethnic, and territorial movements, which take advantage of the transfer of policy competencies to the EU and seize on the efforts to engage "regions" in a limited range of policy areas to experiment with the idea of greater autonomy. But domestic territorial divisions predate the emergence of regional aid and the interest of Brussels in promoting the formation of a subnational level of governance structures. Opposition by the Italian and Belgian regional movements to the postwar system of national unity and social solidarity cannot be attributed to EU meddling in the national affairs of the member states. Territorial leaders appropriated European Commission rhetoric and concern for subnational decisionmaking decentralization to push their own agenda of less spending on distressed regions.

In a similar vein, European institutions also foster national unity. Although statehood no longer counts for as much as it did in the days prior to global financial markets and membership in multilateral supranational organizations, national unity and product markets do facilitate domestic adjustment to external shocks. In a single currency area, the size of the market and its fiscal resources defines the ability of the central government to compensate economic sectors, regions, and employees for hardship caused by external turbulence.

Conflicting developments also describe the area of legal-judicial integration. On the one hand, considering the genuinely transnational scale of drug smuggling, car theft, money laundering, prostitution rings, and so forth, it makes sense for European countries to collaborate on setting common criminal procedures and policing standards. The Maastricht Treaty and the negotiations to revise or broaden that treaty during the 1997 Amsterdam summit pay considerable attention to the development of a European judicial system. On the other hand, governments are reluctant to agree on a shared system of policing because they do not fully trust the court systems and law enforcement principles of other member states. The public is concerned about organized crime, and elected leaders have recurrently stated that safe streets and safe jobs are very high priorities.

Yet seemingly unbridgeable disagreements that reflect genuine differences over basic principles of state-society relations, civil liberties, and democratic accountability have led to an impasse. Any further steps toward institutionalized cross-border police cooperation will evolve slowly. The emergence of a European judicial space must be sufficiently compatible with the national norms and values of all member states to be adopted by the European Union. If no prior consensus and harmonization exist, there should be no European legal and judicial standards or norms. Since a reconciliation of divergent definitions of civil liberties, policing, and democratic rights has not yet been achieved, it is preferable to have a poorly functioning third pillar and to leave law enforcement and the judiciary in the hands of national officials accountable to an electorate. A final observation therefore is that the impact of EU institutions and integration on national democracy has been mostly indirect and frequently inadvertent.

NOTES

I am especially grateful to Erik Jones and Bart Kerremans for their assistance in locating some last-minute facts and figures on Belgium.

1. Paulette Kurzer, *Business and Banking: Political Change and Economic Integration in Western Europe* (Ithaca: Cornell University Press, 1993).

2. Marino Regini, *Uncertain Boundaries: The Social and Political Construction of European Economies* (New York: Cambridge University Press, 1995).

3. Torben Iversen, "Power, Flexibility, and the Breakdown of Centralized Wage Bargaining," *Comparative Politics* 28 (1996): 399–436.

4. Jelle Visser, "European Trade Unions: The Transition Years," in *New Frontiers in European Industrial Relations*, Richard Hyman and Anthony Ferner, eds. (Cambridge: Blackwell, 1994), 82–83.

5. Peter Lange, Michael Wallerstein, Miriam Golden, "The End of Corporatism? Wage Setting in the Nordic and Germanic Countries," in *The Workers of Nations: Industrial Relations in a Global Economy*, Sanford Jacoby, ed. (New York: Oxford University Press, 1995).

6. Neil Buckley, "Belgian Jobs Pact Close to Collapse," *Financial Times*, April 30, 1996, 2.

7. Jacques Vilrokx and Jim van Leemput, "Belgium: A New Stability in Industrial Relations?" in *Industrial Relations in the New Europe*, Anthony Ferner and Richard Hyman, eds. (Cambridge: Blackwell, 1992), 357–392. Organization for Economic Cooperation and Development (OECD), *Economic Survey: BLUE 1997* (Paris: OECD, 1997), 64–68.

8. Jelle Visser, "The Netherlands: The End of an Era and the End of a System," in *Industrial Relations in the New Europe*, Ferner and Hyman, eds., 323–353.

9. Emma Tucker, "Workers Pay for Europe's Rigidities," *Financial Times*, February 13, 1998, 2.

10. Anton C. Hemerijck, "Corporatist Immobility in the Netherlands," in *Organized Industrial Relations in Europe? What Future*, Colin Crouch and Franz Traxler, eds. (Brookfield, Vt.: Ashgate, 1995), 183–226.

11. Robert Cox, "From Safety Net to Trampoline: Labor Market Activation in the Netherlands and Denmark," *Governance* (forthcoming).

12. Centraal Planbureau (CPB), Netherlands Bureau for Economic Policy Analysis, *Challenging Neighbours: Rethinking German and Dutch Economic Institutions* (Berlin: Springer, 1997), 214–216.

13. Ibid., 199–205.

14. Romke van der Veen and Willem Trommel, "Managed Liberalization of the Dutch Welfare State," paper presented at the Society for the Advancement of Socioeconomics (SASE) conference, Montreal, July 1997.

15. Single mothers with children over age five are expected to become active labor market participants. Unemployment beneficiaries can no longer reject a job below their level of qualification, and a college graduate is legally obliged to accept unskilled employment after two years of unemployment.

16. Franz Traxler, "Farewell to Labor Market Associations? Organized Versus Disorganized Decentralization as a Map for Industrial Relations," in *Organized Industrial Relations in Europe*, Crouch and Traxler, eds., 3–19; Frans van Waarden, "Persistence of National Policy-Styles: A Study of Their Institutional Foundations," in *Convergence or Diversity? Internationalization and Economic Policy*

Response, Brigitte Unger and Frans van Waarden, eds. (Brookfield, Vt.: Avebury, 1995), 333–335.

17. Paulette Kurzer, "Placed in Europe: Belgium and the Netherlands in the European Union," in *Tamed Power: Germany in Europe*, Peter Katzenstein, ed. (Ithaca: Cornell University Press, 1997), 108–141.

18. Erik Jones, "Is 'Competitive' Corporatism an Adequate Response to Globalization? Evidence from the Low Countries," paper presented at the Eleventh International Conference of Europeanists, Baltimore, February 26–28, 1998.

19. The term refers to a political economy that is not free market, disorganized capitalism or collective, planned socialism. In the 1980s it referred to a policy mix that is not neoliberal monetarist or Keynesian.

20. Assar Lindbeck, *Turning Sweden Around* (Cambridge: MIT Press, 1994); Arthur Gould, "Sweden: The Last Bastion of Social Democracy," in *European Welfare Policy: Squaring the Welfare Circle*, Vic George and Peter Taylor-Gooby, eds. (New York: St. Martin's, 1996), 89–91.

21. Peter Swenson, "Bringing Capital Back In, or Social Democracy Reconsidered: Employer Power, Cross-Class Alliances, and Centralization of Industrial Relations in Denmark and Sweden." *World Politics* 43 (1991): 513–545.

22. Kathleen Thelen, "West European Labor in Transition," *World Politics* 46 (1993): 28–29.

23. Karl Ove Moene and Michael Wallerstein, "How Social Democracy Worked: Labor-Market Institutions," *Politics and Society* 23 (1995): 206–207; Michael Wallerstein and Miriam Golden, "The Fragmentation of the Bargaining Society: Wage Setting in the Nordic Countries, 1950–1992," *Comparative Political Studies* 30 (1997): 699–731.

24. Organization for Economic Cooperation and Development, *Economic Surveys: Sweden 1997* (Paris: OECD, 1997), 87.

25. Ibid., 80. Anders Björklund and Richard B. Freeman, "Generating Equality and Eliminating Poverty, the Swedish Way," in *The Welfare State in Transition*, Richard B. Freeman, Robert Topel, and Birgitta Swedenborg, eds. (Chicago: University of Chicago Press, 1997), 33–78. In March 1998 the metal union and engineering employers agreed to an 8.5 percent pay increase over three years. Many firms claimed this was too high and would lead to further job shedding.

26. Capital outflows were also driven by the removal of currency controls in Sweden.

27. Paul Marginson and Keith Sisson, "The Structure of Transnational Capital in Europe: The Emerging Euro-Company and Its Implications for Industrial Relations," in *New Frontiers*, Hyman and Ferner, eds., 27–29.

28. United Nations Conference on Trade and Development, *World Investment Report: TNCs, Employment, and the Workplace* (New York: United Nations, 1994), 415, 419.

29. Ibid., 178.

30. OECD, *Economic Surveys: Sweden 1997*, 144.

31. Swedish Institute, *Fact Sheet on Sweden: The Swedish Economy* (Stockholm: FS1 w Qad, November 1994).

32. Magnus Blomström and Robert Lipsey, "The Competitiveness of Countries

and Their Multinational Firms," in *Multinationals in the Global Political Economy*, Lorraine Eden and Evan Potter, eds. (New York: St. Martin's, 1993), 133–134.

33. Tim Burt, "Stockholm Faces Corporate Pressure over Membership of EMU," *Financial Times*, March 3, 1998, 2.

34. Mark A. Pollack, "Regional Actors in an Intergovernmental Play: The Making and Implementation of EC Structural Policy," in *The State of the European Union* (vol. 3), Carolyn Rhodes and Sonia Mazey, eds. (Boulder: Lynne Rienner, 1995), 377; Jeffrey Anderson, "Structural Funds and the Social Dimension of EU Policy: Springboard or Stumbling Block?" in *European Social Policy: Between Fragmentation and Integration*, Stephan Leibfried and Paul Pierson, eds. (Washington, D.C.: Brookings Institution, 1995), 143–146.

35. Michael Keating, "Europeanism and Regionalism," in *The European Union and the Regions*, Michael Keating and Barry Jones, eds. (New York: Oxford University Press, 1995), 1–23; Liesbet Hooghe, "Belgian Federalism and the European Community," in *The European Union and the Regions*, Keating and Jones, eds., 135–167. Murray Forsyth, "Federalism and Confederalism," in *Political Restructuring in Europe: Ethical Perspectives*, Chris Brown, ed. (New York: Routledge, 1994), 50–69.

36. Organization for Economic Cooperation and Development, *Economic Surveys: Italy 1996* (Paris: OECD, 1996), 96–97.

37. David Hine, "Federalism, Regionalism, and the Unitary State: Contemporary Regional Pressures in Historical Perspective," in *Italian Regionalism: History, Identity and Politics*, Carl Levy, ed. (Washington, D.C.: Berg, 1996), 109–131.

38. Hans-Georg Betz, *Radical Rightwing Populism in Western Europe* (New York: St. Martin's, 1994).

39. John Fitzmaurice, *The Politics of Belgium: A Unique Federalism* (Boulder: Westview, 1996), 206.

40. Alfred Pijpers and Sophie Vanhoonacker, "The Position of the Benelux Countries," in *The Politics of European Treaty Reform*, Geoffrey Edwards and Alfred Pijpers, eds. (Washington, D.C.: Pinter, 1997), 122.

41. Joseph Farrell and Carl Levy, "The Northern League: Conservative Revolution?" in *Italian Regionalism*, Levy, ed., 131–150; Anna Cento Bull, "Ethnicity, Racism, and the Northern League," in *Italian Regionalism*, Levy, ed., 171–185.

42. Ilvo Diamanti, "The *Lega Nord*: From Federalism to Secession," in *Italian Politics: The Center-Left in Power*, Roberto D'Alimonte and David Nelken, eds. (Boulder: Westview, 1997), 74.

43. Mark Gilbert, *The Italian Revolution: The End of Politics, Italian Style?* (Boulder: Westview, 1995), 57.

44. Diamanti, "The *Lega Nord*," 76–80.

45. Mario Mignone, *Italy Today: A Country in Transition* (New York: Peter Lang, 1995), 126.

46. Carlo Desideri, "Italian Regions in the European Community," in *The European Union and the Regions*, Keating and Jones, eds., 84–85.

47. Erik Jones, "Finding the Balance: The Decentralization of Belgium," unpublished MS, University of Nottingham, 1997.

48. Ellen Ahnfelt and Johan From, "European Policing," in *Making Policy in Europe*, Svein S. Andersen and Kjell A. Eliassen, eds. (Thousand Oaks: Sage, 1993); also Monica den Boer and Neil Walker, "European Policing After 1992," *Journal of Common Market Studies* 31 (1993): 3–27; Malcolm Anderson, Monica den Boer, Peter Cullen, William Gilmore, Charles Raab, and Neil Walker, *Policing the European Union* (Oxford: Clarendon, 1995).

49. Henk Jan van Vliet, "A Symposium on Drug Decriminalization: The Uneasy Decriminalization: A Perspective on Dutch Drug Policy," *Hofstra Law Review* 18 (1990): 723.

50. Constantijn Kelk, Laurence Koffman, and Jos Silvis, "Sentencing Practices, Policy, and Discretion," in *Criminal Justice in Europe: A Comparative Study*, Phil Fennell, ed. (Oxford: Clarendon, 1995), 325–328; and David Downes, *Contrasts in Tolerance: Postwar Penal Policy in the Netherlands, and England and Wales* (New York: Oxford University Press, 1988).

51. Julia Fionda, *Public Prosecutors and Discretion: A Comparative Study* (Oxford: Clarendon, 1995), 99–100.

52. Jos Silvis and Katherine Williams, "Managing the Drug Problem: Prohibition or Tolerance?" in *Criminal Justice in Europe*, Fennell, ed., 156. The flow of prisoners increased faster than the construction of new prison cells. The Ministry of Justice had to release less violent criminals early to make room for more dangerous offenders. Fionda, *Public Prosecutors and Discretion*, 114.

53. Other countries may also waive prosecution of minor crimes, but that is often the result of resource constraints and rising criminal activity rather than the product of deliberate policy evaluations.

54. This was already the situation in the 1980s. Downes, *Contrasts in Tolerance*, 123–162.

55. Vincenzo Ruggiero and Nigel South, *Eurodrugs: Drug Use, Markets, and Trafficking in Europe* (London: UCL, 1995), 91.

Section III

From European Integration
to Regional Integration

10

NAFTA and the EU:
Toward Convergence?

Gustavo Vega-Cánovas

One of the most important trends in the international community has been the steady progress of regionalization in Europe, the Americas, and Asia. But what are the patterns of regionalization among regions, within regions, and between current and potential members of regional arrangements? Will North America follow the pattern of Europe? What is the impact of regionalization on the domestic politics of countries that are members of regional arrangements? What can the North American countries learn from the European experience and vice versa?

This chapter analyzes the North American Free Trade Agreement (NAFTA), the type of regional integration it represents, and its likely future evolution. I also speculate on the impact of NAFTA on the process of democratization in Mexico. I first compare the European Union (EU), a region with progressively "positive" deepening integration in multiple dimensions—political, economic, and institutional—with NAFTA and show that although the EU and NAFTA share important commonalities, they have different origins, goals, structure, and content. These differences, I conclude, make it unlikely that NAFTA will follow Europe's path. I then discuss what I consider the likely pattern of evolution of NAFTA based on the experience of NAFTA's first four years and on the lessons we can draw from the European experience. In the final section I speculate about NAFTA's impact on the process of democratization in Mexico.

A COMPARISON OF EUROPEAN UNION AND NAFTA

Economists usually distinguish between a basic "negative" form of integration, which entails the elimination of discrimination against and restrictions on the free movement of goods and elements of production between countries, and a more advanced "positive" form, which involves the development of common institutions and policies to enable the integrated market to function effectively and to promote collective political and economic objectives. Bela Balassa's classic model, for instance, formulates economic integration as a process in which three cumulative stages of negative, or market, integration (a free trade area, customs union, and common market) are superseded by two stages of positive, or policy, integration (economic union and total economic integration).[1] In principle, each stage incorporates all of the features of the preceding one plus a new element.

From this discussion it is clear that the EU is the most advanced example of deep positive integration, having progressed through all three of Balassa's stages since 1957. The original impetus for the formation of the European Economic Community (EEC) (and before it the European Coal and Steel Community) was political: It was founded to reconcile former bitter enemies—most specifically, France and Germany—who had fought numerous wars over the previous century. The means chosen to achieve political cohesion between these former antagonists were economic, although the ultimate objective was far more ambitious. As a result of a progression from largely negative to increasingly positive forms of integration, relations among Western European nations have been transformed from the traditional state of war to a situation of complex interdependence. Collective economic management takes place through a process of truly supranational decisionmaking within institutions such as the EU Commission, intergovernmental bargaining among members in the Council of Ministers, or a mixed process in which EU-level policies extend and mingle with national politics. National political systems have become porous, as bureaucracies, interest groups, and even political parties have established transnational linkages and direct their activities toward EU institutions. EU decisions, in turn, have a direct impact—often unmediated by national governments—on member states' economies, societies, cultures, and politics.

The Impulse to Regionalization in North America

In North America, a very different regionalization process is under way. The first impulse toward regionalization in North America was the initiation of negotiations for the Canada-U.S. Free Trade Agreement (CUSFTA) in 1985. For over a hundred years Canada had flirted with the idea of a special trade relationship with the U.S. but had always backed away for fear of being overwhelmed economically, politically, and culturally by a country ten times its size or had been rebuffed by the U.S. Congress. After several decades of gradual liberalization of bilateral trade between Canada and the U.S. through multilateral negotiations under the General Agreement on Tariffs and Trade (GATT), as well as limited sectoral accords, Canada faced serious challenges to its exports from rising U.S. protectionism.

Since the 1970s the U.S. had run a large merchandise trade deficit. In the early 1980s the large and growing federal budget deficit contributed to dependence on foreign savings and the misalignment of the U.S. dollar; as a result, the U.S. became the world's largest net debtor. Declining international competitiveness, as evidenced in the trade and current account deficits, eroded U.S. support for liberal trade policy; through 1985 numerous proposals to amend U.S. trade laws were introduced in Congress to make it easier for domestic interests to obtain relief from import competition. This created great concern in Canada over security of access to the U.S. market, and in 1985 it proposed negotiations for a bilateral free trade agreement. Canada's objective was to secure and enhance its market access to the world's largest and wealthiest market.

In responding to the Canadian initiative, the U.S. was driven by broader objectives: specifically, to send a message to the EU and Japan that it was in their best interest to return to the multilateral table and begin a new round of GATT talks. Even staunch multilateralists recognized that GATT-conforming agreements with Canada and possibly Mexico would be consistent with U.S. objectives for liberalized trade. Eventually, a free trade agreement (FTA) was negotiated in 1987 and implemented on January 1, 1989, that went even further than the Uruguay Round negotiations on the GATT. The agreement was comprehensive; it spanned virtually the entire GATT agenda, including most of the new issues such as services and investment but not intellectual property. The FTA also broke new ground by establishing a new bilateral dispute resolution process designed to regulate and manage the U.S.-Canadian economic relationship.

When the negotiations over the Canada-U.S. FTA were launched, each country was the other's largest trading partner and the largest investor in the other's economy. In 1989 Canada's stock of foreign direct investment in the United States was US$50 billion, and the U.S. stock in Canada was US$67 billion. Canada depends on exports for 30 percent of its gross national product (GNP); 70 percent of those exports go to the U.S.[2]

The next stage of regionalization in North America was the initiation of the trilateral NAFTA in spring 1991. Mexico's decision to seek free trade with the United States (and eventually with Canada) was triggered by the economic disaster that followed the collapse of oil prices and the onset of the debt crisis in the early 1980s, which forced Mexico to rethink its import-substitution development strategy and seek new revenues through exports. In less than a decade Mexico was transformed from one of the most closed, state-centric economies in Latin America to one of the most open economies. For Mexico's outward-oriented strategy to succeed, however, secure access to the U.S. market was essential. Concerns about a drift toward protectionism in the United States led Mexican authorities to seek such access. The two countries negotiated a series of bilateral accords, including a 1985 agreement on subsidies and countervailing duties and 1987 and 1989 framework agreements for bilateral consultations on a range of issues. These agreements, combined with Mexico's accession to the GATT in 1986 and indigenous reforms, established a firmer foundation for U.S.-Mexican economic relations.

As with Canada, in the twentieth century Mexico has always been strongly integrated with the U.S. economy. Mexico is currently the third-largest U.S. trading partner, after Canada and the EU, accounting for approximately 8.4 percent of U.S. exports and imports. The United States is Mexico's dominant trading partner, accounting for two-thirds of both exports and imports and far outdistancing Mexico's trade with Europe, Japan, and the rest of Latin America and Canada. The United States is also the major source of foreign investment in the Mexican economy, accounting for nearly 70 percent of the total.[3] Labor market integration between the two countries is also very high. Mexican migrant labor has had a large impact on the U.S. economy, accounting for at least 10 percent of the growth of the U.S. labor supply since World War II.[4]

Thus an important feature of North American integration—one that parallels the European experience—is that Canada, the U.S., and Mexico experienced several decades of informal economic integration, led by investment and trade flows, before establishing any formal institutional arrangements. But in the end these arrangements remained at the lower levels of negative, or market, integration with a minimum of shared institutions. For instance, no serious proposals have been made for a North American customs union, common market, or full economic and monetary union. This point is worth exploring in more detail by turning to the existing institutional features of integration in these two regions.

Institutional Features of Integration in the EU and NAFTA

It is helpful to borrow an analytical scheme from Peter Smith.[5] Specifically, we can compare integration following four basic dimensions. *Scope* is defined as the range of issues and transactions falling under the purview of the integration scheme. *Depth* is the extent of policy coordination or harmonization. *Institutionalization* is the degree to which accommodation and decisionmaking take place in organized and predictable ways. Finally, *centralization* is the extent to which a central supranational decisionmaking apparatus exists to establish common policy. Employing these categories as comparative frames of reference, we find, unsurprisingly, that the EU is a much more complete and ambitious undertaking than NAFTA. The EU covers a broader range of issues, provides for deeper policy coordination, is more institutionalized, and uses more centralized decision-making.

Scope is extremely useful in highlighting the differences between the two arrangements. For example, since 1987 the implementation of the Single European Act has taken the meaning of a uniform customs policy in Europe to new levels; in fact, most EU member governments have eliminated customs checkpoints along their borders. Each country in NAFTA retains its own regulations. Furthermore, the treaties governing the EU provide for the free movement of persons—especially students and laborers—among member nations. NAFTA migration provisions apply only to professionals, businesspersons, and investors, all of whom can transfer temporarily for work in member states. The European treaty framework also covers trade policy, foreign policy, consumer protection, and defense—to name just a few areas unmentioned in the NAFTA agreement.

Depth as a criterion for comparison reveals further striking differences between the EU and NAFTA. The European Union has implemented coordinated decisionmaking mechanisms involving trade agreements with non-member nations (trade agreements are agreed to by the EU rather than individual countries), monetary policy, certain categories of tax policy, occupational health and safety regulations, antitrust and subsidy regulations, and consumer protection. NAFTA countries pursue their own policies in all of these areas.

Considering that both arrangements exist in the form of a diplomatic treaty, it may be unfair to say one is more institutionalized than the other. Nonetheless, the EU allows decisionmaking to take place in more formal, organized, and predictable ways than does NAFTA. For this reason I contend that NAFTA is less institutionalized than the EU. This fact notwithstanding, the legal nature of both organizations provides for much more thorough institutionalization than that offered through Asia-Pacific Economic Cooperation (APEC) or the Andean Pact.

In terms of the degree of centralization, the EU clearly has a much more advanced central decisionmaking process. The Council of Ministers makes decisions by unanimous or qualified majority votes that are binding on all members. No such body exists under the terms of NAFTA. In fact, changes to the treaty are negotiated on an ad hoc basis. Dispute resolution goes to a central trade commission, but its decisions are not binding (although one country can retaliate against another that continues to pursue policies deemed unfair by a binational panel). The North American Free Trade Area also lacks institutions that correspond to the European Commission, the European Court of Justice, and the Court of Auditors. Another aspect of EU policymaking glaringly absent from NAFTA is the existence of a democratically elected body—the European Parliament—that participates in the decisionmaking process, albeit on the margins.

Main Differences between the EU and NAFTA

Clearly, then, the EU and NAFTA are two very different arrangements. Moving beyond Smith's comparative dimensions, other salient differences appear. For example, in NAFTA one country (the United States) can overpower the other two through pure economic might and a disproportionately large population. This is not the case in Europe, where the largest country (Germany) contains less than a quarter of the EU population and earns less than 26 percent of its gross product. Further, the wage and GNP per capita disparities among EU nations (which measure about 3 to 1 between Germany and Spain) are much smaller than those in NAFTA (where a 10 to 1 disparity exists between the United States and Mexico).[6]

We can ask why the two arrangements are so different. After all, both are integration schemes that involve countries with a long tradition of market-based economic policy. One obvious explanation for the difference is that the EU is much older than NAFTA. Although founded in 1957, the EEC did not even attain a truly common market until the late 1960s. If we take this as a guide, we can assume that in thirty years the North American continent will be as integrated as Europe.

This explanation only goes so far, however. The two treaties arose out of very different historical environments. It is foolish to assume a post–Cold War economic pact will develop in North America in the same way the one founded in Europe did during the Marshall Plan era. The needs of European countries in the 1950s were markedly different from those in North America in the 1990s. Perhaps the most pressing reason for integration in the 1950s was the need to strengthen Western Europe so it could resist a Soviet-led invasion. North America faces no such threat today. Further, factories in post–World War II Europe needed to achieve economies of scale if they were to successfully rebuild. The productive plants in Canada, Mexico, and the United States have faced no similar destruction since the Mexican Revolution in the 1920s.

NAFTA was implemented for a unique set of reasons. First, Mexico was saddled with such high debt payments that it had to seek outside capital if it was to develop. Therefore, it sought a trade and investment agreement with the most powerful economy in the world. From a northern perspective, the United States wanted to help stabilize Mexico's economy to prevent the negative shocks that would transfer to Texas and California if their southern neighbor continued experiencing economic and political difficulties. Canada simply wanted to prevent the U.S. from granting Mexico better trade and financial opportunities and from positioning itself as the only viable conduit to trade in the Americas.

Thus, it is perhaps inappropriate to expect the EU and NAFTA to be very similar. They grew out of different eras with different needs and for different reasons. In fact, the EU has always been considered a political union first and an economic union second. The same cannot be said for NAFTA.

Economic Impact of the EU on Member Countries

Regional integration in Western Europe is generally acclaimed to be a major success that in no small part has ushered in one of the longest periods of peace and growing prosperity in recent memory. Each member state's economy has experienced spectacular increases in productivity, specialization, and standard of living. Whereas all members have experienced economic growth and national prosperity that can be attributed to the Common Market, some have profited more than others. In fact, some authorities have stated that if one takes into account the intensity and nature of economic interaction and the level of economic development, one can identify the existence of a core and a periphery in Western Europe.[7] Germany (excluding the former German Democratic Republic), France, the Benelux countries, Denmark, and large portions of England, Italy, and Spain form part of the core group, whereas the less developed countries and regions of the EU are situated in the geographical periphery.

The EU attempts to deal with the regional and national economic disparities through a few redistributive policy instruments, some differentiation in the application of common rules and policies (longer timetables for the weaker economies and temporary derogations have characterized much internal market legislation), and the goal of improving general macroeconomic conditions—which in turn may facilitate the task of economic adjustment. What effect has the EU had on regional disparities more generally? The evidence points to no consistent pattern. Intra-EU income disparities are very large, and they have become wider with each successive enlargement. According to Loukas Tsoukalis, purchasing power parities point to considerable stability in the rank order of GDPs of EU members over a period of thirty years. But they also highlight the remarkable performance of the three southern European newly industrialized countries (NICs)—Greece, Portugal, and Spain—between 1960 and 1975, the steady rise of Italy, and the decline—with some ups and downs—of Denmark, Luxembourg, the Netherlands, and the United Kingdom.[8]

On the other hand, little evidence suggests that economic integration itself has contributed to the widening of disparities. In fact, it appears that intercountry disparities in the EC were narrowed during the 1960s and early 1970s. The trend was reversed during the long recession and continued until the mid-1980s when growth rates in most of the less developed members of the Community picked up again, leading to another narrowing of disparities that coincided with the economic boom of the late 1980s.[9]

NAFTA: THE FIRST FOUR YEARS

NAFTA is basically a trade agreement; therefore, its effect on trade flows (goods and services) is a relevant measure of its success. NAFTA also seeks to encourage investment in the member countries, especially direct investment (in plants and equipment), but most important it is aimed at furthering the integration of the three North American countries through changes in institutions to facilitate cooperation and through procedures to expedite resolution of conflicts.[10] Based on these basic principles, the agreement consists of a set of rules that cover merchandise trade liberalization, deregulation and protection of foreign investment, trade in services, and institutional framework and enforcement.

Most economists and policymakers would probably agree that the full effects derived from the formation of a free trade area take time to develop. One important reason is the structural adjustment each country must undertake: Capacity and employment need to be reduced in some sectors, whereas in others additional investments must be undertaken and new jobs filled with workers with new skills.[11] A second reason the effects of trade liberalization are gradual is that some gradualism is deliberately built into the agreement: Phase-out periods are agreed on for the full elimination of tariffs and the dismantling of nontariff barriers.[12]

These considerations suggest that it may still be too early to make a definite judgment on NAFTA's effects. Furthermore, Mexico's macroeconomic crisis, triggered by an abrupt devaluation of its currency in December 1994, has also affected trade flows among the NAFTA partners over the past several years. To evaluate the relative significance of NAFTA in Mexico-U.S. trade, we need to consider the transition periods in the agreement as well as other factors when we analyze how such trade has evolved since January 1, 1994.

Mexico-U.S. Bilateral Trade

As was expected,[13] trade liberalization under the terms of NAFTA has reinforced the U.S. position as Mexico's main trading partner, whereas Mexico has stabilized as the third-largest trading partner of the U.S. A significant change, however, is that Mexico has become the second-largest market for U.S. exports, overtaking the EU. Total Mexico-U.S. trade (exports and imports) has experienced tremendous growth from $81.6 billion in 1993 to $100.3 billion in 1994, $108.0 billion in 1995, and a record high of $140.4 billion in 1996.[14]

This dramatic growth in bilateral trade has caused a sharp change in the bilateral trade balance. A $2 billion U.S. trade surplus in 1993 and a $1.2 billion surplus in 1994 became a $15.4 billion deficit in 1995 and a $16 billion deficit in 1996.[15] This turn undoubtedly has much to do with the gradual depreciation of the Mexican peso throughout 1994 and the abrupt devaluation at the end of that year.

Mexican Exports to the United States: Sectoral Highlights

Two Mexican manufacturing industries with exceptionally high post-NAFTA rates of export growth were those in which regional integration had progressed significantly even before the agreement entered into force: auto and auto parts (which include the bulk of metal products and machinery) and textiles and apparel.

The Automotive Sector

The automotive industry plays a crucial role in the economies of the three countries in terms of exports, employment generation, and technological and industrial development. The auto industry, which includes vehicle manufacturers and auto parts producers, is the largest industry in each NAFTA country's manufacturing sector, and automotive products are the largest component in bilateral trade among the three North American partners—accounting for 14 percent of total bilateral trade between Mexico and the U.S. and roughly a third of total bilateral trade between Canada and the U.S. in 1990.

These vigorous trade activities should be viewed against the backdrop of increasing integration in the North American automotive industry, which has led to substantial intraindustry specialization. Canada has specialized in the production of large passenger cars and trucks, and Mexico has become the major supplier of engines for vehicle assembly in U.S. and Canadian plants. The United States produces numerous auto parts that are exported to Canada for assembly and manufactures vehicles for all market segments in the U.S. and abroad.

Thus it is not surprising that the automotive sector was singled out as particularly sensitive during the NAFTA negotiations, as discussed later. From the Mexican perspective the sector is not only the largest exporter and importer of manufactured goods, but as such it is also a prime example of the kind of intraindustry trade NAFTA was designed to boost. Free trade allows firms that sell in the entire North American market to relocate their production facilities among the NAFTA countries to minimize costs and take full advantage of specialization and economies of scale.

Given that the automotive industry is particularly sensitive to economic conditions—such as the level of real income, interest rates, and availability of credit—and, in international trade, to shifts in exchange-rate relationships, it is not surprising that domestic demand for automobiles and trucks shrank considerably in Mexico in 1995. The situation in the Mexican industry was not worse that year only because of the increase in exports to the United States; Mexico sold more automotive products in 1995 than it imported, the first time that had happened since 1989.[16] As the Mexican economy recovered in 1996, U.S. exports to Mexico resumed their growth.[17] In any case, total automotive trade between the two countries was increasing before NAFTA and continued its upward trajectory after NAFTA. Total two-way trade figures, combining vehicles and parts, in recent years are as follows: 1991, $13 billion; 1992, $16 billion; 1993, $18 billion; 1994, $23 billion; 1995, $25 billion.[18]

Textiles and Apparel

The liberalization program devised for this sector is based on a basic premise: From the U.S. point of view, regardless of whether quota restrictions were removed and tariffs were eliminated on textile trade with Mexico, the more labor-intensive activities (most notably apparel production) would continue to lose jobs to low-wage countries—many of which were located in the Far East. Moreover, to the extent that those downstream activities moved away from North America, the more competitive segments of the U.S. textile complex (such as yarn and fabric production) would continue to face falling demand for their products: As more and more apparel producers relocated to Asia, they would seek non-U.S. input sources—which, among other things, would allow them to save on transportation costs. Also, anticipation that the Multifiber Agreement would be phased out as a result of the Uruguay Round meant that exempting Mexico from the U.S. quotas would amount to no more than giving Mexico a head start vis-à-vis other suppliers of textiles and apparel to the U.S. market.

In turn, improved access to the U.S. market for its garments and textile products (including full elimination of applicable quotas) was a major NAFTA goal for Mexico. The so-called Special Regime, by which Mexico-assembled apparel from U.S.-formed and -cut fabric benefited from flexible quotas and the application of U.S. tariffs only on non-U.S. value added, had been very successful. Its intensive utilization by Mexican exporters in the years prior to 1994 had been the basis of a fast-growing garment industry and a source of jobs for low-skilled workers. The immediate elimination of quotas (coupled with substantial cuts in certain exceptionally high tariffs as the agreement entered into force) would build on this progress and expand its benefits to Mexican fabric producers, who would become NAFTA-qualifying suppliers.[19]

After four years of textile trade under NAFTA, the sector's performance indicates that those expectations were well-founded. Mexican exports of these products grew at an average yearly rate of 32.2 percent in 1994, 1995, and 1996. This extraordinary growth enabled Mexico to overtake China as the main foreign source of garments sold in the U.S. Moreover, and despite the increased peso cost of foreign yarn and fabric, imports of U.S. textiles, apparel, and footwear into Mexico kept growing at an average rate of nearly 17 percent per annum.[20]

*   *   *

In summary, NAFTA has reinforced the trends toward regional integration in automotive, textile, and apparel products that were previously present in the U.S.-Mexico bilateral trade relationship. The agreement has also opened new opportunities in other sectors that shared some of the labor-intensity competitive advantage of the garment industry and enjoyed additional advantages, such as abundance of quality domestic raw materials or favorable climatic conditions. I turn now to one such sector.

Agriculture and Animal Products

In the spirit that guided Uruguay Round negotiations on this sector, NAFTA replaced standard quantitative restrictions with their tariff equivalents (the so-called tariffication). NAFTA also defined seasonal windows during which U.S. supplies of certain goods (particularly fresh vegetables and fruit) are low. Within those seasonal openings Mexico would be allowed to ship primary products to the U.S. at reduced or null tariffs, which would return to their normal levels when U.S. growers entered the market. In exchange, Mexico would import predetermined amounts of grains (including corn) tariff free; surplus amounts would pay the tariffs that replaced the quantitative restrictions. Also, enhanced cooperation in the area of sanitary and phytosanitary measures would help to minimize the trade-restricting effects of these protective standards. Under these NAFTA conditions, Mexican agricultural exports grew from $2.1 billion in 1993 to $3.4 billion in 1995, nearly doubling the average rate of growth per annum (17.4 percent).[21]

Mexican Imports from the United States

Given the accumulated magnitude of the depreciation of the peso since NAFTA entered into force, the fact that Mexican imports from the U.S. have continued to grow at an average yearly rate of 9.0 percent is striking. A comparative analysis of exports by sector shows not only that the two countries share a considerable volume of two-way trade in certain categories but that the trade balance in these sectors has become fairly even. By

1996, under NAFTA, neither country had a significant trade advantage in a given sector. Instead, the two countries tended to produce together within the same sectors, thereby giving NAFTA nations a competitive advantage over other countries.

Investment

NAFTA, particularly chapter 11, was designed to encourage foreign investment in Mexico. As a condition of NAFTA, however, Mexico was required to phase out the *maquiladora* program, a duty drawback-based system that during the period 1965–1994 resulted in the establishment of more than 2,000 factories—primarily but not exclusively in the border region—with production valued at over $26 billion annually.[22] Although the longer-term effects of NAFTA may be to encourage movement of foreign-owned factories away from the border—particularly if the Mexican domestic market becomes more attractive—the trend over the past few years has been toward increased investment and employment for all *maquilas*, including in the border area.[23] Employment in the *maquila* industry grew 20.3 percent during the first eleven months of 1996, to a total of over 811,000 workers.[24] This growth was undoubtedly caused in part by the peso devaluation—resulting in a more than one-third reduction of Mexican wage costs in dollar terms—but NAFTA's stringent rules of origin with local content requirements, the proposed elimination of the duty drawback in the year 2001,[25] and tariff benefits also contributed. NAFTA's growing impact on parts and components suppliers is reflected in the fact that Mexican value added by *maquilas* in the aggregate is growing at a much faster rate—63 percent more in 1996 than in 1995—than *maquila* employment.[26] Ownership of the *maquilas* remains overwhelmingly U.S. and Mexican.[27]

Asian investment in Mexico has also increased. The Korean television industry has invested over $500 million in television and picture tube facilities since 1991, and electronics industry employment in the Tijuana area alone is estimated at 24,576.[28] Two Korean giants, Daewoo and Samsung, have established highly capital-intensive color picture tube manufacturing facilities in Mexico in addition to television assembly facilities, arguably because for most televisions NAFTA duty benefits are available only when the picture tube is of North American origin. Whether this is desirable depends on one's point of view; NAFTA has helped to create jobs in Mexico—in this instance largely at the cost of jobs in Asia—but economists might well argue that the diversion of TV component production from Asia to Mexico is a distortion of the principle of comparative advantage.

Financial Services

The opening of Mexico's financial services sector is proceeding more rapidly than required under NAFTA because of the country's critical need for additional capital. Under NAFTA, as of January 1, 1994, U.S. banks were permitted to own 8 percent of the Mexican banking industry in the aggregate with an increase to 15 percent after seven years, after which the limit would disappear.[29] The U.S. securities industry was granted an initial 10 percent interest rate, rising in increments to 20 percent over the seven-year period,[30] with all restrictions eliminated thereafter.[31] Existing U.S. and Canadian insurance joint ventures in Mexico were authorized to acquire 100 percent ownership as of 1996, and new entrants can obtain a majority interest as of 1998.[32] The financial crisis in Mexico beginning in December 1994 has encouraged the Mexican government to increase the extent of equity ownership foreign financial institutions can acquire in Mexican banks—to 49 percent—and in general to accelerate the opening of the Mexican financial sector to foreign investment.[33]

Problems

NAFTA's positive performance, however, has not been free of problems during its first years of existence. These problems have created tensions among the three NAFTA partners and may imperil the agreement in the future. These problems include recurring technical barriers and border controls imposed on both sides of the border, which disrupt trade and frustrate Mexican and U.S. businesses; and a rising number of antidumping actions between both Mexico and the United States and Canada and the United States.

Technical Standards and Border Controls

A variety of restrictions have been imposed on U.S. and Mexican products since 1994 as a result of the application of technical standards, testing procedures, and labeling requirements. Many conflicts have also arisen in the areas of custom administration and rules of origin.[34]

According to U.S. documents, Mexico has established standards—including "emergency" phytosanitary standards—that have impeded the entry of U.S. grains, citrus, cherries, cling peaches, and Christmas trees;[35] Mexico has also insisted on using national testing facilities that are still inadequate and has forced each importer to replicate testing even if another importer had arranged to test the same product. In March 1996 a problem that had created tremendous friction in 1994 and 1995 was finally resolved with an agreement on mutually acceptable test data for new truck and automobile tires, but many problems remain. In the telecommunications field, for example, deadlines have not been met, and standards have been established in a general way rather than in terms of network consistency. Both countries have complained that customs procedures have often been changed with little advance notification.[36]

Mexico, in turn, has objected to several U.S. actions such as the imposition of local content labeling requirements for automobiles, a continued embargo on Mexican tuna under the Marine Mammal Protection Act, the long delay in opening the U.S. market to Mexican avocados, and, once it was open, restriction of sales to selected regions of the United States.[37] But perhaps the most divisive issue has been the U.S. government decision to forbid Mexican trucks from circulating in the states adjacent to Mexico.[38] Sidney Weintraub has pointed out that this decision was made at the eleventh hour, despite a clear obligation in the agreement.[39] The excuse given was that Mexican trucks did not meet U.S. safety standards, but these standards were supposed to have been negotiated over a three-year period.[40] More recently, the United States delayed access for scheduled passenger bus service required under chapter 12 of NAFTA as of December 21, 1996.[41]

How should we interpret these problems? In 1994, when these problems began to appear, some analysts suggested that they stemmed from start-up difficulties, lack of administrative capacity, and poor communication.[42] Weintraub has suggested that these problems are relatively modest and amenable to resolution. Given their recurrence and prevalence, however, we must ask whether NAFTA rules are adequate to prevent the imposition of new technical barriers. To answer this question it is useful to review the purposes of technical standards and the existing regimes that prevent their utilization as trade barriers.

Technical standards are specifications that lay down some or all of a product's properties in terms of quality, purity, nutritional value, performance, dimensions, and other characteristics. Such specifications include, where appropriate, testing methods, regulations concerning safety and durability, and procedures for packaging, marking, and labeling products. Standards ensure minimum levels of control over products offered on the market and are adopted largely by domestic organizations to establish specifications that apply principally within national jurisdictions. Historically, standards have not been intended primarily to restrict trade, but the process of generating standards and certifying products has complicated and inhibited trade in numerous ways. In the worst cases, issues involving standards can become crucial and potentially significant nontariff barriers.

As an illustration of the significance this topic can have for facilitating or preventing free trade, the Cecchini Report, which provided the empirical base for the movement to the European Single Market, identified technical barriers—border controls, standards, rules of origin, and technical requirements—as the main costs of a "non Europe."[43] As a consequence, the EU has utilized several regimes in an attempt to reduce these barriers.

Technical regulations can no longer be used to keep imports out if the other country's technical requirements are "equivalent."[44] Mutual recognition and harmonization of national standards are two other approaches (besides equivalence) the EU has introduced to reduce the barriers of technical regulations.

NAFTA does attempt to deal with these issues in chapter 9, but it is far behind the EU in this area. Article 904 affirms the rights of each party to set "any standards-related measures," although the goods of another NAFTA country receive national and most-favored-nation (MFN) treatment. Article 906.2 requires "to the greatest extent practicable" the compatibility of standards-related measures. Articles 906.4 and 906.6 are key to the effective withdrawal of standards as trade barriers. In these two subsections parties agree that a standard of an "exporting party" is equivalent when that party demonstrates "to the satisfaction of the importing party that its technical regulation adequately fulfills the importing party's legitimate objectives" (906.4) and that parties accept "wherever possible the results of a conformity assessment procedure" conducted in the other country. Article 908.2 requires mutual accreditation of conformity assessment bodies, and procedures are set out (908.33, 909, 910) to ensure nondiscriminatory access to those bodies. Article 913 establishes the joint Committee on Standards-Related Measures, which monitors the implementation and administration of the chapter, provides a forum for consultation, and can establish subcommittees (four have been created).

The differences between the EU's mutual recognition process and chapter 9 of NAFTA are obvious. NAFTA is a host country standard regime, compared to the home country standard regime of the EU. Canada, for example, can require that Mexico must prove that Mexican standards in some area meet Canada's legitimate objectives. In the EU, France can only require that Portugal demonstrate that its standards in some area meet Portugal's objectives. Thus NAFTA does not involve mutual recognition, which entails a home country regime.

NAFTA does remove the obvious uses of standards as trade barriers and does provide for processes that lower the cost of standards setting.[45] The U.S. will accept results of tests in Mexico and Canada "whenever possible." Standards setting in NAFTA, however, is below the standard set in the EU in several ways. First, Article 904 of NAFTA allows individual country standards for a number of goods; the EU has Community-wide standards. Second, in the EU one country cannot prevent the import of goods that meet different member country standards (except for reasons of safety, health, and the environment); in NAFTA imported goods with different standards can be kept out. Finally, an individual country interprets what the "legitimate objective" of a standard is and what "practicable" means for comparability across countries.[46] I predict recurring and divisive conflicts over these definitions.

Antidumping Cases

Antidumping (AD) cases have also been a recurring problem, causing deep frustration among businesses in the three North American countries during the first years of the agreement. Most trade and economic policy analysts have concluded that AD procedures are among the most pressing areas for reform in the international trading system; by reform analysts mean elimination or at least a major circumscription.[47] Calls for reform have been particularly prominent in North America. The most that has been achieved so far has been the establishment of a special dispute resolution mechanism that was set up in chapter 19 of NAFTA. This chapter was negotiated as a compromise solution to a proposal by Canada and Mexico to suspend the application of AD laws among the three countries.[48]

Chapter 19 of NAFTA allows domestic judicial review of the national investigating authority's final determinations regarding AD and countervailing duty (CVD) to be replaced with a binational panel of five panelists with at least two panelists from each country. The fifth panelist is selected by agreement between the parties and by lot if agreement is not reached. One of the main purposes of the chapter 19 dispute resolution process is to monitor the use of antidumping and countervailing duties laws and thus increase the certainty of access to North American markets by establishing a process of revision of the antidumping final determinations of national investigating authorities that is "just, speedy, and inexpensive."[49]

Such a process of revision is assured through several means. First, five expert panelists from both countries are likely to make objective, fair decisions and to be less subject to political pressures.[50] Additionally, the process is aimed at discouraging frivolous claims and lax resolutions by helping private individuals and administrative authorities to recognize that their claims or decisions would be either rejected or amended, respectively, if they were not in accordance with the law. Low cost and speediness would be assured by establishing a 315-day period to conclude the revision.[51]

In the CUSFTA chapter 19 was originally intended to serve as a temporary mechanism while a working group developed a substitute system of rules for dealing with unfair transborder pricing practices and government subsidization, but the group failed to agree on a substitute system.

In NAFTA chapter 19 became a permanent mechanism. In December 1993, however, the three NAFTA parties issued a joint statement in which they agreed to "seek solutions that reduce the possibility of disputes concerning the issues of subsidies, dumping and the operation of the trade remedy laws regarding such practices" and to set up a working group to complete that work by December 31, 1995.[52] The group was established at the request of Canadian Prime Minister Jean Chrétien as part of his commitment to implement NAFTA. The deadline was met, but the work is far from complete and the parties have extended the group beyond the deadline.

What has happened in this area over the past several years? First, despite chapter 19, the incidence of AD cases has not significantly decreased and may even have increased since January 1994. Forty-nine cases were filed under the CUSFTA between January 1989 and December 1993, thirty of which reviewed U.S. investigating authorities' determinations and nineteen of which reviewed decisions by Canadian investigating authorities. As of March 1998, thirty-five requests for binational panel review had been filed under NAFTA, fifteen relating to U.S. agency determinations, eleven to Canadian determinations, and nine to Mexican agency determinations.[53] These figures suggest that the binational panel review process has had little or no deterrent effect on the initiation of trade remedy actions. Even though no systematic evidence exists of the cost of the review process, it appears to be very expensive to participants.

Second, even though the binational panel's record in disputes between Canada and the United States under CUSFTA was positive (in terms of being relatively expeditious, uncontroversial, and fair),[54] NAFTA's chapter 19 record shows it is clearly not making expeditious and noncontroversial decisions. Several high-profile disputes between Canada and the U.S. remain to be resolved.[55] In disputes between Mexico and the U.S. and between Mexico and Canada, the system has had difficulties serving its original purpose.[56]

Third, the uncertainty surrounding the invocation and application of these laws has not secured predictable access to North American markets, one of the original objectives of chapter 19. Only by eradicating the market distortions and commercial uncertainty caused by trade remedy laws will North American exporters have secure access to NAFTA markets.

In summary, NAFTA's four-and-a-half years of existence have been marked by vigorous expansion of trade and investment. NAFTA has also served as a vehicle for government cooperation on a variety of regulatory matters and has provided a valuable context for resolving several controversies. This positive performance, however, has not been free of problems, which have surfaced during the process of implementing the agreement and establishing NAFTA-related institutions. In seeking to address such problems and to strengthen the positive dimensions of regional integration, what can we learn from the European experience?

NAFTA'S FUTURE EVOLUTION: LESSONS FROM THE
EUROPEAN EXPERIENCE

Despite the obvious differences between NAFTA and the EU, the European experience can offer lessons on how important problems impeding the progress of an integration effort can be surmounted. It is worth recalling that NAFTA is facing the same problems that became major issues within the EU—namely, problems involving technical standards and other nontariff barriers such as antidumping. The EU addressed these issues by adopting a variety of regimes that have required a deepening of the integration arrangement and the relinquishing of domestic sovereignty in a number of critical areas. Are the three North American countries likely to adopt a similar approach to NAFTA's pending problems—namely, the adoption of positive integration à la the EU?

A long-standing debate in the literature has discussed the political and economic impacts of economic integration in the countries involved. The question is whether once the process of integration is initiated at the lower level it tends to move more or less automatically from one stage to the next. Political theories of integration have often asserted such a logic, whereas pure economic theory remains more skeptical.[57] Taking the EU as an example, one could argue that indeed economic integration has an inexorable logic even though the reactions of the Danish, French, and English electorates clearly prove that the progress beyond the customs union is unlikely to be smooth. If one takes other examples, such as the free trade agreements forged on an individual basis between what at that time was the EC and members of the European Free Trade Association (EFTA) (Iceland, Norway, Sweden, Finland, Austria, and Switzerland), one could reasonably argue that free trade areas can achieve stable equilibrium at levels that do not entail significant elements of supranationality—that is, that economic integration can be managed and contained at an early stage at least for a long time as the case of the EFTA countries shows.[58]

In principle, it is clear that NAFTA countries have intentionally chosen the EFTA rather than the EU route, but to what extent can the problems of nontariff barriers that have surfaced in North America be managed with the regime in place in NAFTA? I believe they cannot and that political and economic elites in the region will have to recognize that at the present time NAFTA is in an unstable equilibrium that may imperil the agreement in the future. But then, what direction is North American regional integration likely to take?

Contrary to what political theories of integration have asserted, it is not preordained that NAFTA will proceed productively or that North American regional integration will continue to deepen, although the chances that they will deepen are better than ever because of the objective realities in place. These realities include the growing vested interest in NAFTA by powerful traders and investors in the three countries; the impossibility for Mexico to revert to a state-led, protectionist model without paying an exorbitant price; and similarly, the high costs to the United States of withdrawing into protectionism given the global economic interests of its multinational corporations.

Mexico entered NAFTA with little internal debate, and the outcome may or may not have been the same if the agreement had been subjected to widespread public discussion. We must ask, therefore, whether the growing democracy in Mexico is favorable or unfavorable to the deepening of NAFTA. The answer is uncertain, but a full-blown debate will likely reveal NAFTA's importance to Mexico's trade and, hence, to its well-being. Likewise, in the United States, even though one of the reasons for President Bill Clinton's inability to obtain fast-track negotiating authority in 1997 was a perception among members of Congress that NAFTA was a failure, it would be as difficult for the United States to eliminate NAFTA's trade and investment arrangements as it would be for Mexico.

Nevertheless, two options are possible as one looks ahead. The first is the demise of NAFTA, which is conceivable without further deepening of the agreement. Arrangements within NAFTA must be dynamic because the economic situations of the member countries are continually changing. The obstruction of progress in any of the three countries will more likely lead to the atrophy of the agreement than to outright elimination, but the end result would be much the same. NAFTA could also come to an end if a major political fallout occurs among the member countries.

The second and much more likely outcome is the further deepening of the agreement. If it occurs, this will be a process of gradual change as the situation demands. In what areas is this evolution likely to take place?

Transformation of NAFTA into a Customs Union

This option implies one additional degree of political engagement by the member countries but not an overwhelming one. External tariffs are likely to merge in any event because retaining higher barriers against the import of intermediate and capital goods prejudices a country's competitiveness. The same is true of the use of nontariff barriers, which worsen the competitive position of domestic producers.

The most difficult aspect of moving to a customs union (CU) is the adoption of a common commercial policy. If the United States continues to use economic sanctions promiscuously as in the past, none of the NAFTA countries would want a common commercial policy. The countries can move to a common external tariff without a common commercial policy, which may be the form the deepening takes.

The main advantage of a CU is that most rules of origin can be eliminated, which would significantly simplify economic integration in North America and eliminate many of the border problems that have surfaced in recent years. Canada and Mexico would have to lower their external tariffs to the U.S. level if a common external tariff (CET) were adopted because it would be uneconomic for the United States to raise its tariff to accommodate the other two countries and also because of the worldwide nature of U.S. trade compared with that of Mexico and Canada.

Replacing the North American AD-CVD Regime

The replacement of the AD and CVD regime in North America would be as difficult to accomplish as moving from a free trade agreement to a CU, and it would be just as significant. In theory, AD measures are intended to combat predatory pricing, but as practiced in the U.S. and increasingly in Mexico, the real purpose is protectionism. This form of protection has powerful political support, which makes its elimination exceedingly difficult.

The one possible advantage of the increasing use of AD measures by Mexico is that those measures punish U.S. suppliers and may set up powerful countervailing political forces. U.S. apple producers, for example, lost a prime season for export to Mexico in 1997–1998 because of questionable AD duties. Mutual destruction is not the best rationale for dealing with AD practices, but it may be the only one that will work.

Dealing with government subsidies is different than treating private dumping. Much progress has been made on this issue in the context of the World Trade Organization.

The most effective way to eliminate the protectionist bias of the AD regime in North America would be to replace it with competition laws. Originally, AD remedies were conceived as the international extension of the anti–price discrimination laws under national jurisdiction. Over time, the approaches to the implementation of AD measures and domestic anti–price discrimination laws have evolved in different fashions,[59] especially in the U.S. Although it has become easier to obtain relief from imports through AD measures, it has become more difficult to obtain relief under the anti–price discrimination and anticompetitive laws. The U.S. Council of Economic Advisors has observed that AD laws often restrict trade and increase prices, unlike antitrust and anticompetition laws, which seek increased competition and lower prices. The council argues that making sound competition policies more easily enforceable against foreign misconduct would be a more appropriate response to restrictive business practices.[60]

The option of replacing antidumping with competition laws is feasible because "there already is similarity in the substantive price discrimination and predatory pricing laws of the United States, Canada and Mexico; however, there remain some key differences."[61] Thus for the replacement to take place, the three countries would have to agree to harmonize or converge their laws. This could happen, but it will take some time because, as mentioned previously, the type of protection implied by antidumping has powerful political support in the United States and increasingly in Mexico as well.

Freer Movement of Labor

Many Mexicans argue that if capital and goods can move freely under economic integration, why not labor? At present, however, extending NAFTA to include labor mobility is a political nonstarter in the United States. This can be explained by the wide income disparities among the three NAFTA countries.[62] Under current conditions free labor movement would reduce the wages of low-skilled U.S. workers, and no U.S. administration could adopt a policy that would hurt a large segment of its population and help a similarly situated group in another country.

Some developments in Mexico may reduce emigration pressures over time. The most important of these is the reduction in Mexico's birth rate, which, if continued, would reduce the pressure for job creation to accommodate new entrants into the labor force. This development, if coupled with consistently high real rates of economic growth of 5 to 6 percent a year over ten to fifteen years, should sharply reduce the push for emigration to the United States.

NAFTA AND DEMOCRATIZATION IN MEXICO

During the negotiations over NAFTA and particularly at the time of its ratification in the United States it was frequently asked whether the agreement would stimulate democratic development in Mexico. Supporters of NAFTA predicted increased democratization,[63] whereas opponents argued that NAFTA would strengthen authoritarianism.[64]

No clear answer to this question can be given because the relationship between economic integration and the political system is not necessarily direct or consistent.[65] Nevertheless, over the past two decades and even before, Mexico has been undergoing an important process of political change that has profoundly affected the norms and rules that traditionally regulated political practices and processes. These changes have been triggered primarily by the dramatic and profound process of economic restructuring the Mexican government imposed unilaterally as a way to resolve the economic crisis that followed the plummeting of oil prices and the debt crisis in the early 1980s.

Since NAFTA is an important part of economic reforms and in fact was negotiated to lock in such reforms, this section will identify and isolate the impact NAFTA negotiations and implementation have had on the dramatic political change in Mexico since the 1980s. I will first explore the nature of the political reforms and discuss the extent to which they can be understood to lead toward a democratic transition. Second, I will investigate NAFTA's impact on this change and show that although indirectly, it has supported the process of democratization in Mexico.

The Mexican Political System

Since the late 1970s the practices, norms, and institutions that for decades underpinned the world's oldest hegemonic party system have significantly eroded. Although Mexico's Institutional Revolutionary Party (PRI) showed renewed vitality with the election of Ernesto Zedillo in the 1994 presidential election, symptoms of instability preceded and followed the election, and the exercise of political control by the PRI seemed increasingly incompatible with government efficiency. To understand the dramatic changes that have taken place in the political arena, I will summarize the rules and institutions that governed political behavior in Mexico for more than four decades.

Mexico's Political Order During PRI Hegemony

Two basic maxims lay at the core of Mexico's postrevolutionary political system: One was the exchange of loyalties for political and economic gain; the other was the supremacy of the presidency. These two traits characterized Mexico for decades, and they go a long way toward explaining the longevity of the PRI and of the political norms, practices, and institutions that lie at its core; the country's economic ascent over the years, particularly from the 1940s to the early 1970s; and its current troubles.

The core institution of the political system after the 1920s was the presidency. Regardless of the system's formal structure, the presidency was its centerpiece. Everything was related to the presidency, and almost every institution was built to interact with it—either as a mechanism to channel demands to and negotiate with the president or as a means through which the president could act. Although a host of formal structures existed, from the legislature to the political parties, they all operated around the presidency. The presidency gained such relevance immediately after the revolutionary years when a host of strongmen brought about a concentration of political and military power. Álvaro Obregón (1920–1924) began to pacify the country, a process from which he emerged as strongman. But it was Plutarco Elías Calles (1924–1928) who shaped the political system by creating the National Revolutionary Party, which was eventually transformed into the PRI.

Calles's construct was an exceptional piece of political engineering. He succeeded not only in drawing into a single organization virtually all of Mexico's relevant political groups, clusters, political parties, militias, unions, and politicians but also in creating a mechanism whereby they all benefited from remaining under the PRI umbrella. As the party evolved, its foremost traits began to emerge. First, the central role of the president became paramount. When Calles was ousted as *líder máximo*, the party became institutionalized, giving way to a continual shift of coalitions. Successive presidents became the centerpiece of the system, each sustained in power by a different coalition of groups, politicians, and organizations. The president was the undisputed leader during his term, but that privilege ended when the term ended. The constant change of coalitions constituted a source of oxygen for the system at large, making it not only representative of and legitimate in the eyes of most of those in the political arena but also exceptionally effective.

The second trait of the political system was its success in maintaining the loyalty of most of the country's politicians and the leaders of numerous organizations. The system functioned around the principle that all politicians would be loyal to the system and the system would be loyal to them. The principle became an effective instrument for exerting discipline over the party membership and also nourished the expectation that one day, through discipline, an individual would have his or her own chance to access power. PRI members were exceptionally disciplined, largely because they expected—credibly—that discipline and loyalty would eventually allow them to enjoy valued privileges.

The system Calles invented and Lázaro Cárdenas (1934–1940) perfected by creating the so-called sectors (labor, the peasantry, popular, and initially, the military) was indeed exceptionally representative. It succeeded in bringing on board virtually all relevant political groups and was also representative of Mexicans at large. In fact, the PRI's success lay precisely in the fact that it brought all of the politically active groups and politicians into its core, thereby drawing enough support to maintain peace and stability and, as a result, to foster economic development.

Onset of the Decline of the PRI's Hegemony

For decades, these rules and institutions worked together smoothly and kept the political system in place. With the collapse of the import-substitution strategy and the debt crisis, however, discontent with PRI hegemony came to the fore. The introduction of market reforms undermined the traditional structures of single-party dominance—decentralizing decisionmaking, eroding corporatist controls, and awakening civil society. Economic reform inevitably required political reform, to an extent unanticipated by the economic reformers who began the process.[66]

President Miguel de la Madrid (1982–1988), as a first measure to regain public confidence, carried out a campaign for the "moral renovation of society." Yet the impact of economic adjustment in the electoral arena and the advance of the Partido Acción Nacional (PAN) in the north forced the government to consider new electoral reforms.[67] The 1988 presidential election again made clear the limits of a strategy implemented within the context of economic adjustment and stabilization policies.[68] Although the PRI's 1991 electoral recovery seemed to suggest the return of hegemonic rule, the party's performance could not easily eclipse two important changes: the gradual consolidation of opposition parties as effective political actors and related changes in the relative power of the main political actors. In sum, the ruling party's control over the process of political liberalization was increasingly questioned as the need for political opening became the main object of dispute between the regime and opposition parties.

The start of negotiations with Canada and the U.S. over NAFTA further complicated this situation by adding new actors and external linkages to Mexican politics and ending the isolation of PRI rule.[69] Although NAFTA did not attach an institutional or a formal commitment to democratic and human rights standards to Mexico's accession, its negotiation—including the parallel agreements and the ensuing process of ratification—produced important changes in the practices and strategies of political actors.[70] Political actors increasingly used the U.S. Congress and academic fora as an external arena of Mexican politics. As the Mexican government championed lobbies in Washington, opposition parties vigorously campaigned to denounce the government's authoritarian practices in the U.S. Congress, the media, and several universities.[71] This was an important shift in the traditional isolation enjoyed during the period of PRI hegemony.

Despite Salinas's effort to fine-tune political change, the political opening and the internationalization of domestic politics undermined the system's capacity to adjust to the demands of new actors seeking changes in the system, as well as of those negatively affected by the changing political circumstances. An increasingly complex dynamic was unleashed, characterized by the regime's effort to appease the opposition while preserving its own bases of support. NAFTA also undoubtedly played an important role in this dynamic, as it entered the government's calculation and influenced its decision to allow the opposition some electoral victories to smooth the road to negotiation.[72]

By the end of the Salinas administration, the main legacy of this dynamic was, on the one hand, the erosion of rules and institutions that in the past had fostered orderly political behavior and, on the other, the emergence and consolidation of new political actors, with important implications for the prevailing distribution of power. Indeed, the context created by NAFTA and, subsequently, the Chiapas uprising further accelerated the internationalization of Mexican politics and offered a window of opportunity the opposition seized to reopen electoral reform. This juncture altered the relative power of political actors and enabled opposition parties to realize an important change within the Federal Electoral Authority.

The Zedillo Administration and Democratization

When the new administration of President Zedillo took over in December 1994, prospects for democratization looked bright, but the complex and unexpected course of events since that time has led to increased uncertainty, polarization, and crisis. Although the Mexican government is still committed to liberal economic reforms, those reforms have not yet resulted in positive social gains. On the contrary, the December 1994 peso devaluation plunged Mexico into a new economic crisis that left most Mexicans in an increasingly perilous position.

Few societies could view with equanimity the dramatic declines in living standards implied by wage freezes, a devaluation of 40 to 50 percent in the value of the peso versus the dollar, higher interest rates (50 percent or more) on many outstanding loans, and increases of 30 to 50 percent in sales tax, the price of gas, and basic services such as transportation and utilities. The shock of yet another emergency austerity program after Mexicans had come to believe in promises of prosperity under NAFTA made the disillusionment worse. The crisis has exacerbated social conflicts in the short term. At least for the immediate future, it appears unlikely that the economy can create sufficient jobs for those displaced by international competition, who lose their jobs because of a wave of bankruptcies caused by high interest rates on private business debt, or who enter the Mexican job market for the first time—approximately 1 million workers each year.

Further, protest has not followed democratic means. The guerrilla movement that surfaced in January 1994 deliberately timed its first strike to occur on the date NAFTA went into effect and condemned the trade agreement's impact, especially on the peasants of southern Chiapas. Violent and highly confrontational protests, in turn, may undermine both economic recovery and political stability. In such circumstances, even if democratic construction occurs as a political solution to escalating social conflict, it will be difficult to consolidate a stable democracy.

CONCLUSION

In sum, Mexican society is in flux. Many of its traditional parameters appear unsettled. Since the beginning of 1995, there has been a qualitative transformation of the nature of demands against the government, as well as an extraordinary explosion of the media. Fundamental institutions of society have collapsed, as evidenced by ever increasing personal-security problems and concerns. Nevertheless, numerous political uncertainties represent some hope for democratization.

First, the erosion of undemocratic practices has widened the possibilities for democratic alternatives and has strengthened opposition voices.

Second, the regime's realization that traditional bases of stability are endangered has stimulated liberalization moves aimed at protecting stability. The most outstanding example of these efforts is the major political-electoral reform agreed to by the three major political parties in 1996 and carried out to assure competitive and fair elections. Most elections since the reform was put in place have been seen as fair and have been uncontested. Further, it was because of such reform that in the July 6, 1997, election, the opposition Party of the Democratic Revolution could win the governorship of Mexico City and the PRI could lose—for the first time since its founding in 1929—the majority in the Chamber of Deputies.[73] It is no longer unthinkable that a non-PRI candidate could win the presidential election in the year 2000.

Third, the vitality of civil society and some freedoms (e.g., media freedom) have expanded. Middle-class, business, and even grassroots populist groups have organized more autonomously and have become more critical of the regime, and a third sector of private nonprofit organizations and nongovernmental organizations is developing.

Fourth, unwritten rules that regulated U.S.-Mexican relations in the past have undergone important changes that favor democratization in Mexico. Although NAFTA did not contemplate the creation of a supranational institutional framework or condition Mexico's accession on formal democratic commitments, it has unleashed a dynamic that has intensified the interaction between the U.S. and Mexican political systems in a democratic direction. The visibility of Mexican politics and corruption in the U.S. media have become foremost sources of domestic pressure. The visibility of U.S. politics, particularly U.S. elections, on Mexican television constitutes a natural point of comparison those in Mexico cannot ignore. In 1994, for instance, presidential candidates held the first preelection debate in Mexican history, and such a debate is now a staple in most races. U.S. (and Canadian) unions, the staunchest opponents of NAFTA, have shifted their energies and instead of opposing free trade are now attempting to join Mexican unions and to transfer "technology" to those unions and enhance their ability to fight.[74] Technology, the Internet, the media, special interests, and U.S. congressional criticism have all played a significant role in shaping the Mexican democratization process.

In conclusion, even though Mexico has long been an authoritarian state, the situation is changing in a democratizing direction. This process, however, is arduous. The status quo ante seems to be dead. PRI dominance is a thing of the past. These changes have coincided with economic liberal reform and the first four years of NAFTA. There may not be causation, but there is surely interaction between economic and political liberalization.

NOTES

1. Bela Balassa, *The Theory of Economic Integration* (London: Allen and Unwin, 1962).

2. Jeffrey Schott and Murray Smith, *The Canada–United States Free Trade Agreement: The Global Impact* (Washington, D.C.: Institute for International Economics, 1988), 4–5, 41–42. See also Gustavo del Castillo and Gustavo Vega-Cánovas, *The Politics of Free Trade in North America* (Ottawa: Carleton University Center for Trade Policy and Law, 1995), 91–98.

3. See Office of the United States Trade Representative (USTR) and Related Entities, *Study on the Operation and Effect of the North American Free Trade Agreement* (Washington, D.C.: USTR, June 1997), 1 27.

4. A. Jorge Bustamante, Clark Reynolds, and Raul Hinojosa Ojeda, eds., *U.S.-Mexico Relations: Labor Market Interdependence* (Stanford: Stanford University Press, 1992), 1–18.

5. H. Peter Smith, ed., *The Challenge of Integration: Europe and the Americas* (New Brunswick: Transaction Publishers, 1993).

6. Gary Hufbauer and Jeffrey Schott, *North American Free Trade: Issues and Recommendations* (Washington, D.C.: Institute for International Economics, 1992), 3–9.

7. W. Wallace, *The Transformation of Western Europe* (London: Royal Institute for International Affairs, 1990); Loukas Tsoukalis, *The New European Economy: The Politics and Economics of Integration* (Oxford: Oxford University Press, 1993), 333–350.

8. Ibid.

9. Norbert Vanhove and Leo Klaassen, *Regional Policy: A European Approach*, 2d ed. (Aldershot: Avebury, 1987); also, Commission of the EC, *The Regions in the 1990s* (Luxembourg: Office for Official Publications of the European Communities, 1991).

10. Sidney Weintraub, *NAFTA at Three* (Washington, D.C.: Center for Strategic and International Studies, 1997), 17ff.

11. Although this always takes time, the intensity of the adjustment will tend to be greater and may take longer the smaller, less developed, and more highly protected an economy is prior to trade liberalization.

12. NAFTA established a four-stage program for phasing out tariff rates—immediate, 5 years, 10 years, and 15 years.

13. Most studies undertaken before NAFTA went into effect predicted that the agreement would benefit the three countries through increased exports, output, and employment. See Gary Hufbauer and Jeffrey Schott, *NAFTA: An Assessment* (Washington, D.C.: Institute for International Economics, 1994); also, Nora Lustig, Barry Bosworth, and Robert Lawrence, eds., *Assessing the Impact of North American Free Trade* (Washington, D.C.: Brookings Institution, 1992).

14. Bureau of the Census, Foreign Trade Division, *Top Ten Countries With Which the U.S. Trades* (Washington, D.C.: U.S. Government Printing Office, November 1996).

15. Bureau of the Census, Foreign Trade Division, *Exports, Imports and Balance of Goods by Selected Countries and Geographic Areas* (Washington, D.C.: U.S. Government Printing Office, November 1996).

16. Mexican production of cars and trucks for the domestic market dropped by 70 percent in 1995, some of which was offset by the 38 percent increase in exports, largely to the U.S. See Weintraub, *NAFTA at Three*, 39. Even though the drastic reduction of domestic demand in Mexico implied a 42 percent fall in U.S. automotive product exports to Mexico from the previous year, such exports nevertheless were double the pre-NAFTA level. See U.S. Department of Commerce, International Trade Administration, "Impact of the North American Free Trade Agreement on U.S. Automotive Exports to Mexico," *Report to Congress* (Washington, D.C.: U.S. Government Printing Office, June 1996). Bilateral trade data for 1995 reported by the Department of Commerce were U.S. vehicle exports to Mexico, $394 billion; parts exports, $6.7 billion; vehicle imports from Mexico, $7.8 billion; parts imports, $10.5 billion. On the general topic of NAFTA and automobiles, see Gustavo Vega-Cánovas, "NAFTA and the Auto Sector," in *The Politics of Free Trade*, del Castillo and Vega-Cánovas, eds., 159–183.

17. U.S. passenger vehicle exports during the first quarter of 1996 were 111 percent above those of the first quarter of 1995, and truck exports were 339 percent higher. The big three (General Motors, Ford, and Chrysler) shipped a record 26,533 vehicles to Mexico from U.S. and Canadian plants in the first five months of 1996, compared with 19,863 in the first five months of 1994 and only 10,574 during the same period in 1995. U.S. Department of Commerce, International Trade Administration, "Impact of the North American Free Trade Agreement."

18. Weintraub, *NAFTA at Three*, 40.

19. The basic rule of origin adopted under NAFTA was the so-called yarn-forward rule: To qualify for preferential treatment, textile goods had to be made from North American spun or extruded yarn. This rule of origin was acceptable to Mexico because slightly over half of Mexican fabric production was done by firms that also operated yarn-producing facilities.

20. The positive conditions NAFTA created for Mexico's apparel industry have also led to the establishment of new forms of production in the rural *ejidos*, which are plots of land set aside under the Mexican constitution for use (but not ownership) by peasant communities. Under the auspices of Mexican producer Compañía Manufacturera Libra, fifteen *ejidatario* owned and operated assembly plants have

been opened on *ejidos* in the Mexican states of Coahuila, Durango, and Oaxaca—generating more than 2,000 jobs and selling competitively priced, quality garments to major U.S. retailers.

21. See Office of the United States Trade Representative (USTR) and Related Entities, *Study on the Operation and Effect of the North American Free Trade Agreement*, 1–57.

22. *U.S.-Mexico Free Trade Report*, September 1, 1994, at 4 (citing 1994 data, Research Department, El Paso Branch–Federal Reserve Bank of Dallas).

23. *Maquila* employment increased by 9.8 percent in 1995 over 1994, to approximately 639,000 workers, according to the National Council of Maquila Industries, reported by *El Financiero International Edition* (May 27–June 2, 1996): 14. Total direct investment declined from approximately $10.972 billion in 1993 to $6.984 in 1995—still a very impressive figure. Although no separate data are given, it is reasonable to assume that a substantial portion of that investment was in the *maquila* industries. Bank of Mexico data.

24. "Maquiladora Employment Rose 20.3 Percent in November," *Journal of Commerce* (January 31, 1997): 3A, citing Mexican government data.

25. NAFTA, Article 303. Under duty drawback and similar duty deferral programs, import duties on parts and components may be refunded to the importer when the finished goods using the parts and components are exported. Under NAFTA, after January 1, 2001, refunds on parts and components imported from outside the region will be limited to the smaller of the duties on finished goods exported to another NAFTA country, or duties on imported parts and components. Thus if the finished goods are duty free under NAFTA, as will be the case with most intraregional trade by 2001, no duty refunds on parts and components will be available, and duty-free parts and components from within the region will gain a significant comparative advantage.

26. "Maquiladora Employment Rose 20.3 Percent in November," *Journal of Commerce* (January 31, 1997): 3A.

27. Of 1995 registrations 37.7 percent were U.S. owned, 14.0 percent were mixed U.S. and Mexican ownership, 42.6 percent were Mexican owned, 2.0 percent were Japanese, and 3.7 percent were owned by others. Mexican Ministry of Trade data quoted in "Fed Economist Credits NAFTA with Job Growth in Textile Apparel Maquiladoras," *International Trade Daily* (January 9, 1997): D6.

28. Anthony de Palma, "Economics Lesson in a Border Town," *New York Times* (May 23, 1996): C1, C5.

29. NAFTA Annex VII (B)(5),(9)(Mexico), VII-M-13,14,17.

30. Ibid.

31. During the ensuing four-year period, Mexico has the right to freeze the aggregate foreign capital percentage at 25 percent for commercial banks and 30 percent for securities firms for a maximum of three years. NAFTA Annex VII(B)(9) (Mexico), VII-M-17.

32. NAFTA Annex VII(C)(4)(Mexico), VII-M-20.

33. "Amendments to the Law to Regulate Financial Groups and the Law of the Securities Market," *Diario Oficial of the Government of Mexico* (February 15, 1995), reprinted in *Inter-American Trade and Investment* (February 24, 1995): 255.

34. The calculations required to demonstrate a particular regional value content—necessary under the NAFTA rules of origin for some import-sensitive products—have proven onerous, particularly for smaller exporters and importers that lack extensive in-house accounting expertise. A mistaken decision to claim NAFTA benefits exposes the importer not only to a difficult and expensive audit but also to subsequent payment of duties, interest, and possible penalties. Anecdotal evidence suggests that many smaller traders, whose goods would be subject to low U.S. tariffs even without NAFTA, are foregoing NAFTA tariff benefits because of the costs of record keeping and the risk of audits.

35. U.S. Trade Representative, *Foreign Trade Barriers* (Washington, D.C.: U.S. Government Printing Office, 1995, 1996).

36. Ibid.

37. The reason given was concern over the sanitary safety of Mexican avocados despite a U.S. Department of Agriculture finding that no such concern was warranted. See Weintraub, *NAFTA at Three*.

38. The negotiations over liberalizing trucking services were among the most important for Mexico. Clearly, for imports to compete with domestically produced goods, especially in a world of "just-in-time" production, timely and low-cost delivery is crucial. Once this provision is finally implemented, Mexico will enjoy a crucial comparative advantage.

39. Weintraub, *NAFTA at Three*. NAFTA requires that as of December 18, 1995, Mexican trucks should have direct access to the four U.S. border states and U.S. trucks should have access to the ten Mexican border states. See NAFTA, Annex I-M-69,70, I-U-20. As of October 1998, this provision had not yet been implemented.

40. Weintraub, *NAFTA at Three*.

41. BNA, *International Trade Daily* (January 3, 1997): D2. The U.S. Department of Transportation is expected to issue rules that will allow scheduled Mexican buses to obtain operating authority. Again, the principal concern is safety, but U.S. officials believe that Mexican standards for buses are higher than those for trucks and so the problem is less complex. "International Trade Outlook: Agriculture, Mexican Buses, Among Many NAFTA Issues," BNA, *International Trade Daily* (January 27, 1997): D10.

42. U.S. International Trade Commission, *The Year in Trade* (Washington, D.C.: U.S. Government Printing Office, 1995).

43. Indeed, within the EC until the 1970s, technical standards were the classic means of maintaining national barriers to Community trade. The European Court of Justice (ECJ), in two benchmark cases (*Cassis de Dijon* in 1979 was the most famous), greatly reduced EC members' ability to protect domestic producers on the basis of differing technical requirements. See reference to the Cecchini Report in Victoria Curzon Price, "1992: Europe's Last Chance? From Common Market to Single Market," *Occasional Paper* 81 (London: Institute of Economic Affairs, December 1988).

44. During 1990 thirty-nine ECJ rulings were delivered on issues involving the free movement of goods and the operation of the Customs Union.

45. NAFTA also sets up a Working Committee on Trade in Goods that annually

brings together officials concerned with border issues, although this mechanism is likely insufficient. Additionally, NAFTA does contain a dispute resolution process—the binational panels—but this process is costly and can take up to a year. One cannot rely on new agreements or costly binational panels to resolve border disputes, especially those involving minor issues; further, one cannot rely on "good faith" to establish convergence on customs issues. One possible avenue for minimizing the number of disputes is to have the working group meet monthly, provide it with a staff, and have informal discussions of different interpretations and potential conflicts before they become official disputes.

46. The EU has been careful to state that non-EU products are treated identically to EU products. Thus once a product has been accepted in France, for example, home country equivalence means that product is exportable across the EU. No similar language exists in NAFTA.

47. An extensive literature has developed that is critical of the protectionist bias of antidumping procedures, regulations, and statutes. See, for example, Jagdish Bhagwati, *Protectionism* (Cambridge: MIT Press, 1989), 123; W. Robert McGee, "The Case to Repeal the Antidumping Laws," *Northwestern Journal of International Law and Business* 13 (1993): 491–527; Beatriz Leycegui, William Robson, and S. Dahlia Stein, eds., *Trading Punches: Trade Remedy Law and Disputes Under NAFTA* (Washington, D.C.: National Planning Association, 1995). Further, most experts agree that dumping is rare in a free trade area once tariffs and other barriers have been eliminated.

48. Canada under CUSFTA and then Mexico under NAFTA were convinced that to gain secure and stable access to the U.S. market they would need to be excluded from U.S. legislation on antidumping, subsidies, and countervailing duties. In their perception, U.S. legislation in these matters had increasingly protectionist overtones; therefore, they both needed special treatment in the form of exclusion. Canada and Mexico reached this conclusion because by the mid-1980s the United States was the largest single user of administrative trade law remedies. See Anne Krueger, *American Trade Policy: A Tragedy in the Making* (Washington, D.C.: American Enterprise Institute Press, 1995), 35. In an address to the Mexican Senate at the conclusion of the NAFTA negotiations, Mexican Minister of Commerce Jaime Serra stated that "a fundamental aspect of the negotiation was to make sure that Mexican exporters would not be subject to an arbitrary and unjustifiable application of defense measures against unfair trade practices by the United States." See Javier Garciadiego, *El TLC a día a día* (Mexico: Miguel Angel Porrua Grupo Editorial, 1994).

49. See rule 2 of the North American Free Trade Agreement Rules of Procedure for Article 1904 of NAFTA.

50. Some indicators that would serve to measure the objectivity and fairness of the panel decisions would be a high technical quality of the decisions by the panels and that such decisions did not reflect a bias against or for trade remedy legislation, or a nationalistic bias.

51. This brief time period would give rise to savings in time and money, especially in attorney fees.

52. *Inside NAFTA* (Washington, D.C.: Inside Washington Publishers, December 17, 1993).

53. Sección Mexicana del Secretariado de los Tratados de Libre Comercio, *Informe de los Casos de Solución de Controversias del Capítulo XIX y XX del Tratado de Libre Comercio de América del Norte* (Mexico City: Seccion Mexicana del Secretariado del TLC, March 1998).

54. Michael Trevilcock and Thomas Bodez, "The Case for Liberalizing North American Trade Remedy Laws," *Minnesota Journal of Global Trade* 4, no. 1 (1995): 6.

55. The panel system has failed to resolve several high-profile disputes relating to products and sectors that involve the highest value of trade between Canada and the U.S. within politically powerful industries.

56. The binational panels involving Mexico have been less timely than those between Canada and the U.S. Of the active and completed cases reviewing U.S. and Mexican agency determinations in December 1996, more than 80 percent had been suspended or had asked for postponement of the original 315-day limit. In addition, some of the cases have been controversial; in one case the panel's decision led to the presentation of an Amparo (a judicial procedure aimed at providing a remedy against the final decisions of all judges or administrative authorities), which if granted by the Mexican courts may jeopardize Mexico's participation in chapter 19. See Beatriz Leycegui and Gustavo Vega-Cánovas, "Eliminating Unfairness Within the North American Region: A Look at Antidumping," in *Finding Middle Ground: Reforming the Antidumping Laws in North America*, Michael Hart, ed. (Ottawa: Centre for Trade Policy and Law, Carleton University, 1997), 251–304.

57. Charles Pentland, "North American Integration and the Canadian Political System," in *The Politics of Canada's Economic Relations with the United States,* Denis Stairs and Gilbert Winham, eds. (Toronto: University of Toronto Press, 1985), 95–126.

58. Victoria Curzon Price has aptly demonstrated that the free trade technique successfully managed the relationship between the EC and the EFTA countries where the latter group "had no stomach for the highly intensive form of economic integration on which the EC was prepared to embark [and wanted] to keep a free hand not only in trade policy but in . . . industrial policy." See her "Free Trade Areas: The European Experience. What Lessons for Canadian-U.S. Trade Liberalization?," *Observation* 31 (Toronto: C. D. Howe Institute, 1987). EFTA countries' recent accession to the EU seems to support the inexorable logic of economic integration. The fact that accession took so long to develop, however, would support the notion that free trade areas can be sustained, at least for many years.

59. Murray Smith, "The Evolution of Trade Remedies in NAFTA," in *Finding Middle Ground*, Hart, ed., 18–83.

60. U.S. President, *Economic Report of the President Transmitted to the Congress* (Washington, D.C.: U.S. Government Printing Office, 1994), 239.

61. American Bar Association, *Report of the Task Force of the ABA Section of Antitrust Law on the Competition Dimension of NAFTA* (Chicago: ABA, 1994).

62. As Hufbauer and Schott have pointed out, the European Community spanned a wide divide when it incorporated Spain and Portugal, whose per capita GNP levels at the time of accession (January 1986) were $4,860 and $2,250, re-

spectively, or 40 percent and 19 percent, respectively, of West German per capita GNP. By comparison, in 1989 Mexico's per capita GNP was only 12 percent that of the United States and Canada combined. See G. Hufbauer and J. Schott, *North American Free Trade: Issues and Recommendations* (Washington, D.C.: Institute for International Economics, 1992), 7–8. This differential may have widened as a result of the economic crisis that started in Mexico in 1994.

63. NAFTA supporters relied on the assumption that economic liberalization would be a catalyst for political opening in a democratic direction through the gradual erosion of the long-standing control by the center, the greater decentralization and delegation of economic policymaking, and the articulation of new coalitions, as well as the setting of limits to arbitrariness and presidentialism. Two representatives of this view are M. Delal Bael, "North American Free Trade," *Foreign Affairs* 70, no. 4 (1991): 132–149; and Luis Rubio, "Mexico in Perspective: An Essay on Mexico's Economic Reform and the Political Consequences," *Houston Journal of International Law* 12, no. 2 (1990).

64. NAFTA opponents predicted increased authoritarianism based on the increase in the negative sociopolitical consequences economic reforms were producing; they believed the agreement would accelerate the long-standing resilience of the Mexican authoritarian regime, and furthermore pointed out that the U.S. government has played an important role in supporting Mexico's authoritarian system. Two representatives of this view are Cuauhtémoc Cárdenas, "Free Trade Is Not Enough," *New Perspectives Quarterly* (winter 1991): 62–80; and Jorge Castañeda, "Can NAFTA Change Mexico?" *Foreign Affairs* 72, no. 4 (1993).

65. This argument is cogently demonstrated in Peter Smith, "The Political Impact of Free Trade in Mexico," *Journal of Inter-American Studies and World Affairs* 34, no. 1 (1992): 1–25.

66. It is easy to understand why profound political reforms were necessary. Economic restructuring and the need to transfer resources abroad to meet debt obligations produced sharp drops in living standards during the 1982–1988 stabilization program. These declines affected not only the poor but also the middle class. This was the first setback faced by this influential group since the 1930s. Naturally, most Mexicans blamed the political authorities for the nation's dire economic situation. As a result, passive resentment turned into active voting for opposition parties, particularly the *Partido Acción Nacional*, a conservative party that had taken a strong anticorruption and free market stance.

67. In 1982 minor electoral reforms were aimed at bolstering the regime and containing electoral protest rather than providing for orderly competition. As the PAN gained momentum and captured the protest vote in state and local elections in 1984, the PRI decided to rig the electoral results, thereby confirming the belief that democracy was not among de la Madrid's priorities. The 1986 electoral reform again reinforced PRI hegemony by introducing proportional representation in the Federal Electoral Commission and the vertical appointment of commission officers. These reforms were justified on the basis of creating stability. See Juan Molinar, *El tiempo de la legitimidad. Elecciones, autoritarismo y democracia en México* (Mexico City: Cal y Arena, 1991).

68. The PAN was supplanted as a catalyst for discontent by the 1988 presiden-

tial candidacy of Cuauhtémoc Cárdenas, son of one of Mexico's most revered presidents, Lázaro Cárdenas. In fact, the young Cárdenas captured the voters' imagination by invoking memories of his father and running on a platform opposed to PRI economic reform, which he described as a betrayal of the Mexican Revolution's heritage. The outcome of the 1988 presidential elections, which many claimed to be fraudulent, left the incoming administration of Carlos Salinas (1988–1994) with problems of legitimacy.

69. Unlike the EC, where government representatives became key actors in forging the Treaty of Rome and interest groups seem to have played no part, the process in NAFTA has been different. Although the NAFTA negotiations may have been led from the top, the impending accord catalyzed a wide range of interests and pressure group activity—including social mobilization in Mexico, trade union demands and political party debates in the United States, and the emergence of unprecedented cross-border coalitions to promote expanded and more effective environmental social provisions. See Cathryn Thoroup, "The Politics of Free Trade and the Dynamics of Cross-Border Coalitions in U.S.-Mexican Relations," *Columbia Journal of World Business* 26, no. 2 (summer 1991): 12–26.

70. In fact, this lack of a democratic requirement foreclosed for Mexico the route to democracy that has been called "democracy by convergence," which takes place through the enlargement of a preexisting democratic community of sovereign states. The new entrant must agree to a democratic test to qualify as a member. In the case of NAFTA the U.S. did not impose such a test on Mexico, and its main concern seems to have been Mexican political stability. Here again we find another important difference between regional integration in North America and that in Europe. European integration in the post–World War II period was defined by overlapping concerns with economic growth, military security, and democratic community. In North America regional integration reflects more pragmatic and plural loyalties. See Lawrence Whitehead, "Democracy by Convergence in Southern Europe," in *Encouraging Democracy: The International Context of Regime Transition in Southern Europe*, Geoffrey Pridham, ed. (Leicester: Leicester University Press, 1991), 45–62.

71. This trend was first seen after the disputed 1986 Chihuahua gubernatorial in which the PAN candidate was believed to have been denied a legitimate victory. Frustrated PAN activists went to Washington without the authorization of their national headquarters, met with several U.S. senators and other leaders, and held a conference at the National Press Club to call attention to their grievance. They also filed a formal complaint with the Human Rights Commission of the Organization of American States. In 1988, Cardenas toured the U.S. for the same purpose. See M. Delal Baer and Sydney Weintraub, eds., *The NAFTA Debate: Grappling with Unconventional Trade Issues* (Boulder: Lynne Rienner, 1994).

72. The impact of this calculation was evident during the 1991 midterm and gubernatorial elections in the states of Guanajuato and San Luis Potosí and the gubernatorial election in Michoacán in 1992. The resignations of the apparently victorious candidates reflected sensitivity to external pressure at a time when the outcome of NAFTA negotiations was uncertain. See ibid., 177.

73. The 1997 midterm elections represent a significant advance toward democ-

racy. With only a few exceptions, the major political parties accepted both the process and the results of the elections. Opposition victories by the Party of the Democratic Revolution in the governor's race for Mexico City and the PAN in gubernatorial races in Querétaro and Nuevo León were promptly recognized by the regime. Mexicans turned out in record numbers, demonstrating a high degree of civic enthusiasm. In Mexico City participation rates approached 75 percent; nationally they hovered around 60 percent.

74. A number of concrete examples of trade union organizational cooperation have been seen under NAFTA. For example, the United Electrical Workers Union has entered into a Strategic Organizing Alliance with the Frente Autentico del Trabajo (FAT), an independent Mexican union organization that organizes workers along the border who work for U.S. multinationals such as GE and Honeywell. This alliance eventually led to the first NAFTA complaint under the Side Agreement on Albor Cooperation. The United Steelworkers of America-Canada has been supporting union expansion and leadership training with the FAT since 1994, and FAT has participated in major national conferences. See other examples of trade union organizational cooperation under NAFTA in Canadian Labor Congress, *Social Dimensions of North American Economic Integration: Impacts on Working People and Emerging Responses. A Report Prepared for the Department of Human Resources Development* (Ottawa: CLC, 1996), 76–82.

11

Mercosur: Democratic Stability and Economic Integration in South America

José Augusto Guilhon Albuquerque

Following the so-called lost decade of the 1980s, South American political leaders were increasingly aware of their countries' need to meet the new requirements for partnership in the post–Cold War era. They were proud of their new democratic institutions, sound macroeconomic policies, and fresh credibility after a decade of spiraling inflation and uncontrolled external debt. As regional leaders became increasingly aware of the costs implied in their domestic agendas, they became more concerned about the region's failure to remain at the forefront of world concern.

In the early 1990s Europe's Maastricht initiative provoked diverse reactions in South America. Some viewed the European Union (EU) as a new superpower—indeed, as an alternative partner for those countries whose relations with the United States were strained. Some felt reassured by common ancestral ties to Europe. They longed for a Latin fraternity as a protection from market challenges. Others feared a European fortress—that is, a new protectionism emerging around the dismantled internal barriers. The decline of Western European investment in South America seemed to suggest the dissolution of significant economic relations with the European continent.

The fall of the Soviet empire was another matter of concern. Central Europe now appeared much more attractive as a partner for investments formerly undertaken with countries such as Brazil and Argentina. First, a close cultural proximity exists between Western and Central Europe. Second, Europeans clearly felt a moral need to assist their neighbors who had long been in distress. Finally, the new prospective market had an industrial and technological base supposedly more developed than that in Latin America.

Privileged links between Europe and its former colonies in South America are also a permanent source of anxiety. Some have proposed extending to Latin America the status granted by the Lomé Agreements instead of demanding the end of trade barriers. This idea is ambiguous, associated with the expectation of privileged entry into Europe through the Iberian countries. Among other things, such status would shift existing trade with Germany, for instance, to Spain and Portugal. It would mean more alienation from, rather than proximity to, the most dynamic poles of growth.[1]

The prospect of vanishing from the U.S. and European world map is so threatening that those who had blamed imperialist strategic interests for Latin America's backwardness and dependency are now decrying the problems generated by imperialism's unwillingness to continue to exploit those countries. Throughout its history South America has been linked to the dynamic core of the world economy. Born as part of the Iberian economic world, the region belonged to the first global economy. In the nineteenth century South America was integrated into the British Empire, the only empire in that century of imperialisms with the ability to implement its vision of a balance of power in Europe and hegemony around the world. In the twentieth century the region was incorporated into the American empire.

South America's unexpected situation of nondependency on existing trade blocs can be considered from several viewpoints. First, it could mean being condemned to a marginal position of no return. The situation could also mean the possibility of establishing cooperative links with every trade bloc or free trade agreement (FTA) and even the ability to choose among different forms of integration into each area or bloc.[2] Nondependency could also allow South America to demand true multilateralism.[3]

Among the countries not integrated into the major trading areas, the most developed countries in the Southern Cone of South America—Argentina, Brazil, and Chile—represent the most viable options for short-term market expansion from the point of view of the United States, Japan, and the EU countries.[4] The countries of South America's Southern Cone are in the best position to rapidly absorb massive flows of capital, whether in production, commerce, or finance. In fact, in contrast to Eastern Europe, Argentina, Brazil, and Chile possess an entrepreneurial elite, somewhat freely organized unions with considerable potential for industrial bargaining, a banking community that endured despite the volatility of monetary policies in Argentina and Brazil during the 1980s, and relatively widespread social affluence.

Nevertheless, the attractiveness of the Southern Cone to major global investors has been offset by a number of constraints. Democratic institutions in those countries are still undergoing an unfinished process of transition from authoritarian rule.[5] Their history is one of great economic and political instability. Their new democratic governments are facing a wide range of social welfare problems with different levels of success (or failure). Finally, Argentina and Brazil are struggling to fully recover international credibility as a result of their pressing foreign debt and the volatility of their monetary and exchange policies in the recent past.

Whatever the outcome, we can hardly assume that the Southern Cone is entirely off the world economic map. Its integration into the new dynamic economic relationships depends substantially on its ability to consolidate economic and political stability through institutional reforms. Those were the goals explicitly sought by Argentinean and Brazilian leaders when they initiated the bilateral cooperation that later led to the creation of Mercosur.

In this chapter I describe the dramatic efforts of South American leaders to reassess their countries' role in international relations, the importance of a balanced and stable economy, and the relevance of democratic institutions to the long road back from stagnation. In this context, regional integration appears to be a stepping stone to adjustment to a changing domestic and international environment. Mercosur is a response to this complex, multilevel challenge, and the chapter analyzes its impact on both the region's relationships with its major international partners and the domestic processes of consolidation of democratic institutions.

MERCOSUR: ORIGINS AND MAJOR FEATURES

The idea of regional economic integration seems like just another panacea. Why not stabilize the economy and politics first and *then* integrate those national economies that have recovered their economic dynamism? Does it make sense to integrate in a context of industrial backwardness, limited markets, and limited regional trade?

These criticisms apply more to the traditional conception of Latin American integration, a notion strongly associated with the theory of import substitution and deeply entangled in Third World ideology.[6] They do not apply to the policies guiding Mercosur, the origins of which lie in a shift in bilateral relations between Brazil and Argentina during the 1980s. These countries openly competed for hegemony in the Southern Cone of South America and in Latin America as a whole during the 1960s and 1970s. In 1979, however, both countries, along with Paraguay, signed an agreement regulating common use of the Paraná River. In 1980 an agreement on cooperation in nuclear energy was signed, followed by the establishment of regular political consultations between the foreign ministers of the two countries to occur on an ongoing basis.

After the election of new democratic governments in Argentina (Raul Alfonsín) and Brazil (José Sarney, elected vice president of Tancredo Neves), cooperation between the two countries intensified. The two presidents met in 1985 to announce the *Ata do Iguaçu* (Protocols of Iguaçu), which established a high-level joint committee to study trade integration between the two countries, as well as broader economic issues. This was followed in 1986 by the Economic Integration and Cooperation Joint Program, which included twelve protocols addressing specific policy areas such as trade, customs, technical regulations, taxation and monetary affairs, transportation, industrial competitiveness, technology, agriculture, and energy.

In 1988 the two governments signed a bilateral Treaty on Integration, Cooperation and Development, ratified by both national Congresses the following year, which called for the creation of an FTA between Brazil and Argentina within ten years. In 1990 new presidents were in power in both countries: Carlos Menem in Argentina and Fernando Collor in Brazil. The two signed the *Ata de Buenos Aires* (Protocols of Buenos Aires), which set December 31, 1994, as the deadline for the establishment of a common market—a more ambitious goal than an FTA. Finally, in 1991 the two men signed the Treaty of Asunción, which opens Mercosur to Paraguay and Uruguay under the same deadline.[7]

The common market provided for in the Treaty of Asunción entailed:

- Free circulation of goods, services, and factors of production among the member states through the elimination of all tariff, nontariff, and similar barriers
- A customs union including common external tariffs, common commercial policies toward third countries, and coordination of policies to be adopted by multilateral economic and commercial forums
- Coordination of macroeconomic and sectoral policies, such as external trade, and agricultural, industrial, fiscal, monetary, and exchange policies to assure the leveling of conditions for competition among member states
- Commitment of member states to harmonization of domestic legislation in areas relevant to regional integration.

A transition period was fixed before the December 31, 1994, deadline when the common market was to be fully enforced. Several measures were adopted to achieve the goals:

1. A Trade Liberalization Program consisting of an automatic, progressive, and linear reduction of all tariffs and the elimination of nontariff and

similar barriers to attain zero tariff, as well as the total elimination of other barriers to intra-Mercosur trade by December 31, 1994. Although more than 90 percent of tariffs were included in the program, a list of exceptions was adopted, along with special regimes applying to sensitive industries. In 1994 a new Protocol of Agreement was signed in Ouro Preto (Brazil) establishing a 10-year delay for the elimination of exceptions and special regimes. Paraguay and Uruguay were given longer delays, a slower progression of tariff reduction, and longer lists of exceptions.

2. Coordination of macroeconomic policies, to be adopted gradually and consistently with trade liberalization. The growing interdependence among the economies, particularly between Brazil and Argentina, provided the basis for informal consultations and prompt information concerning major government decisions expected to influence another country's economic stability. No formal mechanisms of coordination were created, however.

3 A common external tariff. The Protocol of Ouro Preto downgraded the full-fledged common market, to be completed by 1995, into a customs union, to be enforced by the same date. The external tariffs of the four countries were then converted to a common level, averaging the higher Brazilian tariffs and the lower tariffs of the three other countries, but similar exceptions and special regimes applied. A ten-year transition period was adopted to eliminate exceptions, and new exceptions would apply pending consultation among the four countries.

4. Sectoral agreements, aimed at optimizing factors and scales of production. From labor to the environment, to transportation and technical standards, sectoral task groups met continually from the beginning of Mercosur. This is probably the aspect in which integration developed the most.

The treaty did not provide a finalized institutional framework for Mercosur. A provisional organizational structure was created to monitor the transition to a full fledged common market, which would then adopt new permanent institutions. Article 18 of the treaty states that prior to the establishment of the common market by December 1994, the member states would meet to decide on the permanent institutional structure and decisionmaking system of Mercosur.

Meanwhile, Mercosur was given two bodies—the Common Market Council[8] and the Common Market Group[9]—both of which make decisions on a consensus basis—a situation that makes Mercosur more of a forum for permanent intergovernmental negotiations than a supranational organization. The Protocol of Ouro Preto postponed discussions of and decisions concerning the final institutional framework of Mercosur, which continues as a permanent forum for negotiations plus a set of ill-defined new bodies: the (powerless) Administrative Secretariat; the Socioeconomic Forum, a consultative panel designed to integrate economic and social actors; and the Parliamentary Commission, conceived as a stepping stone to a future common legislative body.

MAJOR OBSTACLES TO THE FORMATION OF MERCOSUR

Four main arguments were raised against the viability of Mercosur in the early 1990s. First, critics pointed to the conspicuous imbalance among the relevant countries in terms of population, size of economy, and level of industrial development. Brazil is several times larger than its three partners combined; only Argentina can be compared to Brazil in terms of economic modernization, although its dynamic sector continues to be agriculture. From the beginning these imbalances have resulted in different rates of trade liberalization and tariff and nontariff reduction. Further, negotiations over the common external tariff and the customs union often dealt with contrasting conditions that were difficult to reconcile—not between industries of different scale and competitiveness, as is typically the case in Europe, but between a struggling industry and no industry at all.[10] These concerns about the heterogeneity of the Mercosur group are similar to objections raised against NAFTA: The imbalance between the economies was such that, to paraphrase Ross Perot, either a "sucking" of jobs from high-wage to low-wage economies, or the total destruction of the smaller, less competitive economies would occur.

A related argument takes the EU as a reference point to imply the necessity of transferring compensatory funds from wealthier (Brazil) to poorer economies, which would make the cost of Mercosur unbearable (and for that matter far less desirable) for a developing economy such as Brazil. This complaint, like the previous one, has yet to meet the burden of proof.

Second, critics have complained that the pace of integration was pushed too quickly by the current governments of Brazil and Argentina and ratified too soon by the other two countries. Even if no other obstacles existed to the full implementation of the program, it is unlikely that a highly complex process of supranational institutionalization could be accomplished in two or three years. The organization of the EU started with a much greater level of economic cooperation and was far less ambitious. In the case of Mercosur, speed became a liability rather than an asset.

Critics also point out that Mercosur still lacks solid experience in trade negotiations, political coordination, and institution building. The four countries' academic, business, and political classes do not know each other's history, economies, and culture. A strong generation of "South Americanists" has yet to be formed.

The rapid pace of integration in South America is a direct consequence of the electoral rhythm affecting presidential mandates in plebiscitarian democracies such as Brazil and Argentina.[11] Ten years was too long a delay when presidential terms were four or seven years and reelection was prohibited.[12] The common market, which was to be accomplished in four years, has been postponed for ten more years. A set of exceptions to be eliminated in four years has been extended ten more years.

One of the most strongly criticized aspects of the pace of integration has proved to be an important asset. The linear progressive tariff reduction—a reduction of 25 percent each year, with a target of zero tariff by 1995—actually worked: Over 95 percent of tradable items produced in Mercosur are now subject to a zero tariff inside the treaty area. The loosening of all other measures of trade liberalization following the Protocol of Ouro Preto—ten more years for the elimination of exceptions to internal and external tariffs, ten more years for the elimination of special regimes—together with delays of up to fifteen years to adopt specific areas of the agreement between Mercosur and Chile, suggest that a slower pace of internal tariff reduction would have given rise to stronger pressures to postpone liberalization still further.

A third obstacle to Mercosur involves the electoral pace already mentioned. The inclusion of Paraguay and Uruguay clearly increased the imbalance among the partners and the difficulties of negotiation. Exclusion from Mercosur, however, would have been too heavy an electoral burden for the incumbent presidents of the two smallest countries of the Southern Cone; their premature entry into Mercosur indicates their governments' limited ability to resist domestic pressure for change.

The last argument concerns the volatility of public policies, which is generally associated with presidential powers, particularly in plebiscitarian presidential regimes. Monetary, fiscal, and foreign exchange policies are not subject to effective legislative control and depend only on the president and his or her many— and not always concurring—advisers. Coordination of macroeconomic policies between the two leading countries of Mercosur was therefore a practical impossibility from the beginning. Indeed, the only mechanisms provided for such coordination have been intergovernmental committees, which suffer from the same congenital disease as the domestic policy process.[13]

MAJOR ARGUMENTS OF MERCOSUR SUPPORTERS

I now turn to arguments advanced by supporters of economic integration in the Southern Cone.[14] Complementarity of exports and imports between countries was a major requirement of the earlier theory of Latin American integration. By contrast, present regional economic integration in different areas is based on overall competitiveness and intrasectoral complementarity. In this sense, Mercosur is not intended to enhance exchanges of, for instance, Argentinean wheat for Brazilian water power plants; instead, it is supposed to stimulate Argentinean or Uruguayan investments in the Brazilian sugar cane industry, or to induce the creation of multinational Mercosur joint ventures to compete in foreign markets where Brazilian contractors already operate.

Therefore, Southern Cone economic integration should be regarded not as a defensive strategy but as an active policy. Integration was not to be designed as a new autarkic response to trade blocs that excluded South American countries. Its aim was to link the most dynamic and competitive sectors of Southern Cone countries to enhance their ability to compete in international trade.

Brazil and Argentina, the leading countries of Mercosur, have been adjusting their economies to fit a post-import-substitution era. At different speeds and with different results, they have followed steps similar to the economic adjustments undertaken in other Latin American countries such as Chile and Mexico: opening the economy to foreign trade, privatizing state-owned enterprises, and cutting public deficits.

The coordination of macroeconomic policies required by regional integration in Mercosur should place additional pressure on national governments to continue to pursue these adjustment policies. At the least, this need for coordination should constitute an extra obstacle to sudden shifts in national macroeconomic policies. Moreover, international agreements often remove specific issues from the domestic political agenda. In every successful economic integration framework based on international agreements or treaties, strong motivations have been present to remove the issues included in those treaties from domestic politics.

The first institutional framework for the European Community, the European Coal and Steel Community, was designed to support deep national economic adjustments in coal and steel policies that would otherwise have met strong domestic opposition. Canada and Mexico experienced difficult domestic adjustments in a shift away from import-substitution policies before they joined the United States in trade agreement negotiations. In both countries opposition to adjustment was such that the governments feared having to make concessions that would undermine the original reforms. In such cases reform-minded leaders welcomed the opportunity to remove the controversy regarding adjustment from the domestic arena.

If removing specific conflictual issues over adjustment from the domestic arena is a significant stimulus for international agreements, we can respond to two major criticisms of Mercosur. The first concerns the volatility of macroeconomic policies in plebiscitarian democracies such as the presidential system of Brazil and Argentina. Rather than waiting for prior stabilization of policies as a prerequisite for multipartite coordination, we could expect that the need for coordination imposed by international agreements would be a powerful inducement for stabilizing domestic macroeconomic policies.

The second criticism concerns the strong opposition to liberalizing reforms that emerged in these countries. Complete liberalization of the Southern Cone countries' economies is supposed to be a precondition for sound regional trade agreements. But a thorough liberalization program could be abandoned in the face of strong domestic and foreign interests. In contrast, international agreements requiring liberalizing policies could effectively remove those policies from the domestic agenda, thereby contributing to their continuity and eventual success.

THREE CONVERGING CRISES: CREDIBILITY, STABILITY, AND LEGITIMACY

Latin America entered the 1990s facing three converging crises. The first, which flowed from the problem of external debt, was a credibility crisis in international financial circles, which accounts for the reduction in capital flows to Latin America during the 1980s and early 1990s. When renegotiations of major Latin American countries' debts were concluded, international capital flows to the region increased again. Volatile capital and then productive investments followed; direct investments in Mercosur grew from a low of $3 billion in 1991 to an expected $8 billion in 1998.

The second crisis was caused by hyperinflation, a widespread problem among Latin American countries. Instead of monetary instability, however, the critical factor was the volatility of macroeconomic policies. In the case of Brazil, for instance, succeeding governments—and even succeeding finance ministers and central bank presidents within the same government—issued no less than six anti-inflation stabilization plans from 1986 to 1994. The plans had a common result: a growing lack of credibility. Monetary policy was frequently adjusted, as were the exchange rate and trade rules. Importers, exporters, and external investors complained about the absence of clear, unchanging rules.

The third crisis involved legitimacy. In all areas of transnational opinion during the period—whether human rights, indigenous populations' rights, environmental protection, and, later, democracy, Latin American governments were in debt across the board.

Each of these crises enveloped individual countries, as well as the region as a whole. Prospects for successful regional integration through Mercosur were constrained by Brazil's inability to follow the region's pace of trade liberalization and monetary stabilization. This inability supposedly resulted in an interruption of investment flow as a consequence of Brazil's low international credibility.

The main factor weakening Brazilian and, as an extension, Mercosur's credibility was the instability of Brazil's macroeconomic policies. As a result, the country's external political influence was limited, investors were overcautious, and negotiations with external creditors were wearisome. With an unmanageable external debt, hyperinflation, political instability, and a poor performance in the area of human rights, Brazil had multiple vulnerabilities in terms of international opinion—each of which seemed closely linked to the volatility of its macroeconomic policies.

This context changed dramatically with the successful adoption of the Real Plan, the monetary stabilization program issued in July 1994, which followed a steady opening of the economy that had started in the early 1990s. This plan represented the culmination of six years of continual economic liberalization, with an incremental but steady opening to foreign trade, a predictable exchange rate policy, and, for the third year in a row, monetary stability with a declining inflation rate.

In fact, international expectations had changed even before the Brazilian government announced the launching of the Real Plan. The ascension of the current president, Fernando Henrique Cardoso, to the Ministry of the Economy in 1993 marked a shift in expectations. The renewed credibility that resulted ensured favorable conditions for the renegotiation of Brazil's foreign debt and created friendlier conditions for multilateral talks—inside the World Trade Organization (WTO), with partners in Mercosur, and even within the hemispheric arrangements.

International considerations and commitments, in turn, reinforced domestic constraints on politicians opposed to the interconnected policies of commercial, financial, and economic openness. They have become strong counterarguments against legislators who are resisting economic reforms, especially those concerning deregulation and privatization.

The impact of these changes in policy on the political process has been immense, especially for the electorate, which had internalized a widely shared belief that monetary stability is a societal value to be preserved at any cost. That belief was the most influential factor in Cardoso's election to the presidency; he garnered a majority of popular votes and a level of congressional support unparalleled since the mid-twentieth century.

An entire cycle was complete for Mercosur. Brazil, the country with the largest economy and the most attractive market, was also the most vulnerable to the rampant crises in Latin America—whether a crisis of credibility, instability, or legitimacy. But once it achieved monetary stability and its political stability had improved, Brazil replaced Chile and Argentina as the symbol of the region's international trustworthiness.

Mercosur as such followed from a cycle of regional arrangements in the

Southern Cone that started under the aegis of democracy, the rather conspicuous motivation for the bilateral agreements on technical and economic cooperation between Argentina and Brazil established by Presidents Alfonsín and Sarney. Emerging from long periods of authoritarian rule, both governments felt vulnerable to destabilizing pressures originating from socioeconomic unrest and felt their political processes would benefit from growing economic interdependence between the two countries.

Surprisingly, the effects of cooperation, especially the liberalization of bilateral trade, overran the two governments' expected political goals. Commercial interdependence pushed both countries—simultaneously attracting their closest neighbors, Uruguay and Paraguay—toward growing integration, which, in turn, raised the need for macroeconomic convergence and, above all, macroeconomic concertation. External and domestic pressures for Brazilian stabilization tended to rise accordingly.

A cycle is closed when the fruits of political stabilization in Brazil are such that they warrant a pact aimed at controlling inflation. Brazilian stability impinges on Mercosur's and the entire region's credibility. Essentially a politically motivated regional arrangement, Mercosur ends up creating strong integrative mechanisms that reinforce economic interdependence among the economies, thus increasing pressures toward the convergence of macroeconomic policies. These pressures, in turn, reinforce the drive to enhance political stability, which serves as an asset to attract investments and business opportunities.

This combination of internal and external pressures conducive to measures favoring economic and political stability was present in at least three situations directly linked to Mercosur. First, after the Mexican exchange crisis in December 1994, a similar fear pervaded both Brazilian and Argentinean monetary authorities, who intensified informal consultations before deciding how to cope with the challenges to their respective currencies. The public was aware that because of the growing interdependence between the two leading countries in Mercosur, if the "tequila effect" affected one of them it would trigger similar effects in the other. As a result, strong defensive measures to depress economic activity and contain the growth of the external deficit faced no major criticism from either political class, except from the opposition parties.

The second situation involves Brazil's adoption of an "automotive regime" patterned on a similar regime adopted previously by Argentina. Brazil imposed quotas on foreign imports, and provided export assistance to domestic automobile and parts manufacturers. Mercosur members immediately protested, and Brazil's actions prompted immediate negotiations among the four Mercosur countries to accommodate their interests.

A third situation involves the way Brazil's decisionmakers reacted to the Southeast Asian and Asia-Pacific countries' financial crisis. Brazil's political analysts generally believe that the government's energetic defense of the Real in the immediate aftermath of the Asian stock market collapse was driven by fears of the effect devaluation would have on the Argentine economy.

From a domestic standpoint, congressional approval of the executive's strong fiscal measures aimed at reducing the fiscal deficit, limiting import growth, and fostering the net flow of external capital was surprisingly rapid. Limits on pension programs, job security in the public sector, and other welfare entitlements—all of which entailed formal constitutional amendments and had been subject to various procedural roadblocks for more than two years—finally passed during an extraordinary series of sessions convened during the congressional vacation.

Cardoso's central argument in favor of the amendments and the new legislation was that external credibility was essential to cope with a growing external deficit and that it required significant domestic monetary stability, which, in turn, was directly related to political stability. A clear domestic consensus and willingness to preserve an unchanged agenda of reforms were prerequisites for meeting external credibility requirements.

Argentina's vulnerability to Brazil's responses, whether devaluation or a tightening of exports, was not officially mentioned. That, however, did not prevent the press and progovernment economists from commenting on the dual responsibility of Brazilian monetary authorities to domestic constituencies and their Mercosur partners.

MERCOSUR'S INFLUENCE ON PARAGUAY'S FAILED COUP

In Brazil the growth of economic and political stability and the strengthening of democracy clearly paralleled the growth and consolidation of Mercosur. In this section I turn to a second case that demonstrates how the existence of Mercosur and the functioning of its institutions and political and economic mechanisms had a tangible bearing on democratic stability. That case is Paraguay, the first Mercosur member to experience an attempted military coup.

The Presidential Declaration of Democratic Commitment in Mercosur was signed by the presidents of the four member states on June 25, 1996. The declaration's main clauses follow.

1. Fully operational democratic institutions are an essential precondition for cooperation under the Treaty of Asunción, its protocols and subsidiary acts.
2. Any disruption of the democratic order is an unacceptable obstacle

to the continuation of the process of integration in course as well as for the affected member State.

3. The Parties shall immediately consult each other, in ways and manners they find befitting, whenever a disruption or a risk of disruption of the democratic order occurs in a member State. The Parties shall proceed in mutual coordination to consult the member State referred to.

4. Should the consultations mentioned in the above clause be ineffectual, the Parties shall consider implementation of relevant measures. Such measures may range from suspending the right of participation in the forums of Mercosur, to suspending the rights and obligations deriving from the norms of Mercosur as well as from the agreements accorded between each one of the Parties and the member State where the disruption of the democratic order occurred.

5. The Parties shall include a clause professing a commitment to the democratic principles in all agreements between Mercosur and other countries or groups of countries.

Two months prior to the issue of this declaration, on April 25, the president of Paraguay—under strong pressures from both domestic and external forces to resist a coup attempt by the commander of the army—finally gained the upper hand. For the first time, a member state of Mercosur was facing an attempted military coup, and for the first time Mercosur was challenged not only as a trade community dealing with common and interdependent economic issues but as a political body whose commitment to democracy was an inherent part of its charter, the Treaty of Asunción.

During the military crisis in Paraguay, the governments of the other three Mercosur countries acted promptly, exerting strong pressure against the coup and immediately applying coercive diplomacy. They sustained the constitutional government of President Juan Carlos Wasmosy after the coup had been aborted. Two months later, at the first official meeting of the Mercosur Council, a presidential declaration was issued on the democratic commitment embodied in Mercosur, followed by another presidential declaration on political consultations among the member states. Simultaneously, the two governments then engaged in talks with Mercosur, Bolivia and Chile, issued a joint protocol indicating adherence to the Declaration of Democratic Commitment in Mercosur that had been signed by the member states.

The crisis broke out on April 22, 1996, when the commander of the army, General Lino Oviedo, who was seeking the nomination of the ruling party as a presidential candidate, rebelled against his dismissal by the president who charged him with engaging in partisan politics while in the service. Threatening to stage a military coup with the support of the army,

Oviedo demanded the resignations of the president and vice president and the removal of his major opponent as a presidential candidate of the Colorado Party.[15]

President Wasmosy was given immediate support by the navy and air force, the Congress—including all opposition parties—and public opinion. Thousands of middle-class citizens and students from Asunción rallied before the presidential palace in support of Wasmosy. Initially, the president appeared inclined to submit to Oviedo, then he began negotiations with the rebel who demanded an appointment as minister of the army in exchange for his dismissal from active service. The threat of a military coup remained if Oviedo's demands were not met.[16]

Wasmosy accepted the demands, and Oviedo transferred command of the army to his successor and flew to the presidential palace with his supporters, expecting to take over his promised appointment. There he found a large crowd opposing him and heard a presidential radio announcement withdrawing the appointment. It was April 25.[17] The constitutional government had overcome the attempted coup.

Two sets of arguments are useful in understanding how a president who seemed prepared to abase himself to the extent of appointing as minister of the army a military officer who had first rebelled against the president's authority, then demanded his resignation, and finally threatened his ouster succeeded in prevailing. One argument involves domestic reasons, the other deals with external factors.

First I consider the domestic political process in Paraguay. In contrast to other Latin American countries, the authoritarian regime and the transition to democracy in Paraguay are conspicuously absent from the relevant literature, as Charles Gillespie has pointed out.[18] Gillespie believes the reason for this omission is that Paraguay's regime was party-based rather than a military-based authoritarian regime. The relevant literature "focuses on the question [of] how the military withdraws from politics as a precondition to democratization."[19] This research agenda does not embrace Paraguay.

Additionally, in Paraguay liberalization was not the result of a coalition joining the liberal wing of the ruling faction with the opposition, as scholars argue prevailed in other compacted transitions in Latin America.[20] Rather, liberalization was the result of an internal division that triggered a military coup supported by the majoritarian faction of the ruling Colorado Party. The Paraguayan democratizers were not altogether democrats, and the opposition was not a relevant part of the process.[21]

With the forthcoming succession following Alfredo Stroessner's last term as president, a split occurred in the coterie from which the government, the army, and the Colorado Party were selected. The split provided the basis for Wasmosy's nomination, which Oviedo then supported against his major opponent who controlled the Colorado Party's main faction.[22] The same split was later reported as the main reason for Oviedo's attempted coup. Three candidates were fighting to lead the Colorados in anticipation of the 1998 presidential elections. Luis Maria Argaña, foreign minister during General Andrés Rodríguez's term and leader of the strongest and most traditionalist Colorado faction, won the party's presidency the week following the aborted coup. Angel Roberto Seifart, the party's vice president who was unofficially supported by Wasmosy, was second with just under 34 percent of the votes. Blas Riquelme, Oviedo's champion, was third with only 11 percent of the votes.

Thus the government's modernizing faction, the army, and the core of Colorado traditionalists ran on three separate tickets in seeking to control the party. Oviedo's concern about the party's presidency is understandable because traditionally whoever controls the Colorado Party controls the presidential elections.

The essential unity behind the three ruling segments of the authoritarian regime—the executive, the army, and the party—whose break led to Stroessner's ouster, could no longer be drawn on for new ventures, military or otherwise. Gillespie's hypotheses regarding a similar cleavage prior to Wasmosy's nomination and election, when *tradicionalistas* (traditionalists) and *renovadores* (reformers) struggled for control of the party,[23] is still accurate: "The outcome of this crisis would seem to bode well for the future of democracy by breaking the *tradicionalistas'* lock on the ruling party. The more pluralistic the Colorados become, the more the prospects improve for pluralism in Paraguay as a whole."[24]

One could argue that a precondition for pluralism among the Colorados is the emergence of separation among the government, the army, and the party itself. For separation to occur, each group must develop a separate stake in the Colorado Party, if not in different parties. Oviedo's endeavor and his failure were results of that continued split, which reflected on the results of the election for party leadership.

Regarding the external components of the crisis, three factors must be considered: bilateral pressure, multilateral diplomatic coercion, and vulnerability to strong international public opinion. Brazil and the United States exerted most of the bilateral pressure. In the first few hours of the attempted coup, President Wasmosy moved to the U.S. Embassy in Asunción, where he remained for most of the crisis, accompanied by the U.S. and Brazilian ambassadors. Both the Brazilian and U.S. foreign services issued firm statements condemning the disruption of the democratic order and threatening retaliation. Brazilian officials leaked a supposed decision to suspend free access to Brazilian harbor facilities for Paraguayan imports and exports. The Brazilian press reported a telephone call from Brazil's president to Wasmosy enjoining him not to implement the accord with the rebels. Within days of the flawed coup, Wasmosy visited Brasilia to acknowledge his colleague's support.

Multilateral pressure came from both the Organization of American States (OAS) and Mercosur. The OAS secretary-general, who was also Colombia's former president, Cesar Gaviria, traveled to Asunción on the grounds that the new organization's charter mandated the suspension of any member state in which democratic institutions were disrupted. With no permanent secretariat and only a small administrative body in Montevideo, Mercosur issued no official statement; it acted through discreet pressure by diplomatic representatives of its member states in Asunción and through well-orchestrated leaks to the press in each member state capital. Mercosur's message could not have been clearer: The ouster of President Wasmosy would be considered a violation of the club's agreed rules, prompting automatic suspension of membership. The sanctions announced in the Presidential Declaration of Democratic Commitment in Mercosur two months later can be read as a retrospective threat to Oviedo's followers, as well as a prospective threat to other Paraguayans unhappy with democracy and a constitutional government, whether civilian or military.

International public opinion was overwhelmingly negative, making transparent the state's new vulnerability to transnational pressure. Crowds of citizens in Asunción rallied to welcome—indeed, to press for—external intervention to bolster the continuity of the democratic order.

Since the Colorado Party no longer provided a common arena for reconciling political issues of the state bureaucracy, the armed forces, and the ruling social strata, stable authoritarian rule became increasingly difficult to achieve in Paraguay. The faction that has the best showing in Colorado Party internal elections will be strong enough to govern in a democratic environment but not to rule undisputedly in an authoritarian one.

This fundamental split within the Paraguayan authoritarian coalition not only made it necessary to make the presidential election an open contest but also lowered the chances for a successful coup. Most important, even in the case of a successful coup, such a divide would make it impossible to institutionalize the new government and render it stable without massive concessions to democratic rules, including open elections.

The external component adds a supplementary deterrent, one that reinforces formal respect for constitutional rules and provides additional inducements for a speedier denouement. A large array of possible unsuccessful outcomes faced the rebels, ranging from instant defeat and full recovery of the president's constitutional authority to a long transitional period of unrest leading to democracy without Wasmosy. The split among the ruling coterie can account for the entire range of such outcomes. The external component, especially the new role played by Mercosur, on the other hand is far more consistent with the actual outcome—full respect for constitutional rule—than with any unrealized scenario involving compromise between the constitutional incumbents and the de facto rulers.

The presidential nomination that triggered Oviedo's attempted coup was won not by the most traditional leadership of the Colorados but, surprisingly, by Oviedo himself. Both of his major rivals, Wasmosy and Argaña, immediately accused him of fraud. President Wasmosy, who had previously succeeded in breaking the armed forces' cohesiveness, arrested Oviedo and staged a trial by a specially appointed military court. Initially accused of criticizing his commander-in-chief, Wasmosy, Oviedo was later accused of rebellion.[25]

Still running for the presidency from prison, Oviedo faced elimination from the race if convicted. The voiding of Oviedo's candidacy would also prevent the the Colorado Party from contesting the presidency, since there were no constitutional provisions for appointing another candidate at this late stage in the race.

By mid-February 1998, with little time left before the presidential elections scheduled for May 10, Wasmosy, now with the support of his previous rival, Argaña, suggested that the elections should be postponed[26] to accommodate a constitutional imbroglio: The Electoral Court ruled that Oviedo was the legal candidate of the Colorado Party and could not be replaced unless convicted; the specially appointed military court was not prepared to rule in time for a legal replacement to be named; the Colorado Party leadership refused to accept a legal replacement for Oviedo even if naming one was constitutionally possible, but it could not appoint Argaña without the consent of the Electoral Court; Wasmosy could put his rival candidate in prison but could not prevent him from running; and if the latter were convicted, Wasmosy could not appoint his own candidate.

Mercosur as such took no direct part in the external action concerning the constitutional imbroglio, but the member states' foreign services became increasingly involved beginning in early February 1998 when it became clear that the elections were not going to follow a clear constitutional path until May 10. As such, Mercosur's role in protecting democracy in Paraguay at this stage in the crisis differed from its role during the attempted coup.

The Brazilian ambassador in Asunción, who played a major role in 1996 by supporting Wasmosy against Oviedo's coup attempt, was conveniently replaced as soon as Oviedo's nomination was confirmed by Colorado Party internal elections. This meant clearly that Brasilia did not claim links to particular domestic factions in Paraguay but remained committed to democratic procedural rules. On February 10 the new Brazilian ambassador questioned President Wasmosy about the coup d'état rumors at a formal ceremony. The ambassador later issued a note that should be interpreted against the backdrop of a secular Latin American tradition of lip service to nonintervention and formal respect for national sovereignty.

> It is crucial to warrant continuity to the process of democratic transition initiated with the government of President Andrés Rodríguez and followed during President Juan Carlos Wasmosy's government. The respect for institutions and the maintenance of democratic institutions are essential conditions for membership in Mercosur.[27]

A week later Argentina's Menem sent his special adviser for strategic issues to Brasilia where he openly discussed the Paraguayan crisis with his Brazilian counterparts and announced future sanctions levied by Mercosur members on Asunción if the elections were postponed. Brazilian sources, however, acknowledged that such a postponement would not be considered a break in the democratic process if the decision were made by a legitimate body, such as the Congress or the judiciary.[28]

By the end of the week, Wasmosy was issuing conflicting signals. In an interview with Brazilian journalists, he dismissed the possibility of sanctions by Mercosur—"gossip," he said[29]—whereas he formally assured the OAS representative in Asunción that "the elections shall not be postponed."[30]

Mercosur member states' actions became both more open and less clear. In 1996 Argentinean and Brazilian ambassadors to Asunción exerted more discreet and precise pressure, with a clear goal: to maintain Wasmosy's mandate and sanctions against the rebels. In the more recent imbroglio, officials from both Brazil and Argentina defended Paraguayan democracy and even threatened domestic factions in Paraguay who might have sought to break institutional rules.

Contrasting with this diplomacy, in which officials expressed open discomfort with Paraguayan leaders' low level of commitment to democratic procedures, was a less than clear definition of Mercosur's goals. Would Mercosur enforce rule number three of its democratic clause: Whenever a "disruption or risk of disruption of democratic order" occurs, it will implement "relevant measures [that] may range from suspending the right of participation in the forums of Mercosur, to suspending the rights and obligations deriving from the norms of Mercosur"?

In the end, Mercosur was spared these difficult decisions. Oviedo was eventually convicted by the special military court and ruled ineligible for the presidency by the Electoral Court. The Colorado Party, contrary to Wasmosy's and Argaña's expectations, confirmed the nomination of Raul Cubas Grau, the vice-presidential candidate chosen by Oviedo, and appointed Argaña to run for the vice-presidency on the same ticket. Despite an unexpected surge by the liberal opposition, Cubas won the elections on

May 10. Before the month was out, the newly installed president released Oviedo from prison and ruled his conviction illegal. This political accommodation, however, did not come at the expense of central features of Paraguayan democracy—namely, open elections and a free opposition.

CONCLUSION

I have briefly reviewed two cases in which clear growth of economic and political stability and a strengthening of democracy paralleled the growth and consolidation of Mercosur. In the case of Paraguay—a small country traditionally vulnerable to influence from strong neighbors—Mercosur played a decisive role in strengthening internal resistance to antidemocratic moves. In Brazil domestic factors were determinant. Nonetheless, as external credibility became a crucial ingredient of domestic stability, Brazilian international commitments—particularly those concerning Mercosur—provided a protected environment in which the government could foster economic and political reforms.

What can I add to my earlier hypothesis that Mercosur was not only inspired by the need to consolidate democracy in the Southern Cone but also provided an external stimulus for reinforcing a domestic drive to stabilize the economy and enforce stable democratic institutions?

First, Mercosur allowed political leaders to remove from the domestic agenda issues considered relevant to both economic and political stability. Thus, the Brazilian government finds it less difficult to resist pressure to raise tariffs or loosen public expenditure, whereas the Paraguayan government finds greater support to enforce open elections because both governments can claim they are complying with international commitments.

An example is seen in the Brazilian legislation on intellectual property, adopted in 1995 after five long years of congressional resistance echoing domestic pressure groups. It is generally acknowledged that the legislation would not have passed if the government had not stressed the need to comply with international standards. Another example applies specifically to Mercosur. In 1995 the Brazilian government adopted new legislation on the automobile industry that critics argue is not in compliance with Mercosur and WTO rules. Brazilian trade representatives have since been engaged in extensive talks with both the Mercosur partners and WTO members most concerned about automobile exports to Brazil. As a consequence, the Brazilian legislation has since been adjusted.

Second, Mercosur has enhanced subregional interdependence, which reinforced neighboring countries' influence in other states' domestic policies. Growing trade interdependence forced both Brazil and Argentina to be more considerate of each other's domestic needs. Paraguay and Uruguay became even more aware of the Brazilian and Argentine governments and public opinion.

As mentioned earlier, South American countries have no tradition of regional studies, academic or otherwise. Cross-country surveys are rare or nonexistent, making it difficult to assess public reactions to Mercosur as such. The evidence that does exist suggests important supranational effects. A study of the Argentinean elite showed a positive perception of Mercosur within the government, the business community, and academia. Moreover, regardless of Mercosur's positive and negative impacts on specific industrial sectors, regional integration is perceived as inevitable and more of an asset than a liability.[31]

In Paraguay, as already mentioned, public reaction to regional intervention during the attempted coup provides a good indication of Mercosur's benign character, at least as perceived by Paraguayans. On the other hand, angry reactions to Brazilian enforcement of customs standards along the Paraguayan border have been linked to Mercosur.

In Brazil the press has noted a contrast in attitudes between the northeastern states and those next to the Southern Cone. The elite from "Nordeste," accustomed to huge fiscal transfers and regional subsidies, allegedly perceive Mercosur as just another source of subsidies and federal investments, but this time to the advantage of the states bordering Argentina, Uruguay, and Paraguay. Among the northern states, Venezuela's sudden interest in acceding to Mercosur caused excitement among local governments and business communities.

A meeting of the Common Market Council in 1997 in Fortaleza, the capital city of the northeastern state of Ceará in Brazil, seems to have signaled a change in the local perception of Mercosur. Six presidents were present—those of the four member states of Mercosur plus those of Chile and Bolivia—which indicated the importance of the meeting. For the first time in Mercosur's brief history, the meeting was preceded by a major cultural event: an international seminar on cultural and social integration in Mercosur—a clear effort to reach out to the local elite.

By becoming more aware of each other's domestic political, social, and economic processes, public opinion in these countries has begun to echo regionally international concerns about such areas as democracy, human rights, and sound environmental policies. Transnational networks in place in Mercosur can rapidly transmit local concerns on these issues outside the region. Mercosur has also increased its member states' vulnerability to transnational influence.

Democratic stability is increasingly perceived by Latin American leaders as an asset that is linked to external credibility. As noted earlier, the fight of Latin American peoples for democratization and their leaders' efforts to keep institutions stable are assumed as essential by governments in the region as a part of their homework prior to joining the new international environment. In the case of Mercosur, Uruguay initiated a process of constitutional and subconstitutional reforms aimed at creating stronger parties and more responsive governments. Argentina reformed its constitution mainly to eliminate the prohibition on incumbents seeking reelection. A similar ban existed in Brazil, and an amendment to lift it has been approved in the Congress. The common rationale for these initiatives is to create more stable institutions.

Finally, Mercosur has provided member countries with flexible, expeditious mechanisms to carry out informal consultations and make political decisions in intra- and extraregional affairs. Mercosur issued no formal statement on the Paraguayan crisis, probably because the audience was prepared to acknowledge Mercosur's willingness to intervene even though its intentions remained unofficial.

What Mercosur does not and cannot offer is a replacement for domestic political processes and institutions. Mercosur cannot supply the Brazilian political system with a new party system and new electoral rules. It cannot change the Paraguayan ruling elite into a more pluralistic one that is more committed to democracy. These and other relevant accomplishments of the body politic depend on domestic political action by both collective and individual actors.

NOTES

Amancio Jorge de Oliveira collected the relevant information and publications on the Paraguayan crisis.

1. This is one of the driving forces behind the political and economic accord between the EU and Mercosur. The Framework Agreement was signed in Madrid in December 1995, the first of an interregional nature. The agreement conveys the intent that a free trade area involving both continents will be in place by the year 2007.

2. Latin American countries are engaged in hemispherewide talks to create a free trade area on the continent by 2005. Note 1 describes a Mercosur-EU Framework Agreement for a free trade area early in the twenty-first century. Japan has proposed talks about the creation of a free trade area with Brazil, since extended to include Mercosur.

3. Leading Latin American countries' attitudes toward multilateral trade forums have changed. During the final phase of the Uruguay Round of General Agreement on Tariffs and Trade talks, Argentina and Brazil—as well as Mexico—were much more cooperative and less inclined to push demands for protectionism for developing economies. Their participation in the creation of the new WTO was conspicuously constructive. Another indicator of this new trend in Latin America is Mexico's accession to the Organization for Economic Cooperation and Development, which is expected to be followed by that of Brazil and Argentina.

4. I first developed these points in "O fim da guerra fria e os novos conflitos internacionais," *Série Política Internacional*, São Paulo, Programa de Política Internacional e Comparada, no. 5 (June 1991), 22.

5. See J. A. Guilhon Albuquerque, "Unfinished Reforms," in Werner Baer and Joseph S. Tulchin, eds., *Brazil and the Challenge of Economic Reform* (Washington, D.C.: Woodrow Wilson Center Press, 1993), 149–154.

6. See Robert Packenham, *The Dependency Movement: Scholarship and Politics in Development Studies* (Cambridge: Harvard University Press, 1993), chapters 6, 8; and Gert Rosenthal, "Treinta Años de Integración en América Latina: Un Examen Crítico," Economic Commission for Latin America and the Caribbean, Brasilia, 1994.

7. See Rubens António Barbosa, "A evolução do processo de integração na América do Sul," *Série Política Internacional*, São Paulo, Programa de Política Internacional e Comparada, no. 2 (June 1991); and Francisco Thompson Flores Neto, "Integração e Cooperação Brasil-Argentina," *Série Política Internacional*, São Paulo, Programa de Política Internacional e Comparada, no. 3 (June 1991).

8. Composed of the ministers of foreign relations and of the economy of the member states and, once a year, of their presidents.

9. Composed of representatives of the Ministries of Foreign Relations and of the Economy, associated areas, and national Central Banks.

10. A substantial part of Paraguayan gross national income has been associated with illegal trade with neighboring countries. Some of this is tolerated in Brazil, where a nationwide sector of informal business survives by "legally" smuggling small amounts of goods across the border in handbags. In downtown Brasilia, the federal capital of Brazil, the Paraguayan Market-Place is a conspicuous choice for the purchase of "imported" goods. On one occasion, domestic measures adopted in Brazil to minimize illegal trade across the border prompted threats of retaliation through the blockage of all current negotiations in the Common Market Council.

11. I have described the general features of plebiscitarian presidentialism in "Le présidentialisme plébiscitaire et l'instabilité des démocraties," *Série Política Comparada*, São Paulo, Programa de Política Internacional e Comparada, no. 1 (June 1991). See also J. A. Guilhon Albuquerque, "La inestable democracia brasileña. Un caso de presidencialismo plebiscitario," in *La consolidación democratica en América Latina*, Anna Balletbó, ed., Tercero Fórum de la Fundación Internacional Olof Palmë (Barcelona: Hacer Editorial, 1994), 262–277.

12. Menem has since successfully sought a constitutional amendment allowing him to run for a second term, and he was reelected. Brazilian President Fernando Henrique Cardoso is making a similar bid.

13. As described later, the coordination of macropolicies has never constituted a prior condition for further integration in Mercosur, nor did it pose an obstacle to regional growth. Roberto Lavagna has argued extensively that regional growth and intraregional trade developed strongly despite a sharp divergence in Brazilian and Argentinean macroeconomic policies during the late 1980s and the 1990s. For Lavagna's arguments, see "Estratégias defensivas e coordenação macroeconómica no Mercosur," in *Symposium: O Sul das Américas* (Brasilia: Fundaçao Alexandre Gusmão, May 1995). A thorough assessment of macroeconomic coordination in

Mercosur is found in Marcelo Garriga and Pablo Sanguinetti, "Coordinación Macroeconómica en el Mercosur: Ventajas, desventajas y la práctica," *PROSUR*, Buenos Aires, Fundación Friedrich Ebert (1996).

14. See J. A. Guilhon Albuquerque, "A Opção Continental do Brasil," *São Paulo em Perspectiva* 1 (1995): 58–64.

15. See *Gazeta Mercantil*, São Paolo, April 23, 1996; *O Estado de São Paulo*, April 23, 1996; *El País*, Madrid, April 24, 1996.

16. *El País*, April 25, 1996; *O Estado de São Paulo*, April 25, 1996; *Gazeta Mercantil*, April 25, 1996; *Folha de São Paulo*, April 25, 1996.

17. *El País*, April 26, 1996; *Gazeta Mercantil*, April 26, 1996; *Folha de S. Paulo*, April 26, 1996.

18. One exception is Gillespie himself in his "Democratizing a One-Party State," *Journal of Democracy* 1 (fall 1990): 49–58, on which I rely for the present analysis.

19. Ibid., 50.

20. See, for instance, Guillermo O'Donnell, Philippe Schimitter, and Lawrence Whitehead, eds., *Transitions from Authoritarian Rule: Latin America* (Baltimore: Johns Hopkins University Press, 1986).

21. In both free elections held after the ouster of former president Stroessner in 1989, the Colorados elected the president in a landslide. Oviedo's coup was less about the current administration than about control of the Colorado Party.

22. *El País*, April 30, 1996; *Carta Internacional*, São Paulo, May 1996.

23. Argaña was then the *tradicionalistas*' candidate, and Wasmosy could win the nomination only with the support of Oviedo's faction (and the unstated consent of the army).

24. Gillespie, "Democratizing a One-Party State," 56.

25. *O Estado de São Paulo*, February 20, 1998; *Folha de São Paulo*, February 20, 1998.

26. *Folha de São Paulo*, February 20, 1998. The new alliance was consolidated during an extraordinary convention of the Colorados on February 19 at which both Wasmosy and Argaña made clear that the elections were not to take place until the Colorados could replace Oviedo in time to mount another candidate (probably Argaña himself). See *Folha de São Paulo*, March 1, 1998.

27. *Folha de São Paulo*, February 20, 1998. The Brazilian ambassador in Asunción, Bernardo Pericás, had been ambassador to the OAS where he played a major role in the reform of the OAS charter, which includes a democratic clause that entitles its secretary-general to initiate investigations in member states concerning respect for democratic processes and institutions.

28. *Folha de São Paulo*, February 20, 1998; see also *O Estado de São Paulo*, February 20, 1998.

29. *Folha de São Paulo*, March 6, 1998.

30. Ibid.

31. Janina Onuki, "O governo e o empresariado argentino. A percepção política do Mercosur," M.S. thesis, Department of Political Science, University of São Paulo, São Paulo, 1996. See also Maria Cláudia Drummond, "O Mercosur e a articulação de atores sociais. O caso brasileiro (1991–1994)," M.S. thesis, Department of International Relations, University of Brasilia, Brasilia, 1994.

12

Conclusion

Jeffrey J. Anderson

The European nation-state shows no signs of withering away. As Thomas Biersteker persuasively argues (chapter 2), however, integration, along with larger forces of globalization, has transformed the meaning of sovereignty as it is exercised by European Union (EU) member governments. Examples of "ceding authority, changing recognition of authority claims, and emerging competing authorities"[1] abound in contemporary Europe, and much of this can be traced directly to dynamics associated with an ongoing integration process. To quote Wolfgang Merkel, "Whereas the supranational sovereign is still a fiction, the principles of the national sovereign have already eroded."[2]

The transformation of national sovereignty launched in the 1950s was not accompanied by an extension of the mechanisms of democratic control to the new supranational level. As integration progressed, opening up new areas of coordinated activity and enveloping the member governments in multilateral decisionmaking processes, the democratic deficit widened.

For individual citizens, the democratic implications of integration were even more far-reaching. The emergence of a system of multilevel governance in Europe[3] produced in its wake a system of multilevel citizenship in which the twentieth-century trinity of political, economic, and social rights of the individual—historically lodged within the nation-state—came unbundled.[4] Increasingly, the European Community (EC) took over as the locus of economic citizenship rights, whereas political and social rights remained tied mostly to the nation-state. Integration proceeded primarily on the foundations of economic citizenship rights—in the absence of any direct guidance from the *demos*—and eventually stretched to the breaking point existing national mechanisms of democratic accountability and control flowing from political and social citizenship rights.

Always problematic from the standpoint of classical democratic theory, the democratic deficit contained a silver lining for the European project, endowing elites with considerable autonomy, which they used to push integration forward. As Merkel elegantly points out (chapter 3), the democratic deficit contributed to a more efficient path to integration, one that despite the absence of democratic controls enjoyed widespread, albeit diffuse, support and legitimacy among Europe's citizenries up through the Maastricht summit in 1991.

How have national democratic arrangements fared in the midst of this ongoing transformation of sovereignty and the yawning democratic deficit at the supranational level? A complete answer must begin with the salutary effects of integration on national models of democratic capitalism that (re)emerged from the rubble of World War II. By enabling political elites to solve both internal and external problems now beyond the reach of purely national instruments, the European project, to quote Alan Milward, rescued the European nation-state.[5]

We also need to acknowledge the benefits of membership, both actual and anticipated, for the string of new democracies that emerged on the continent during the postwar period. In the freshly minted Federal Republic of Germany, the goal of economic and political *Westintegration* provided a strong orientation point for conservative political elites and during the 1950s served as an ineluctable pole of attraction for moderate forces on the left; European integration ultimately became part and parcel of the cross-party consensus that shaped postwar democratic politics in the Bonn republic.

In Portugal, Spain, and Greece, where elites took up the difficult challenge of "crafting" democracy on terrain occupied by faltering but still potent authoritarian regimes,[6] European integration transmitted benign impulses to the process. The impact of the European Community was rarely direct and almost always contextual; during democratic transitions national elites employed the Community in myriad ways to facilitate crafting—as a pool of proven democratic practices and institutions, as an external reference point for forging a new democratic Europeanist identity, and as an economic lever against skeptics and outright opponents of democracy.[7] Based on António Barreto's analysis (chapter 5), Europe clearly contributed to the development of a system of mutual security during the Portuguese transition to democracy.[8]

Similar dynamics can be observed in Hungary where, according to Péter Gedeon (chapter 6), political elites have internalized European values of democracy and markets, thereby forging a common political culture within which the peaceful competition for power can unfold. Europeanization has been central to the ability of political elites to extricate themselves successfully from state socialism and to embark on a future "under the umbrella of the concept of Europe."[9] Integration has had comparable effects and served comparable ends in South America.

Beyond its salutary impact on democratization and the early phases of democratic consolidation in Europe, integration has generated a more checkered pattern of effects at the national level. As I and Paulette Kurzer demonstrate in chapters 8 and 9, respectively, for much of the postwar period Germany and many of the smaller members managed to achieve a more comfortable fit between their democratic institutional arrangements—which place a premium on consensus politics and decentralization—and the emerging supranational governance system in Europe; among other things, the higher degree of institutional and normative congruence between the two levels rendered the transfer of national sovereignty claims to Brussels less problematic for political elites who were accustomed to working within "semi-sovereign" frameworks back home.[10]

Member governments such as Britain and France, however, have often chafed under the dynamics of integration. Jack Hayward (chapter 7) explains this with reference to their long political histories of centralized, untrammeled sovereignty; their entrenched traditions of adversarial politics; and their conceptions of democratic legitimacy based not on ethnicity but on citizenship. In these established democracies, integration has often sparked intense political debates over national sovereignty and democratic accountability.

Such concerns are in no way limited strictly to established members; several authors sound cautionary notes about the consequences of integration for young democracies. Across the EU the creation of a supranational governance system has allowed political executives to escape the control of their national political systems. This general phenomenon has especially worrisome implications for a country such as Portugal, which unlike many of its fellow member states cannot fall back on a long tradition of a strong, independent parliament, active regional governments, political parties with established democratic credentials, or robust civic institutions. Barreto's conclusion is sobering: "Through the European institutions, long-standing, relatively undemocratic administrative and political habits have been encouraged."[11] These problems of democratic institutions are compounded by the uneven economic effects of market integration in many regions of Portugal, which despite the level of transfers received from Brussels have strained otherwise solid public support for European integration. Barreto's dour assessment could well apply with equal force to Spain, Greece, and prospective EU members in Central and Eastern Europe.

Picking up on this last point, "informal" integration, as Kurzer describes the market dimension of the process, has been at the center of a

subtle shift in the balance of power between the state and the social partners throughout Europe. The creation of the internal market in the 1950s,
and the subsequent completion of the internal market and the push for economic and monetary union in the 1980s, created incentives that reward
competitive, mobile capital, thereby rendering citizens and governments
more vulnerable to the professed needs of business enterprises. It would
appear that Charles Lindblom's "automatic punishment mechanism" has
been sharpened gradually yet inexorably in Europe during the postwar period.[12]

The range of influences generated by integration on national systems of
democracy narrowed substantially after the Maastricht summit in 1991.
Across the EU, the public response to this collective foray into the sovereign core of the nation-state has been universally cautious, in many quar-
ters deeply skeptical, and for not a few openly hostile. The democratic
deficit is blamed for having allowed Maastricht to come to pass, and fears
are strong that the deficit will continue to widen as the treaty is implemented over the years. The lack of legitimacy, as both Merkel and Gary
Marks point out in chapters 3 and 4, respectively, has already had a chill-
ing effect on the integration process.

What is to be done? One solution is to reduce the size of the deficit or
even to eliminate it altogether "from above"—that is, by converting the
European Union's institutional framework into a democracy modeled
along national lines. An objective near and dear to federalists throughout
Europe, this is almost certainly a pipe dream since democratizing Europe
from above has become synonymous with pushing the integration process
to a (but not necessarily *the*) logical conclusion: a United States of Europe.
Deep-seated opposition in countries such as the United Kingdom and
France, when combined with newfound hesitation in Germany and many
of the smaller member governments, will likely prevent this vision from
ever becoming a reality.

The Maastricht ratification phase during 1992 and 1993 revealed another
solution to the EU's democratic deficiencies—closing the deficit "from
below." National responses to the Treaty on European Union often (but
not always; see chapter 5) contained institutional expressions of a democratic backlash in which national parliaments redrew the balance of intergovernmental power to increase their ability to control the integration
process. In countries as constitutionally diverse as Germany, Italy, Belgium, and the United Kingdom, the latest EC/EU grand bargain also called
forth or intensified a variety of regionalist responses that have wrapped
themselves in the mantle of democratic self-determination.[13] The backlash,
in other words, is occurring at multiple levels—all of which, however, are
located *within* existing national boundaries.

The fact that the EU experienced an element of democratization from below in the wake of Maastricht is perhaps not terribly surprising. It should be emphasized, however, that this process is piecemeal and uneven and does little to close the long-standing democratic deficit at the level of EU institutions. Combined, the results of the democratic backlash represent more of a hedge against the future than a correction of existing flaws. And as Merkel cogently argues, they come at a price: the declining efficiency of the integration process, which, by diminishing the perceived benefits of supranationalism, could further reduce public support for the overarching goal of integration.

Is there a way out of Merkel's democracy-efficiency tradeoff? As with most dilemmas, the answer appears to lie in strategies for breaking entirely free of the Hobson's choice. Merkel and Marks together offer insights into this challenge. By implication, Merkel puts great stock in the role of identity in lending political legitimacy to the integration process, arguing in effect that absent a set of institutional arrangements that can provide acceptable levels of legitimacy, efficiency, and democracy—and thereby stimulate a European identity among citizens—the status quo ante Maastricht is in fact the more legitimate state of affairs.

The political momentum—and therefore the political stakes- -of Economic and Monetary Union (EMU) rule out any return to a pre-Maastricht past for the EU. So accepting Merkel's analysis but foregoing his prescriptions, we should be deeply concerned about the consequences of the European project should the introduction of a single currency fail economically. Should EMU work well or even well enough, however, there is some cause for hope, as Marks's analysis of territorial identities in the European Union suggests. The widespread prevalence of multiple political identities among Europe's citizens—the vast majority of which are supportive of or, at a minimum, indifferent to the basic idea of integration—positions the EU advantageously to escape the worst elements of the democracy-efficiency tradeoff. The economic integration process, according to Marks, has generated forces of identity creation in Europe that although far weaker than those associated with European state building are nonetheless efficacious. Since identity is central to legitimacy, which, in turn, is a prerequisite for further integration, then prudence counsels a "steady state" post-Maastricht. And this in effect is what we have.

The flies in the ointment, as it were, can be found first in the inevitability of eastern enlargement, which will at least temporarily dilute the perceived and actual commonalities experienced by the EU citizenries. Second and more critical are the sharpening domestic debates over convergence criteria and budget austerity—particularly as they apply to welfare programs—within current member states. One can point to many examples, including a novel situation in German politics; for the first time since the political left embraced European integration in the late 1950s, leading figures in the

Social Democratic Party have begun to question elements of the cross-party consensus on Europe, arguing that the cherished German *Sozialstaat* must not be sacrificed to romantic ventures such as EMU. With the prospect of eastern enlargement and the enhanced mobility of Eastern European labor, similar rumblings can already be heard from the German trade union movement. A comparable debate, fed by the trajectory of post-Maastricht Europe, is under way in France and many smaller member states (e.g., Austria, Sweden). Thus integration is now at the center of domestic political conflicts that touch on the core political identities of the postwar generations in Europe. To the extent that "Europe" becomes synonymous in many parts of the EU with the dismantling of the postwar welfare state, the processes of identity creation identified by Marks will surely be overwhelmed and perhaps even entirely reversed.

EXPANDING ON THE EUROPEAN EXPERIENCE

Regional integration is now a global phenomenon. And as chapters 10 and 11 by Gustavo Vega-Cánovas and J. A. Guilhon Albuquerque, respectively, amply demonstrate, states involved in these initiatives have modified and in some instances curtailed their sovereignty claims as a consequence of regionalization. The Westphalian conception of sovereignty is being challenged not only in Europe but all over the world. Moreover, both the North American Free Trade Agreement (NAFTA) and Mercosur embrace, in part (NAFTA) or in whole (Mercosur), countries that have either recently instituted democracy or are in the midst of democratic transitions. What are the parallels and contrasts with the European experience?

Vega-Cánovas describes NAFTA as a distinctive model of regional integrations with few obvious parallels to the European experience. In contrast to the European Economic Community (EEC), NAFTA arose out of a purely economic rationale; political-security concerns were entirely absent from the calculations of national elites. The free trade agreement linking the U.S., Canada, and Mexico represents an effort at negative integration with a minimum of shared institutions. This in and of itself will limit the potential for deepening, as it places the levers controlling the integration process squarely in the hands of national governments. Moreover, and this represents a crucial distinction with regard to the European case, the key member government—the United States—is not only vastly more influential than its counterpart in Europe (Germany), but it projects a much more traditional, even Westphalian, conception of sovereignty than its EU counterpart. This reality will place tight constraints on any spillover process unleashed by the NAFTA treaty framework.

NAFTA's insubstantial institutional component, coupled with the fact that democratic arrangements are not a formal prerequisite for NAFTA membership, will also limit its direct relevance for the democratic transition process in Mexico, according to Vega-Cánovas. Any positive impulses for democratization will almost certainly have to be indirect—that is, transmitted through a restricted version of informal (i.e., market) integration. And since NAFTA, again in contrast to the EC/EU, expressly eschews the principle of supranational transfers from richer to poorer members to compensate for negative externalities generated by market integration, a real possibility exists that the Mexican public will greet any attempts to build on the NAFTA foundation with hostility born of fear and uncertainty.

Mercosur, on the other hand, exhibits many interesting parallels with the European experience. The rationale for embarking on regional integration in the Southern Cone bore many of the same characteristics as the Single European Act—in short, it was conceived as a means of enhancing the region's economic competitiveness and facilitating national economic adjustment in a radically changed international environment. Of course, South Americans defined global competitiveness somewhat differently than the Europeans; for example, they emphasized much more strongly the need to remain attractive as a destination for foreign investment.

The Mercosur initiative also reflected a deep and abiding concern among political elites to create the preconditions for internal and regional stability. A supranational framework of cooperation would provide support for governments engaged in ongoing efforts at democratic consolidation. Moreover, such a framework would create a mechanism for harnessing regional rivalries, particularly between Brazil and Argentina, that in the past had threatened economic development and complicated domestic political reform initiatives. The parallels to the Europe of the late 1940s and 1950s, which successfully confronted the challenges of postwar reconstruction and the specter of renewed Franco-German antagonisms, are in some respects striking.

Perhaps as a direct consequence of the greater weight attached to political objectives, the Mercosur treaty framework is much more robust than NAFTA's. The framework reflects a more ambitious set of goals established by the founding member countries, and it provides for a much higher level of institutionalization as well. Indeed, Albuquerque's analysis reveals the extent to which prospective members modeled their regional initiative on the European template. Not surprisingly, decisionmaking procedures stress unanimity, which is what one would expect drawing on the early history of the EEC. The potential for deepening à l'Europe, particularly in light of the supranational institutional component, clearly exists.

The consequences of Mercosur for national democracy remain at the level of hope and conjecture; it is still too early to trace any firm causal connections between the two. As Albuquerque states, Mercosur was launched under the aegis of democracy. It was designed expressly to advance regional economic prosperity through trade liberalization and to facilitate the coordination of macroeconomic policies that would promote economic and, by extension, political stabilization. Mercosur was also intended to serve an outward-looking purpose as well—namely, to enhance the international credibility of the member governments, something elites believed would foster economic and political reforms.

Albuquerque cautions that when considering the complex processes of democratic consolidation under way in Brazil, Argentina, and other member countries, one should not expect too much from regional integration; Mercosur is not a substitute for domestic political processes and institutions. And looking back across the ocean at the unfolding European experience, one should be sensitive to the potential complications or even harm that can befall young democracies as they find their way within an evolving supranational project. Brazil is not Portugal, but if Mercosur today is helping the cause of democracy by taking divisive issues such as protectionism and budget austerity off the domestic agenda, then it is surely within the realm of the possible that tomorrow it will imprison democracy by strengthening the political executive, the civil bureaucracy, and mobile capital at the expense of parliament, trade unions, and civil society.

*　　*　　*

Integration is a double-edged sword for democracy. As long as nation-states remain undigested by an evolving supranational framework—and this appears to be the case everywhere where regionalization is occurring—tensions will exist between the objectives and obligations of integration on the one hand and the rights and responsibilities of territory-based democracy on the other. If the recent experience in Europe demonstrates anything, it is that national institutions of democracy, however imperfect, still perform one of their elemental purposes: to check and control the power and autonomy of political leadership. These controls extend upward to the supranational level in often Byzantine and inefficient ways, but they do work. And as such, they represent an obvious starting point for ruminations on reconciling national democracy with regional integration.

NOTES

1. Biersteker in this volume, p. 35.
2. Merkel in this volume, p. 51.
3. Gary Marks, Liesbet Hooghe, and Kermit Blank, "European Integration Since the 1980s: State-Centric Versus Multi-Level Governance," *Journal of Common Market Studies* 34 (September 1996): 341–378.

4. Here I take my cue from T. H. Marshall, *Citizenship and Social Class and Other Essays* (Cambridge: Cambridge University Press, 1950).

5. Alan Milward, *The European Rescue of the Nation-State* (Berkeley: University of California Press, 1992).

6. See Giuseppe DiPalma, *To Craft Democracies* (Berkeley: University of California Press, 1990).

7. The standard argument made by pro-democratic elites in these countries was relatively straightforward: The European Community, through its markets and direct sources of aid, offered a means of modernizing the national economy, but to realize this potential the nation had to adopt a democratic form of government. Democracy, in short, was the entry ticket to the riches of the Common Market.

8. Robert Dahl, *Polyarchy* (New Haven: Yale University Press, 1971).

9. Gedeon, p. 127.

10. The term *semisovereign* is Katzenstein's; see Katzenstein, *Policy and Politics in West Germany.*

11. Barreto in this volume, p. 117.

12. Charles Lindblom, "The Market as Prison," *Journal of Politics* 44 (May 1982): 324–336.

13. It is important to emphasize Paulette Kurzer's point that political integration not only encourages regionalism but contains it as well. Kurzer in this volume, pp. 212–213.

Bibliography

Ahnfelt, Ellen, and Johan From. "European Policing." In *Making Policy in Europe*, eds. Svein S. Andersen and Kjell A. Eliassen. Thousand Oaks: Sage, 1993.

Albuquerque, J. A. Guilhon. "A Opção Continental do Brasil." *São Paulo em Perspectiva*, 1 (1995): 58–64.

———. "La inestable democracia brasileña. Un caso de presidencialismo plebiscitario." In *La consolidación democratica en América Latina*, ed. Anna Balletbó. III Fórum de la Fundación Internacional Olof Palmë. Barcelona: Hacer Editorial, 1994.

———. "Unfinished Reforms." In *Brazil and the Challenge of Economic Reform*, eds. Werner Baer and Joseph S. Tulchin. Washington, D.C.: Woodrow Wilson Center Press, 1993.

———. "Le Présidentialisme plébiscitaire et l'instabilité des démocraties." *Série Política Comparada*, no. 1 (June 1991): 1–23.

———. "O fim da guerra fria e os novos conflitos internacionais." *Série Política Internacional*, no 5 (June 1991): 1–22.

Allen, Christopher. "The Underdevelopment of Keynesianism in the Federal Republic of Germany." In *The Political Power of Economic Ideas*, ed. Peter Hall. Princeton: Princeton University Press, 1989.

Allot, Philip. *Eunomia: New Order for a New World*. New York: Oxford University Press, 1990.

Almeida, Carlos, and António Barreto. *Capitalismo e Emigração em Portugal*. Lisbon: Edições Prelo, 1969.

Almond, Gabriel and G. Bingham Powell. *Comparative Politics: A Developmental Approach*. Boston: Little, Brown, 1966.

Almond, Gabriel, and Sidney Verba. *The Civic Culture*. Princeton: Princeton University Press, 1963.

"Amendments to the Law to Regulate Financial Groups and the Law of the Securities Market." *Diario Oficial* (Mexico City, February 15, 1995). Reported in *Inter-American Trade and Investment* (February 24, 1995): 255.

American Bar Association. *Report of the Task Force of the ABA Section of Antitrust Law on the Competition Dimension of NAFTA*. Chicago: ABA, 1994.

Anderson, Benedict. *Imagined Communities: Reflections on the Origin and Spread of Nationalism*. London: Verso, 1983.

Anderson, Christopher, and Karl Kaltenthaler. "The Dynamics of Public Opinion

Toward European Integration." *European Journal of International Relations* 2 (1996): 175–199.

Anderson, Jeffrey. "German Industry and the European Union in the 1990s." In *Quest for Economic Empire: European Strategies of German Big Business in the Twentieth Century*, ed. Volker Berghahn. Oxford: Berghahn Books, 1996.

———. "Structural Funds and the Social Dimension of EU Policy: Springboard or Stumbling Block?" In *European Social Policy: Between Fragmentation and Integration*, eds. Stephan Leibfried and Paul Pierson. Washington, D.C.: Brookings Institution, 1995.

Anderson, Malcolm, Monica den Boer, Peter Cullen, William Gilmore, Charles Raab, and Neil Walker. *Policing the European Union*. Oxford: Clarendon, 1995.

A nemzeti megújhodás programja. Budapest, 1990.

Armingeon, Klaus. "The Democratic Deficit of the European Community: A Comment." *Außenwirtschaft* 1 (1995): 67–76.

———. "Die Regulierung der kollektiven Arbeitsbeziehungen." In *Staat und Verbände*, PVS-Sonderheft 25, ed. Wolfgang Streeck. Opladen: Westdeutscher Verlag, 1994.

Ashley, Richard K. "Untying the Sovereign State: A Double Reading of the Anarchy Problematique." *Millennium: Journal of International Studies* 17 (summer 1988): 227–262.

Baer, M. Delal. "North American Free Trade." *Foreign Affairs* 70, no. 4 (1991): 132–149.

Baer, M. Delal, and Sydney Weintraub, eds. *The NAFTA Debate: Grappling with Unconventional Trade Issues*. Boulder: Lynne Rienner, 1994.

Baer, Werner, and António Nogueira Leite. "The Peripheral Economy, Its Performance in Isolation and with Integration: The Case of Portugal." *Luso-Brazilian Review* 29 (1992): 1–43.

Balassa, Bela. *The Theory of Economic Integration*. London: Allen and Unwin, 1962.

Balázs, Péter. "A periferizáció határai. *Európa Fórum* 5 (December 1995): 87–104.

———. "Az EK közép-kelet-európai és mediterrán társulásainak összehasonlítása." *Európa Fórum* 2 (December 1993): 3–19.

Barbosa, Rubens António. "A evolução do processo de integração na América do Sul." *Série Política Internaciona,* no. 2 (June 1991): 1–22.

Barreto, António. *A Situão Social em Portugal, 1960–1995*. Lisbon: Instituto de Ciências Sociais, 1996.

Bartelson, Jens. *A Genealogy of Sovereignty*. Cambridge: Cambridge University Press, 1995.

Berend, Iván T. "Európa! De miért?" *Népszabadság* (Budapest, January 28, 1995): 17.

Berger, Suzanne. "Comments." In *Regional Integration: The West European Experience*, ed. William Wallace. Washington, D.C.: Brookings Institution, 1994.

Berger, Suzanne, and Ronald Dore, eds. *National Diversity and Global Capitalism*. Ithaca: Cornell University Press, 1996.

Berger, Thomas. "Norms, Identity, and National Security in Germany and Japan."

In *The Culture of National Security: Norms and Identity in World Politics*, ed. Peter J. Katzenstein. New York: Columbia University Press, 1996.

Betz, Hans-Georg. *Radical Rightwing Populism in Western Europe*. New York: St. Martin's, 1994.

Bhagwati, Jagdish. *Protectionism*. Cambridge: MIT Press, 1989.

Biersteker, Thomas J. "Globalization and the Modes of Operation of Major Institutional Actors." *Oxford Development Studies* 26 (February 1998): 15–31.

Biersteker, Thomas (with Christine Kearney). "The Global Setting of Contemporary Democratization and Political Reform." Unpublished manuscript, Brown University, April 1994.

Biersteker, Thomas J., and Christine A. Kearney. "International Sources of Contemporary Democratization." In *International Dimensions of Economic Liberalization and Democratic Consolidation*, ed. Laurence Whitehead. Oxford: Oxford University Press, forthcoming.

Björklund, Anders, and Richard B. Freeman. "Generating Equality and Eliminating Poverty, the Swedish Way." In *The Welfare State in Transition*, eds. Richard B. Freeman, Robert Topel, and Birgitta Swedenborg. Chicago: University of Chicago Press, 1997.

Blair, P. *Federalism and Judicial Review in West Germany*. Oxford: Clarendon, 1981.

Blomström, Magnus, and Robert Lipsey. "The Competitiveness of Countries and Their Multinational Firms." In *Multinationals in the Global Political Economy*, eds. Lorraine Eden and Evan Potter. New York: St. Martin's, 1993.

Bosch, Agusti, and Kenneth Newton. "Economic Calculus or Familiarity Breeds Content?" In *Public Opinion and Internationalized Governance*, eds. Oskar Niedermayer and Richard Sinnot. Oxford: Oxford University Press, 1995.

Bozóki, András. "Hungary's Road to Systemic Change: The Opposition Roundtable." *East European Politics and Societies* 7 (spring 1993): 276–308.

Brittan, Samuel. "The Economic Contradictions of Democracy." *British Journal of Political Science* 5 (1975): 129–159.

Bruszt, László, and David Stark. "Remaking the Political Field in Hungary: From the Politics of Confrontation to the Politics of Competition." *Journal of International Affairs* 45 (June 1991): 201–245.

Bull, Anna Cento. "Ethnicity, Racism, and the Northern League." In *Italian Regionalism: History, Identity and Politics*, ed. Carl Levy. Washington D.C.: Berg, 1996.

Bull, Hedley. *The Anarchical Society*. New York: Columbia University Press, 1977.

Bulmer, Simon. "European Integration and Germany: The Constitutive Politics of the EU and the Institutional Mediation of German Power." In *Tamed Power*, ed. Peter Katzenstein. Ithaca: Cornell University Press, 1997.

Bulmer, Simon, and William Paterson. *The Federal Republic of Germany and the European Community*. London: Allen and Unwin, 1987.

Bundesverband der Deutschen Industrie. "Antworten des BDI auf den Fragenkatalog zur Standortdiskussion der CDU/CSU-Bundestagsfraktion." Cologne, April 1992.

Bureau of the Census, Foreign Trade Division. *Exports, Imports and Balance of Goods by Selected Countries and Geographic Areas*. Washington, D.C.: U.S. Government Printing Office, November 1996.

———. *Top Ten Countries With Which the US Trades*. Washington, D.C.: U.S. Government Printing Office, November 1996.

Bustamante, A. Jorge, Clark Reynolds, and Raul Hinojosa Ojeda, eds. *U.S.-Mexico Relations: Labor Market Interdependence*. Stanford: Stanford University Press, 1992.

Canadian Labor Congress. *Social Dimensions of North American Economic Integration: Impacts on Working People and Emerging Responses. A Report Prepared for the Department of Human Resources Development*. Ottawa: CLC, 1996.

Caporaso, James. "The European Union and Forms of State: Westphalian, Regulatory or Post-Modern?" *Journal of Common Market Studies* 34 (March 1996): 29–52.

Cárdenas, Cuauhtémoc. "Free Trade Is Not Enough." *New Perspectives Quarterly* (winter 1991).

Carreira, Henrique Medina. *As Políticas Sociais em Portugal, 1960–1995*. Lisbon: Edições Gradiva, 1996.

Castañeda, Jorge. "Can NAFTA Change Mexico?" *Foreign Affairs* 72, no. 4 (1993): 66–80.

Christiansen, Thomas. "The Länder Between Bonn and Brussels: The Dilemma of German Federalism in the 1990s." *German Politics* 2 (August 1992): 239–263.

Cohen, Benjamin J. "Phoenix Risen: The Resurrection of Global Finance." *World Politics* 48 (January 1996): 268–296.

Commission of the EC. *The Regions in the 1990s*. Luxembourg: Office for Official Publications of the European Communities, 1991.

Cox, Robert. "From Safety Net to Trampoline: Labor Market Activation in the Netherlands and Denmark." *Governance* (forthcoming).

Csaba, László. "A rendszerváltozás második fordulója és az EU keleti kibövülése." *Valóság* 39 (August 1996): 1–20.

Csepeli, György, and Tibor Závecz. "Várakozások, remények, félelmek: Az Európai Unió képe a magyar közvéleményben." In *Magyarorszg Politikai Évkönyve 1996-ról*, eds. Sándor Kurtán, Péter Sándor, and László Vass. Budapest: Demokrácia Kutatások Magyar Központja Alapítvány, 1997.

Curzon Price, Victoria. "1992: Europe's Last Chance? From Common Market to Single Market." *Occasional Paper* 81. London: Institute of Economic Affairs, December 1998.

———. "Free Trade Areas: The European Experience. What Lessons for Canadian-U.S. Trade Liberalization?" *Observation* 31. Toronto: C. D. Howe Institute, 1987.

Dahl, Robert A. "A Democratic Dilemma: System Effectiveness Versus Citizen Participation." *Political Science Quarterly* 109 (1994): 23–34.

———. *Democracy and its Critics*. New Haven: Yale University Press, 1989.

———. *Polyarchy*. New Haven: Yale University Press, 1971.

De Michelis, G. "Die EG als Gravitationszentrum. Für ein Europa der vier Kreise." *Integration* 4 (1990): 141–147.

del Castillo, Gustavo, and Gustavo Vega-Cánovas. *The Politics of Free Trade in North America*. Ottawa: Carleton University Center for Trade Policy and Law, 1995.

den Boer, Monica, and Neil Walker. "European Policing After 1992." *Journal of Common Market Studies* 31 (1993): 3–27.

De Palma, Anthony. "Economics Lesson in a Border Town." *New York Times* (May 23, 1996): C1, C5.

Desideri, Carlo. "Italian Regions in the European Community." In *The European Union and the Regions*, eds. Michael Keating and Barry Jones. New York: Oxford University Press, 1995.

Deudney, Daniel. "The Philadelphian System: Sovereignty, Arms Control, and Balance of Power in the American States-Union, Circa 1787–1861." *International Organization* 49 (spring 1995): 191–228.

Deutsch, Karl W. *Nationalism and Social Communication*. New York: Wiley, 1953.

Deutsch, Karl W. et al. *Political Community and the North Atlantic Area*. Princeton: Princeton University Press, 1968.

Diamanti, Ilvo. "The *Lega Nord*: From Federalism to Secession." In *Italian Politics: The Center-Left in Power*, eds. Roberto D'Alimonte and David Nelken. Boulder: Westview, 1997.

Di Palma, Giuseppe. *To Craft Democracies*. Berkeley: University of California Press, 1990.

Downes, David. *Contrasts in Tolerance: Postwar Penal Policy in the Netherlands, and England and Wales*. New York: Oxford University Press, 1988.

Drummond, Maria Cláudia. "O Mercosur e a articulação de atores sociais. O caso brasileiro (1991–1994)." M.S. thesis in International Relations, University of Brasilia. Brasilia, 1994.

Dyson, Kenneth "West Germany: The Search for a Rationalist Consensus." In *Policy Styles in Western Europe*, ed. Jeremy Richardson. London: George Allen and Unwin, 1982.

Easton, David. *A Systems Analysis of Political Life*. Chicago: John Wiley and Sons, 1965.

Eatwell, Roger. "Europe of the 'Nation States'? Concepts, Theories and Reflections." In *European Political Culture*, ed. Roger Eatwell. London: Routledge, 1997.

Ebbinghaus, Bernhard, and Jelle Visser. "Barrieren und Wege 'grenzenloser Solidarität': Gewerkschaften und Europäische Integration." In *Staat und Verbände*, PVS-Sonderheft 25, ed. Wolfgang Streeck. Opladen: Westdeutscher Verlag, 1994.

Eichenberg, Richard, and Russel Dalton. "Europeans and the European Community: The Dynamics of Public Support for European Integration." *International Organization* 47, no. 4 (1993): 507–534.

Esser, Josef, and Wolfgang Fach (with Kenneth Dyson). " 'Social Market' and Modernization Policy: West Germany." In *Industrial Crisis: A Comparative Study of the State and Industry*, eds. Kenneth Dyson and Stephen Wilks. New York: St. Martin's, 1983.

Falkner, Gerda, and Michael Nenntwich. "Das Demokratiedefizit der EG und die Beschlüsse von Maastricht 1992." *Österreichische Zeitschrift für Politikwissenschaft* 3 (1992): 273–289.

Farrell, Joseph, and Carl Levy. "The Northern League: Conservative Revolution?" In *Italian Regionalism: History, Identity and Politics*, ed. Carl Levy. Washington, D.C.: Berg, 1996.

Fionda, Julia. *Public Prosecutors and Discretion: A Comparative Study*. Oxford: Clarendon, 1995.

Fitzmaurice, John. *The Politics of Belgium: A Unique Federalism*. Boulder: Westview, 1996.

Flickinger, Richard S., and Donley T. Studlar. "The Disappearing Voters? Exploring Declining Turnout in Western European Elections." *West European Politics* 2 (1992): 1–16.

Forsyth, Murray. "Federalism and Confederalism." In *Political Restructuring in Europe: Ethical Perspectives*, ed. Chris Brown. New York: Routledge, 1994.

Franklin, Mark N., Cees Van Der Eijk, and Michael Marsh. "Referendum Outcomes and Trust in Government: Public Support for Europe in the Wake of Maastricht." In *The Crisis of Representation in Europe*, ed. Jack Hayward. London: Frank Cass, 1995.

Frieden, Jeffry. "Invested Interests: The Politics of National Economic Policies in a World of Global Finance." *International Organization* 45 (autumn 1991): 425–451.

Friedrich, Carl J. *Europe: An Emergent Nation?* New York: Harper and Row, 1969.

Gabel, Matthew, and Harvey Palmer. "Understanding Variation in Public Support for European Integration." *European Journal of Political Research* 27 (1995): 3–19.

García, Soledad, and Helen Wallace. "Conclusion." In *European Identity and the Search for Legitimacy*, ed. Soledad García. London: Pinter, 1993.

Garrett, Geoffrey. "International Cooperation and Institutional Choice: The European Community's Internal Market." *International Organization* 2 (1992): 533–560.

Garriga, Marcelo, and Pablo Sanguinetti. "Coordinación Macroeconómica en el Mercosur: Ventajas, desventajas y la práctica," *PROSUR*. Buenos Aires: Fundación Friedrich Ebert, 1996.

Garton Ash, Timothy. *In Europe's Name*. New York: Random House, 1993.

Gellner, Ernest. *Nations and Nationalism*. Ithaca: Cornell University Press, 1983.

Gilbert, Mark. *The Italian Revolution: The End of Politics, Italian Style?* Boulder: Westview, 1995.

Gillespie, Charles. "Democratizing a One-Party State." *Journal of Democracy* 1 (fall 1990): 49–58.

Glotz, Peter. *Die falsche Normalisierung*. Frankfurt: Suhrkamp, 1994.

Goodman, John. *Monetary Sovereignty: The Politics of Central Banking in Western Europe*. Ithaca: Cornell University Press, 1992.

Gordenker, Leon, and Thomas Weiss. "Pluralizing Global Governance: Analytical Approaches and Dimensions." In *NGOs, the UN, and Global Governance*, eds. Leon Gordenker and Thomas Weiss. Boulder: Lynne Rienner, 1996.

Gould, Arthur. "Sweden: The Last Bastion of Social Democracy." In *European Welfare Policy: Squaring the Welfare Circle*, eds. Vic George and Peter Taylor-Gooby. New York: St. Martin's, 1996.

Gourevitch, Peter. *Politics in Hard Times*. Ithaca: Cornell University Press, 1986.

Grabitz, Eberhard, ed. *Abgestufte Integration—eine Alternative zum herkömmlichen Integrationskonzept?* Kehl: Engel, 1984.

Greven, Michael Th., ed. *Macht in der Demokratie*. Baden-Baden: Nomos, 1991.

Grimm, Dieter. *Braucht Europa eine Verfassung?* Themen. vol. 60. Munich: Carl Friedrich von Siemens Stiftung, 1994.

Gunlicks, Arthur. *Local Government in the German Federal System*. Durham: Duke University Press, 1986.

Haas, Ernst B. "The Study of Regional Integration: Reflections on the Joy and Anguish of Pretheorizing." In *Regional Integration: Theory and Research*, eds. Leon N. Lindberg and Stuart A. Scheingold. Cambridge: Harvard University Press, 1970.

―――. "The Uniting of Europe and the Uniting of Latin America." *Journal of Common Market Studies* 5 (1967): 315–343.

―――. *Beyond the Nation State. Functionalism and International Integration*. Stanford: Stanford University Press, 1964.

―――. *The Uniting of Europe*. Stanford: Stanford University Press, 1958.

Habermas, Jürgen. *Faktizität und Geltung*. Frankfurt a.M.: Suhrkamp, 1992.

Halfmann, Jost. "Social Change and Political Mobilization in West Germany." In *Industry and Politics in West Germany*, ed. Peter Katzenstein. Ithaca: Cornell University Press, 1989.

Hall, Peter. *Governing the Economy*. Oxford: Oxford University Press, 1986.

Hallstein, Walter. *Die Europäische Gemeinschaft*. Düsseldorf: Econ Verlag, 1979.

―――. *Der unvollendete Bundesstaat*. Düsseldorf: Econ Verlag, 1969.

Hanrieder, Wolfram. *Germany, America, Europe*. New Haven: Yale University Press, 1989.

Hart, Michael, ed. *Finding Middle Ground: Reforming the Antidumping Laws in North America*. Ottawa: Centre for Trade Policy and Law–Carleton University, 1997.

Hedetoft, Ulf. *Signs of Nations: Studies in the Political Semiotics of Self and Other in Contemporary European Nationalism*. Aldershot: Dartmouth, 1995.

Hemerijck, Anton C. "Corporatist Immobility in the Netherlands." In *Organized Industrial Relations in Europe: What Future?*, eds. Colin Crouch and Franz Traxler. Brookfield, Vt.: Ashgate, 1995.

Hine, David. "Federalism, Regionalism, and the Unitary State: Contemporary Regional Pressures in Historical Perspective." In *Italian Regionalism: History, Identity and Politics*, ed. Carl Levy. Washington, D.C.: Berg, 1996.

Hinsley, F. H. *Sovereignty*, 2d ed. Cambridge: Cambridge University Press, 1986.

Hobsbawm, Eric. "Nation, State, Ethnicity, Religion: Transformations of Identity." In *Nationalism in Europe Past and Present*, vol. 1, eds. Justo G. Beramendi, Romón Máiz, and Xosé M. Núñez. Santiago de Compostela: University of Santiago de Compostela, 1994.

Hoffmann, Stanley. "Delusions of World Order." *New York Review of Books* (April 9, 1992).

―――. "Obstinate or Obsolete? The Fate of Nation State and the Case of Western Europe." *Daedalus* 95 (1966): 862–915.

―――. "The European Process at Atlantic Cross-Purposes." *Journal of Common Market Studies* 3 (1965): 85–101.

Hoffmann, Stanley, and Robert O. Keohane, eds. *The New European Community: Decision Making and Institutional Change*. Boulder: Westview, 1991.

Hollingsworth, J. Rogers, and Robert Boyer, eds. *Contemporary Capitalism: The Embeddedness of Institutions*. New York: Cambridge University Press, 1997.

Hooghe, Liesbet. "Building a Europe with the Regions: The Changing Role of the European Commission." In *European Integration, Cohesion Policy, and Subnational Mobilisation*, ed. Liesbet Hooghe. Oxford: Oxford University Press, 1996.

―――. "Belgian Federalism and the European Community." In *The European Union and the Regions*, eds. Michael Keating and Barry Jones. New York: Oxford University Press, 1995.

Hsu, Michael J. "Institutional Learning: A Study of the World Bank Inspection Panel." B.A. honors thesis, Department of Political Science, Brown University, May 1997.

Hufbauer, Gary, and J. Schott. *NAFTA: An Assessment*. Washington, D.C.: Institute for International Economics, 1994.

―――. *North American Free Trade: Issues and Recommendations*. Washington, D.C.: Institute for International Economics, 1992.

Huntington, Samuel. *The Third Wave: Democratization in the Twentieth Century*. Norman: University of Oklahoma Press, 1991.

―――. "Will More Countries Become Democratic?" *Political Science Quarterly* 99 (summer 1984): 193–218.

Hurrell, Andrew. "International Relations and the Promotion of Democracy and Human Rights." Paper presented at the Queen Elizabeth House conference, "The Third World After the Cold War: Ideology, Economic Development and Politics," Oxford University, Oxford, July 5–8, 1995.

Inotai, András. "A társulási egyezménytöl a teljes jogú tagság felé?" *Gazdaság* 29 (spring 1996): 28–51.

―――. "The System of Criteria for Hungary's Accession to the European Union." Budapest: Institute for World Economics of the Hungarian Academy of Sciences, 1994.

International Trade Commission. *The Year in Trade*. Washington, D.C.: U.S. Government Publishing Office, 1995.

Ipsen, Hans Peter. *Europäisches Gemeinschaftsrecht*. Tübingen: Mohr Verlag, 1972.

Iversen, Torben. "Power, Flexibility, and the Breakdown of Centralized Wage Bargaining." *Comparative Politics* 28 (1996): 399–436.

Jachtenfuchs, Markus, and Beate Kohler-Koch, eds. *Europäische Integration*. Opladen: Leske und Budrich, 1996.

―――. "Regieren im dynamischen Mehrebenensystem." In *Europäische Integration*, ed. Markus Jachtenfuchs and Beate Kohler-Koch. Opladen: Leske und Budrich, 1996.

Jackson, Robert. *Quasi-States: Sovereignty, International Relations and the Third World*. Cambridge: Cambridge University Press, 1990.

James, Alan. *Sovereign Statehood: The Basis of International Society.* London: Allen and Unwin, 1986.

Janning, Josef. "Europa braucht verschiedene Geschwindigkeiten." *Europa Archiv* 18 (1994): 527–536.

Jarausch, Konrad. *The Rush to German Unity.* New York: Oxford University Press, 1994.

Jeffery, Charlie. "The Länder Strike Back: Structures and Procedures of European Integration Policy-making in the German Federal System." Discussion Papers in Federal Studies FS94/4, University of Leicester, September 1994.

Jepperson, Ron, Alexander Wendt, and Peter J. Katzenstein. "Norms, Identity, Culture and National Security." In *The Culture of National Security: Norms and Identity in World Politics*, ed. Peter J. Katzenstein. New York: Columbia University Press, 1996.

Jones, Erik. "Is 'Competitive' Corporatism an Adequate Response to Globalization? Evidence from the Low Countries." Paper presented at the Eleventh International Conference of Europeanists, Baltimore, February 26–28, 1998.

———. "Finding the Balance: The Decentralization of Belgium." Unpublished manuscript, University of Nottingham, 1997.

Kádár, Béla. "Cui prodest Európai Unió?" *Magyar Tudomány* 103 (February 1996): 153–165.

———. "A magyar átalakulás optikája: kívülről és belülről." *Külgazdaság* 39 (September 1995): 53–58.

Kapstein, Ethan B. "We Are US: The Myth of the Multinational." *National Interest* 26 (winter 1991–92): 55–62.

Katzenstein, Peter. "Stability and Change in the Emerging Third Republic." In *Industry and Politics in West Germany*, ed. Peter Katzenstein. Ithaca: Cornell University Press, 1989.

———. *Policy and Politics in West Germany: The Growth of a Semi-Sovereign State.* Philadelphia: Temple University Press, 1987.

———. *Corporatism and Change.* Ithaca: Cornell University Press, 1984.

———. *Small States in World Markets.* Ithaca: Cornell University Press, 1985.

Katzenstein, Peter, ed. *Between Power and Plenty.* Madison: University of Wisconsin Press, 1978.

Keating, Michael. *Nations Against the State: The New Politics of Nationalism in Quebec, Catalonia and Scotland.* London: Macmillan, 1996.

———. "Europeanism and Regionalism." In *The European Union and the Regions*, eds. Michael Keating and Barry Jones. New York: Oxford University Press, 1995.

Kelk, Constantijn, Laurence Koffman, and Jos Silvis. "Sentencing Practices, Policy, and Discretion." In *Criminal Justice in Europe: A Comparative Study*, ed. Phil Fennell. Oxford: Clarendon, 1995.

Kende, Péter. "A Trianon-szindróma és a magyar külpolitika." *Külpolitika* 3–4 (fall-winter 1995): 3–16.

Keohane, Robert O. *After Hegemony: Cooperation and Discord in the World Political Economy.* Princeton: Princeton University Press, 1984.

Kielmansegg, Peter Graf. "Integration und Demokratie." In *Europäische Integration*, ed. Markus Jachtenfuchs and Beate Kohler-Koch. Opladen: Leske und Budrich, 1996.

———. "Legitimität als analytische Kategorie." *Politische Vierteljahresschrift* 3 (1971): 367–401.

King, Anthony. "Overload: Problems of Governing in the 1970s." *Political Studies* 23 (1975): 162–74.

Klatt, Hartmut. "German Unification and the Federal System." In *Federalism, Unification, and German Integration*, ed. Charlie Jeffery and Roland Sturm. London: Frank Cass, 1993.

Kobrin, Stephen J. "Beyond Symmetry: State Sovereignty in a Networked Global Economy." In *Governments, Globalization and International Business*, ed. John H. Dunning. Oxford: Oxford University Press, 1997.

Kohler-Koch, Beate. "Die Gestaltungsmacht organisierter Interessen." In *Europäische Integration*, ed. Markus Jachtenfuchs and Beate Kohler-Koch. Opladen: Leske und Budrich, 1996.

Kohler-Koch, Beate, ed. *Regime in den Internationalen Beziehungen*. Baden-Baden: Nomos Verlag, 1989.

Kornai, János. "Transformational Recession." Discussion Papers no. 1, Collegium Budapest/Institute for Advanced Studies, June 1993.

Központi Statisztikai Hivatal. *Magyar Statisztikai Zsebkönyv 1997*. Budapest: Központi Statisztikai Hivatal, 1998.

Krasner, Stephen D. "Sovereignty and Intervention." In *Beyond Westphalia? State Sovereignty and International Intervention*, eds. Gene M. Lyons and Michael Mastanduno. Baltimore: Johns Hopkins University Press, 1995.

———. "Structural Causes and Regime Consequences: Regimes as Intervening Variables." In *International Regimes*, ed. Stephen D. Krasner. Ithaca: Cornell University Press, 1993.

———. "Westphalia." Unpublished manuscript, Stanford University, 1991.

———. "Sovereignty: An Institutional Perspective." *Comparative Political Studies* 21 (1988): 66–94.

Kratochwil, Friedrich. "The Concept of Sovereignty: Sovereignty as Property." Unpublished manuscript, University of Pennsylvania, 1992.

Kreile, Michael, ed. *Die Integration Europas*, PVS-Sonderheft 23. Opladen: Westdeutscher Verlag, 1992.

Krueger, Anne. *American Trade Policy: A Tragedy in the Making*. Washington, D.C.: AEI, 1995.

Kurzer, Paulette. "Placed in Europe: Belgium and the Netherlands in the European Union." In *Tamed Power: Germany in Europe*, ed. Peter Katzenstein. Ithaca: Cornell University Press, 1997.

———. *Business and Banking: Political Change and Economic Integration in Western Europe*. Ithaca: Cornell University Press, 1993.

Laffan, Brigid. "The Politics of Identity and Political Order in Europe." *Journal of Common Market Studies* 34 (March 1996): 81–102.

Lange, Peter. "The Politics of the Social Dimension." In *Euro-Politics*, ed. Alberta Sbragia. Washington, D.C.: Brookings Institution, 1991.

Lange, Peter, Michael Wallerstein, and Miriam Golden. "The End of Corporatism? Wage Setting in the Nordic and Germanic Countries." In *The Workers of Nations: Industrial Relations in a Global Economy*, ed. Sanford Jacoby. New York: Oxford University Press, 1995.

Lavagna, Roberto. "Estratégias defensivas e coordenação macroeconómica no Mercosur," *Symposium: O Sul das Américas*. Brasilia: Fundaçao Alexandre Gusmão, May 1995.

Lehmbruch, Gerhard. *Parteienwettbewerb im Bundesstaat*. Stuttgart: Verlag W. Kohlhammer, 1976.

Leibfried, Stephan, and Paul Pierson, eds. *European Social Policy: Between Fragmentation and Integration*. Washington, D.C.: Brookings Institution, 1995.

Lepsius, Rainer M. "Institutionenanalyse und Institutionenpolitik." In *Politische Institutionen im Wandel*, ed. Birgitta Nedelmann. Sonderheft der Kölner Zeitschrift für Soziologie und Sozialpsychologie 35. Opladen: Westdeutscher Verlag, 1995.

———. "Nationalstaat oder Nationalitätenstaat als Modell für die Weiterentwicklung der Europäischen Gemeinschaft." In *Staatswerdung Europas? Optionen für eine Europäische Union*, ed. Rudolf Wildenmann. Baden-Baden: Nomos Verlag, 1991.

Levi, L. "Recent Developments in Federal Theory." *The Federalist: A Political Review* 2 (1987): 97–136.

Leycegui, Beatriz, and Gustavo Vega-Cánovas. "Eliminating Unfairness Within the North American Region: A Look at Antidumping." In *Finding Middle Ground: Reforming the Antidumping Laws in North America*, ed. Michael Hart. Ottawa: Centre for Trade Policy and Law–Carleton University, 1997.

Leycegui, Beatriz, William Robson, and S. Dahlia Stein, eds. *Trading Punches: Trade Remedy Law and Disputes under NAFTA*. Washington, D.C.: National Planning Association, 1995.

Lijphart, Arend. *Democracies: Patterns of Majoritarian and Consensus Government in Twenty-One Countries*. New Haven: Yale University Press, 1984.

Lindbeck, Assar et al. *Turning Sweden Around*. Cambridge, MA: MIT Press, 1994.

Lindberg, Leon N. *The Political Dynamics of European Integration*. Stanford: Stanford University Press, 1963.

Lindberg, Leon, and Stuart Scheingold. *Regional Integration, Theory and Research*. Cambridge: Harvard University Press, 1971.

———. *Europe's Would-Be Polity: Patterns of Change in the European Community*. Englewood Cliffs, N.J.: Prentice-Hall, 1970.

Lindblom, Charles. "The Market as Prison." *Journal of Politics* 44 (May 1982): 324–336.

Linz, Juan J. *Conflicto en Euskadi*. Madrid: Espasa Calpe, 1986.

Linz, Juan, and Alfred Stepan, eds. *The Breakdown of Democratic Regimes*. Baltimore: Johns Hopkins University Press, 1978.

Lipschultz, Ronnie D. "Reconstructing World Politics: The Emergence of Global Civil Society." *Millennium* 21 (winter 1992): 389–420.

Loewenstein, Karl. *Verfassungslehre*. Tübingen: Mohr Verlag, 1969.

Lopes, José da Silva. *A Economia Portuguesa, 1960–1995*. Lisbon: Edições Gradiva, 1996.

Lourenão, Eduardo. *Nós e a Europa*. Lisbon: Imprensa Nacional-Casa da Moeda, 1988.

———. *O Labirinto da Saudade*. Lisbon: Edições Dom Quixote, 1978.

Lübbe, Hermann. "Föderalismus und Regionalismus in der Europäischen Union." In *Reform der Europäischen Union*, ed. Werner Weidenfeld. Gütersloh: Bertelsmann, 1995.

Ludlow, Peter. "The European Commission." In *The New European Community*, eds. Stanley Hoffmann and Robert O. Keohane. Boulder: Westview, 1991.

Luke, Timothy. "The Discipline of Security Studies and the Codes of Containment: Learning from Kuwait." *Alternatives* 16 (1991): 315–344.

Lustig, Nora, Barry Bosworth, and Robert Lawrence, eds. *Assessing the Impact of North American Free Trade*. Washington, D.C.: Brookings Institution, 1992.

Lyons, Gene M., and Michael Mastanduno. *Beyond Westphalia? State Sovereignty and International Intervention*. Baltimore: Johns Hopkins University Press, 1995.

Mäding, Heinrich. "Die föderativen Finanzbeziehungen im Prozeß der deutschen Einigung." In *Verwaltungsreform und Verwaltungspolitik im Prozeß der deutschen Einigung*, eds. Wolfgang Seibel, Arthur Benz, and Heinrich Mäding. Baden-Baden: Nomos Verlagsgesellschaft, 1993.

Mahler, Vincent, Bruce Taylor, and Jennifer Wozniak. "Economics and Public Support for the European Union, 1976–1992: An Analysis at the National, Regional and Individual Levels." Paper presented at the European Community Studies Association meeting, Charleston, May 1995.

Marginson, Paul, and Keith Sisson. "The Structure of Transnational Capital in Europe: The Emerging Euro-Company and Its Implications for Industrial Relations." In *New Frontiers in European Industrial Relations*, eds. Richard Hyman and Anthony Ferner. Cambridge: Blackwell, 1994.

Markovits, Andrei. *The Politics of the West German Trade Unions*. New York: Cambridge University Press, 1986.

Marks, Gary, and Richard Haesly. "Thinking Through Territorial Identity in Europe with Reference to Some Evidence." Paper presented at the International Conference of Europeanists, Chicago, March 1966.

Marks, Gary, Liesbet Hooghe, and Kermit Blank. "European Integration Since the 1980s: State-Centric Versus Multi-Level Governance." *Journal of Common Market Studies* 34 (September 1996): 341–378.

Marks, Gary, and Iván Llamazares. "La Transformación de la Movilización Regional en la Unión Europea." *Revista de Estudios Políticos* 22 (1995): 149–170.

Marshall, T. H. *Citizenship and Social Class and Other Essays*. Cambridge: Cambridge University Press, 1950.

Martins, Herminio. "Portugal." In *Contemporary Europe: Class, Status and Power*, eds. Margaret Scotford Archer and Salvador Giner. London: Weidenfeld and Nicholson, 1971.

Martonyi, János. "Csatlakozásunk az Európai Közösséghez." *Európa Fórum* 2 (June 1992): 3–11.

McCormick, John. *The European Union: Politics and Policies*. Boulder: Westview, 1996.

McGee, W. Robert. "The Case to Repeal the Antidumping Laws." *Northwestern Journal of International Law and Business* 13 (1993): 491–527.

Mignone, Mario. *Italy Today: A Country in Transition*. New York: Peter Lang, 1995.

Milner, Helen, and Robert Keohane. "Internationalization and Domestic Politics: An Introduction." In *Internationalization and Domestic Politics*, eds. Helen Milner and Robert Keohane. New York: Cambridge University Press, 1996.

Milward, Alan. *The European Rescue of the Nation-State*. Berkeley: University of California Press, 1992.

Moene, Karl Ove, and Michael Wallerstein. "How Social Democracy Worked: Labor-Market Institutions." *Politics and Society* 23 (1995): 206–207.

Molinar, Juan. *El tiempo de la legitimidad. Elecciones, autoritarismo y democracia en México*. Mexico City: Cal y Arena, 1991.

Molnár, Zoltán and Antal Tóth. "Közép- és kelet-európai vélemények gazdaságról, politikáról és az európai együttmüködésről." In *Magyarország politikai évkönyve*, eds. Sándor Kurtán, Péter Sándor, and László Vass. Budapest: Demokrácia Kutatások Magyar Központja Alapítvány, 1995.

Moravcsik, Andrew. "The Sources of Informal Influence: Entrepreneurial Leadership and European Integration." Unpublished manuscript, Harvard University, March 1997.

———. "Preference and Power in the European Community: A Liberal Intergovernmentalist Approach." *Journal of Common Market Studies* 4 (1994): 473–524.

———. "Why the European Community Strengthens the State: Domestic Politics and International Cooperation." Paper presented at the annual meeting of the American Political Science Association, New York, 1994.

———. "National Preference Formation and Interstate Bargaining in the European Community, 1955–1986." Ph.D. dissertation, Department of Government, Harvard University, 1992.

———. "Negotiating the Single European Act: National Interests and Conventional Statecraft in the European Community." *International Organization*, 45 (Winter 1991): 19–56.

Müller-Armack, Alfred. *Wirtschaftslenkung und Marktwirtschaft*. Hamburg: Verlag für Wirtschaft- und Sozialpolitik, 1948.

Murphy, Alexander B. "The Sovereign State System as Political-Territorial Ideal: Historical and Contemporary Considerations." In *State Sovereignty as Social Construct*, eds. Thomas J. Biersteker and Cynthia Weber. Cambridge: Cambridge University Press, 1996.

Nedelmann, Birgitta, ed. *Politische Institutionen im Wandel*, Sonderheft der Kölner Zeitschrift für Soziologie und Sozialpsychologie 35. Opladen: Westdeutscher Verlag, 1995.

Netherlands Bureau for Economic Policy Analysis. *Challenging Neighbours: Rethinking German and Dutch Economic Institutions*. Berlin: Springer, 1997.

Neto, Francisco Thompson Flores. "Integração e Cooperação Brasil-Argentina." *Série Política Internacional* no. 3 (June 1991): 1–26.

Neunreither, Karl-Heinz. "Legitimationsprobleme der Europäischen Gemeinschaft." *Zeitschrift für Parlamentsfragen* 7 (1976): 245–258.

Neves, João Cèsar das. *The Portuguese Economy*. Lisbon: Universidade Católica Portuguesa, 1994.

Newman, Michael. *Democracy, Sovereignty, and the European Union*. New York: St. Martin's, 1996.

Niedermayer, Oskar, and Richard Sinnot, eds. *Public Opinion and Internationalized Governance*. Oxford: Oxford University Press, 1995.

Nye, Joseph S. "Comparing Common Markets: A Revised Neo-Functionalist Model." In *Regional Integration: Theory and Research*, ed. Leon A. Lindberg and Stuart A. Scheingold. Cambridge: Harvard University Press, 1971.

Obradovic, Daniela. "Political Legitimacy and the European Union." *Journal of Common Market Studies* 34 (June 1966): 191–221.

O'Donnell, Guillermo, Philippe Schimitter, and Lawrence Whitehead, eds. *Transitions from Authoritarian Rule: Latin America*. Baltimore: Johns Hopkins University Press, 1986.

Offe, Claus. "Capitalism by Democratic Design?" *Social Research* 58 (winter 1991): 865–892.

Office of the United States Trade Representative (USTR) and Related Entities. *Study on the Operation and Effect of the North American Free Trade Agreement*. Washington, D.C.: USTR, June 1997.

Ohmae, Kenichi. *The End of the Nation State: The Rise of Regional Economies*. New York: Free Press, 1995.

Olson, Mancur. *The Rise and Decline of Nations*. New Haven: Yale University Press, 1982.

———. *Die Logik kollektiven Handelns*. Tübingen: Mohr Verlag, 1968.

Onuf, Nicholas Greenwood. "Sovereignty: Outline of a Conceptual History." *Alternatives* 16 (1991): 425–446.

Onuki, Janina. "O governo e o empresariado argentino. A percepção política do Mercosur." M.S. thesis in Political Science, University of São Paulo, São Paulo, 1996.

Organization for Economic Cooperation and Development (OECD). *Economic Survey: BLUE 1997*. Paris: OECD, 1997.

———. *Economic Survey: Sweden 1997*. Paris: OECD, 1997.

———. *Economic Survey: Italy 1996*. Paris: OECD, 1996.

Packenham, Robert. *The Dependency Movement: Scholarship and Politics in Development Studies*. Cambridge: Harvard University Press, 1993.

Pentland, Charles. "North American Integration and the Canadian Political System." In *The Politics of Canada's Economic Relations with the United States*, eds. Denis Stairs and Gilbert Winham. Toronto: University of Toronto Press, 1985.

Pfetsch, Frank R. *Entwicklung und Evaluation. Empirische Dimensionen des Politischen*. Darmstadt: Wissenschaftliche Buchgemeinschaft, 1995.

Pierson, Paul, and Margaret Smith. "Bourgeois Revolutions?" *Comparative Political Studies* 25 (January 1993): 487–520.

Pijpers, Alfred, and Sophie Vanhoonacker. "The Position of the Benelux Countries." In *The Politics of European Treaty Reform*, eds. Geoffrey Edwards and Alfred Pijpers. Washington, D.C.: Pinter, 1997.

Pinder, John. "Positive Integration and Negative Integration: Some Problems of Economic Union in the EEC." *World Today* 24 (1968): 88–110.

Pollack, Mark A. "Regional Actors in an Intergovernmental Play: The Making and Implementation of EC Structural Policy." In *The State of the European Union*, vol. 3, eds. Carolyn Rhodes and Sonia Mazey. Boulder: Lynne Rienner, 1995.

Puhle, Hans-Jürgen. "Nation States, Nations, and Nationalisms in Western and Southern Europe." In *Nationalism in Europe Past and Present*, vol. 2, eds. Justo G. Beramendi, Romón Máiz, and Xosé M. Núñez. Santiago de Compostela: University of Santiago de Compostela, 1994.

Putnam, Robert. *Making Democracy Work*. Princeton: Princeton University Press, 1993.

Rácz, Margit. "EK-csatlakozás: Magyar érdekek és közösségi feltéelek." *Európa Fórum* 4 (November 1994): 77–91.

Rattinger, Hans. "Public Attitudes to European Integration in Germany After Maastricht: Inventory and Typology." *Journal of Common Market Studies* 32 (December 1994): 525–40.

Regini, Marino. *Uncertain Boundaries: The Social and Political Construction of European Economies*. New York: Cambridge University Press, 1995.

Reich, Robert. *The Work of Nations*. New York: Knopf, 1991.

Reif, Karlheinz. "Cultural Convergence and Cultural Diversity as Factors in European Diversity." In *European Identity and the Search for Legitimacy*, ed. Soledad García. London: Pinter, 1993.

Ress, George. "The Constitution and the Maastricht Treaty: Between Cooperation and Conflict." *German Politics* (December 1994): 48–74.

Richter, Emanuel. *Die Expansion der Herrschaft*. Opladen: Westdeutscher Verlag, 1994.

———. "Die Komplexität der Gesellschaft und die Reduktion von Legitimität. Machtstrukturen in der Europäischen Gemeinschaft." In *Macht in der Demokratie*, ed. Michael Th. Greven. Baden-Baden: Nomos Verlag, 1991.

Risse-Kappen, Thomas. "Exploring the Nature of the Beast: International Relations Theory and Comparative Policy Analysis Meet the European Union." *Journal of Common Market Studies* 34 (March 1996): 53–80.

———. "Ideas, Communicative Processes, and Domestic Political Change in Europe: A Conceptual Framework and Some Preliminary Results." Paper presented at the International Conference of Europeanists, Chicago, March 1996.

Rogowski, Ronald. *Commerce and Coalitions*. Princeton: Princeton University Press, 1989.

Rosenau, James N. "Sovereignty in a Turbulent World." In *Beyond Westphalia? State Sovereignty and International Intervention*, eds. Gene M. Lyons and Michael Mastanduno. Baltimore: Johns Hopkins University Press, 1995.

Rosenthal, Gert. "Treinta Años de Integración en América Latina: Un Examen Crítico." *ECLAC*, 1994.

Rosow, Stephen J. "On the Political Theory of Political Economy: Conceptual Ambiguity and the Global Economy." *Review of International Political Economy* 1 (autumn 1994): 465–488.

Rubio, Luis. "Mexico in Perspective: An Essay on Mexico's Economic Reform and the Political Consequences." *Houston Journal of International Law* 12, no. 2 (1990).

Ruggie, John Gerard. "Multilateralism: The Anatomy of an Institution." In *Multilateralism Matters*, ed. John Gerard Ruggie. New York: Columbia University Press, 1993.

———. "Territoriality and Beyond: Problematizing Modernity in International Relations." *International Organization* 47 (winter 1993): 139–175.

———. "International Regimes, Transactions, and Change: Embedded Liberalism in the Postwar Economic Order." *International Organization* 36 (spring 1982): 379–415.

Ruggiero, Vincenzo, and Nigel South. *Eurodrugs: Drug Use, Markets, and Trafficking in Europe*. London: University College London Press, 1995.

Sahlins, Peter. *Boundaries: The Making of France and Spain in the Pyrenees*. Berkeley: University of California Press, 1989.

Sbragia, Alberta. "From 'Nation-State' to 'Member-State': The Evolution of the European Community." In *Europe After Maastricht: American and European Perspectives*, ed. Paul M. Lutzeler. Providence: Berghahn, 1994.

———. "Thinking About the European Future: The Uses of Comparison." In *Euro-Politics*, ed. Alberta Sbragia. Washington, D.C.: Brookings Institution, 1991.

Scharpf, Fritz W. "Negative and Positive Integration in the Political Economy of European Welfare States." In *Governance in the European Union*, eds. Gary Marks, Fritz Scharpf, Philippe Schmitter, and Wolfgang Streeck. London: Sage, 1996.

———. "Autonomieschonend und gemeinschaftsverträglich: Zur Logik einer europäischen Mehrebenenpolitik." In *Optionen des Föderalismus in Deutschland und Europa*, ed. Fritz W. Scharpf. Frankfurt: Campus Verlag, 1994.

———. *Optionen des Föderalismus in Deutschland und Europa*. Frankfurt: Campus Verlag, 1994.

———. "Europäisches Demokratiedefizit und deutscher Föderalismus." In *Jahrbuch zur Staats- und Verwaltungswissenschaft*, vol. 6, eds. Thomas Ellwein, Dieter Grimm, Renate Mayntz, and Fritz Scharpf. Baden-Baden: Nomos Verlag, 1993/1994.

———. *Crisis and Choice in European Social Democracy*. Ithaca: Cornell University Press, 1991.

———. "Die Handlungsfähigkeit des Staates am Ende des zwanzigsten Jahrhunderts." *Politische Vierteljahresschrift* 4 (1991): 621–634.

———. "The Joint-Decision Trap: Lessons from German Federalism and European Integration." *Public Administration* 66 (autumn 1988): 239–278.

———. "Die Politikverflechtungsfälle: Europäische Integration und deutscher Föderalismus im Vergleich." *Politische Vierteljahresschrift* 26 (1985): 323–356.

Schirm, Stefan. "Transnational Globalization and Regional Governance: On the Reasons for Regional Cooperation in Europe and the Americas." Center for European Studies, Program for the Study of Germany and Europe, Working Paper no. 6.2, July 1996.

Schmidt, Manfred. "The Domestic Political Economy: Germany in the Post-1989

Period." Paper presented at the meeting of the International Political Science Association, Kyoto, Japan, March 25–27, 1994.

Schmitter, Philippe. "How to Democratize the Emerging Euro-Polity: Citizenship, Representation, Decision-Making." Unpublished manuscript, 1998.

———. "Examining the Present Euro-Polity with the Help of Past Theories." In *Governance in the European Union*, eds. Gary Marks, Fritz Scharpf, Philippe Schmitter, and Wolfgang Streeck. London: Sage, 1996.

———. "Imagining the Future of the Euro-Polity with the Help of New Concepts." In *Governance in the European Union*, eds. Gary Marks, Fritz Scharpf, Philippe Schmitter, and Wolfgang Streeck. London: Sage, 1996.

———. *The European Community as an Emergent and Novel Form of Political Domination*. Working Paper of the Centro de Estudios Avanzados en Ciencias Sociales 26, Madrid, 1991.

———. "A Revised Theory of Regional Integration." In *Regional Integration. Theory and Research*, eds. Leon Lindberg and S. A. Scheingold. Cambridge: Harvard University Press, 1971.

Schmitter, Philippe and Wolfgang Streeck. "Organized Interests and the Europe of 1992." In *Political Power and Social Change*, eds. Norman Ornstein and Mark Perlman. Washington, D.C.: American Enterprise Institute, 1991.

Schott, Jeffrey, and Murray Smith. *The Canada–United States Free Trade Agreement: The Global Impact*. Washington, D.C.: Institute for International Economics, 1988.

Sección Mexicana del Secretariado de los Tratados de Libre Comercio. *Informe de los casos de solución de controversias del Capítulo XIX y XX del Tratado de Libre Comercio de América del Norte*. Mexico City: Secofi, March 1998.

Secretaría de Comercio y Fomento Industrial. *El TLC a día a día*. Mexico City: Porrúa-Secofi, 1994.

Shore, Chris. "Inventing the 'People's Europe': Critical Approaches to European Community 'Cultural Policy.' " *Man* 28, no. 4 (December 1993): 779–799.

Sieyés, Emanuel J. *Politische Schriften*. Darmstadt: Lucherhand, 1975.

Sikkink, Kathryn. "Human Rights, Principled Issue Networks, and Sovereignty in Latin America." *International Organization* 47 (summer 1993): 411–441.

Silvis, Jos, and Katherine Williams. "Managing the Drug Problem: Prohibition or Tolerance?" In *Criminal Justice in Europe: A Comparative Study*, ed. Phil Fen nell. Oxford: Clarendon, 1995.

Smith, Anthony D. *Nations and Nationalism in a Global Era*. Cambridge: Polity, 1995.

———. "The Nations of Europe After the Cold War." In *Governing the New Europe*, eds. Jack Hayward and Edward C. Page. Durham: Duke University Press, 1995.

———. *The Ethnic Revival*. Cambridge: Cambridge University Press, 1981.

Smith, H. Peter, ed. *The Challenge of Integration: Europe and the Americas*. New Brunswick: Transaction, 1993.

———. "The Political Impact of Free Trade in Mexico." *Journal of Inter-American Studies and World Affairs* 34, no. 1 (1992): 1–25.

Smith, Michael. "The European Union and a Changing Europe: Establishing the

Boundaries of Order." *Journal of Common Market Studies* 34 (March 1996): 5–28.

Smith, Murray. "The Evolution of Trade Remedies in NAFTA." In *Finding Middle Ground: Reforming the Antidumping Laws in North America*, ed. Michael Hart. Ottawa: Centre for Trade Policy and Law–Carleton University, 1997.

Sobisch, Andreas, and David Patterson. "Public Support for European Integration: A Longitudinal Analysis." Paper presented at the American Political Science Association meeting, Chicago, September 1995.

Soskice, David. "Wage Determination: The Changing Role of Institutions in Advanced Industrialized Countries." *Oxford Review of Economic Policy* 6 (1990): 36–62.

Stark, David. "Recombinant Property in East European Capitalism." *American Journal of Sociology* 101 (January 1996): 993–1027.

———. "Path Dependence and Privatization Strategies in East Central Europe." *East European Politics and Societies* 6 (winter 1992): 17–54.

Stone-Sweet, Alec, and Wayne Sandholtz. "European Integration and Supranational Governance." *Journal of European Public Policy* 4 (September 1997): 297–317.

Strange, Susan. *The Retreat of the State: The Diffusion of Power in the World Economy*. Cambridge: Cambridge University Press, 1996.

Streeck, Wolfgang. "German Capitalism: Does It Exist? Can It Survive?" In *Political Economy of Modern Capitalism: Mapping Convergence and Diversity,* eds. Colin Crouch and Wolfgang Streeck. London: Sage, 1997.

———. "Neo-Volunteerism: A New European Social Policy Regime?" In *Governance in the European Union*, eds. Gary Marks, Fritz Scharpf, Philippe Schmitter, and Wolfgang Streeck. London: Sage, 1996.

———, ed. *Staat und Verbände*, PVS-Sonderheft 25. Opladen: Westdeutscher Verlag, 1994.

Streeck, Wolfgang, and Philippe C. Schmitter. "From National Corporatism to Transnational Pluralism: Organized Interests in the Single European Market." *Politics and Society* 19 (1991): 133–164.

Swedish Institute. *Fact Sheet on Sweden: The Swedish Economy*. Stockholm: FS1 w Qad, November 1994.

Swenson, Peter. "Bringing Capital Back In, or Social Democracy Reconsidered: Employer Power, Cross-Class Alliances, and Centralization of Industrial Relations in Denmark and Sweden." *World Politics* 43 (1991): 513–45.

Tannenwald, Nina. "The Nuclear Taboo: The Normative Basis of Nuclear Non-Use." Unpublished manuscript, Watson Institute, Brown University, 1996.

Taylor, Paul. "The European Community and the State: Assumptions, Theories and Propositions." *Review of International Studies* 17 (April 1991): 109–126.

———. *The Limits of European Integration*. New York: Columbia University Press, 1983.

Thelen, Kathleen. "West European Labor in Transition." *World Politics* 46 (1993): 23–49.

———. *Union of Parts: Labor Politics in Postwar Germany*. Ithaca: Cornell University Press, 1991.

Thoroup, Cathryn. "The Politics of Free Trade and the Dynamics of Cross-Border Coalitions in U.S. Mexican Relations." *Columbia Journal of World Business* 26, no. 2 (summer 1991): 12–26.

Traxler, Franz. "Farewell to Labor Market Associations? Organized Versus Disorganized Decentralization as a Map for Industrial Relations." In *Organized Industrial Relations in Europe: What Future?* eds. Colin Crouch and Franx Traxler. Brookfield, Vt.: Ashgate, 1995.

Trevilcock, Michael, and Thomas Bodez. "The Case for Liberalizing North American Trade Remedy Laws." *Minnesota Journal of Global Trade* 4, no. 1 (1995): 6.

Tsoukalis, Loukas. *The New European Economy: The Politics and Economics of Integration.* Oxford: Oxford University Press, 1993.

U.N. Conference on Trade and Development. *World Investment Report: TNCs, Employment, and the Workplace.* New York: United Nations, 1994.

U.S. Department of Commerce, International Trade Administration. "Impact of the North American Free Trade Agreement on U.S. Automotive Exports to Mexico." *Report to Congress* (June 1996).

US-Mexico Free Trade Reporter (September 1, 1994).

U.S. President. *Economic Report of the President Transmitted to the Congress.* Washington, D.C.: U.S. Government Printing Office, 1994.

U.S. Trade Representative. *Foreign Trade Barriers.* Washington, D.C.: U.S. Government Printing Office, 1995, 1996.

van der Veen, Romke, and Willem Trommel. "Managed Liberalization of the Dutch Welfare State." Paper presented at the Society for the Advancement of Socioeconomics conference, Montreal, July 1997.

van Vliet, Henk Jan. "A Symposium on Drug Decriminalization: The Uneasy Decriminalization: A Perspective on Dutch Drug Policy." *Hofstra Law Review* 18 (1990): 723.

van Waarden, Frans. "Persistence of National Policy-Styles: A Study of Their Institutional Foundations." In *Convergence or Diversity? Internationalization and Economic Policy Response*, eds. Brigitte Unger and Frans van Waarden. Brookfield, Vt.: Avebury, 1995.

Vanhoe, Norbert, and Leo Klaassen. *Regional Policy: A European Approach*, 2d ed. Aldershot: Avebury, 1987.

Veen, Hans-Joachim, and Carsten Zelle. "National Identity and Political Priorities in Eastern and Western Germany." *German Politics* 4 (April 1995): 1–26.

Vega-Cánovas, Gustavo. "NAFTA and the Auto Sector." In *The Politics of Free Trade in North America*, eds. Gustavo del Castillo and Gustavo Vega-Cánovas. Ottawa: Carleton University Center for Trade Policy and Law, 1995.

Vilrokx, Jacques, and Jim van Leemput. "Belgium: A New Stability in Industrial Relations?" In *Industrial Relations in the New Europe*, eds. Anthony Ferner and Richard Hyman. Cambridge: Blackwell, 1992.

Visser, Jelle. "European Trade Unions: The Transition Years." In *New Frontiers in European Industrial Relations*, eds. Richard Hyman and Anthony Ferner. Cambridge: Blackwell, 1994.

Wade, Robert. "Globalization and Its Limits: Reports of the Death of the National

Economy Are Greatly Exaggerated." In *Convergence or Diversity? National Models of Production and Distribution in a Global Economy*, eds. Suzanne Berger and Ronald Dore. Ithaca: Cornell University Press, 1995.

Walker, R.B.J. *Inside/Outside: International Relations as Political Theory*. Cambridge: Cambridge University Press, 1993.

Wallace, Helen. "The Best Is the Enemy of the 'Could': Bargaining in the European Community." In *Agricultural Trade Liberalization and the European Community*, eds. Secondo Tarditi et al. Oxford: Clarendon, 1989.

Wallace, William. *The Transformation of Western Europe*. London: Royal Institute for International Affairs, 1990.

Wallace, William, and Julie Smith. "Democracy or Technocracy? European Integration and the Problem of Popular Consent." *West European Politics* 18 (July 1995): 137–157.

Wallerstein, Michael, and Miriam Golden. "The Fragmentation of the Bargaining Society: Wage Setting in the Nordic Countries, 1950–1992." *Comparative Political Studies* 30 (1997): 699–731.

Waltz, Kenneth. *Man, the State and War*. New York: Columbia University Press, 1959.

Weber, Cynthia. *Simulating Sovereignty: Intervention, the State, and Symbolic Exchange*. Cambridge: Cambridge University Press, 1995.

Weber, Cynthia, and Thomas J. Biersteker. "Reconstructing the Analysis of Sovereignty: Concluding Reflections and Directions for Future Research." In *State Sovereignty as Social Construct*, eds. Thomas J. Biersteker and Cynthia Weber. Cambridge: Cambridge University Press, 1996.

Weber, Max. *Wirtschaft und Gesellschaft*. Tübingen: Mohr, 1956.

Weidenfeld, Werner. "Kernpunkte der Reform." In *Reform der Europäischen Union*, ed. Werner Weidenfeld. Gütersloh: Bertelsmann, 1995.

———. "Zur Rolle der Europäischen Gemeinschaft in der Transformation Europas." In *Die Integration Europas*, ed. Michael Kreile. Opladen: Westdeutscher Verlag, 1992.

———, ed. *Reform der Europäischen Union*. Gütersloh: Bertelsmann, 1995.

———, ed. *Europa '96. Reformprogramm für die Europäische Union*. Gütersloh: Bertelsmann, 1994.

———, ed. *Die Identität Europas*. Bonn: Europa Union Verlag, 1985.

Weiler, Joseph, Ulrich R. Haltern, and Ranz C. Mayer. "European Democracy and Its Critique." In *The Crisis of Representation in Europe*, ed. Jack Hayward. London: Frank Cass, 1995.

———. "Journey to an Unknown Destination: A Retrospective and Prospective of the European Court of Justice in the Arena of Political Integration." *Journal of Common Market Studies* 31, no. 4 (1993): 417–446.

———. "After Maastricht: Community Legitimacy in Post-1992 Europe." In *Singular Europe*, ed. William James Adams. Ann Arbor: University of Michigan Press, 1992.

———. "Problems of Legitimacy in Post-1992 Europe." *Außenwirtschaft* 46 (1991): 411–437.

Weintraub, Sidney. *NAFTA at Three*. Washington, D.C.: Center for Strategic and International Studies, 1997.

Wessels, Wolfgang. "Staat und (westeuropäische) Integration." In *Integration Europas*, ed. Michael Kreile. Opladen: Westdeutscher Verlag, 1992.

————. "The EC Council." In *The New European Community: Decisionmaking and Institutional Change*, eds. Robert Keohane and Stanley Hoffmann. Boulder: Westview, 1991.

Westle, Bettina. *Politische Legitimität—Theorien, Konzepte, empirische Befunde*. Baden-Baden: Nomos Verlag, 1989.

Whitehead, Lawrence. "Democracy by Convergence in Southern Europe." In *Encouraging Democracy: The International Context of Regime Transition in Southern Europe*, ed. Geoffrey Pridham. Leicester: Leicester University Press, 1991.

Wieland, Beate. *Ein Markt—zwölf Regierungen?* Baden-Baden: Nomos Verlag, 1992.

Wiener, Antje, and Vincent Della Sala. "Constitution-Making and Citizenship Practice—Bridging the Democracy Gap in the EU." *Journal of Common Market Studies* 35 (December 1997): 593–614.

Wildenmann, Rudolf, ed. *Staatswerdung Europas? Optionen für eine Europäische Union*. Baden-Baden: Nomos Verlag, 1991.

Williams, Shirley. "Sovereignty and Accountability in the European Community." In *The New European Community*, Robert Keohane and Stanley Hoffmann, eds. Boulder: Westview, 1991.

Wood, David and Birol Yesilada. *The Emerging European Union*. White Plains, N.Y.: Longman, 1996.

Zellentin, Gerda. "Der Funktionalismus—eine Strategie gesamteuropäischer Integration." In *Die Integration Europas*, ed. Michael Kreile. Opladen: Westdeutscher Verlag, 1992.

Zimmerling, Ruth. *Externe Einflüsse auf die Integration von Staaten*. Freiburg: Alber, 1991.

Zürn, Michael. "Über den Staat und die Demokratie im Europäischen Mehrebenensystem." *Politische Vierteljahresschrift* (37) no. 1 (1996): 27–55.

Index

317

About the Editors and Contributors

José Augusto Guilhon Albuquerque is professor of political science at the University of São Paulo and director of the University Research Center for International Relations. He is the author of *Sessenta Anos de Politica Externa Brasileira* (1997), a four volume study of contemporary Brazilian foreign policy, as well as numerous book chapters and journal articles published in Portuguese, English, Spanish, French, and German, on hemispheric integration, foreign policy, and political behavior.

Jeffrey J. Anderson is associate professor of political science at Brown University. He is author of *The Territorial Imperative* (1992) and *German Unification and the Union of Europe* (forthcoming 1999), as well as numerous book chapters and articles on comparative political economy and European integration.

António Barreto, a sociologist, is a researcher at the Instituto de Cincias Sociais of the Lisbon University, and a professor of law at the New Lisbon University. He is author of *Tempo de Mudança* (1996) and *A Situação Social em Portugal, 1960–1995* (1997). He has been a member of Parliament and member of government.

Thomas J. Biersteker is Henry R. Luce Professor of Transnational Organizations, professor of political science, and director of the Watson Institute for International Studies at Brown University. His most recent books include *Dealing with Debt: International Financial Negotiations and Adjustment Bargaining* (1993), *State Sovereignty As Social Construct,* coedited with Cynthia Weber (1996), and *Argument Without End: In Search of Answers to the Vietnam Tragedy,* in which he co-drafted the concluding chapter (forthcoming). He has also written extensively about issues in international relations theory and international political economy.

Péter Gedeon is professor of economics at Budapest University of Economic Sciences in Hungary. He is author of several book chapters and

333

journal articles on political economy and social theory. His recent publications in English include "Market and Democracy: The Dilemmas of Postsocialist Transition," *Society and Economy* (1995); "The Economics of Transition and the Transition of Economics," *Economic Systems* (1997); and "Hungary: German and European Influences on the Postsocialist Transition," in Peter Katzenstein (ed.), *Mitteleuropa: Between Europe and Germany* (1997).

Jack Hayward is emeritus professor of politics and emeritus fellow of St. Antony's College, Oxford University. He is the author and editor of numerous books on France and comparative European politics, including *Industrial Enterprise and European Integration* (1995) and *Elitism, Populism and European Politics* (1996).

Paulette Kurzer is associate professor of political science at the University of Arizona. She is the author of *Business and Banking* (1993) as well as numerous articles and book chapters on the impact of European integration on small member states.

Gary Marks is professor of political science at the University of North Carolina at Chapel Hill and director of the UNC Center for European Studies. He is currently chair of the European Community Studies Association. His most recent books are *Governance in the European Union* (1996, co-edited with Fritz Scharpf, Philippe Schmitter, and Wolfgang Streeck) and *Continuity and Change in Contemporary Capitalism* (forthcoming, co-edited with Herbert Kitschelt, Peter Lange, and John Stephens).

Wolfgang Merkel is professor of political science at Heidelberg University. He is the author of numerous articles and books on European politics, social democracy, and democratic transitions. Among them are *Ende der Sozialdemokratie?* (1993) and *Systemtransformation* (forthcoming). He is also the editor of the five-volume *Systemwechsel* (1994–1999).

Gustavo Vega-Cánovas is professor of political science at El Colegio de Mexico in Mexico City. He is the co-author of *The Politics of Free Trade In North America* (1995) and *Mexico's Trade Policy in the Changing International Economy* (forthcoming), as well as numerous book chapters and articles on North American economic relations and Mexican foreign and economic policies.